HOW TO USE THIS BOOK

The directory includes all the butterflies that regularly live and breed in Europe, together with most of the moths that habitually fly by day. Moths that normally fly only around day-break and sun-set have not been included. Some of the smaller and less conspicuous day-flying moths have also been omitted, although representatives of most of the day-flying families are described.

The brief introduction to each family, omitted in a few instances where only a single species is involved, outlines the characteristics common to the species within that family, and this introduction is followed by an account of each species. Each account is accompanied by one or more illustrations.

The adult butterflies are illustrated in a standard format, with the upperside on the left and the underside on the right. Both sexes are shown if they are significantly different ($\male$ = male and $\female$ = female), and important variations are also illustrated. Larvae (caterpillars) are pictured for most butterfly species, but the young stages are still unknown for quite a few butterflies. Eggs and pupae are illustrated for selected species, merely to give some idea of the range of form occurring in each family.

The moths are depicted in various ways, but one half of the painting usually shows the characteristic resting position of the front wing – the position in which most moths are found when feeding. Larvae are illustrated for selected species.

Illustrations of eggs are obviously much enlarged, but the other pictures are life sized unless otherwise stated.

In each species account the English vernacular name appears first (if it exists), followed by the scientific name (see. p. 24) in italics: e.g.

SMALL TORTOISESHELL *Aglais urticae*
All the European butterflics have been given English names by earlier writers, but many of the smaller moths are still known only by their scientific names. Many of the larger non-British moths also lack English names at present.

As a quick check, a symbol in the margin denotes the occurrence of a species in Britain and Ireland.

▲ Widely distributed, in suitable habitats, throughout Britain.

△ Confined to the southern half of Britain.

△ Confined to the northern half of Britain.

△ An occasional visitor to the British Isles, possibly quite numerous in some years but absent in others.

The dividing line between northern and southern Britain has been arbitrarily fixed at about 54.5°N – a line running approximately from St Bee's Head in the west to Whitby in the east and thus passing through the Lake District. This line holds good for most species, although a few *small populations* may be found outside the indicated areas. Of course, species shown to occupy southern Britain may actually occupy only a very small area and this is indicated on the maps.

In order to present as much information as possible in the space available, many of the facts have been presented in abbreviated form. The codes have been devised so that the reader will rapidly learn to read the information without difficulty.

The scientific name of each species is followed by one or more diagnostic features. These are the most useful points by which a butterfly or moth may be *distinguished from other*

continued on the inside back cover

Collins

New Generation Guide

TO THE

BUTTERFLIES AND DAY-FLYING M

OF

BRITAIN AND EUROPE

The Lepidoptera have been the most watched, and unfortunately colle
the insect orders. The interest shown in them has resulted in numerous
fascinating facets of their biology being revealed, giving a greater insigh
the general biology of the insect world. Butterflies are also the most bea
the insects and have long intrigued by their ability to metamorphose fro
caterpillar to the intricate beauty of the adult.

The NEW GENERATION GUIDE TO THE BUTTERFLIES AND D
FLYING MOTHS is the first book ever to not only give the user a compl
guide to the eggs, caterpillars, pupa and adults of the European butterfli
and day-flying moths, but also to look behind the identification of each sp
and give an insight into why a species looks like it does, why it behaves lik
as well as what is going on inside the insect. This guide is for the new gene
of naturalists, who no longer wish to collect, but want to identify and then
understand the life of a butterfly.

Collins

New Generation Guide

TO THE

BUTTERFLIES AND DAY-FLYING MOTHS

OF

BRITAIN AND EUROPE

Michael Chinery

GENERAL EDITOR
Sir David Attenborough

COLLINS
8 Grafton Street, London W1

STS

an Hargreaves
enys Ovenden
ophie Allington
John Wilkinson

Frontispiece: Heathland is a habitat rich in butterflies and moths but, with the continuing destruction of heathland, many of these species are threatened with extinction

Also in the New Generation series

Birds of Britain and Europe by Christopher Perrins
Wild Flowers of Britain and Northern Europe by Alastair Fitter
Fungi of Britain and Europe by Stefan Buczacki

First published 1989

ISBN 0 00 219785 5 Hardback
ISBN 0 00 219787 1 Paperback

William Collins Sons & Co. Ltd
London · Glasgow · Sydney · Auckland · Toronto · Johannesburg

Typeset by Rowland Phototypesetting Ltd, Bury St Edmunds, Suffolk

Colour and black and white reproduction by Alpha Reprographics Ltd, Perivale, London

Printed and bound in Great Britain by William Collins Sons & Co. Ltd, Glasgow

CONTENTS

FOREWORD

Sir David Attenborough

The first question that comes to my mind when I see a butterfly or a day-flying moth fluttering through a wood or across a meadow is 'What is it?' Answering that is, surely, the primary function of any field guide and this New Generation Guide certainly claims to do so. But, like all the Guides in this series, it also aims to do considerably more.

Naming a species can seem to be a very arbitrary process unless the logic which underlies a classification is understood. At its best, of course, a classification seeks to reflect the degree to which species are related to one another, and therefore the evolutionary history of the whole group to which they belong. This guide therefore begins with an account of butterfly evolution.

Once that initial question is answered, however, many other questions will occur to a thoughtful naturalist. Why is it brightly coloured? Why does it visit this flower and not that? How old is it likely to be and how long will it live? Why does it settle with its wings in one position and, on another occasion, in a different way? The answers to such questions can only come from a knowledge of the general biology of butterflies. So another section follows the descriptions of individual species which describes in detail the life history of butterflies from the egg through the caterpillar stage to the reproduction and ultimate death of the butterfly. And to make sure that particularly interesting aspects of any one species will not be missed, there are cross references between the species descriptions and the encyclopedia section.

Like most wildlife these days, butterflies are becoming rarer and rarer in Britain and in many other parts of Europe. That must be a source of concern and dismay to almost everyone who is likely to use this guide. Consequently, its final pages are devoted to methods of conserving and encouraging the spread of butterflies.

All of us who have contributed to the New Generation Guide hope that this volume, with its three sections, will enable anyone who uses it to find a deeper appreciation of these lovely insects.

HOW TO USE THIS BOOK

The directory includes all the butterflies that regularly live and breed in Europe, together with most of the moths that habitually fly by day. Moths that normally fly only around day-break and sun-set have not been included. Some of the smaller and less conspicuous day-flying moths have also been omitted, although representatives of most of the day-flying families are described.

The brief introduction to each family, omitted in a few instances where only a single species is involved, outlines the characteristics common to the species within that family, and this introduction is followed by an account of each species. Each account is accompanied by one or more illustrations.

The adult butterflies are illustrated in a standard format, with the upperside on the left and the underside on the right. Both sexes are shown if they are significantly different ($\male$ = male and $\female$ = female), and important variations are also illustrated. Larvae (caterpillars) are pictured for most butterfly species, but the young stages are still unknown for quite a few butterflies. Eggs and pupae are illustrated for selected species, merely to give some idea of the range of form occurring in each family.

The moths are depicted in various ways, but one half of the painting usually shows the characteristic resting position of the front wing – the position in which most moths are found when feeding. Larvae are illustrated for selected species.

Illustrations of eggs are obviously much enlarged, but the other pictures are life sized unless otherwise stated.

In each species account the English vernacular name appears first (if it exists), followed by the scientific name (see. p. 24) in italics: e.g.

SMALL TORTOISESHELL *Aglais urticae*
All the European butterflies have been given English names by earlier writers, but many of the smaller moths are still known only by their scientific names. Many of the larger non-British moths also lack English names at present.

As a quick check, a symbol in the margin denotes the occurrence of a species in Britain and Ireland.

▲ Widely distributed, in suitable habitats, throughout Britain.

⬕ Confined to the southern half of Britain.

▲ Confined to the northern half of Britain.

△ An occasional visitor to the British Isles, possibly quite numerous in some years but absent in others.

The dividing line between northern and southern Britain has been arbitrarily fixed at about 54.5°N – a line running approximately from St Bee's Head in the west to Whitby in the east and thus passing through the Lake District. This line holds good for most species, although a few *small populations* may be found outside the indicated areas. Of course, species shown to occupy southern Britain may actually occupy only a very small area and this is indicated on the maps.

In order to present as much information as possible in the space available, many of the facts have been presented in abbreviated form. The codes have been devised so that the reader will rapidly learn to read the information without difficulty.

The scientific name of each species is followed by one or more diagnostic features. These are the most useful points by which a butterfly or moth may be *distinguished from other*

continued on the inside back cover

Collins

New Generation Guide

BUTTERFLIES AND DAY-FLYING MOTHS

OF

BRITAIN AND EUROPE

The Lepidoptera have been the most watched, and unfortunately collected, of the insect orders. The interest shown in them has resulted in numerous fascinating facets of their biology being revealed, giving a greater insight into the general biology of the insect world. Butterflies are also the most beautiful of the insects and have long intrigued by their ability to metamorphose from a caterpillar to the intricate beauty of the adult.

The NEW GENERATION GUIDE TO THE BUTTERFLIES AND DAY-FLYING MOTHS is the first book ever to not only give the user a complete guide to the eggs, caterpillars, pupa and adults of the European butterflies and day-flying moths, but also to look behind the identification of each species and give an insight into why a species looks like it does, why it behaves like that, as well as what is going on inside the insect. This guide is for the new generation of naturalists, who no longer wish to collect, but want to identify and then understand the life of a butterfly.

Collins

New Generation Guide

BUTTERFLIES AND DAY-FLYING MOTHS

OF

BRITAIN AND EUROPE

Michael Chinery

GENERAL EDITOR
Sir David Attenborough

COLLINS
8 Grafton Street, London W1

ARTISTS

Brian Hargreaves
Denys Ovenden
Sophie Allington
John Wilkinson

Frontispiece: Heathland is a habitat rich in butterflies and moths but, with the continuing destruction of heathland, many of these species are threatened with extinction

Also in the New Generation series

Birds of Britain and Europe by Christopher Perrins
Wild Flowers of Britain and Northern Europe by Alastair Fitter
Fungi of Britain and Europe by Stefan Buczacki

First published 1989

Text copyright © Michael Chinery 1989
Illustration copyright © William Collins Sons & Co. Ltd 1989

ISBN 0 00 219785 5 Hardback
ISBN 0 00 219787 1 Paperback

William Collins Sons & Co. Ltd
London · Glasgow · Sydney · Auckland · Toronto · Johannesburg

Typeset by Rowland Phototypesetting Ltd, Bury St Edmunds, Suffolk

Colour and black and white reproduction by Alpha Reprographics Ltd, Perivale, London

Printed and bound in Great Britain by William Collins Sons & Co. Ltd, Glasgow

CONTENTS

PREFACE

Michael Chinery

This new type of natural history guide, already familiar to birdwatchers and flower enthusiasts, is aimed at the naturalist who wants to do more than just put names to things. During more than 40 years of collecting and studying insects I have rarely been satisfied with just a name. I always wanted to know why an insect flew where it did, how it got there, and what it was doing. Over the years it has become obvious that many other people feel the same way, and when Crispin Fisher invited me to write this book for Collins I jumped at the chance of answering some of these questions for future generations of butterfly watchers.

The inclusion of day-flying moths, suggested by Sir David Attenborough, adds a further, most useful dimension to the book – not to mention the extra pages! While leading field trips I have been shown scores of insects with the plea 'This isn't in my butterfly book: what is it please?'. Most of the 'butterflies' turned out to be day-flying moths, so the inclusion of these diurnal species in this book should make life somewhat easier for the beginner. Space does not permit the inclusion of all the day-flying moths of Europe, but the book does cover all the major groups and virtually all the more colourful species that might be confused with butterflies are included.

A vast amount of research has been carried out on butterfly natural history in recent years, and in writing this book I have drawn heavily on the published works of many specialists. I thank them all for the information.

Staff at the British Museum (Natural History) have been most helpful in pointing me to the right books and cabinets and in making specimens available for the artists. David Carter has been particularly helpful and patient in answering my numerous queries, and I have had valuable help from Paul Whalley and from Dr P Hattenschwiler who was most helpful with advice on the biology and distribution of the Psychidae.

Much of the information on population dynamics has been extracted from the results of the Institute of Terrestrial Ecology's Butterfly Monitoring Scheme. Dr Ian McLean of the Nature Conservancy Council has also made helpful suggestions concerning butterfly conservation.

The information concerning butterfly legislation was gathered by the IUCN Conservation Monitoring Centre, and I am most grateful to Dr Mark Collins for making this information available. Other information on the status of butterflies has been drawn largely from *Threatened Rhopalocera (butterflies) in Europe* by the late John Heath (Nature and Environment Series No. 23, published by the Council of Europe).

I have greatly enjoyed working with Crispin Fisher and Myles Archibald at Collins, receiving enthusiastic support and encouragement from them throughout the project. I have equally enjoyed many hours with my artist colleagues and I thank them all for their meticulous attention to detail. Brian Hargreaves' butterflies and Denys Ovenden's moths form the backbone without which the book could never have taken shape.

The Evolution of Butterflies and Moths

BUTTERFLY ORIGINS

The butterflies are certainly the most popular and probably the most familiar of insects in the temperate parts of the world. Long admired for their beauty and elegance, butterflies have been collected for centuries, and generations of children have been introduced to the pleasures of natural history through chasing the insects with home-made nets and jam-jar prisons. Only the birds and the flowers have more fans among naturalists today. Although nets have now largely given way to cameras, the chase is no less rewarding and, being conducted at a less furious pace, enables the enthusiast to learn a good deal more about butterfly behaviour than can be gleaned from netting an insect and popping it in a killing bottle.

Much has been written on the origin of the word butterfly, including the suggestion that it is a shortened version of 'butter-coloured fly' – which *might* have been applied to the Brimstone and other yellow species. This seems unlikely, as yellow butterflies are not the commonest of those around us and it is fairly implausible that the name would be extended to include the non-yellow species. This theory is not as daft as some that have been put forward; one absurd idea even suggested that butterflies are so called because many species void a yellowish fluid when they leave the chrysalis! Slightly more plausible is the suggested derivation from 'batter-fly' – possibly used in the past and based on the way the insects flutter or bat their wings up and down in flight. The explanation is probably much simpler. Chaucer, writing in the fourteenth century, called the insect a 'boterflye', which is not too different from the Old English 'buttor-fleoge'. Neither is far removed from the Old French word 'biaute' meaning beauty, suggesting that butterfly simply means

'beautiful fly'. A descriptive name understood and appreciated by anyone, it makes no reference to specific colours and it would have been readily accepted into everyday use.

BUTTERFLIES AND MOTHS

The butterflies and moths form the order Lepidoptera which, with about 165,000 known species, is the second largest of all the insect groups. Only the beetles have more species. The main characteristic of the Lepidoptera is the possession of minute scales which clothe the wings and body and give the wings their colourful patterns (see p. 18). Lepidoptera literally means 'scale-wings'. Scales occur in some other insect groups, but never form such a dense and extensive covering as they do in the butterflies and moths. The other major feature of these insects is the slender proboscis or drinking tube (see p. 257), although this is not present in all moths.

The long-standing and widely-used division of the order into butterflies and moths suggests that the two groups are of equal standing, but this is far from the truth. It is simply a division of convenience, based on little more than superficial observation and with no real scientific basis. The butterflies form just two, admittedly well-defined, superfamilies (see p. 24) of the twenty two that make up the Lepidoptera, and they account for only about 360 of the 5,000 or so species that live in Europe. There is just as much difference between a butterfly and a hawkmoth as there is between that hawkmoth and a burnet moth. Nevertheless, the division into butterflies and moths is deeply entrenched in our books and other literature and is unlikely to be discarded.

So what *is* the difference between butterflies and moths? There is no

The Gatekeeper (left) and Burnet (centre) show the characteristic resting position of a butterfly and a moth. The frenulum (right), on the underside of the wing, is found only in moths

single feature separating all the butterflies on the one hand from all the moths on the other, but the antennae are the most useful aids to identification. Almost all butterflies, including all the European species, have clubbed antennae, hence the name Rhopalocera (meaning 'club-horns') commonly applied to these insects. Moth antennae are much more variable and the insects are sometimes known as the Heterocera (= various horns). Some moths, notably the burnets (see p. 154), have clubbed antennae – although the shape is somewhat different from that of butterfly antennae – but the majority of moths have hairlike or feathery antennae. Any lepidopteran with unclubbed antennae is clearly a moth; one with clubbed antennae could be a moth but is more likely to be a butterfly. If there is still doubt, the next diagnostic feature is found on the wings. Many moths link the two wings on each side with a bristle or cluster of stout hairs called the frenulum (see above). Not all moths have a frenulum, but as far as the European species are concerned all those with clubbed antennae do have one. Apart from one Australian skipper, no butterfly ever has a frenulum.

It is commonly stated that butterflies are brightly coloured and fly by day, while moths are drab and fly at night. There is certainly plenty of truth in this observation, which is probably the basis for the original separation of the two groups, but there are also lots of exceptions. The European butterflies certainly all fly by day, but the well-named Dingy Skipper demonstrates that not all butterflies are brightly coloured. There are also plenty of brightly coloured, day-flying moths, including the burnets and some of the tigers.

Resting attitudes may also help to distinguish butterflies from moths. Butterflies normally roost at night and in dull weather with their wings brought together and held vertically over the body, whereas most moths hold their wings in a tent-like fashion or even wrap them round the body. But again there are exceptions: many thorn moths, for example, close their wings vertically above the body, while the Dingy Skipper rests with its wings draped around its body like a cloak – just like many moths.

Mouffet's *Theatrum Insectorum*, published in 1634, did not recognise any fundamental divide between the butterflies and moths and merely treated the latter as 'nocturnal butterflies'. Many European languages retain this simple approach: in German there are *Tagfalter* and *Nachtfalter*, while in French there are *papillons diurnes* and *papillons nocturnes* (or *papillons de nuit*). It is worth remembering that in the far north, where it does not get dark in summer, they all fly in daylight!

BUTTERFLY EVOLUTION

Over the years many theories have been put forward concerning the possible ancestors of the Lepidoptera, and nearly every other order of insects has been considered for this role. Most of the suggestions are purely conjectural, for the fossil record is too fragmentary to build up a clear picture, but it is certain that the closest relatives of the butterflies and moths are the caddis flies of the order Trichoptera. This does not mean that the caddis flies were the ancestors of the Lepidoptera, but it does seem likely that the two groups evolved from a common ancestor – probably during the Permian Period, almost 250 million years ago.

A few moth-like fossils are known from the Triassic rocks, but it is difficult to say whether they represent primitive moths or caddis flies. Primitive moths were flying among the Jurassic dinosaurs about 150 million years ago, although very few fossils of this age have yet been discovered. The Lower Cretaceous rocks, laid down about 120 million years ago, have yielded richer finds, representing quite a wide range of primitive moths, and the evolution of the Lepidoptera was clearly well under way by that time, although we have no butterfly fossils from the Cretaceous rocks. The earliest butterfly fossils come from Eocene rocks and are a mere 50 million years old! By early Oligocene times, about 40 million years ago, all the major butterfly families were in existence and the general form of the fossil species is very similar to that of the butterflies flying today. Clearly, the butterflies must have put in an appearance long before this – possibly way back in Cretaceous times, 100 million years ago. There is no hard evidence for this earlier origin of the butterflies, but the distribution of modern butterfly families does suggest that they were already well along their evolutionary paths before the continents finally separated towards the end of the Cretaceous.

It is generally agreed that the butterflies arose from some kind of moth, and lots of moth families have been suggested as butterfly ancestors, but in the absence of fossils it is difficult to draw any firm conclusion. The venation of butterflies is fairly complete (see p. 17), and this suggests a derivation from one of the moth families with more primitive origins. The Castniidae has often been put forward as a major candidate, for its members – now confined to tropical America and the Indo-Pacific – are colourful, day-flying insects with clubbed antennae. Other features, however, clearly place this family with the moths, and detailed studies of both adult and larval anatomy indicate that the Castniidae cannot be regarded as butterfly ancestors. Current opinion is that the butterflies, and most of the larger moths, evolved from a common ancestor, which, as yet, has not been identified.

The study of fossils can tell us nothing about the flying habits of the early Lepidoptera, and it is not possible to say with certainty whether they flew by night or by day. Members of the families with more primitive origins are generally day-flying, however, and it is thus likely that the

One of the oldest butterfly fossils, Nymphalites zeuneri, *is 50 million years old*

earliest moths were also active by day. So why did some become nocturnal? It was probably as the result of predation by birds, which were increasing rapidly in Cretaceous and early Tertiary times when lepidopteran evolution was in full swing. Mammals, lizards, and amphibians would also have contributed to predation and their combined effect would surely have been sufficient to encourage the evolution of nocturnal habits in many moth families. But some families, including the burnets (Zygaenidae), have remained diurnal – protected by distasteful properties and warning colours (see p. 277). It also seems certain that day-flying members of families that are today predominantly nocturnal have secondarily reverted to diurnal life – perhaps in response to predation by bats – after a period of night duty. These day-fliers include some of the tiger moths, protected by acrid tastes and warning colours, and the bee hawkmoths (p. 184) which gain protection by mimicking bees. We do not know whether the butterflies' ancestors were nocturnal or diurnal, but the most plausible theory is that the butterflies evolved directly from some group of day-flying moths and have never passed through a nocturnal stage. But this theory is based on the assumption that the early Lepidoptera were diurnal.

As with the burnet moths, bright colours and distasteful properties would have helped many butterflies to remain (or to become) diurnal, and it has been suggested that at least some butterfly families flourished through adopting poisonous food-plants in the larval stage and sequestering the poisons in their bodies for use in the battle against predators. This happens in the Monarch and its relatives and in several other brightly coloured butterflies (see p. 277), but certainly not all butterflies rely on such strategy. The browns, for example, acquire no poisons from their grass food-plants and they rely mainly on camouflage to escape their enemies.

The evolution of butterflies is clearly very closely linked with that of

Monarch

Jersey Tiger

Bumble Bee

Bee Hawkmoth

Nettle-tree

Warning colours (top), mimicry and camouflage all help to protect butterflies and moths from predation

The Hummingbird Hawkmoth probes a flower for nectar and picks up pollen on its tongue in the process

the flowering plants on which they feed. Early butterflies would have been able to feed from extra-floral nectaries and also on other sources of sugar, such as honeydew, and possibly had relatively short tongues. Long tongues evolved as the flowers began to secrete their nectar in less accessible places. Conversely, tubular flowers which rely on long-tongued butterflies and moths for pollination could not have evolved until the insects had started to develop their probing tongues. The fossil record tells us that the first flowering plants appeared early in Cretaceous times, about 130 million years ago. The Lepidoptera had already been around for some time but, like today's *Micropterix* species (see p. 152), they all had biting jaws and were pollen-feeders. By 100 million years ago the flowering plants occupied most of the earth's surface and flies and beetles were the earliest pollinators of this floral profusion. Moths with undoubted tongues joined the act a little later and we can assume that the flowers had already evolved insect-attracting nectar. But it was not until early Tertiary times, some 65 million years ago, that the flowering plants and the butterflies and moths really started to branch out into the wide range of forms that we know today, and this co-evolution was undoubtedly due to their mutual dependence.

There has also been co-evolution of flowering plants and Lepidoptera in terms of caterpillars and their food-plants, but here the 'partnership' is distinctly one-sided: having its leaves nibbled is of no benefit to the plant and plant evolution has been guided along the path of avoiding or at least reducing such damage. Many plants have achieved this through the development of poisonous or distasteful compounds in their leaves, but evolution is a continuing process and some caterpillars have 'caught up' with their food-plants by evolving enzymes capable of breaking down the poisons. These caterpillars are specialist feeders, concentrating on just one plant species or on a group of closely related species. At the same time the adult butterflies or moths have developed the ability to recognise the plant compounds and to use them as stimuli when laying eggs (see p. 201). The poisons can also be used in other ways: with or without change, they can be used to deter predators (see p. 277) and they can also be used to manufacture specific pheromones which are then used in courtship. This again is demonstrated by the Monarch, which synthesises the pheromone danaidone from alkaloids obtained from the larval food-plant.

There can be no doubt that the evolution of the Lepidoptera and the flowering plants has proceeded hand in hand over the last 100 million years or so, with each group influencing the development of the other, but there are a few plant families that have managed to stay well ahead of the caterpillar army. The bedstraw family (Rubiaceae), for example, contains about 6,000 species and yet virtually no butterfly caterpillar feeds on them. Admittedly, a few moth larvae, including those of the Hummingbird Hawkmoth and the Bedstraw Hawkmoth, feed on bedstraws, but the high concentrations of alkaloids such as caffeine and quinine found in the plants of this family protect them from the majority of caterpillars. Butterfly caterpillars also generally avoid the bitter-tasting leaves of the cucumber and grape families.

THE BUTTERFLY BODY

The butterfly body, like that of any other insect, has three main regions – the head, thorax, and abdomen. The wings and all the legs are attached to the thorax.

The head is small and rounded and a large part of its surface is occupied by the compound eyes – so called because each is composed of hundreds or even thousands of minute lenses. Each lens has its own light-sensitive layer and its own connection with the brain, and the whole unit is known as an ommatidium. The working of the compound eye is described on p. 254. Many butterflies and moths also have a pair of simple eyes, known as ocelli, just above or behind the compound eyes. The ocelli cannot form images, and in any case are usually concealed by the scales and hairs that clothe the head, but they are very sensitive to changes in light intensity and are thought to control the working of the compound eyes in some way.

The antennae spring from between the eyes and are composed of numerous small segments. As we have already seen, moth antennae are rather variable, ranging from minute bristles to elaborate 'feathers', and they are often markedly different in the two sexes. Butterfly antennae are much more uniform and always clubbed at the tip, although the size and shape of the club vary a good deal. The antennae are usually clothed with scales and carry a complex array of sense organs designed to pick up chemical and tactile signals (see p. 255).

Jaws and mandibles are completely lacking in almost all the Lepidoptera and are functional only in the pollen-eating Micropterigidae (see p. 152). The rest of the moths and all of the butterflies are liquid feeders, although quite a number of moths do not feed in the adult state. Nectar is the principal food of almost all species (see p. 257) and it is taken through a slender 'drinking straw' known as the tongue or, more accurately, the proboscis. Formed from parts of the maxillae, the proboscis is actually in two halves which have to be zipped together to complete the tube when it leaves its chrysalis. The proboscis is often as long as the body, and in some tropical hawkmoths it is more than 30cm long, but when not in use it is coiled up out of sight underneath the head. The working of the proboscis is explained in more detail on p. 257.

The adult butterfly shows all the major anatomical characteristics of an insect

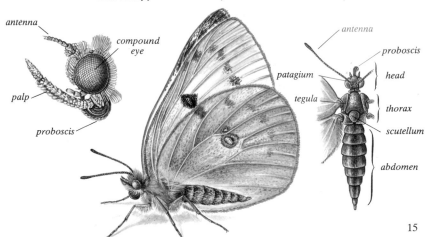

antenna

compound eye

palp

proboscis

antenna

patagium

tegula

proboscis

head

thorax

scutellum

abdomen

15

Sticking forward and upward from the lower side of the head and looking like two short horns are the labial palps, usually referred to simply as the palps although some moths actually have a pair of maxillary palps as well. They are densely clothed with stout hairs and the coiled proboscis is normally hidden between them. Well supplied with sense organs, the palps play a major role in identifying food-plants (see p. 201). In the Nettle-tree Butterfly they are as long as the head and thorax together, but they are usually much shorter and in many moths they are hardly visible from above. There are normally three segments to each palp, although the segmentation is usually concealed by the hairs.

The thorax, densely clothed with hair in most species, consists of three segments of very unequal size. The prothorax at the front is relatively large in some of the more evolutionary primitive groups of moths, but in the butterflies and the larger moths it forms little more than a collar just behind the head. It carries the first pair of legs but never bears wings. The middle section – the meso-thorax – is the largest, and carries the front wings and the middle pair of legs. At the front of each side, over-lying the wing-base, there is a tri-angular 'shoulder-pad' known as the tegula. It is a horny plate clothed with scales and rather easily detached in dried specimens. Its function seems to be simply the protection of the delicate articulation of the wing. At the rear of the mesothorax there is a more or less oval plate called the scutellum, which partly overlaps the much smaller metathorax. This is the third segment of the thorax and it bears the hind wings and the last pair of legs. The thorax as a whole is much firmer than the abdomen as a result of its much thicker and stronger outer skeleton – essential for the proper anchorage and working of the legs and the flight muscles (see p. 260).

The legs of butterflies and moths all have the same basic structure, although in the Nymphalidae – the 'brush-footed butterflies' – and some other families the front legs are re-duced and useless for walking. Among the swallowtails and most of the skippers the front tibia bears a broad, scaly spur, known as an epiphysis, which is used for cleaning the antennae and the proboscis.

The abdomen consists of ten seg-ments, although not all of them are visible externally, and bears no limbs. In most species it is well covered with scales and hairs. The hind end con-tains the genitalia. Males are en-dowed with a pair of claspers which surround the terminal opening, but these are not usually very obvious and there is little external difference be-tween the two sexes – although freshly emerged females tend to be plumper than their mates because they are full of eggs. Each species has its own distinctive genitalia, ensuring that it can not normally link up with the wrong mate. The detailed struc-ture of the genitalia is thus of great value in separating closely related species, notably some of the fritil-laries, which are difficult or even impossible to separate with certainty on external features alone.

WINGS AND SCALES

The butterflies and moths have two pairs of thin wings, of which the front pair are usually the larger. Only in some of the more evolutionary primi-tive groups of moths are all four wings of similar shape and size. The two wings on each side are linked together and function as one unit in flight. Among the butterflies and some of the larger moths – notably the eggars and emperors (see p. 178) – the link-age is achieved simply by a large overlap of the wings, while most moths employ a frenulum to couple the wings. The frenulum is a stout bristle in the male and normally a cluster of more slender bristles in the female. Springing from the 'shoulder' of the hind wing, it runs obliquely forward under the forewing, where it is held in place by a small hook or by a group of stiff hairs or scales (see p. 11).

It is easy to assume that the but-terfly wing is a single sheet of tissue,

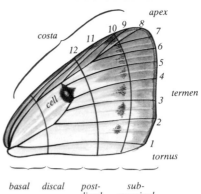

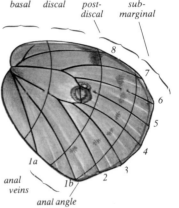

The veins and areas of a butterfly's wing

but it is actually more like a flattened paper bag, with two distinct sheets or membranes separated by a very narrow space. Minute struts connect the two layers at various points and keep them close together. Each wing is supported by a number of veins, whose arrangement varies from family to family and is of great value in classification – although examination of the veins is not necessary to name our European butterflies. A little alcohol dropped onto the wings will make the veins stand out better.

The wing veins have been given names by various entomologists over the years, but the names have not been standardised. Many lepidopterists now adopt a simpler system of numbering the veins that reach the wing margin. Most butterflies have twelve such veins in the forewing, although vein 7 is missing from the lycaenids. The hind wing normally has nine long veins, although these are numbered from 1 to 8; the two hindmost veins, known as the anal veins, are numbered 1a and 1b. Vein 1a is absent from the swallowtails and their relatives, while vein 5 is missing from many of the skippers. Vein 8 in the hind wing normally has a short spur near the base. Known as the precostal or humeral vein, its function is to support the bulge that creates the wing overlap.

The spaces between the veins are known as cells, or sometimes simply as spaces, and they are numbered according to the veins behind them except in the region of the anal veins. These spaces are commonly mentioned in the detailed descriptions of butterflies, especially when referring to the presence or absence of spots. The most prominent of the cells is the discal cell – generally referred to simply as the cell – which is always present near the centre of the wing and often has a dark spot – the discal spot – at its outer end.

It is often convenient to refer to more general areas of the wings when describing the insects. The front edge of the wing is known as the costa, while the hind edge is called the inner margin or dorsum. The outer margin,

furthest from the body, is called the termen, and the angle between it and the rear edge is called the tornus. In the hind wing, the region of the anal veins is called the anal region.

Because bits can be torn from the wings without apparent harm to the insect, it is commonly assumed that the wings are dead structures like our own nails and hair, but they are actually living membranes and they remain so throughout the insect's life. Although the wings become very dry when they are fully expanded, the veins continue to carry blood and they also contain functional nerves and air-carrying tracheae. The fact that many scales give off scent (see p. 20) is a sure indication that living processes are going on in the wings. The flight mechanisms of butterflies and moths are described on p. 260.

17

Both upper and lower surfaces of the wings are clothed with scales and a low-power microscope will reveal that in all but a few of the more primitive moths they are arranged in overlapping rows, very much like the tiles or slates on a roof. At a higher magnification it can be seen that each scale has a tiny stalk that fits neatly into a pocket in the wing membrane. But the attachment of the scales is not a very secure one and, as anyone who has handled butterflies can confirm, they are easily dislodged – either removed from their sockets entirely or snapped off at the base. Many scales are actually lost during flight and older specimens may look very worn. The day-flying bee hawkmoths lose nearly all their scales during their first flight and then resemble the bumble bees very closely. Their flight is in no way impaired by the loss of scales, but some butterflies do find flight a little difficult when they have lost a large proportion of their scales. It seems likely that in these cases the loss of scales prevents the butterflies from warming up properly. The importance of the scales in regulating the body temperature is not generally appreciated. Many butterflies have to raise their body temperature to about 30°C before they can take off, and they generally do this by sun-bathing with their wings wide open. Such sun-bathing is especially noticeable in the morning and in freshly-emerged butterflies. The system works well even in cool weather, as long as there is some sunshine, and dark scales absorb heat much more efficiently than pale ones – explaining why butterflies from mountainous regions tend to be darker than their lowland relatives. Those species that hibernate as adults and emerge early in the spring also tend to be rather dark, although the Brimstone is an obvious exception. Night-flying moths, with no sunshine available, normally warm themselves up by 'shivering' – powerful muscular activity which sets the whole body quivering as it prepares for flight.

The scales can be likened to minute flat bags, each containing a number of

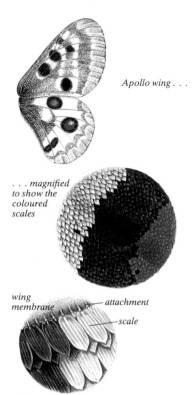

Apollo wing . . .

. . . magnified to show the coloured scales

wing membrane — *attachment*

— scale

Butterfly colours are provided by scales which spring from small pockets in the wing membrane

Broad-bordered Hawkmoth before (left) and after its first flight, during which it loses its wing scales

partitions and chambers. Most of them contain some kind of pigment and they are responsible for the colours and intricate patterns of the wings. Common pigments include the melanins, which are brown and black, and the pteridines. The latter, which are particularly common in the Pieridae, produce most of the yellows and oranges and many of the reds seen in butterfly wings. Some pteridines are white, but these rarely contribute to the wing colours. White wings or patches are almost all produced by the reflection and scattering of light from the numerous internal surfaces of empty scales – empty in the sense that they contain no pigment, although their chambers are full of air. The same phenomenon causes snow to appear white. The silver spots on the undersides of many of the fritillaries are produced in a similar way, but here the reflecting surfaces are arranged in a much more regular pattern inside the scales and they send out brighter reflections than we see from the normal matt white wings.

The brilliant metallic colours, notably the iridescent blues and purples, that we see in many butterfly wings are also due to the structure of the scales rather than to any pigment contained in them. The scales carry, either inside or on the surface, numerous extremely thin plates or lamellae – visible only under the electron microscope – which each reflect light. The reflections 'interfere' with each other and blot out some wavelengths, leaving just one or two colours to reach our eyes – and those of other insects. These colours are thus known as interference colours and they are usually some shade of blue or purple. Because they are very pure they appear bright and metallic. They change in hue and intensity as the angle of view changes and, as in the Purple Emperor, they may disappear altogether at certain angles. The colours are also destroyed by damaging the scales, or even by dropping water on them. Pigmentary colours are not altered in this way. The flashing of the structural colours in flight undoubtedly plays a big role in

The scales making up the spots on a fritillary's wing contain numerous internal reflectors parallel to the surface. Multiple reflections from these surfaces produce the silver colour seen in these, and other butterflies, in much the same way as silvery reflections are produced by a roll of cling film

communication between butterflies, and recent work has shown that the visible interference colours are accompanied by intense ultra-violet displays, which are invisible to us but clearly visible to the butterflies themselves. Some butterflies, including many of the whites, produce 'spectacular' iridescent displays that are entirely in the ultra-violet range. Males normally put on better shows than females and in many species, including the Purple Emperor, the females display no iridescence at all.

The slender scent scales (right) form dark patches on the forewings of male Gatekeepers

Male butterflies possess a number of specialised scent scales or androconia, which play an important role in courtship (see p. 288). They are very variable in shape, but most end in a minute tuft or fringe. The base is connected to a tiny scent gland in the wing membrane and the scent travels along the scale to diffuse into the air from the terminal tuft or fringe. The scent is, of course, a chemical messenger or pheromone, and it is normally released only when the male is chasing or courting a female. If she is a virgin, it excites her and persuades her to accept the male and continue the courtship. The androconia may be scattered all over the wing surface, but in many species they are concentrated in certain areas known as sex brands. These are often darker than the surrounding parts of the wing and are particularly prominent in the Gatekeeper and some of the other brown butterflies, making it very easy to distinguish the sexes at a glance. In some of the fritillaries and skippers the androconia are packed into raised folds which form dark streaks on the forewings. In some other skippers the androconia are packed into a groove along the front edge of the fore-wing.

The distribution of scales and pigments is, like all other features, controlled by the genes and is characteristic for each species and sex. There are lots of minor variations, particularly concerning the sizes of spots, which do not alter the general appearance of the insect, but major mistakes do sometimes occur during the development and they lead to the abnormal colours and patterns that we call aberrations (see p. 298). Much sought after by collectors, these freaks include albinos and others with totally different colours and also specimens with abnormal numbers of spots. Very occasionally the hind-wing pattern is carried on the forewing or vice-versa, while it is quite common for male and female patterns to be mixed in one individual. Such a mixed-up insect is called a gynandromorph and commonly has one half male and the other half female, with the dividing line running right down the middle of the body. The most striking gynandromorphs are those belonging to species in which the sexes have totally different colours, such as the blues.

gynandromorph

A male, a female and gynandromorph Common Blue, with the gynandromorph showing a male righthand and female lefthand side

THE BUTTERFLY LIFE CYCLE

Butterflies and moths are holometabolous insects, meaning that they undergo a complete change or metamorphosis in their body form during development. They all pass through four distinct stages – the egg, caterpillar or larva, chrysalis or pupa, and adult or imago. This is rather different from the hemimetabolous life cycle of a grasshopper or an earwig, in which there are only three stages – the egg, the nymph, which resembles the adult except that it has no wings, and the adult itself.

The eggs are usually laid on suitable food-plants by the female parent (see p. 200) and they usually hatch within a couple of weeks. The worm-like caterpillar that struggles out of the egg has no wings and no compound eyes and it has biting jaws instead of the hair-like proboscis of the adult. It is so unlike the adult butterfly that one could be forgiven for thinking that it is a totally different creature. As well as the three pairs of true legs on the thorax, it has a number of stumpy prolegs on the abdomen (see p. 211). The caterpillar soon gets to work on its food-plant and within a few days it is almost bursting at its seams. As the tough outer coat of the insects does not grow, it has to be changed periodically for a larger one (see p. 214). This process, known as moulting or ecdysis, takes place four or five times during the caterpillar's life. At the final moult the caterpillar's skin peels back to reveal the chrysalis or pupa. But before this change can take place the caterpillar must make certain preparations. Many moth larvae, for example, burrow into the ground where each hollows out a snug chamber in which pupation – the change from larva to pupa – finally takes place. Other moth caterpillars spin silken cocoons around themselves before pupation. A few butterfly larvae spin flimsy cocoons, usually on the ground at the base of the food-plant, but the majority pupate naked after attaching themselves to the food-plant or some other suitable support with silk. Some pupate hanging upside-down, while others are held upright against the support by a silken safety belt.

The life-cycle of the Purple Emperor butterfly

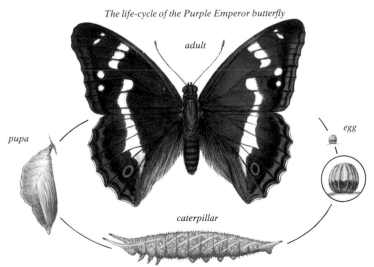

adult

pupa

egg

caterpillar

The pupa or chrysalis is often said to be a resting stage, because it does not feed and rarely moves, but internally it is a cauldron of activity as the tissues are liquefied and then re-built to the adult pattern (see p. 236). This marvellous transformation commonly takes two or three weeks, although the White Admiral can complete the change within seven days in warm weather. There are, of course, many species that spend the whole winter in the pupal stage, but development is suspended for most of this time (see p. 236) and construction of the adult body may still be carried out in just a few weeks. The wings of the adult can often be seen quite clearly through the pupal skin in the later stages and, although they are small and folded, you can often pick out their patterns well enough to identify the species. At emergence, the pupal skin splits and the limp adult appears. After pumping up its wings from limp bags into the fully extended structures the adult flies off to feed and mate.

ONE BROOD OR TWO?

Many butterflies produce just one brood or generation each year, with the adults flying at a particular season. The actual time of appearance may vary according to the locality, with northern populations on the wing later than southern ones. There are two flight periods in those species, such as the Brimstone, that hibernate as adults, but there is still only one brood of larvae in a year. Well known single-brooded species include the Orange-tip, the Peacock, and the Silver-washed Fritillary. Most of the skippers are also single-brooded.

A large number of species are double-brooded, with two generations in a year and usually two distinct flight periods – although the two generations sometimes overlap. The flight periods for the two generations are commonly early and late summer. The second brood is often only a partial one, meaning that only some of the individuals grow rapidly enough to reach maturity in the summer. The rest delay their develop-

The flight periods of the Orange-tip (single brooded), Peacock (single brooded + hibernation) and the Small Tortoiseshell (double brooded + hibernation)

ment and pass the winter as larvae or pupae before maturing in the following spring or summer just like normal single-brooded species. Some species, including the Small White and the Small Copper, even have three broods, although the third brood is usually only a partial one and may be abandoned altogether in a poor season. Adults from the third brood are frequently rather small, perhaps as a direct result of high temperatures or perhaps through having to make do with rather old plants in the larval stage.

Many species that produce two or even three broods in the warmer parts of their range are single-brooded in the north and in the mountains where the growing season is too short for more than one generation to be reared. Familiar examples include the Duke of Burgundy and the Pearl-bordered Fritillary. But climate is not the only factor involved here. It is clear that, at least in some species, there are genetic distinctions between single-brooded and double-brooded populations. The Green-veined White provides us with an interesting example. In most parts of the British Isles it is double-brooded, although the second brood is only a partial one with no more than about 40% of pupae developing directly into adults, and there may be a partial third generation in a good season. In many parts of Scotland, however, and also in some upland areas of northern England, there are colonies that are entirely single-brooded. Double-brooded colonies exist in the same area, suggesting that the differences are genetically controlled and not just the result of the cooler climate.

In the far north and in high mountain regions there are butterflies that take two years to mature, as a result of low temperatures and very short summers (see p. 248). This does not mean that the species is on the wing only every two years: there are usually two populations which mature in alternate years.

WHY METAMORPHOSE?

As we have seen, not all insects go through the dramatic transformation from larva to imago experienced by the butterflies and moths. So what is the advantage of this complete metamorphosis? Why do the butterflies and moths not grow up in the same way as the grasshoppers, in which little wing buds sprout from the back in the early stages and then get larger at each moult? This method, which is the more primitive of the two types of life cycle, does not involve any major bodily change and the youngsters generally eat the same kinds of food as the adults. Caterpillars, on the other hand, feed in a totally different way from the adults and take totally different foods – and here is the big advantage of complete metamorphosis. By using different foods, adults and young do not compete with each other. A given environment can thus support greater numbers of each species than it could if all stages used the same foods and occupied the same ecological niches. It is worth pointing out that the largest insect groups – the beetles, the flies, and the bees and wasps as well as the butterflies and moths – are all holometabolous, although many beetle larvae do actually eat the same foods as the adults.

Six-spot Burnet

Meadow Brown

Small Tortoiseshell

Adults and caterpillars use different parts of the plant, and usually even different species, thereby reducing competition between them

CLASSIFICATION

Butterflies and moths are arranged in a large number of families, whose members all share a number of common features. Professional entomologists place great emphasis on the arrangement of the wing veins when allocating the insects to their families, and the form of the front legs is also important in the classification of the butterflies. Venation is rarely needed in the identification of European butterflies as the legs and other more obvious features are usually sufficient.

The families are split into genera (singular: genus), and the genera contain a number of closely related species – although there are many genera with just a single species. Some families are also split into sub-families – groups containing genera that are more closely related to each other than to the rest of the genera in the family.

The names of families always end in . . . idae, while sub-family names end in . . . inae. The European butterflies are commonly allotted to nine families. The skippers (family Hesperiidae) stand somewhat apart from the rest of the butterflies and in some respects are intermediate between them and the moths. For this reason they are placed in their own superfamily – the Hesperoidea. The rest of the butterflies are much more closely related to each other and most entomologists place them in a single superfamily – the Papilionoidea. European moths belong to about 50 different families, distributed among 18 superfamilies, although not all of the families contain day-flying species.

Each species or individual kind of insect receives a scientific name (always printed in italics) consisting of the name of its genus, always starting with a capital letter, and the specific name which starts with a small letter. The Brimstone, for example, has the scientific name *Gonepteryx rhamni* and the Cleopatra is known as *Gonep-*

teryx cleopatra. The scientific names thus reveal immediately that the two butterflies are closely related (see p. 46) – a fact that is not apparent from the English or common names. Scientific names also have the big advantage of internationality, for they are used by biologists all over the world.

From this it would be reasonable to assume that the scientific names would be permanent, but unfortunately the nomenclature has not yet reached this desirable state of affairs and names change with alarming frequency; of the eight skipper butterflies in the 1941 edition of South's *Butterflies of the British Isles* only two – the Chequered Skipper and the Lulworth Skipper – have retained their full scientific names, although most still have their original specific names.

Frustrating as it may be for amateur naturalists, there are several sound reasons for changing names. Since Linnaeus first established the binomial system of labelling living things with both generic and specific names, thousands of new species have been discovered and named by various people and, because communication between biologists was not always good, it often happened that several names were given to the same insect. Many of these names simply became lost in obscure literature, but when they come to light again, usually through the researches of specialists, the rules of zoological nomenclature dictate that the earliest name is the correct one – even when it means abandoning a long-used and well-known name. But the specialists must be quite sure that the two names do refer to the same species, and this means checking the descriptions – and the original specimens if possible – in great detail. Names also have to be changed when it is discovered that the same name has been given to two different species.

Another type of name-changing

stems from our increasing knowledge of the insects – often through microscopic and biochemical studies unthinkable when the insects were originally named. Whereas whole groups of superficially similar species were once lumped together in a single genus, detailed studies have often revealed significant differences between them and the specialists have then decided that new genera were needed. A good example of this concerns the 'cabbage' whites and their relatives, all of which were originally placed in the genus *Pieris*. Examination of the scent scales or androconia, however, reveals that those of the Large White are long and slender, while those of the smaller species, including the Small White and the Green-veined White, are broad and Y-shaped. On this basis, some entomologists keep the Large White in the genus *Pieris* and put all the others in a new genus called *Artogeia*. But this can only be an opinion. Other entomologists do not believe that differences in the shape of the scent scales are sufficient to warrant putting the butterflies into different genera and they still regard them all as species of *Pieris*. The limits of the genera and families are all matters of opinion and there will always be 'lumpers', who favour large groups, and 'splitters' who prefer lots of smaller groups.

VARIATION

A good number of butterfly and moth species exist in two or more varieties in different parts of their range (see p. 301), and when these varieties exhibit constant visible differences – although still able to interbreed when and where they meet – they are known as sub-species. A third part is then added to the scientific name. The typical form of the Small Tortoiseshell, found almost everywhere in Europe, is thus known to lepidopterists as *Aglais urticae urticae*, while the Corsican and Sardinian populations, which lack the black spots in the hind part of the forewing, belong to the sub-species *Aglais urticae ichnusa*. But all are Small Tortoiseshells, species *Aglais urticae*.

Seasonal variation occurs in several species, with the two generations (see p. 22) differing markedly in appearance. The Comma (see p. 84) is a familiar example, but the most striking seasonal variation is shown by the Map Butterfly (see p. 300). The two generations are so different that they could easily be mistaken for two distinct species. In this case the spring or early summer brood is known as *Araschnia levana* f. *levana* and the late summer brood is known as *Araschnia levana* f. *prorsa*, with f. standing for form. The term form is also used for genetically produced varieties that occur regularly in a population and make up a fairly constant proportion of that population. Good examples are provided by the Silver-washed Fritillary, in which 10–15% of the females are the greenish f. *valezina* (see p. 298), and by the Clouded Yellow, in which a similar proportion of females are the pale f. *helice* instead of the normal deep yellow.

One-off or irregularly occurring freaks, from whatever cause, are known as aberrations. Some of these have received names, which are then preceded by the abbreviation 'ab.'. Abnormal temperatures, both high and low, during the pupal stage are known to cause aberrations by interfering with pigment formation or deposition, and it is possible that the large number of aberrations of the Silver-washed Fritillary that appeared in England in the summer of 1976 were the result of the extremely high temperatures experienced during pupation. But not all aberrations are caused by environmental factors: many are genetically engineered and, although most are detrimental in the wild, they are readily passed on to succeeding generations in captivity.

The word variety was once used instead of form, and you will find the pale form of the Clouded Yellow referred to as var. *helice* in older books. It has no scientific meaning and is now used for anything that departs significantly from the normal appearance of a species.

BUTTERFLIES

With the exception of a few recently discovered species, all the European butterflies are described and illustrated in the following 126 pages. Each of the nine families also has a brief description preceding those of the individual species.

FAMILY PAPILIONIDAE – THE SWALLOW-
TAILS AND APOLLOS   This family contains mainly large and colourful butterflies, whose hind wings often bear 'tails' on the rear margin. There is only one anal vein in the hind wing and the inner margin is strongly concave, leaving a clear gap between wings and body when the wings are outstretched. The antennae are relatively short and the club is often rather weak. All six legs are fully developed in both sexes and the front tibia bears an epiphysis.

The apollos (sub-family Parnassiinae, pp. 30–32), which are essentially montane butterflies, are reluctant aeronauts and spend most of their waking hours sipping nectar or basking on the ground. Even when they do take off, their flight is surprisingly slow and laboured. The swallowtails (sub-family Papilioninae, pp. 26–28), on the other hand, despite their apparently lazy drifting from flower to flower, can show a fine turn of speed when necessary. After mating, female apollos carry a large horny pouch under the abdomen. Known as the sphragis, this serves to prevent further mating (see p. 295).

The eggs are hemispherical and the larvae are endowed with a brightly coloured osmeterium which is thrust out from behind the head to ward off enemies when the caterpillar is alarmed (see p. 231). The pupae of the swallowtails are attached to the food-plant or other support by a silken girdle, but those of the apollos and the festoons (sub-family Zerynthiinae, pp 28–29) are wrapped in flimsy cocoons on the ground.

Most of the 600 or so species in the family are tropical creatures. Only eleven occur in Europe and some of these have very restricted distributions. Only the Swallowtail itself is found in the British Isles, where it maintains a precarious hold on life in a few parts of the Norfolk Broads.

Young caterpillar

Swallowtail

▲SWALLOWTAIL *Papilio machaon*. Upf has large dark basal patch. HAB flowery places; confined to fenland in B. ALT sl–2200. FLIGHT 4–9 in 1–3 broods. FP various umbellifers, especially fennel, milk parsley, and wild carrot. EGG 5–9; solitary on upper parts of fp. LARVA 5–10; like bird dropping at first, becoming green after 2nd moult. PUPA 1–12; succinct on plant stems close to ground; WINTER pupa. VAR summer broods have black areas dusted with paler scales; abdomen black in 1st brood, yellow with a black stripe in later broods; British specimens are darker with wavier edges to submarginal band of unf. NOTES The British race (*P. m. britannicus*) requires a moist habitat for the proper functioning of the male claspers. STATUS E; Czech., Denmark: V; B: R; Lux. LP; Czech., W. Germany, B, Hungary, Liech., Switz. Poland. SEE ALSO p. 207, 217, 250, 261, 267, 269, 282, 286, 301, 305, 312.

CORSICAN SWALLOWTAIL *Papilio hospiton*. Like Swallowtail but with shorter tails and smaller red spot at rear of uph; unf has very wavy edges to submarginal band. HAB flowery hillsides. ALT 600–1500. FLIGHT 5–7. FP fennel and other umbellifers. EGG 5–7; solitary on leaves and stems. LARVA 6–9. PUPA 9–6; succinct on stems. WINTER pupa. STATUS E. LP; Corsica. SEE ALSO p. 304.

SOUTHERN SWALLOWTAIL *Papilio alexanor*. Upf has yellow base; ups clearly striped. HAB mountain slopes: very local. ALT <1500. FLIGHT 4–7. FP various umbellifers, especially fennel. EGG 4–7; solitary on stems and leaves. LARVA 5–8. PUPA 1–12; succinct on fp. WINTER pupa. NOTES Adult very fond of thistles. STATUS E; Greece, Italy. V; elsewhere. LP; Greece.

Swallowtail

Corsican Swallowtail

Southern Swallowtail

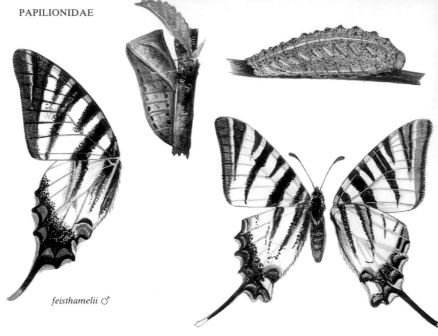

feisthamelii ♂

Scarce Swallowtail

SCARCE SWALLOWTAIL *Iphiclides podalirius*. Upf has 6 dark stripes in an unmistakable pattern; tails of hw are much longer than in *Papilio* spp. HAB open country, both wild and cultivated. ALT sl–2000. FLIGHT 3–9 in 2 broods. FP blackthorn and other rosaceous trees, including cultivated fruit trees. EGG 4–9; solitary on fp. LARVA 5–10. PUPA 1–12; succinct on fp and neighbouring supports. WINTER pupa. VAR ground colour of 1st brood much yellower than summer brood; ground colour of ♂ is almost white in both broods in Iberia and S.W. France (*I. p. feisthamelii*). NOTES Vagrants occasionally reach B and Scandinavia. STATUS E; Czech., Lux., Poland. V; Belgium, W. Germany. LP; Belgium, Czech., W. Germany, Hungary, Liech., Poland, Switz. SEE ALSO p. 228, 229, 230, 251, 253, 260, 275, 276, 286.

SPANISH FESTOON *Zerynthia rumina*. Upf has red spots in and at the end of the cell; clear 'window' towards wing-tip. HAB rough hillsides, especially near the coast. ALT sl–1500. FLIGHT 2–5. FP birthworts. EGG 3–5. LARVA 4–6: ground colour fawn to dark grey. PUPA 6–4; fixed to the ground by a few silken threads. WINTER pupa. VAR ground colour sometimes more orange, especially in ♀. NOTES Overlaps with Southern Festoon only in Provence. STATUS V. LP; France. SEE ALSO p. 250, 251.

SOUTHERN FESTOON *Zerynthia polyxena*. Like Spanish Festoon but upf has no red in cell and no clear 'window' near tip. HAB Rough, stony places. ALT sl–1100. FLIGHT 2–5. FP birthworts. EGG 3–5. LARVA 4–6: ground colour fawn to dark grey. PUPA 6–4; fixed to the ground by a few silken threads. WINTER pupa. VAR blue sub-marginal markings often missing from uph; *Z. p. cassandra* of France and Italy is darker and upf lacks red spot near the front. NOTES Overlaps with Spanish Festoon in France. STATUS E; Czech. LP; Czech., Greece, Hungary. Decline thought due to intense cultivation of vineyards, fp habitat.

EASTERN FESTOON *Zerynthia cerisyi*. Hw deeply scalloped; often a short tail on v4. HAB rough hillsides. ALT sl–1500. FLIGHT 4–7. FP birthworts. EGG 4–6. LARVA 5–7. PUPA 7–5; attached to the ground by a few silken threads. WINTER pupa. VAR *Z. c. cretica* from Crete is smaller and yellower, with no obvious tail. STATUS V; Bulgaria: R; Greece. LP; Greece.

Spanish Festoon

♂

cassandra

♀

♀

Southern Festoon

♂

♀

Eastern Festoon

Apollo

False Apollo

FALSE APOLLO *Archon apollinus*. Wing pattern is unique. HAB rough hillsides. ALT <1500. FLIGHT 3–4. FP birthworts. EGG 3–5. LARVA 4–7. PUPA 7–4. WINTER pupa. STATUS V & LP in whole range.

APOLLO *Parnassius apollo*. Wings thinly scaled with a characteristic pattern; ♀ often has greyer ground colour; antennae pale grey with darker rings. HAB exposed mountain slopes with plenty of flowers. ALT 500–2000; often lower in Scandinavia. FLIGHT 7–8. FP stonecrops and houseleeks. EGG 7–9; occasionally overwintering until 4; solitary or in small groups. LARVA 8–4, most obvious in spring; feeds only in sunshine. PUPA 5–7; in loose cocoon, usually concealed under stones or debris. WINTER hibernating larva or as fully formed young larva within the egg-shell. VAR spot size varies and red may be replaced by yellow or orange. Many varieties. NOTES Flight is slow and laboured and the insects are easy to approach when feeding at flowers. STATUS E: Czech., Finland, W. Germany & Poland. V; elsewhere, although may be locally common. LP; Bulgaria, Czech., Finland, France, W. Germany, Greece, Leich., Switz. & Poland. Afforestation major reason for decline. SEE ALSO p. 18, 208, 233, 234, 249, 276, 301.

SMALL APOLLO *Parnassius phoebus*. Like Apollo but smaller and upf usually with a red spot near front margin; ♂ uph has no dark marks beyond red spots; ♀ ups more heavily marked; antennae white with black rings. HAB grassy mountain slopes. ALT >1800. FLIGHT 5–8. FP houseleeks and saxifrages. EGG 7–9, occasionally over-wintering until 4; solitary or in small clusters. LARVA 8–6, feeding in sunshine. PUPA 5–7; in a loose cocoon concealed under stones or plant debris. WINTER hibernating larva or egg with fully formed larva inside. VAR ♀ upf generally has black spot near hind margin; f. *cardinalis* of Eastern Alps is heavily dusted with black and has more red on hw. STATUS V. LP; France, W. Germany & Leich. SEE ALSO p. 295.

Spanish race

Apollo

♂

Small Apollo

f. *cardinalis*

31

athene

Clouded Apollo

CLOUDED APOLLO *Parnassius mnemosyne*. Lacks red spots of other apollos and resembles Black-veined White at a distance, but latter has no spots and inner margin of hw is not concave. HAB open hillsides and mountain slopes; also damp meadows in the north. ALT sl (Scand.)–2200. FLIGHT 5–7. FP corydalis. EGG 1–12; solitary on fp. LARVA generally 4–5, but some eggs hatch in summer and then larva is found all year. PUPA 4–5; dull yellow amongst debris on ground. WINTER generally as fully formed larva inside the egg, but occasionally as partly grown larva. VAR some ♀♀ are heavily dusted with grey or brown, especially on high mountains; *P. m. athene* of southern areas has white spots in grey apical patch of upf. STATUS E; Denmark (possibly extinct), E. Germany, Lith. & Sweden. V; elsewhere. LP; Czech., Finland, W. Germany, Greece, Hungary, Leich., Poland, Switz.

FAMILY PIERIDAE – THE WHITES AND YELLOWS The European members of this family are largely white or yellow. The sexes usually differ to some extent – markedly so in the Brimstone and the Orange tip – although in most species the differences revolve around the presence or absence of spots. There are two anal veins in the hind wings, the inner margin of which is slightly convex. When at rest, the abdomen is completely concealed by the hind wings. Each hind wing has a broad groove into which the abdomen fits snugly when the wings are closed.

All six legs are fully developed in both sexes. The antennae are very slender, with a slim, elon-gate rather indistinct club.

The eggs are skittle-shaped and usually strongly ribbed. The caterpillars are markedly cylindrical, without any obvious taper or outgrowths and no more than a short coat of fine hairs. The larvae of most of the whites feed on plants of the cabbage family, while the yellows nearly all use plants of the pea family. The pupa, with a single sharp point at the head end, is held upright on its support by a silken girdle.

About 40 species live in Europe. Only six are resident in the British Isles although four more, including the Clouded Yellow, arrive in variable numbers each year from the continent.

BLACK-VEINED WHITE *Aporia crataegi*. Conspicuous black (♂) or brown (♀) veins; wings thinly scaled, especially in ♀, and often becoming transparent with age. HAB flowery places in open country, often in hills. ALT sl–2000. FLIGHT 5–7. FP blackthorn and hawthorn and other rosaceous shrubs. EGG 6–7; clustered on upper sides of leaves. LARVA 7–5; gregarious in silken nests until after hibernation. PUPA 5–7; succinct on fp. WINTER hibernating larvae in dense silken tent. NOTES Adult is very fond of drinking from wet ground, often in large numbers. Became extinct in B early in 20th Century. STATUS E; Holland. V; Lux. (extinct?) & Norway. R; Leich. LP; only in Lux. & parts Austria. Sometimes orchard pest in S. SEE ALSO p. 204, 213, 217, 225, 253, 258, 294, 304, 306.

▲**LARGE WHITE** *Pieris brassicae*. Much larger than any similar butterfly; black apical patch on upf reaches back at least to vein 3. HAB all flowery places but especially common in and around gardens. ALT sl–2200. FLIGHT 4–10: 2–3 broods. FP mainly cultivated brassicas; also garden nasturtiums. EGG 4–9; bright yellow in batches of 50–100, usually on underside of leaves. LARVA 5–11; gregarious in early instars. PUPA 1–12; succinct on fences and other supports: sometimes plain green. WINTER pupa. VAR unh ground colour yellow in 1st brood, but much paler in later broods; summer broods have intense black apical markings. STATUS An abundant pest. SEE ALSO p. 25, 200, 201, 202, 204, 224, 225, 239, 248, 252, 260, 262, 264, 266, 277, 279, 289.

Black-veined White

Large White

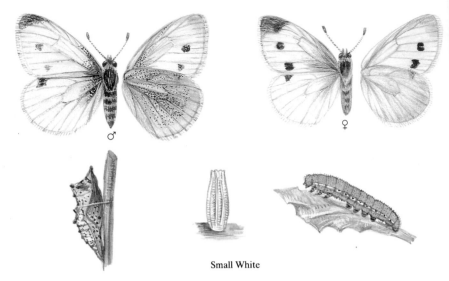

Small White

▲**SMALL WHITE** *Pieris rapae*. Like Large White but smaller; apical patch reaches back only to vein 6. HAB flowery places everywhere, but especially common around gardens. ALT sl–2000. FLIGHT 3–10; 2–4 broods. FP wild and cultivated brassicas, including rape; also garden nasturtiums. EGG 3–10; solitary on both surfaces of leaf. LARVA 1–12, mainly 3–11; solitary and very well camouflaged. PUPA 1–12; succinct on fences and other vertical supports. WINTER pupa, although in mild years larvae can be found throughout the winter. VAR summer broods have darker markings on ups than spring ones and fewer grey scales on unh. NOTES Larvae very like those of Green-veined White, but distinguished in later instars by the yellow line along the back. STATUS An abundant pest. SEE ALSO p. 22, 25, 202, 203, 222, 223, 224, 252, 264, 266, 267, 268.

MOUNTAIN SMALL WHITE *Pieris ergane*. Like Small White but unf has no black spots (upf markings may show through). HAB rough, flowery grassland. ALT sl–2000. FLIGHT 3–10 in 2 or 3 broods. FP aethionema. EGG 4–10. LARVA 4–11. PUPA 1–12. WINTER pupa. STATUS V. LP; France, Greece, Hungary.

▲**GREEN-VEINED WHITE** *Pieris napi*. Unh has lines of green or greyish scales along veins. HAB light woodland, hedgerows, gardens, damp meadows, and river banks. ALT sl–2500. FLIGHT 3–11; 1–3 broods. FP various crucifers, especially garlic mustard, cuckooflower, and watercress; rare on cultivated brassicas. EGG 3–9; solitary on leaves. LARVA 4–10; no yellow stripe on the back (see Small White). PUPA 6–3; succinct on fp or other support. WINTER pupa. VAR summer broods are less strongly marked than spring ones; in some alpine areas ♂ ups are strongly veined and ♀ ups are heavily dusted with brown (*P. n. bryoniae*). NOTES Northern and western populations in B are largely restricted to damp meadows and riversides. STATUS LP; Hungary (*P. n. bryoniae* only) and in parts of Austria. SEE ALSO p. 23, 25, 237, 242, 243, 245, 247, 249, 250, 252, 259, 266.

Green-veined White

Mountain Small White

2nd brood ♂   2nd brood ♀

bryoniae ♂   *bryoniae* ♀

Green-veined White

Kreuper's Small White ▶

1st brood ♀

2nd brood ♀

Southern Small White

2nd brood ♂

SOUTHERN SMALL WHITE *Pieris mannii*. Like Small White but apical patch of upf extends down the edge at least to vein 4; pd spot in S3 of upf often crescent-shaped (never round) and in ♀ usually linked to margin by dark streaks, especially in summer broods. HAB rough flowery places. ALT sl–1600. FLIGHT 3–11; 3–4 broods. FP various wild crucifers. EGG 4–10. LARVA 1–12. PUPA 1–12. WINTER larva or pupa. VAR summer insects are larger than spring ones, with larger black markings. STATUS E; Czech. V; Hungary. LP; Hungary.

KREUPER'S SMALL WHITE *Pieris kreuperi*. Upf has triangular black spot near tip. HAB rocky slopes. ALT sl–2000. FLIGHT 3–10; 2–4 broods. FP golden alyssum. EGG 4–10. LARVA 4–11. PUPA 1–12. WINTER pupa. STATUS V; Bulgaria. R; elsewhere. LP; Greece.

△**BATH WHITE** *Pontia daplidice*. Unf has a large discal spot reaching to front margin and two prominent black spots near outer margin; apical markings of unf are green; ♀ usually much blacker than ♂. HAB rough flowery places. ALT sl–2000. FLIGHT 2–10; 2–4 broods. FP various wild crucifers and mignonette. EGG 3–9; solitary on leaves and flowers. LARVA 1–12, mainly 3–10. PUPA 1–12; succinct on fp. WINTER larva or pupa. VAR summer insects often paler and with yellower uns than spring ones. NOTES Migrates northwards each summer; a few vagrants reach B in most years. STATUS E; Lux. (extinct?). Common in S. SEE ALSO p. 268, 288.

SMALL BATH WHITE *Pontia chloridice*. Like Bath White but unf discal spot does not reach front margin; unh has an almost continuous white pd band and elongate white marginal spots; ♀ usually has heavier black markings than ♂. HAB rocky flower-rich places. ALT sl–1500. FLIGHT 4–6: 2 broods. FP various crucifers. EGG ? LARVA ? PUPA ? WINTER ? STATUS V. LP; Greece.

PEAK WHITE *Pontia callidice*. Unh has pd series of white or yellowish arrow-head marks; fw rather more pointed than in other similar species. HAB montane grassland. ALT >2000. FLIGHT 6–8. FP dwarf treacle mustard; Pyrenean mignonette. EGG 6–8. LARVA 7–9. PUPA 9–6; succinct on fp or other support. WINTER pupa. STATUS E; Austria.

Bath White

♀

Bath White

♂

Bath White

Small Bath White

♀

2nd brood ♂
Small Bath White

Peak White

Peak White

♂

♀

Peak White

Dappled White

DAPPLED WHITE *Euchloe ausonia*. Upf discal spot joins dark patch on front margin; unf discal spot comma-shaped with a pale centre; front edge of hw strongly angled. HAB alpine meadows. ALT 1000–2000. FLIGHT 6–7. FP candytuft and other crucifers. EGG 6–8; solitary on fp. LARVA 7–9. PUPA 9–6; sandy coloured and succinct on fp. WINTER pupa. STATUS ?

FREYER'S DAPPLED WHITE *Euchloe simplonia*. Like Dappled White but upf discal spot rarely meets front margin; unh white spots often shiny. HAB flowery fields and hillsides. ALT sl–1400. FLIGHT 3–6 in 2 broods. FP candytuft and other crucifers. EGG 3–7. LARVA 3–8. PUPA 1–12. WINTER pupa. STATUS ?

CORSICAN DAPPLED WHITE *Euchloe insularis*. Smaller than most similar species; upf discal spot slender and linked to grey patch on front margin; unf discal spot very small. HAB mountain slopes. ALT sl–1200, usually 800–1000. FLIGHT 5–6. FP hoary mustard. EGG 5–6. LARVA 6–7. PUPA 1–12. WINTER pupa. STATUS ?

PORTUGUESE DAPPLED WHITE *Euchloe tagis*. Like Dappled White but white spots are completely enclosed in the dark apical patch of upf; front margin of hw smoothly rounded. HAB stony places, usually in the hills. ALT sl–1000. FLIGHT 2–5. FP candytuft. EGG 2–5. LARVA 3–6. PUPA 1–12. WINTER pupa. VAR specimens from southern Spain and Portugal have very little spotting on unh. STATUS R; Portugal.

GREEN-STRIPED WHITE *Euchloe belemia*. Unf apex green with transverse white stripes; unh usually with prominent stripes; unf discal spot large and enclosing a slender white crescent. HAB rough flowery places. ALT sl–1000. FLIGHT 2–5; 2 overlapping broods. FP candytuft, rockets (*Sisymbrium* spp), and other crucifers. EGG 3–6; solitary on fp. LARVA 4–6; PUPA 1–12; succinct on fp. WINTER pupa. VAR 2nd brood often has poorly defined stripes on unh and less pointed fw than 1st brood. STATUS ? SEE ALSO p. 251.

▲**ORANGE-TIP** *Anthocaris cardamines*. ♂ upf has orange tip on a white background; ♀ fw is distinctly rounded at apex, with a more or less solid black tip on upper side and greyish or yellowish tip on underside. HAB Woodland margins, hedgerows, gardens, and damp flowery meadows. ALT sl–1500. FLIGHT 4–6. FP various crucifers, but mainly garlic mustard and cuckooflower in the wild; also *Reseda* spp. and, in gardens, honesty and sweet rocket. EGG 5–6; white at first, soon becoming orange; solitary in flowerheads. LARVA 5–8; well camouflaged on flowers and developing fruits; cannibalistic. PUPA 7–5; succinct; green or brown and extremely well camouflaged on fp. WINTER pupa. NOTES Mainly associated with cuckooflower in damp meadows in N & W of range. STATUS Generally common. LP; W. Germany. SEE ALSO p. 22, 202, 205, 206, 207, 215, 217, 228, 229, 233, 243, 251, 252, 295.

GREENISH BLACK-TIP *Elphinstonia charlonia penia*. Distinguished from all other yellow butterflies by the large black discal spot linked to front margin of upf. HAB rocky slopes. ALT sl–500. FLIGHT 4–6; 2 broods. FP stocks. EGG 4–7. LARVA 4–8. PUPA 1–12: has a very obvious head prominence. WINTER pupa. STATUS E; Yugoslavia. V; Greece.

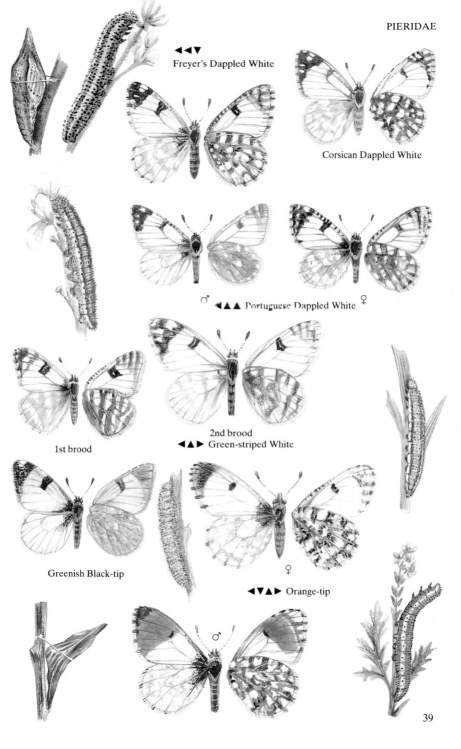

◄◄▼
Freyer's Dappled White

Corsican Dappled White

♂ ◄▲▲ Portuguese Dappled White ♀

1st brood

2nd brood
◄▲► Green-striped White

Greenish Black-tip

♀

◄▼▲► Orange-tip

♂

39

♂   ♀

Moroccan Orange-tip

♂   ♀

Eastern Orange-tip

MOROCCAN ORANGE-TIP *Anthocaris belia euphenoides*. Orange apical patch on upf of ♀ is distinctive; ♂ coloration is unique in SW Europe, but see Eastern Orange-tip. HAB rough, flowery hillsides. ALT sl–1500. FLIGHT 3–6. FP flowers and seed pods of buckler mustard and other crucifers. EGG 4–6; solitary on fp. LARVA 4–7. PUPA 6–4; succinct on fp. WINTER pupa. STATUS V; Italy. SEE ALSO p. 251, 288.

EASTERN ORANGE-TIP *Anthocaris damone*. Like Moroccan Orange-Tip but unh has a more extensive dark pattern; ♂ unf has a broader orange patch and ♀ upf lacks orange tip. HAB rocky hillsides: local. ALT sl–1500 but generally around 1000. FLIGHT 4–5. FP woad. EGG 4–5. LARVA 5–7. PUPA 6–4. WINTER pupa. STATUS R. LP; Greece.

GRUNER'S ORANGE-TIP *Anthocaris gruneri*. Like Orange-Tip but smaller; ♂ ups pale yellow; ♀ upf has a large discal spot linked to costal margin and dark apical patch reaching almost to tornus. HAB rough, stony places. ALT sl–1600. FLIGHT 4–6. FP burnt candytuft. EGG 4–6. LARVA 5–7. PUPA 7–5. WINTER pupa. STATUS R; Yugoslavia. LP; Greece.

SOOTY ORANGE-TIP *Zegris eupheme*. Orange patch in black tip of upf is unique. HAB rough, flowery places. ALT sl–1000. FLIGHT 4–5. FP hoary mustard. EGG 4–6. LARVA 5–7. PUPA 7–4: in flimsy cocoon. WINTER pupa. STATUS ?

MOUNTAIN CLOUDED YELLOW *Colias phicomone*. Ups pale greyish yellow heavily suffused with black, especially in ♂; pale spots in dark marginal bands; uph has a prominent yellow spot in the centre. HAB flowery mountain slopes. ALT >1800. FLIGHT 6–9. FP vetches and other leguminous plants. EGG 7–8; solitary on upper surfaces of leaves. LARVA 8–5. PUPA 5–7; succinct. WINTER hibernating larva. NOTES There is nothing similar in the mountains of Western Europe. STATUS Generally abundant. V; Austria. LP; W. Germany.

PALE ARCTIC CLOUDED YELLOW *Colias nastes*. Like Mountain Clouded Yellow but with less black suffusion; uph has at most a very small yellow spot; ranges of the two species do not overlap. HAB rough hillsides. ALT 300–500. FLIGHT 5–7. FP alpine milk-vetch and *Vaccinium* spp. EGG 6–8. LARVA 6–4. PUPA 4–6; succinct. WINTER hibernating larva. STATUS R; Norway. SEE ALSO p. 222, 288.

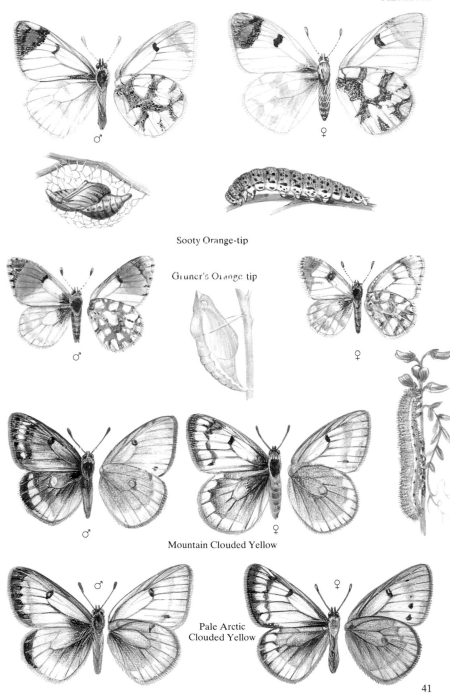

♂ ♀

Sooty Orange-tip

Gruner's Orange-tip

♂ ♀

♂ ♀

Mountain Clouded Yellow

♂ ♀

Pale Arctic
Clouded Yellow

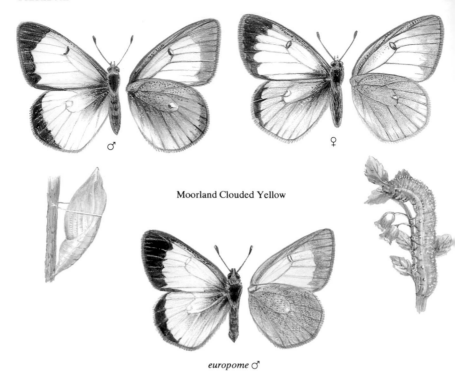

Moorland Clouded Yellow

europome ♂

MOORLAND CLOUDED YELLOW *Colias palaeno*. Pale to dirty yellow in ♂; white in ♀; both sexes with solid black borders. HAB bogs and moorland. ALT 300(N)–600. FLIGHT 6–7. FP bilberry and bog bilberry. EGG 7–8, but sometimes not hatching until spring; solitary on fp. LARVA 8–5. PUPA 4–6; succinct on low-growing vegetation. WINTER larva, occasionally as egg. VAR ♂ very pale in north (*C. p. palaeno*), darker in central regions with white or black discal spot on upf. (*C. p. europome*); smaller and darker in Alps, without discal spot on upf (*C. p. europomene*). STATUS E; Belgium (Ex?), Poland. V; one of the commonest butterflies in N. LP; France, W. Germany.

LESSER CLOUDED YELLOW *Colias chrysotheme*. Uns of both wings carry small dark pd spots; ♀ upf has broad greyish green costal margin. HAB waste places and grassy hillsides. ALT <900m. FLIGHT 5–8 in 2 broods. FP hairy tare. EGG 5–9. LARVA 1–12. PUPA 4–8. WINTER larva. STATUS V; Austria. R; elsewhere.

GREEK CLOUDED YELLOW *Colias libanotica*. ♂ ups dull orange with a purplish sheen when seen at certain angles; ♀ uns uniformly yellowish green; ♀ unh largely grey. HAB rough mountain grassland. ALT 1800–2500. FLIGHT 5–7. FP *Astragalus* spp. EGG 6–8. LARVA 7–5. PUPA 4–6; succinct. WINTER hibernating larva. VAR ♀ occasionally white. STATUS V; Greece.

DANUBE CLOUDED YELLOW *Colias myrmidone*. Like Clouded Yellow but upf more orange and ♂ has no yellow veins crossing black border; uns with small dark pd spots or none at all. HAB lowland heaths and dry grassland, mainly in Danube basin. ALT up to 1000. FLIGHT 5–8; 2 broods. FP brooms, mainly *Cytisus capitatus*. EGG 5–9. LARVA 6–4. PUPA 4–8; succinct on fp. WINTER small larva. STATUS E; Czech., V; elsewhere. LP; W. Germany, Hungary.

♂ ♀

Greek Clouded Yellow

♂ ♀

Lesser Clouded Yellow

♂ ♀

Danube Clouded Yellow

Clouded Yellow

f. *helice*

▲**CLOUDED YELLOW** *Colias crocea*. Ups bright yellow with wide black borders crossed by yellow veins; unf has large black pd spots; ♀ ups always with yellow spots in marginal bands. HAB flowery places. ALT sl–2200. FLIGHT 4–10 in several broods. FP clovers, vetches, and other leguminous plants. EGG 4–10; solitary on upper sides of leaves; yellow at first, becoming orange later. LARVA 1–12. PUPA 3–9; succinct on stems of fp; occasionally found in late autumn in northern parts of the range, but these individuals do not survive. WINTER hibernating larva, although it may remain active in mild winters in far south; it cannot survive winters north of the Alps. VAR ~10% of ♀♀ are creamy white (f. *helice*). NOTES Flight very fast. Like other clouded yellows, rarely opens wings when resting. Resident in S; migrates N in spring, then produces one or more summer generations. Size of population in far N depends on numbers arriving in spring and breeding success of summer generations. STATUS LP; W. Germany. SEE ALSO p. 25, 246, 265, 299, 308.

BALKAN CLOUDED YELLOW *Colias balcanica*. Ups like Greek Clouded Yellow but no yellow veins cross the dark margins and uns are yellower, especially in ♀; ♂ has a prominent pale oval sex brand at front of upf. (Other species have a sex brand, but it is much less prominent.) HAB open woodland. ALT >1600. FLIGHT 6–7. FP ? EGG ? LARVA ? PUPA ? WINTER ? VAR f. *rebeli* is a pale ♀, very similar to f. *helice* of the Clouded Yellow, but it is not common. STATUS V. LP; Bulgaria.

NORTHERN CLOUDED YELLOW *Colias hecla*. Smaller than the other orange species and the only one of this colour in the far north; ups have a rosy reflection at certain angles; unh largely greyish green. HAB rough grassland. ALT sl–1000. FLIGHT 6–7. FP alpine milk-vetch and *Vaccinium* spp. EGG 6–8. LARVA 1–12; 2-year life cycle? PUPA 4–6; 1–12 in W; succinct on fp. WINTER larva (twice) or pupa. STATUS R; Norway. SEE ALSO p. 222, 247.

△**PALE CLOUDED YELLOW** *Colias hyale*. Pale ups and bright yellow unh distinguish this butterfly from all others except Berger's Clouded Yellow; black patch at base of upf usually invades base of cell; ♀ is like f. *helice* of Clouded Yellow but has less black, especially on uph. HAB flowery fields and hillsides; very fond of lucerne and clover fields. ALT sl–2000. FLIGHT 5–9; 2 broods. FP lucerne, vetches, and other leguminous plants. EGG 5–10; solitary on fp. LARVA 6–4. PUPA 4–8; succinct on fp. WINTER larva. NOTES Resident in C. and S.E. Europe, migrating northwards each spring; a sporadic mainly coastal visitor to B. STATUS R; Lux. (as a resident). LP: W. Germany, Greece. SEE ALSO p. 241, 299.

Balkan Clouded Yellow

 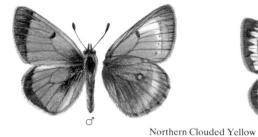 

Northern Clouded Yellow

Clouded Yellow larva

▲▼ Pale Clouded Yellow

45

Berger's Clouded Yellow

△**BERGER'S CLOUDED YELLOW** *Colias australis*. Very similar to Pale Clouded Yellow but ♂ uph usually brighter yellow with a much darker discoidal spot; ♀ unh generally greener than in the Pale Clouded Yellow; upf usually without black in the base of the cell. HAB rough flowery places, usually in hilly areas. ALT sl–2000. FLIGHT 5–9; 2 broods; occasionally a 3rd brood 9–10 in far south. FP horseshoe vetch and crown vetch. EGG 5–10; solitary on fp. LARVA 1–12. PUPA 3–8 (9); succinct on fp. WINTER hibernating larva. NOTES Only recently distinguished from Pale Clouded Yellow, no single adult feature reliable enough to separate the two. Larvae are quite different. Resident in S & C, migrating northwards in spring; a sporadic visitor to B. STATUS V; Lux. (as a resident). LP; Belgium, W. Germany.

EASTERN PALE CLOUDED YELLOW *Colias erate*. Ups butter yellow; fw rather pointed; ♀ has pale spots in margin of fw. HAB lowland grassland. ALT ? lowland. FLIGHT 5–9; 2 broods; all European specimens are 2nd brood, suggesting that the species migrates into the area from Asia. FP ? EGG ? LARVA ? PUPA ? WINTER ? STATUS ?.

▲**BRIMSTONE** *Gonepteryx rhamni*. ♂ unmistakable; ♀ greenish white and often mistaken for a Large White in flight. HAB open woods, rough, flowery places, and gardens. ALT sl–1800. FLIGHT 2–9; adults emerging in summer before parents have died. FP buckthorn and alder buckthorn. EGG 5–6; cream and skittle-shaped; solitary on buds or the underside of young leaves. LARVA 6–7; well camouflaged when resting along leaf mid-rib, but revealing its presence by characteristic perforations of the leaves. PUPA 6–8; succinctly fixed to underside of a leaf and resembling a curled leaf. WINTER hibernating adult, usually in holly or ivy where its leaf-like underside affords it good camouflage. VAR slightly larger in south (f. *meridionalis*). NOTES Strong purposeful flight often takes it far from its breeding haunts, which are often on the edges of woods. STATUS LP; Greece, N. Ireland. SEE ALSO p. 22, 24, 242, 243, 244, 251, 260, 261, 271, 273, 274, 289.

CLEOPATRA *Gonepteryx cleopatra*. ♂ unmistakable; ♀ very much like Brimstone but uph often slightly yellower and unf has a faint orange streak running through the cell. HAB open woodland and scrub in hilly regions. ALT sl–1500, usually 500–1000. FLIGHT 2–7, new adults on the wing in early summer before overwintered parents have died; occasionally a 2nd brood in autumn, especially in Spain. FP buckthorn. EGG 3–4, occasionally 6–7; solitary under leaves of fp. LARVA 4–5, occasionally 7–8. PUPA 5–7, occasionally 8–9; succinct on fp. WINTER adult. NOTES The adults mate before going into hibernation, but do not lay their eggs until the spring. STATUS ? SEE ALSO p. 24, 271.

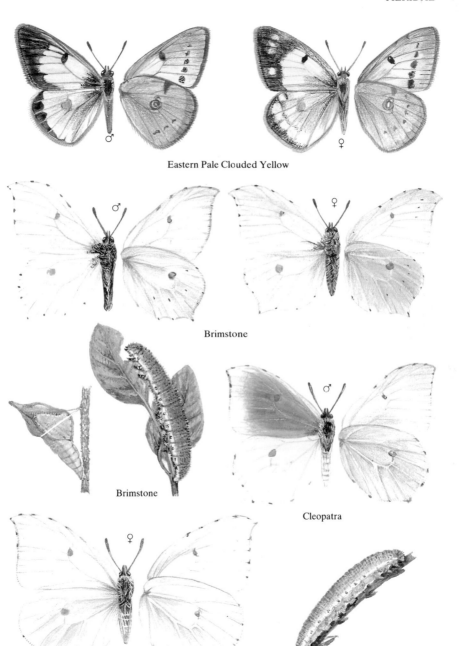

Eastern Pale Clouded Yellow

Brimstone

Brimstone

Cleopatra

Cleopatra

47

POWDERED BRIMSTONE *Gonepteryx farinosa*. Like Brimstone but ♂ uph paler than upf; hw more strongly toothed than Brimstone. HAB scrubby hillsides. ALT < 2200. FLIGHT 5–6. FP buckthorn. EGG ? LARVA ? PUPA ? WINTER ? STATUS ?

▲**WOOD WHITE** *Leptidea sinapis*. A flimsy species not closely related to the 'cabbage whites'; antennal club black with a chestnut brown tip and a white spot beneath it. HAB sheltered woodland rides and glades in B, but more open areas, such as woodland margins and surrounding fields elsewhere, including Ireland. ALT sl–2000. FLIGHT 4–9; 1–3 broods; 1 brood in B, but may be a partial 2nd brood in warm years. FP meadow vetchling and a few other leguminous plants such as tufted vetch. EGG 4–9; solitary on underside of leaves of fp. LARVA 4–9; rarely moves far from egg site. PUPA 1–12; succinct on fp. WINTER pupa. VAR ♂ has large grey apical patch on upf in 1st brood; later broods have smaller but blacker patch; 2nd brood ♀♀ almost unmarked; Irish specimens (*L. s. juvernica*) have olive-green unh. NOTES Extending its range in B at present, after a noticeable decrease in the earlier part of this century. STATUS E; Holland. LP; W. Germany. SEE ALSO p. 244, 259, 260, 292–3, 307.

EASTERN WOOD WHITE *Leptidea duponcheli*. Like Wood White but with no white spot under antennal club; ♀ resembles ♂ but has fainter dark markings. HAB upland meadows. ALT <1000. FLIGHT 4–9; 2 broods. FP sainfoin and other leguminous plants. EGG 4–9; solitary on fp. LARVA 4–9. PUPA 6–4; succinct on fp and neighbouring vegetation. WINTER pupa. VAR 2nd brood has smaller apical patch on upf and no black on uns. STATUS R; Yugoslavia. LP; Greece.

FENTON'S WOOD WHITE *Leptidea morsei*. Very like Wood White and difficult to distinguish from it without examining genitalia, but ♀ has slightly pointed wing-tips in 1st brood. HAB lightly wooded valleys. ALT sl–500? FLIGHT 4–7; 2 broods. FP spring pea and black pea. EGG 4–7; solitary on leaves. LARVA 4–8. PUPA most of the year; succinct on fp or neighbouring vegetation. WINTER pupa. VAR 2nd brood slightly larger and with less black. STATUS E; Austria, Czech.: V; elsewhere.

FAMILY LYCAENIDAE – HAIRSTREAKS, COPPERS, AND BLUES   This is an immense family with well over 6,000 species – about a third of the world's known butterfly fauna. They are mostly small butterflies – no more than 40mm across the wings in the European species – and many males exhibit gleaming metallic colours, especially among the coppers (sub-family Lycaeninae, pp. 52–56) and the blues (sub-family Polyommatinae, pp. 56–64). Sexual dimorphism is the rule, and particularly striking among the blues where the females are often dressed in brown and quite unlike their shiny blue mates. Female coppers are often quite colourful, although usually less brilliant than the males. Hairstreaks (sub-family Theclinae, pp. 50–52) show fewer differences between the sexes, but where there are differences the female is usually the more colourful. Scent scales or androconia usually occur on the males' forewings, and in some of the hairstreaks they are concentrated into small oval patches – the sexbrands – near the front margin. The hind wings often bear slender 'tails' on the rear of the outer margin. These are short in our European species, but in some tropical lycaenids they are as long as or longer than the body and they resemble antennae (see p. 275).

The antennae are usually conspicuously ringed with white and the club varies from weak to very strong. With little room on the small head, the antennae are attached very close to the eyes and the latter are slightly indented near the top to make room for the bases of the antennae. All six legs are used for walking, but the front legs differ in the two sexes. Those of the male have just one long tarsal segment and a single claw, while the female front leg has the full complement of five tarsal segments and two claws. Flight is rather jerky but, despite their small size, many of the lycaenids can cover the ground quite rapidly. Most of them keep close to the ground.

Lycaenid eggs are generally shaped like tiny buns or doughnuts, although those of the White-letter Hairstreak are rather more flattened and resemble miniature discuses. Intricately sculptured with hexagonal patterns, and often spiny when viewed under high magnification, they are among the most exquisite of insect eggs. The larvae are distinctly flattened and, with a flange along each side, they are shaped rather like woodlice – especially when the small head is withdrawn into the thorax. They have relatively short legs and are clothed with short hairs. Hairstreak larvae all feed on trees and shrubs, copper larvae feed on docks and sorrels, and the blues nearly all use leguminous plants – feeding on flowers and fruits as well as leaves. Many lycaenid larvae are associated with ants, which are attracted by sweet secretions from the abdo-

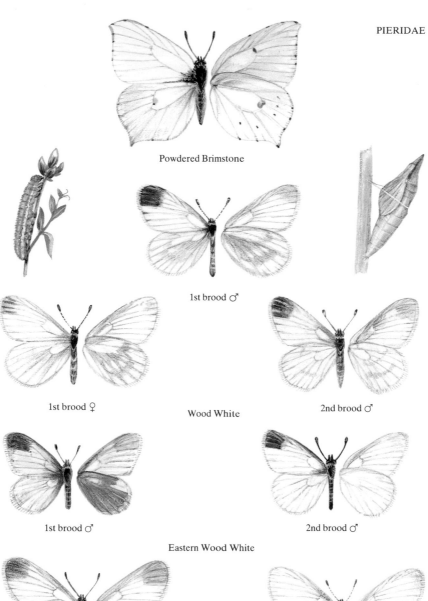

Powdered Brimstone

1st brood ♂

1st brood ♀

Wood White

2nd brood ♂

1st brood ♂

Eastern Wood White

2nd brood ♂

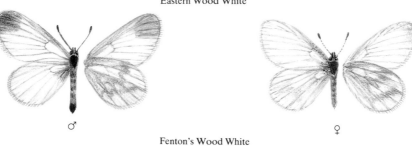

♂

Fenton's Wood White

♀

men (see p. 218). The pupae are dumpy and without any sharp points or corners. They sometimes lie freely just on or under the ground, but are more commonly bound to the food-plant with a silken girdle.

About 90 species occur in Europe. Fifteen are resident in the British Isles, including the artificially maintained Large Copper, although only seven are found in Ireland. Three further species occasionally arrive in Britain as migrants from the continent.

▲**BROWN HAIRSTREAK** *Thecla betulae*. Orange uns, streaked with white, is unmistakable. HAB light woodland and hedgerows, keeping mainly to tree-tops and feeding on honeydew. ALT sl–500. FLIGHT 7–10. FP blackthorn and other *Prunus* spp: occasionally on birch. EGG 8–4: pale grey and hemispherical, solitary or in pairs on twigs. LARVA 4–7: slug-like and hard to spot. PUPA 6–8: smooth and reddish brown, succinctly attached to undersides of leaves. WINTER egg. VAR ♂ upf may have *small* orange patch. STATUS V; Greece, Holland. R; Eire. LP; W. Germany. SEE ALSO p. 244.

▲**PURPLE HAIRSTREAK** *Quercusia quercus*. Uns grey, usually with a distinct white streak: ups with brilliant purple sheen all over in ♂, but restricted to a small patch on fw in ♀. HAB mature woodland, keeping mainly to tree-tops and feeding on honeydew. ALT sl–2200. FLIGHT 6–9. FP oak and occasionally ash. EGG 7–4: flattened grey spheres attached singly or in small groups to buds and twigs. LARVA 4–6: feeding inside buds in 1st instar and later browsing on leaves by night. PUPA 5–7: concealed in bark crevices. WINTER egg. VAR white line on uns often vestigial in Iberia. STATUS V; Lith. LP; W. Germany. SEE ALSO p. 245, 258.

SPANISH PURPLE HAIRSTREAK *Laeosopis roboris*. Like Purple Hairstreak but with brown uns edged with orange: purple less extensive on ups. HAB light woodland and other areas with ash trees. ALT sl–1500. FLIGHT 5–7. FP ash and occasionally privet. EGG 6–4. LARVA 3–5. PUPA 5–6. WINTER egg. STATUS ?

SLOE HAIRSTREAK *Nordmannia acaciae*. Dull brown ups with no sex brand in ♂: unh with orange marginal lunules: white line often indistinct on unf: ♀ has black anal tuft. HAB rough ground with blackthorn bushes, usually in hills. ALT sl–1800. FLIGHT 6–7. FP blackthorn and sometimes oak. EGG 6–8; coated with hairs from ♀. LARVA 7–5. PUPA 4–6. WINTER larva. STATUS E; Lux. V; W. Germany, Italy. R; Austria, Belgium. LP; Belgium, W. Germany. SEE ALSO p. 210.

ILEX HAIRSTREAK *Nordmannia ilicis*. Like Sloe Hairstreak but slightly larger, darker on uns and with red marginal lunules on unh: ♀ lacks black anal tuft: upf with or without the orange patch in both sexes. HAB light woodland and oak scrub; very local in northern parts of range. ALT sl–1500. FLIGHT 6–8. FP oaks, especially the low-growing species. EGG 7–5: solitary on twigs. LARVA 4–6, often attended by ants. PUPA 5–6: succinctly bound to twig or dead leaf and strongly resembling a bird-dropping. WINTER fully formed larva inside the egg-shell. VAR the orange patch is rare in ♂ but quite common in ♀, especially in south. STATUS E; Denmark. R; W. Germany, Lith. LP; W. Germany.

FALSE ILEX HAIRSTREAK *Nordmannia esculi*. Like Ilex Hairstreak but with paler uns and less obvious white streak: red marginal spots on unh not clearly black-edged. HAB rough, scrubby ground. ALT sl–1500. FLIGHT 6–7. FP oaks, especially the low-growing species, and *Prunus* spp. EGG ? LARVA ? PUPA succinctly bound to fp. WINTER ? VAR ♀ may have faint orange patch on upf. STATUS R; Italy.

Spanish Purple
Hairstreak

♂   ♀

Brown Hairstreak

Purple Hairstreak

Sloe Hairstreak

Ilex Hairstreak

Ilex Hairstreak

False Ilex Hairstreak

BLUE-SPOT HAIRSTREAK *Strymonidia spini*. Unh has distinct blue spot at anal angle: ♂ has a small oval sex brand on upf. HAB dry, scrubby fields and hillsides. ALT sl–1800. FLIGHT 6–7. FP blackthorn, buckthorn, and various other shrubs. EGG 7–5: solitary on twigs. LARVA 4–6: commonly attended by ants. PUPA 5–7: succinctly bound to leaf or twig. WINTER egg. VAR ♀ commonly has orange patch on upf, and sometimes on uph as well, in Iberia (f. *vandalusica*): elsewhere these patches are usually absent. STATUS Declining in most areas: E; Lux. R; Belgium, Lith. LP; W. Germany. SEE ALSO p. 275.

▲**WHITE-LETTER HAIRSTREAK** *Strymonidia w-album*. White streak forms a distinct W on unh: ♂ has a small oval sex brand just above the cell on upf. HAB light woodland and hedgerows with elm. ALT sl–1500. FLIGHT 6–8. FP elms, especially wych elm: sometimes on lime. EGG 7–4: dark and button-like, laid singly in forks of twigs. LARVA 4–7: feeding on elm flowers at first and then on leaves. WINTER egg. NOTES Adult is very fond of bramble flowers. STATUS E; Holland, Lux.: V; Czech., S. Greece, Lith: R; N. Greece. LP; W. Germany. SEE ALSO p. 217.

▲**BLACK HAIRSTREAK** *Strymonidia pruni*. Unh has a bright orange submarginal band edged internally with conspicuous black spots: ♂ is smaller and lacks orange flush on upf: oval sex brand present on upf of ♂. HAB old woodland and hedgerows with blackthorn. ALT <1000. FLIGHT 6–8. FP blackthorn. EGG 6–4: like a brown button, laid singly on twigs. LARVA 4–6: chestnut brown at first, becoming green later: feeds on buds at first and transfers to leaves as they open: always very well camouflaged. PUPA 5–6: succinctly attached to leaf or twig and closely resembling a bird-dropping. WINTER egg. VAR unf may or may not have inconspicuous orange submarginal band: ♀ may lack orange flush on upf. STATUS E; Denmark, Lux: R; Greece, Italy, Lith. LP; W. Germany, Greece. SEE ALSO p. 208, 229, 238, 239, 243, 312.

▲**GREEN HAIRSTREAK** *Callophrys rubi*. Ups dark brown, with small oval sex brand on upf of ♂: uns may have an incomplete row of small white spots: scales on front of head are green. HAB open woods, scrub, and heathland. ALT sl–2100. FLIGHT 3–7, occasionally with a partial 2nd generation in late summer in warm areas. FP gorse, broom, heather, rockrose, and other low-growing plants. EGG 4–6: green and doughnut-shaped and laid singly on flowers of fp. LARVA 5–8: feeding on flowers and leaves but partly cannibalistic. PUPA 7–5: brown and bristly, lying on or under the ground where it is commonly attended by ants. WINTER pupa. VAR ups are paler in the south. STATUS Not threatened, although it has declined in many areas through scrub clearance and the reclamation of rough grassland and heathland. LP; W. Germany. SEE ALSO p. 215, 217, 242, 248, 273, 288.

CHAPMAN'S GREEN HAIRSTREAK *Callophrys avis*. Like Green Hairstreak but ups brighter and front of head with reddish brown scales: white line on uns broken only at veins. HAB maquis and other scrubby places. ALT sl–1500. FLIGHT 4–5. FP strawberry tree. EGG 5–6. LARVA 6–8: usually attended by ants. PUPA 7–4: on ground at base of fp: often attended by ants. WINTER pupa. VAR white line may be missing from unf. STATUS V.

PROVENCE HAIRSTREAK *Tomares ballus*. Combination of green unh and coppery unf is unique. HAB rough ground. ALT sl–500. FLIGHT 1–4. FP birds's-foot-trefoil and other *Lotus* spp. EGG 2–5. LARVA 3–6; attended by ants. PUPA 6–3. WINTER pupa/adult. STATUS ? SEE ALSO p. 250, 251.

VIOLET COPPER *Lycaena helle*. ♂ easily recognised by small size and by violet sheen all over ups: ♀ has no violet sheen and is best recognised by the narrow white band just inside the orange submarginal band of unh: ♀ wing-tips are rather more rounded than in other species. HAB damp flowery meadows and moors. ALT sl–1600. FLIGHT 5–10 in 1 or 2 broods. FP sorrels, bistorts and knotgrasses. EGG 6–10: solitary on fp. LARVA 5–10. PUPA 7–5: amongst plant debris on the ground. WINTER pupa. STATUS Declining everywhere through drainage of its habitat: E; Czech., Lux. V; elsewhere. LP; Belgium, France, W. Germany, Hungary.

Blue-spot Hairstreak

f. *vandalusica* ♀

♂

White-letter Hairstreak

Chapman's Green
Hairstreak

Black Hairstreak

Green Hairstreak

♂

Provence Hairstreak

♀

♂

Violet Copper

♀

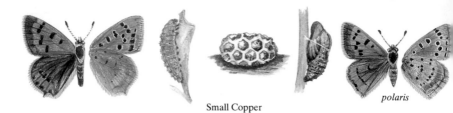

Small Copper

polaris

▲SMALL COPPER *Lycaena phlaeas*. Unh greyish brown with inconspicuous orange-red submarginal lunules: ♀ fw slightly more rounded than that of ♂. HAB flowery places of all kinds, especially waste land and gardens: also on heathland. ALT sl–2500. FLIGHT 2–11: 2–3 broods: 3rd brood insects often very small. FP common and sheep's sorrel: sometimes docks. EGG 3–10: resembles a miniature golf ball: laid singly at base of leaf. LARVA 1–12: usually on underside of leaf. PUPA 2–9: succinctly attached to dead leaves on fp or ground. WINTER young or old larva according to brood. VAR small blue spots are not uncommon on uph: *L. p. polaris* from Lapland has a much greyer unh with prominent black spots: summer broods in south may be very dark: copper occasionally replaced by pale gold or even white. NOTES ♂ adopts a territory each day, often on a flower-head and chases intruders very vigorously. STATUS V; Malta. LP; Germany. SEE ALSO p. 22, 221, 251, 253, 308.

▲LARGE COPPER *Lycaena dispar*. Unh bright bluish-grey: sexes very different on ups and ♀ generally much larger. HAB fens, marshes, and damp grassland in general. ALT sl–1000. FLIGHT 5–9: 1–2 broods. FP docks, especially great water dock. EGG 7–9: solitary on fp. LARVA 8–6. PUPA 6–8: succinctly attached to fp. WINTER small larva in rolled leaf: often submerged. VAR British race (*L. d. dispar*) became extinct about 1850 through drainage of fens. Dutch race (*L. d. batavus*) is large and bright. *L. d. rutilus*, scattered over much of Europe, is the commonest race. Smaller and duller than *batavus*, it has narrower red margins on unh. Only *rutilus* is double-brooded. NOTES The Dutch race, sometimes regarded merely as a form of *L. d. dispar*, has been established at Woodwalton Fen in B, where it is protected on a nature reserve. STATUS All races are becoming rare through drainage of their habitats and the species is endangered throughout its range. LP; Belgium, Finland, France, W. Germany, Holland, Hungary. SEE ALSO p. 243, 304, 305, 306, 308, 312.

SCARCE COPPER *Heodes virgaureae*. Unh greenish or greyish yellow with a few small black and white spots: sexes markedly different on ups. HAB flowery fields and hillsides, especially near streams. ALT sl–1800. FLIGHT 6–8. FP docks and sorrels. EGG 7–4: solitary on fp. LARVA 4–5: often attended by ants. PUPA 4–6: succinctly bound to leaf. WINTER fully formed larva inside egg-shell. VAR smaller and darker in mountains and far north: ♂ ups lightly spotted with black in Spain. STATUS R; Lux. LP; W. Germany. SEE ALSO p. 263.

GRECIAN COPPER *Heodes ottomanus*. ♂ is like Scarce Copper but upf has small black spots near tip: unh lacks green and has prominent red lunules: ♀ is best identified by the short 'tail' on hw and by the red marginal band of unh. HAB rough, flowery places, including roadsides. ALT sl–2200. FLIGHT 3–9 in 2 broods. FP ? EGG 3–9. LARVA 1–12. PUPA 2–9. WINTER larva. STATUS E; Greece. V; Yugoslavia.

SOOTY COPPER *Heodes tityrus*. ♂ ups sooty brown, usually with black spots showing through: ♀ is distinguished from most other coppers by orange upf and brown uph, but yellowish uns should always identify this species. HAB flowery fields and hillsides. ALT sl–2100. FLIGHT 4–10: 2 broods. FP docks and sorrels. EGG 5–10: solitary on fp. LARVA most of the year: closely associated with ants. PUPA 4–8: hidden in plant debris and often attended by ants. WINTER larva. VAR ♀ ups may be sooty all over at high altitudes (*H. t. subalpinus*): orange lunules poorly developed or absent in both sexes: uns greyish. STATUS E; Denmark (extinct?). V; Holland. R; Lith., Lux. LP; W. Germany.

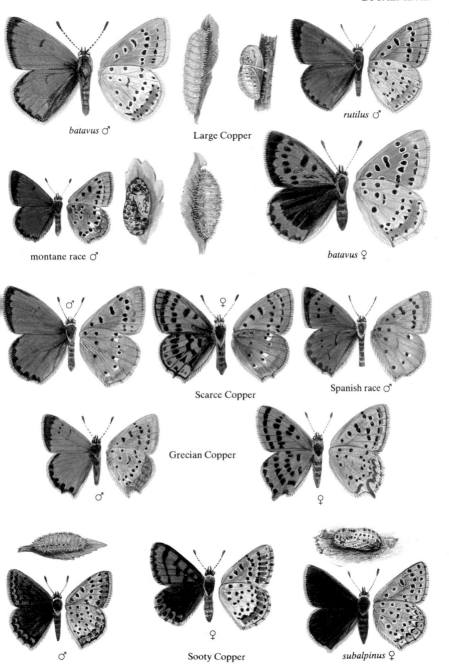

batavus ♂

Large Copper

rutilus ♂

montane race ♂

batavus ♀

♂

♀

Scarce Copper

Spanish race ♂

Grecian Copper

♂

♀

♂

♀

Sooty Copper

subalpinus ♀

55

Purple-shot Copper

PURPLE-SHOT COPPER *Heodes alciphron*. ♂ has violet tinge, of varying depth, all over ups: ♀ ups sooty brown or orange with very irregular pd spots on upf. HAB flowery fields and hillsides. ALT sl–2000. FLIGHT 6–8. FP docks. EGG 6–8: solitary on fp. LARVA 7–5: often attended by ants. PUPA 5–6: bound to leaf in a flimsy cocoon. WINTER larva. VAR *H. a. gordius* from Alps and other upland areas of western Europe (above 1500m) has only a faint purple sheen in ♂ and ♀ ups are orange: in Germany, N.E. France, and to the east of the Alps ♂ has much more purple and ♀ ups are sooty brown. STATUS V; Czech. R; Austria, W. Germany, Greece. LP; W. Germany.

LESSER FIERY COPPER *Thersamonia thersamon*. Narrow black borders to upf, with two almost straight rows of small black spots inside them. HAB rough, flowery places: always very local. ALT sl–1700. FLIGHT 4–9: 2 broods. FP docks and broom. EGG 4–9: solitary on fp. LARVA 6–4: sometimes tended by ants. PUPA 3–7: firmly bound to leaf of fp. WINTER larva. VAR 2nd brood often has a short tail at vein 2 on hw. STATUS R; Greece.

FIERY COPPER *Thersamonia thetis*. ♂ coppery red with black border strongly expanded at tip of upf: unh pale and faintly marked in both sexes: ♀ ups like Lesser Fiery Copper. HAB flowery mountain slopes, especially with thyme. ALT >2000. FLIGHT 7–8, possibly with a 2nd brood in early autumn. FP ? EGG ? LARVA ? PUPA ? WINTER ? VAR slender 'tail' on hw is not always developed. STATUS E & LP; Greece.

PURPLE-EDGED COPPER *Palaeochrysophanus hippothoe*. ♂ upf has a deep purple sheen along front edge: rear of uph very dark with a purple sheen: ♀ upf has dark spots in a smooth curve (very irregular in Purple-shot Copper): ♀ uph always brown with an orange border. HAB damp fields and boggy places. ALT sl–2000. FLIGHT 6–8. FP docks and bistorts. EGG 6–8: solitary on fp. LARVA 7–5: often attended by ants. PUPA 5–6: succinctly bound to leaf, usually near base of fp. WINTER larva, but possibly egg in far north. VAR paler in far north, where ♀ has smaller spots and a prominent marginal band on unh (*P. h. stiberi*): *P. h. eurydame*, flying above 2000m in S & C Alps, lacks purple flush in ♂, while ♀ ups are all brown: *P. h. leonhardi* from Balkans is very large. STATUS E; Hungary and Lux. V; Denmark. LP; W. Germany, Hungary. SEE ALSO p. 247, 304.

△**LONG-TAILED BLUE** *Lampides boeticus*. Slender 'tail' on hw, with prominent black spot near it on uph: ♂ upf rather hairy with androconia: unh has prominent white stripe in both sexes. HAB rough, flowery places. ALT sl–2000. FLIGHT 5–10: 2 or 3 broods. FP bladder senna, lupins, gorse, and other legumes. EGG 4–8: solitary on fp. LARVA 5–9: feeding inside seed pods of fp at first: attended by ants later. PUPA most of the year: concealed in vegetation. WINTER pupa. NOTES Resident in S, migrating each year to C and occasionally reaching B: abundant throughout the warmer parts of the world. STATUS LP; W. Germany.

LANG'S SHORT-TAILED BLUE *Syntarucus pirithous*. Like Long-tailed Blue but slightly smaller and with no single clear white stripe on unh. HAB rough, flowery places. ALT generally lowland, but up to 3000 on migration. FLIGHT 3–10 in several broods. FP broom, lucerne, and various other legumes. EGG 4–8: solitary on fp. LARVA 1–12: regularly tended by ants. PUPA 2–9: concealed in vegetation and debris. WINTER larva. NOTES Resident in S: strongly migratory, but nevertheless rarely seen north of the Alps: very occasionally reaches B. STATUS ?

gordius ♂

gordius ♀

Purple-shot Copper

Fiery Copper

Lesser Fiery Copper

♂

♀

♂

♀

eurydame ♂

eurydame ♀
Purple-edged Copper

leonhardi ♂

stiberi ♀
Purple-edged Copper

♂

♀

Lang's Short-tailed Blue

♂

Long-tailed Blue

♀

57

COMMON TIGER BLUE *Tarucus theophrastus*. Uns pattern is unique in W. Europe. HAB dry scrubby places with *Ziziphus* bushes. ALT sl–500. FLIGHT 4–8: 2 or 3 broods. FP *Ziziphus* bushes, including the cultivated jujube (*Z. jujuba*). EGG solitary on fp. LARVA ? PUPA ? WINTER ? STATUS R. Possibly extinct in Italy.

LITTLE TIGER BLUE *Tarucus balkanicus*. Like Common Tiger Blue but ♂ ups have more black spots and ♀ uph lacks white spots: pd spots of unh are joined to form a line: the ranges of the two species do not overlap. HAB dry, scrubby places with Christ's thorn bushes: mainly coastal. ALT sl–500. FLIGHT 4–9: 2 or 3 broods. FP Christ's thorn. EGG ? LARVA ? PUPA ? WINTER ? STATUS ?

AFRICAN GRASS BLUE *Zizeeria knysna*. Deep violet blue ups with wide brown borders identify ♂: ♀ has variable amounts of blue on brown ups, but poorly marked greyish uns will separate her from most other blues. HAB moist, grassy places: mainly coastal. ALT lowland. FLIGHT 4–9: 2 broods. FP medicks and *Oxalis* spp. EGG ? LARVA ? PUPA ? WINTER ? VAR size is rather variable – possibly due to water supply. STATUS V; Greece, Italy. R; Spain. LP; Greece (Crete).

SHORT-TAILED BLUE *Everes argiades*. Hw has a short 'tail': unf pd spots more or less in a straight line. HAB flowery fields and hillsides, often in damp areas. ALT sl–2000. FLIGHT 4–10: 2–3 broods. FP trefoils and other legumes, including gorse. EGG 4–9, but through winter in N: solitary on fp. LARVA 5–3: green at first, becoming brown during hibernation: feeds on flowers and seeds. PUPA 3–9: succinctly bound to a curled leaf. WINTER generally larva but egg in N. VAR 2nd & 3rd broods are darker, with little or no blue on ♀. NOTES Resident in most of S & C: some northward migration in spring: vagrants very occasionally reach B. STATUS E; Lux. (extinct? as a resident): R; Greece. LP; W. Germany.

EASTERN SHORT-TAILED BLUE *Everes decoloratus*. Tail very short, little more than a point: ♂ upf has a small black discal spot: unf pd spots are not in a straight line. HAB sheltered, flowery hillsides and fields. ALT sl–900, preferring the lower levels. FLIGHT 4–9: 2 broods. FP black medick. EGG ? LARVA ? PUPA ? WINTER ? VAR blue colour rapidly fades and ♂ becomes dingy. STATUS R; Greece.

PROVENCAL SHORT-TAILED BLUE *Everes alcetas*. Tail very short, as in Eastern Short-tailed Blue, but ♂ has much narrower black borders and no discal spot on upf: unf pd spots not in a straight line: unh generally without any trace of orange lunules. HAB open flowery places. ALT sl–1200. FLIGHT 4–9: 2–3 broods. FP crown vetch and other legumes. EGG 4–10. LARVA 1–12. PUPA 3–9: succinctly attached to curled leaf. WINTER larva. STATUS R; Greece.

▲**LITTLE BLUE** *Cupido minimus*. Ups dark brown, with silvery blue scales only in ♂: clear white fringes on ups: unf has pd spots in a smooth curve parallel to wing margin. HAB well-drained grassy slopes, mainly on chalk and limestone. ALT sl–2000. FLIGHT 4–9: 1–2 broods. FP kidney vetch. EGG 5–8: solitary on fp, mainly on flowers. LARVA 1–12: feeding inside seed pods at first and then on the outside: attended by ants. PUPA 3–8: greyish and rather hairy and succinctly bound low down on a grass stem or concealed amongst the leaf litter. WINTER hibernating fully-grown larva in dead flower-heads, under stones, or in crevices in the ground. Larva actually goes into hibernation soon after mid-summer in single-brooded populations. VAR very small and dark in far south: above average size in higher parts of Alps. STATUS E; Holland. LP; W. Germany, N. Ireland.

OSIRIS BLUE *Cupido osiris*. ♂ ups clear violet blue with narrow black margins: ♀ like Little Blue, but larger and unf pd spots almost in a straight line. HAB flowery banks, usually in uplands: very local. ALT 500–1800. FLIGHT 5–8: 1 brood. FP flowers of sainfoin and other legumes. EGG 5–9. LARVA 6–3: attended by ants (*Lasius* spp). PUPA 3–7. WINTER larva. VAR wingspan from 22–35mm. STATUS LP; Hungary.

LORQUIN'S BLUE *Cupido lorquinii*. ♂ ups violet blue with broad black borders: ♀ like Little Blue but ups rather darker: uns very like Little Blue in both sexes, but the two species are likely to be found together only in Portugal. HAB grassy places. ALT sl–1500. FLIGHT 4–6. FP ? EGG ? LARVA ? PUPA ? WINTER ? STATUS V.

Common Tiger Blue

Little Tiger Blue

African Grass Blue

Eastern Short-tailed Blue

Short-tailed Blue

Provencal Short-tailed Blue

Little Blue

Osiris Blue

Lorquin's Blue

▲**HOLLY BLUE** *Celastrina argiolus*. ♂ ups violet blue: ♀ ups paler with broad black borders: unf pd spots distinctly elongate, especially towards the rear. HAB open woods, hedges, and gardens. ALT sl–2000. FLIGHT 4–9: 2 broods. FP holly (spring), ivy (autumn), and various other shrubs including gorse, bell heather, and snowberry. EGG 4–9: solitary on flower buds. LARVA 5–9: rather slug-like and feeding mainly on flowers and developing fruits, but also on young leaves. PUPA 7–4: succinctly attached under a leaf or (in over-wintering generation) in a bark crevice. WINTER pupa. VAR ♀ of summer brood has much more black than 1st brood. NOTES The only British blue likely to be seen in towns and gardens or flying around trees and shrubs. Adults drink honeydew, oozing sap, and carrion juices and rarely visit flowers. STATUS Generally common. V; Denmark. LP; W. Germany. SEE ALSO p. 200, 251, 253, 288, 312.

GREEN-UNDERSIDE BLUE *Glaucopsyche alexis*. Unf has large pd spots but no marginal markings: unh has greenish-blue patch in basal half, more extensive in ♂ than ♀: ♀ ups brown with a basal blue flush. HAB flowery places, generally in uplands. ALT sl–1300m. FLIGHT 4–7. FP milk vetch and other legumes. EGG 4–6: solitary on fp. LARVA 1–12: tended by ants. PUPA 3–6: succinct on fp. WINTER larva. STATUS V; Lith. R & LP; W. Germany.

BLACK-EYED BLUE *Glaucopsyche melanops*. Ups like Green-underside Blue, but unh lacks blue-green flush: uns have some marginal marks. HAB heaths and open woodland: very local. ALT sl–1000. FLIGHT 3–5. FP vetches and other legumes. EGG 3–5. LARVA 1–12: feeding on flowers and seeds of fp and tended by black ants. PUPA 2–4. WINTER larva. VAR marginal markings on uns are fainter in France (*G. m. melanops*) and ups have thinner black borders than Spanish insects (*G. m. algirica*). STATUS ?

ODD-SPOT BLUE *Turanana panagaea*. Pd spots of unf large, in s3 displaced towards the margin. ♀ ups brown. HAB dry mountain slopes. ALT >2300. FLIGHT 6–8. FP prickly thrift. EGG ? LARVA ? PUPA ? WINTER ? VAR ? STATUS E & LP; Greece.

ALCON BLUE *Maculinea alcon*. One of the larger blues: ♂ ups unmarked apart from broad black borders and faint sub-marginal spots: ♀ upf has small pd spots: unh with little or no blue dusting at base. HAB grassy places, both wet and dry. ALT sl–1800. FLIGHT 6–7. FP gentians during the first three instars, but later larvae live in ant nests. EGG 6–8: solitary on fp, but several ♀♀ may lay on one plant. LARVA 8–5: hidden in ant nests for much of this time. PUPA 5–6: in ant nests. WINTER larva in ant nests. VAR *M. a. rebeli*, found mainly in mountain regions, has darker blue ups and broader black borders in ♂: ♀ has more blue and heavier pd spots than elsewhere. STATUS E. LP; Belgium, France, W. Germany. SEE ALSO p. 220, 304.

▲**LARGE BLUE** *Maculinea arion*. One of the largest blues: pd spots of upf distinctly elongate, often very large in ♀: unh has extensive greenish-blue dusting. HAB rough flowery places with wild thyme and ant nests. ALT sl–2000. FLIGHT 6–7. FP wild thyme in first three instars, after which the larvae are taken into ant nests. EGG 6–7: solitary on fp. LARVA 7–5: in ant nests for much of this time. PUPA 5–6: in ant nests. WINTER larva in ant nests. VAR ups of both sexes may be heavily clouded with brown in high parts of Alps (f. *obscura*): ups often very bright in Maritime Alps, but with reduced blue flush on unh (*M. a. ligurica*). NOTES Became extinct in B in 1979, but now re-introduced on protected sites. STATUS E; owing to reduced grazing resulting in changes in ant population. LP; Belgium, B, W. Germany. SEE ALSO p. 217, 218, 219, 220, 243, 250, 304, 305, 311, 312.

Holly Blue

Green-underside Blue

1st brood ♂

1st brood ♀

2nd brood ♀

Holly Blue

♂

♀

Green-underside Blue

♂

Odd-spot Blue

Spanish race
Black-eyed Blue

♂

♀

rebeli ♂

Alcon Blue

rebeli ♀

♂

obscura ♂

♀

Large Blue

SCARCE LARGE BLUE *Maculinea teleius*. Like Large Blue but ups markings smaller and uns brownish with little or no bluish dusting: pd spots of unf much larger than in Alcon Blue, but other unf markings very faint. HAB damp moors and meadows: very local. ALT sl–1800. FLIGHT 6–7. FP great burnet and bird's-foot trefoil in first three instars, older larvae being taken into ant nests. EGG 6–7: solitary on fp. LARVA 7–5: in ant nests for much of this time. PUPA 5–6: in ant nests. WINTER larva in ant nests. STATUS E. LP; Belgium, France, W. Germany. SEE ALSO p. 220, 304, 305.

DUSKY LARGE BLUE *Maculinea nausithous*. Uns dark brown without marginal spots: ♀ ups brown with very little blue at the base. HAB lakesides and other marshy areas: very local. ALT sl–1200, but usually in lowlands. FLIGHT 7. FP great burnet in first three instars, later larvae being taken into ant nests. EGG 7–8: 2 or 3 on fp. LARVA 8–6: in ant nests much of this time. PUPA 6–7: in ant nests. WINTER larva in ant nests. STATUS E. LP; W. Germany, Hungary. SEE ALSO p. 304, 305.

IOLAS BLUE *Iolana iolas*. A very large blue with silvery grey uns. HAB grassy and rocky slopes and light woodland. ALT sl–1800. FLIGHT 5–6: occasionally partial 2nd brood 8–9. FP bladder senna. EGG 5–6, sometimes 8–9: solitary on fp. LARVA 6–8, sometimes 9–10: pink or green: feeding on flowers and seeds of fp: attended by ants. PUPA 8–5: brown with black spots. WINTER pupa. VAR marginal spots may be darker on uns: ♀ ups may be virtually all brown. STATUS E; Hungary, Spain. V; France. Generally rare elsewhere. LP; Hungary.

BATON BLUE *Pseudophilotes baton*. Chequered fringes, especially on unf: unh has orange lunules sandwiched between black spots: ♀ ups black with a slight blue basal flush. HAB flowery slopes. ALT sl–2000. FLIGHT 4–9: 1–2 broods. FP 1st generation on wild thyme: 2nd on various labiates, especially on the flowers. EGG 5–10: solitary on fp. LARVA 1–12, feeding mainly on flowers: tended by ants. PUPA 4–8, but single-brooded races may pass winter as pupae: usually on ground at base of fp, without any girdle. WINTER larva or pupa. NOTES Eastern and western populations are split into 2 sub-species on genitalia structure, but are indistinguishable in the field. *P. barbagiae*, confined to Sardinia, is very similar. STATUS E; Lux. R; Belgium, W. Germany. LP; W. Germany.

PANOPTES BLUE *Pseudophilotes panoptes*. Like Baton Blue but unh darker and rarely with any trace of orange: ups fringes more prominent. HAB rough flowery places in hills. ALT 800–2000. FLIGHT 4–7: 2 broods. FP wild thyme. EGG 4–8: solitary on fp. LARVA ? PUPA ? WINTER ? STATUS ?

FALSE BATON BLUE *Pseudophilotes abencerragus*. Like Panoptes Blue but ♂ ups darker and with broader dark margins: unh may have just a trace of orange: ♀ distinguished from ♀ Panoptes Blue by the much larger pd spots on unf. HAB scrubby, heather-clad areas, usually in hills: very local. ALT sl–800. FLIGHT 4–5. FP wild thyme, *Cleonia lusitanica*, and possibly *Erica* spp., usually feeding on flowers. EGG ? LARVA ? PUPA ? WINTER ? STATUS ?

BAVIUS BLUE *Pseudophilotes bavius*. Ups with strongly chequered margins: uph with bright orange-red lunules: uns silvery white with heavy spots. HAB flowery grassland. ALT sl–1000. FLIGHT 5–7. FP claries. EGG ? LARVA ? PUPA ? WINTER ? STATUS E. LP; Greece. SEE ALSO p. 304.

CHEQUERED BLUE *Scolitantides orion*. White uns with heavy black spots, together with generally dark ups and strong fringes, separate this from all the other blues. HAB dry, stony hillsides: also coastal cliffs. ALT sl–1800. FLIGHT 4–8: 1–2 broods. FP stonecrops. EGG 4–8: solitary or in small groups. LARVA 6–9: tended by ants. PUPA 9–7: at base of fp. WINTER pupa but possibly also larva, under stones, in N. VAR *S. o. orion* of Fennoscandia is much bluer on ups in both sexes. STATUS E; Czech., Hungary. R; elsewhere.

GRASS JEWEL *Freyeria trochylus*. Very small: brown in both sexes with 2–4 orange lunules on uph. HAB dry, stony ground. ALT sl–1000. FLIGHT 3–9; several broods throughout the summer. FP heliotrope. EGG ? LARVA tended by *Pheidole* ants. PUPA ? WINTER ? NOTES One of the world's smallest butterflies. STATUS R & LP; Greece.

Scarce Large Blue

Dusky Large Blue

Panoptes Blue

Iolas Blue

Baton Blue

False Baton Blue

Bavius Blue

Grass Jewel

Chequered Blue

ZEPHYR BLUE *Plebejus pylaon*. A very variable species with few constant features, but uph always has a small black marginal spot at least in s2: no silver in black marginal spots of unh: ♂ tibiae spined. HAB flowery places, mostly in the mountains. ALT sl–2100: usually >1000. FLIGHT 5–8. FP milk vetch. EGG 6–3. LARVA 7–4: tended by ants. PUPA 4–7: tended by ants. WINTER egg or larva. VAR ♂ is a much brighter blue in Balkan region (*P. p. sephirus*): *P. p. trappi* from Alps is larger and ♀ ups have vestigial or no orange lunules. STATUS E; Hungary. V; elsewhere. LP; Hungary.

▲SILVER-STUDDED BLUE *Plebejus argus*. Black marginal spots of unh have shiny green or blue pupils (silver-studded): unf has no black spot in the basal half of the cell: front tibia has a strong spine: ♀ has variable amount of blue dusting. HAB heaths and grassy places. ALT sl–2500. FLIGHT 5–9: 1–2 broods. FP heather and various leguminous plants, including gorse. EGG 6–4: solitary on fp. LARVA 4–8: brown or green: very well camouflaged on young leaves, but more easily seen when on flowers: always tended by black ants. PUPA 4–9: on ground at base of fp, but often buried by ants. WINTER egg. VAR black margins of wings are often much wider at high altitudes: larger in Spain, where ground colour of uns is very pale (*P. a. hypochionus*): in Corsica (*P. a. corsicus*) ♀ has much more blue on ups. STATUS V; Lux. LP; W. Germany.

IDAS BLUE *Lycaeides idas*. Very like Silver-studded Blue but front tibia lacks spine. HAB heaths and other rough, flowery places, mainly in uplands. ALT sl–2500. FLIGHT 5–8: 1–2 broods. FP assorted leguminous plants: also sea buckthorn in French Alps. EGG 6–8. LARVA 6–4: tended by various ants. PUPA 4–8: in ant nests. WINTER larva in ant nests. VAR smaller in far north, where ♀ is largely blue (*L. i. lapponicus*): very large in parts of Greece, with broad black margins in ♂ and complete orange lunules in ♀ (*L. i. magnagraeca*). Corsican specimens (*L. i. bellieri*) are very heavily marked. NOTES Often gathers in large numbers to drink at muddy pools. STATUS E; Lux. (extinct?). V; Holland. R; Belgium. LP; Belgium, W. Germany. SEE ALSO p. 289.

REVERDIN'S BLUE *Lycaeides argyrognomon*. Very like Idas Blue and difficult to separate on external features, although black chevrons inside orange band on unh are generally much flatter (usually triangular in Idas Blue): genitalia distinctly different. HAB flowery slopes. ALT sl–1500. FLIGHT 5–9: usually 2 broods. FP crown vetch and other legumes. EGG 6–3. LARVA 3–8: associated with large black ants. PUPA 4–8: yellow and green and succinctly attached to fp. WINTER egg or, occasionally, 1st instar larva. STATUS E; Norway. V; Sweden. R; Belgium, Greece. LP; Belgium, W. Germany.

CRANBERRY BLUE *Vacciniina optilete*. A prominent orange-red submarginal lunule in s2 of unh, often with smaller ones on each side as well: ♂ is a deeper violet than other blues in the Arctic: ♀ ups dark brown with a violet flush at base. HAB moorland and mountain slopes. ALT sl(N)–2500. FLIGHT 7. FP bog bilberry and heaths. EGG 7–8. LARVA 8–6. PUPA 5–7: green and yellow with red hairs: amongst moss. WINTER half-grown larva. STATUS E; Holland, Poland. V; elsewhere. LP; W. Germany, Greece.

CRETAN ARGUS *Kretania psylorita*. Ups with yellow submarginal lunules, best developed in ♀ and sometimes missing from ♂ upf: uns very pale, with small spots. HAB rocky slopes. ALT 1600–1800. FLIGHT 5–8. FP milk vetches. EGG ? LARVA ? PUPA ? WINTER ? STATUS V & LP; Greece.

Zephyr Blue

Cranberry Blue

♂

♀

Zephyr Blue

trappi ♂

♂

♀

hypochionus ♂

Silver-studded Blue

hypochionus ♀

♂

♀

bellieri ♂

magnagraeca ♂

Idas Blue

Cretan Argus

Reverdin's Blue

GERANIUM ARGUS *Eumedonia eumedon*. Ups plain brown in both sexes, with traces of blue at base in ♂ and occasionally a trace of orange near anal angle of uph in ♀: unh generally with a short white streak from discal spot to pd spots. HAB rough, damp grassland and moors, usually in hills. ALT sl–2500. FLIGHT 6–8. FP meadow cranesbill and other *Geranium* spp. EGG 6–8: solitary on flowers or upper leaves. LARVA 7–4: tended by ants. PUPA 4–7 in flimsy cocoon on ground. WINTER larva. VAR white stripe often absent from unh in N & E: orange sub-marginal lunules on unh may be larger in SE. STATUS R; W. Germany, Greece, Lith. LP; W. Germany, Hungary.

▲**BROWN ARGUS** *Aricia agestis*. Ups deep brown in both sexes: unf with the two front pd spots one above the other to form a colon-like mark. HAB heaths and open grassy places. ALT sl–2200, generally <1000. FLIGHT 4–9: 2–3 broods. FP rockrose, stork's-bills, and other low-growing members of the geranium family. EGG 5–10: solitary on undersides of leaves. LARVA 1–12: well camouflaged, but always tended by ants. PUPA 3–9: green with a pink stripe: formed in leaf litter below fp, but quickly buried by ants. WINTER small hibernating larva. VAR orange lunules larger and uns much browner in Iberia (*A. a. cramera*): larva feeds on leguminous plants. NOTES Rockrose is the normal foodplant on calcareous soils, with stork's-bills and related plants used on sands and clays. The different foodplants may result in slightly different coloration, and may also affect the rate of development. STATUS V; Holland, Malta: R; Lith. LP; W. Germany. SEE ALSO p. 289.

▲**MOUNTAIN ARGUS** *Aricia artaxerxes*. Very like the Brown Argus but orange lunules are generally poorly developed and often absent from upf. HAB rough grassland. ALT sl–2500: usually >1000 in S. FLIGHT 6–7: single-brooded. FP rockrose and occasionally *Erodium* and *Geranium* spp. EGG 6–8: solitary on upper surfaces of leaves. LARVA 7–6: tended by ants in spring. PUPA 5–6: buried by ants. WINTER hibernating larva. VAR British race (*A. a. artaxerxes*) usually has a white discal spot on upf and almost pure white spots on uns: Spanish race (*A. a. montensis*) has very pale uns and better developed lunules on ups (yellow in ♀). The northern and mountain race (*A. a. allous*) may lack orange lunules on ups. NOTES The range of this species, also called the Northern Brown Argus, does not overlap with that of the Brown Argus in B. STATUS E; Hungary, Poland: V; Denmark: R; Lith. LP; W. Germany and Hungary.

SPANISH ARGUS *Aricia morronensis*. Like Mountain Argus but with chequered fringes and smaller, yellower lunules on uns. HAB rough hillsides: local. ALT 900–2000. FLIGHT 5–8: 2 broods. FP ? EGG ? LARVA ? PUPA ? WINTER ? STATUS ?

BLUE ARGUS *Aricia anteros*. ♂ upf shiny blue with a prominent black discal spot: unf has no black spot in cell: ♀ not easily distinguished from other *Aricia* spp, but two front pd spots on unh are not one above the other to form a colon (see Brown Argus). HAB flowery mountainsides. ALT 1000–2000: occasionally lower. FLIGHT 5–8. FP ? EGG ? LÂRVA ? PUPA ? WINTER ? STATUS V.

SILVERY ARGUS *Pseudaricia nicias*. Pale blue ups with very wide dark margins characterise ♂: both sexes have a broad white stripe, almost wedge-shaped, along vein 4 of unh. HAB sunny mountain slopes: light woodland in north. ALT 900–2000 in Alps and Pyrenees: lower in the N. FLIGHT 7–8. FP cranesbills. EGG 7–4: solitary. LARVA 4–6. PUPA 6–7: green with red stripes and succinctly fixed to leaf litter or to base of fp. WINTER egg. VAR dark borders are somewhat narrower in Fennoscandia (*P. n. scandica*). STATUS V; Spain. R; Italy. Locally common elsewhere.

ALPINE ARGUS *Albulina orbitulus*. Unf greyish brown and almost unmarked: unh with plain white spots: ♀ ups brown. HAB alpine meadows. ALT 900–2800. FLIGHT 7–8. FP milk vetch. EGG 7–8. LARVA 8–5. PUPA 5–7. WINTER larva. STATUS V; France. SEE ALSO p. 249.

Geranium Argus

♂

Brown Argus

cramera ♀

allous ♂

allous ♀

British race ♂

Mountain Argus

montensis ♂

Spanish Argus

♂

Blue Argus

♀

Silvery Argus

♂

Alpine Argus

GLANDON BLUE *Agriades glandon*. ♂ ups like Silvery Argus but wide border has a very blurred inner margin on upf: unf has a black spot in cell and greyish, somewhat indistinct sub-marginal spots. HAB grassy places in mountains and tundra. ALT <2400. FLIGHT 6–8. FP rock-jasmines, snowbells, and, in N, alpine milk vetch. EGG 6–7. LARVA 7–5: on flowers and leaves, mainly by night. PUPA 5–6: grey with yellow markings and found mainly under stones. WINTER larva. VAR proportions of blue and black vary in ♂, with darkest specimens in high mountains: unh with large white spots in far N. (*A. g. aquilo*) and in Bavarian Alps (f. *alboocellatus*). STATUS R; Finland, Italy, Norway. LP; W. Germany.

GAVARNIE BLUE *Agriades pyrenaicus*. Like Glandon Blue but ♂ ups silvery with narrower margins and ♀ ups with pale submarginal lunules: unf has black submarginal spots, not grey as in Glandon Blue. HAB montane grassland: local. ALT 1500–2400. FLIGHT 7. FP snowbells and rock-jasmines. LARVA 8–5. PUPA 5–7. WINTER larva. VAR white submarginal lunules of ups especially well marked in Cantabrian Mountains of northern Spain (*A. p. asturiensis*): ♂ ups greyish brown in Balkans. STATUS E; Bulgaria, Yugoslavia: V; elsewhere.

MAZARINE BLUE *Cyaniris semiargus*. Like Green-underside Blue but ♂ ups with narrower margins: uns with smaller spots and little blue flush: uns darker than in Osiris Blue, and pd spots of unf in a distinct curve rather than in a straight line. ♀ is brown. HAB flowery meadows and hillsides. ALT sl–2000. FLIGHT 5–8: 1–2 broods. FP various leguminous plants. EGG 6–9: solitary on fp. LARVA 7–5: feeds on flower-heads and developing fruits in summer and on young shoots in spring. PUPA 4–8: succinctly attached low down on fp. WINTER small larva. NOTES One of the commonest butterflies at muddy puddles and seepages. Became extinct in B about 100 years ago. STATUS E; Holland. LP; W. Germany. SEE ALSO p. 306.

GREEK MAZARINE BLUE *Cyaniris helena*. Ups like Mazarine Blue but unh very distinctive. HAB mountain slopes. ALT <1900. FLIGHT 5–7. FP kidney vetch and perhaps a few other leguminous plants. EGG ? LARVA ? PUPA ? WINTER ? STATUS LP.

DAMON BLUE *Agrodiaetus damon*. Unh yellowish brown (♂) or coffee-coloured (♀), with a clear white stripe in centre extending to well beyond pd spots. HAB mountain slopes, mainly on limestone: local. ALT <3000. FLIGHT 7–8. FP sainfoins. EGG 7–8: solitary on fp. LARVA 9–6: tended by ants. PUPA 6–7: dull yellow and hidden in leaf litter. WINTER small larva. VAR ♂ ups very deep blue in Poland (*A. d. ultramarinus*). STATUS E; Belgium, Czech., Hungary. R; Austria, E. & W. Germany, Greece. LP; W. Germany, Hungary.

CHELMOS BLUE *Agrodiaetus iphigenia*. ♂ ups shiny blue with narrow black margins: ♀ ups brown with orange lunules on both wings: uns pale yellowish grey in both sexes with a white stripe running through the centre of unh: orange lunules not always well developed on unh. HAB mountain slopes. ALT 1300–1800. FLIGHT 6–7. FP ? EGG ? LARVA ? PUPA ? WINTER ? STATUS E.

FURRY BLUE *Agrodiaetus dolus*. ♂ ups pale blue to almost white, but always with an extensive light brown patch of androconia in basal half of upf: ♀ ups brown with white fringes: unh with or without a pale stripe in both sexes. HAB rough meadows and hillsides. ALT sl–1800. FLIGHT 6–8. FP lucerne and sainfoin. EGG 7–8: solitary on fp. LARVA 8–5: often tended by ants. PUPA 5–6: in leaf litter. WINTER small larva. VAR *A. d. virgilius* of peninsular Italy has white or very pale blue ups in ♂, with no pale stripe on unh: *A. d. vittatus*, from west of the Rhône, has pale ups in ♂ with extensive brown suffusion, and a prominent stripe on unh. STATUS V; France. R; Italy.

FORSTER'S FURRY BLUE *Agrodiaetus ainsae*. (Not illustrated.) Like Furry Blue and distinguished only by its lower chromosome number. HAB rough hillsides. ALT <1500. FLIGHT 7–8. FP ? EGG ? LARVA ? PUPA ? WINTER ? VAR ? STATUS R.

Glandon Blue

aquilo ♂

Glandon Blue

Mazarine Blue

asturiensis ♂

asturiensis ♀

Gavarnie Blue

Mazarine Blue

Damon Blue

Greek Mazarine Blue

Chelmos Blue

♂

Furry Blue

♀

vittatus ♂

Furry Blue

virgilius ♂

69

ANOMALOUS BLUES   The following eight species, confined mainly to the Mediterranean region, have brown uppersides in both sexes and are very difficult to separate. The only sure way may be to examine the chromosome numbers in the cells – a job for a well-equipped laboratory!

RIPART'S ANOMALOUS BLUE *Agrodiaetus ripartii.* ♂ upf has a hairy patch of androconia in basal half: unh has a central white stipe, especially well marked in ♀, which also has paler fringes. ♀ resembles ♀ Damon Blue but uns are slightly less heavily marked. HAB rough, sunny slopes. ALT <1900. FLIGHT 6–8. FP sainfoins, especially rock sainfoin. EGG 6–8. LARVA 7–5. PUPA 5–7. WINTER larva. NOTES Adults are very fond of lavender. STATUS E; Italy. V; Poland. R; Spain. LP; Greece.

ANDALUSIAN ANOMALOUS BLUE *Agrodiaetus violetae* (Not illustrated). Like Ripart's Anomalous Blue but uns much paler: ♂ upf has an extensive patch of androconia: unh usually has a pale stripe in centre, but this is less prominent in ♀. HAB rocky and grassy slopes in uplands. ALT >1000. FLIGHT 7–8. FP ? EGG ? LARVA ? PUPA ? WINTER ? STATUS ?

HIGGINS'S ANOMALOUS BLUE *Agrodiaetus nephohiptamenos* (Not illustrated). Ups relatively pale, with darker veins and pale fringes: white stripe prominent on unh. HAB grassy slopes. ALT >1600. FLIGHT 7–8. FP ? EGG ? LARVA ? PUPA ? WINTER ? NOTES A very similar butterfly from S. Italy (*A. galloi*), may be conspecific with the present species. STATUS V (although Italian race not uncommon).

ANOMALOUS BLUE *Agrodiateus admetus.* Like Ripart's Anomalous Blue but unh has no white stripe, although often a wedge-shaped white spot near the centre: ♂ upf has a large patch of hairy androconia: ♀ uph generally has faint orange lunules near anal angle. HAB rocky hillsides. ALT <1800. FLIGHT 6–8. FP sainfoin. EGG ? LARVA ? PUPA ? WINTER ? STATUS V; Hungary. LP; Greece.

OBERTHUR'S ANOMALOUS BLUE *Agrodiaetus fabressei.* Like Anomalous Blue but uns with much heavier pd spots: marginal spots very faint. HAB sunny mountain slopes. ALT 900–1200. FLIGHT 6–8. FP sainfoins. EGG ? LARVA ? PUPA ? WINTER ? STATUS ?

GRECIAN ANOMALOUS BLUE *Agrodiaetus aroaniensis.* Like Oberthur's Anomalous Blue but pd spots are smaller and unf lacks marginal spots. HAB flowery slopes and meadows. ALT <1800. FLIGHT 6–8. FP ? LARVA ? PUPA ? WINTER ? VAR unh sometimes has faint marginal spots. STATUS ?

AGENJO'S ANOMALOUS BLUE *Agrodiateus agenjoi.* ♂ rather large: veins of ups often rather prominent, especially in ♀: uns resemble Oberthur's Anomalous Blue but spots are smaller. HAB dry hillsides: very local. ALT <500. FLIGHT 7–8. FP ? EGG ? LARVA ? PUPA ? WINTER ? STATUS ?

PIEDMONT ANOMALOUS BLUE *Agrodiaetus humedasae* (Not illustrated). Larger than most anomalous blues, with small dark marginal spots on unh. HAB montane meadows. ALT >800. FLIGHT 7–8. FP ? EGG ? LARVA ? PUPA ? WINTER ? STATUS ? A recently discovered species.

ESCHER'S BLUE *Agrodiaetus escheri.* ♂ ups sky blue with a pale costa and several pale veins near front of upf: fringes of uph chequered, at least in posterior half: unf lacks black spot in cell: ♀ ups usually has a complete series of orange marginal lunules. HAB grassy places, usually in hills. ALT sl–1800. FLIGHT 6–8. FP milk-vetch, thyme and possibly sainfoins. EGG 6–8. LARVA 7–5: attended by ants. PUPA 4–7. WINTER larva. VAR often rather small in mountains of C Italy (*A. e. splendens*): *A. e. dalmaticus* of Yugoslavia and Greece has much wider black borders on ♂ ups and paler uns. STATUS ?

AMANDA'S BLUE *Agrodiaetus amanda.* A relatively large species resembling some forms of Escher's Blue but without chequered fringes on uph: basal spots on unh rather small: ♀ upf lacks orange lunules and uns much browner than in Escher's Blue. HAB flowery slopes. ALT <2100. FLIGHT 5–7. FP tufted vetch. EGG 7–8: solitary on fp. LARVA 7–4: attended by ants. PUPA 4–6: succinct on fp or amongst dead leaves. WINTER small larva on leaf litter. VAR ♀ uph may lack orange lunules. STATUS V; France: R; Denmark, W. Germany. LP; W. Germany.

Anomalous Blue

Ripart's Anomalous Blue

Oberthur's Anomalous Blue

Grecian Anomalous Blue

Agenjo's Anomalous Blue

Escher's Blue

dalmaticus ♂
Escher's Blue

Amanda's Blue

Amanda's Blue

CHAPMAN'S BLUE *Agrodiaetus thersites*. ♂ ups have a violet tinge and are like Common Blue but are rather furry: unf has no black spot in cell: ♀ not easily distinguished from other species. HAB flower-rich fields and hillsides. ALT sl–1750. FLIGHT 5–9: 2–3 broods. FP sainfoins. EGG 5–10. LARVA 1–12: tended by various ants. PUPA 4–9. WINTER larva. VAR ♂ unh often has a basal blue flush, especially in 1st brood: orange lunules often absent from ♀ upf. STATUS LP; W. Germany.

PONTIC BLUE *Neolysandra coelestinus*. ♂ ups intense blue: black margins 2–3mm wide: ♀ ups brown with traces of orange lunules at rear of uph: unh has more greenish suffusion than Mazarine Blue and pd spots in a smooth curve. HAB mountain slopes. ALT 1200–1500. FLIGHT 6. FP vetches. EGG ? LARVA ? PUPA ? WINTER ? STATUS V.

TURQUOISE BLUE *Plebicula dorylas*. ♂ ups pale shining blue, with outer parts of veins black: margins of uns distinctly white with vestigial markings. HAB flowery fields and hillsides. ALT <2000: mainly above 1000. FLIGHT 5–9: 1–2 broods. FP assorted leguminous plants and wild thyme. EGG 5–9: solitary on fp. LARVA 1–12: tended by ants. PUPA 4–8: succinct on fp. WINTER small larva in dead flower heads. VAR ♀ upf occasionally has orange lunules. STATUS E; Belgium, Lux. V; Lith.. R & LP; W. Germany.

NEVADA BLUE *Plebicula golgus*. Like Turquoise Blue but a little smaller and ♂ ups more violet: ♀ ups brown, with or without orange lunules on uph. HAB rocky slopes in mountains. ALT 2000–2500. FLIGHT ? FP ? EGG ? LARVA ? PUPA ? WINTER ? NOTES Does not overlap with Turquoise Blue. STATUS E.

MOTHER-OF-PEARL BLUE *Plebicula nivescens*. ♂ ups shiny powder blue with grey spots on margin of uph: ♀ resembles Turquoise Blue but usually has orange lunules on upf: both sexes can be distinguished from all the chalkhill blues by the absence of a black spot in unf cell. HAB mountain slopes. ALT 1000–2000. FLIGHT 6–7. FP clovers and other legumes. EGG 6–7. LARVA 7–4. PUPA 4–6. WINTER larva. STATUS ?

MELEAGER'S BLUE *Meleageria daphnis*. Hw scalloped at rear, especially in ♀: no spot in cell of unf. HAB flowery hillsides. ALT sl–1800. FLIGHT 5–8. FP wild thyme, milk-vetch, and other legumes. EGG 7–8: solitary on fp. LARVA 8–5: tended by ants. PUPA 4–6 in leaf litter. WINTER egg or small larva. VAR ♀ sometimes very dark grey on ups (f. *steeveni*). STATUS V; France: R & LP; W. Germany.

▲CHALKHILL BLUE *Lysandra coridon*. Silvery blue ups and chequered fringes distinguish ♂ from most other blues except the Provence Chalkhill Blue (see Notes): no other British blue has this coloration: ♀ is more difficult to distinguish but the presence of a black spot in the cell of unf separates the *Lysandra* spp from other blues of similar size. HAB flowery hillsides on chalk and limestone. ALT sl–2000. FLIGHT 6–8. FP small legumes, especially horseshoe vetch. EGG 6–4: solitary on or near fp. LARVA 4–6: crepuscular: tended by ants for most of its life. PUPA 5–7: brown and yellow and formed naked on ground, although quickly buried and guarded by ants. WINTER egg, with fully formed larva inside: it usually falls from vegetation in autumn. VAR ♀ is commonly heavily suffused with blue (f. *syngrapha*): ♂ is often much brighter blue in parts of Spain (f. *caelestissima*), while *L. c. graeca* from the mountains of Greece has yellowish grey ups in ♂. NOTES Although visually almost indistinguishable from the Provence Chalkhill Blue, in the areas where the two species overlap the Chalkhill Blue flies 6–7, between the two broods of its relative. STATUS R; Lith. LP; W. Germany. SEE ALSO p. 218, 247, 269.

Chalk-hill Blue   f. *caelestissima* ♂

Chapman's Blue

Pontic Blue

Mother-of-Pearl Blue

Turquoise Blue

Nevada Blue

Meleager's Blue

f. *steeveni* ♀

Meleager's Blue

Chalk-hill Blue

f. *syngrapha* ♀

Chalk-hill Blue

73

PROVENCE CHALKHILL BLUE *Lysandra hispana*. Very like Chalkhill Blue, although ♂ often a little darker: ♀ uph often has small grey patches just before the orange lunules: flight time differs from Chalkhill Blue. HAB flowery slopes. ALT <1000. FLIGHT 4–6, 8–9. FP horseshoe vetch. EGG ? LARVA ? PUPA ? WINTER ? STATUS ?

MACEDONIAN CHALKHILL BLUE *Lysandra philippi* (Not illustrated). ♂ has shiny blue ups and is exactly like Chalkhill Blue from Cantabrian Mountains of Spain, but chromosomes differ. HAB mountain slopes. ALT 700–1900. FLIGHT 7–8. FP ? EGG ? LARVA ? PUPA ? WINTER ? NOTES Possibly a race of False Eros Blue. STATUS V.

SPANISH CHALKHILL BLUE *Lysandra albicans*. Like Chalkhill Blue but larger and ♂ is much paler: ♀ uph often has small grey patches just before the orange than normal: inner row of greyish spots on uph often vestigial in both sexes. HAB rough grassy slopes. ALT 900–1500. FLIGHT 6–7. FP horseshoe vetch and other legumes. LARVA tended by ants. PUPA ? WINTER ? VAR somewhat bluer at higher altitudes, but still much paler than Chalkhill Blue in this area. STATUS ?

▲**ADONIS BLUE** *Lysandra bellargus*. ♂ ups intense sky blue: fringes chequered in both sexes: ♀ like Chalkhill Blue but richer brown and with blue (not white) scales outside dark marginal spots on uph. HAB flowery hillsides on chalk and limestone. ALT sl–1800. FLIGHT 5–9: usually in 2 broods. FP horseshoe vetch: other low-growing legumes on the continent. EGG 5–10: solitary under leaflets of fp. LARVA 6–4: usually feeding by day and always tended by ants. PUPA 4–8: always buried by ants and often in their nests. WINTER small larva. STATUS E; Lux. R; Lith. LP; Belgium, France, W. Germany. SEE ALSO p. 218, 243, 246, 269, 308, 312.

▲**COMMON BLUE** *Polyommatus icarus*. ♂ ups violet blue: ♀ ups brown with greater or lesser amount of violet or purplish blue: unf has a black spot in the cell and another just below it in s1b. HAB flowery grasslands of all kinds, including dunes, heaths, roadsides and waste ground. ALT sl–2500. FLIGHT 4–10: 2–3 broods: single-brood, 6–8, in far N. FP clovers and other small legumes, especially bird's-foot trefoil. EGG 5–10: solitary on terminal shoots and leaflets of fp: sometimes on flowers: greenish at first, becoming white later. LARVA 1–12: often tended by ants. PUPA 4–10: on the ground, but quickly buried by ants, often in their nests. WINTER small larva. VAR aberrations affecting spot pattern are not uncommon. STATUS One of the commonest European butterflies and certainly the commonest of the blues. E; Malta. LP; W. Germany. SEE ALSO p. 20, 217, 242, 244, 247, 251, 258, 295, 302.

FALSE EROS BLUE *Polyommatus eroides*. Like Common Blue but ♂ less violet and with wider black margins: uph with small black spots on black margins: ♀ lacks any blue suffusion. HAB mountain slopes. ALT 1200–1800. FLIGHT 6–7. FP ? EGG ? LARVA ? PUPA ? WINTER ? STATUS E; Bulgaria, Czech. V; Poland. R; Greece.

EROS BLUE *Polyommatus eros*. Like Common Blue but ♂ ups more silvery and less violet: smaller than False Eros Blue: ♀ ups lighter brown than Common Blue with bright blue suffusion or none at all: orange lunules usually poorly developed: black spot in cell of unf distinguishes it from most similar blues. HAB mountain slopes. ALT 1200–2500. FLIGHT 6–8. FP milk-vetch and other legumes. EGG 6–8. LARVA 7–5: often tended by ants. PUPA 4–7. WINTER larva. STATUS V & LP; Greece.

Provence Chalkhill Blue

Spanish Chalkhill Blue

Adonis Blue

Common Blue

False Eros Blue

Eros Blue

FAMILY RIODINIDAE – THE DUKE OF BURGUNDY   There is only one European member of this family – the Duke of Burgundy, also misleadingly called the Duke of Burgundy Fritillary because of its coloration. Most of the 1,200 or so species in the family are found in Tropical America. They are often known as metalmarks butterflies because of the bright metallic splashes on the wings of many species. The family is closely related to the Lycaenidae, of which it is sometimes treated as a sub-family, but there are a number of differences between the two groups – notably in the legs. Whereas all six legs are fully functional in both sexes among the lycaenids, male riodinids have only four walking legs. Their front legs are very short and useless for walking, having only one short tarsal segment and no claws. The females' front legs are fully formed, although slightly shorter than the others, and all six are used for walking.

▲DUKE OF BURGUNDY *Hameais lucina.* Superficially like some of the smaller fritillaries, but readily distinguished by the two prominent white bands on unh. HAB open woodland and scrubby places. ALT sl–1200, but mainly lowland. FLIGHT 5–9: 1–2 broods: darts rapidly over low vegetation, basking on leaves but paying little attention to flowers. FP cowslip and, less often, primrose. EGG 5–6: spherical and pearly, usually in twos and threes on underside of leaf. LARVA 6–8, and again 9–10 in S: light brown at first, becoming darker and hairier later. PUPA 7–5: fawn with black spots, succinct on underside of leaf. WINTER pupa. VAR larger in S, where 2nd brood is often very dark, especially on uph. NOTES Often called the Duke of Burgundy Fritillary, although not a true fritillary. STATUS Declining in B, especially in woodland. E; Denmark. V; Lith. R; Greece, Lux. LP; W. Germany. SEE ALSO p. 23, 207, 211, 233, 237.

FAMILY LIBYTHEIDAE – THE NETTLE-TREE BUTTERFLY   This small, but widely distributed family, sometimes treated as a sub-family of the Nymphalidae, has only one European member, the Nettle-tree Butterfly, which is easily recognised by its coloration and by the strongly toothed margin of the forewing. The palps of this and the other dozen or so members of the family point forward and are extremely long – usually about half the length of the abdomen. The antennae are not strongly clubbed. All six legs are functional in the female, but the front legs of the male are very small and clawless and useless for walking.

NETTLE TREE BUTTERFLY *Libythea celtis.* Wing shape and pattern unique: very long palps. HAB open woods and scrub, also in small towns and villages. ALT sl–1800, but usually below 1000. FLIGHT 6–9 and again 3–5 after hibernation. FP nettle trees, occasionally cherry. EGG 3–4: in small groups on fp. LARVA 4–8: brown or green, in small groups. PUPA 5–9: suspended. WINTER adult. NOTES May be 2 broods in some areas. STATUS LP; Hungary. Fairly common in S, where nettle tree is often planted for shade. SEE ALSO p. 13, 16, 271, 272.

FAMILY NYMPHALIDAE – TORTOISE-SHELLS, FRITILLARIES, AND ADMIRALS
This is a huge family with over 3,000 species of mostly medium-sized to large butterflies. The European species have wingspans ranging from about 30mm to over 80mm. The family boasts some of our most colourful butterflies, including the Purple Emperor, the Peacock, and the Painted Lady as well as those mentioned in the above heading. The fritillaries are a fairly distinct group with black patterns on an orange-brown background and often with silvery spots on the underside. Most of the nymphalids are fast and powerful in the air, although many can also glide for considerable periods without flapping their wings.

The nymphalids are sometimes referred to as the brush-footed butterflies, as the front legs are short and often rather furry, especially in the males. They are quite useless for walking and remain tucked up under the front of the thorax. This feature is also shared by the next two families. The antennae are rigid, although often very slender, and the club is always very distinct. With a few exceptions, including the Purple Emperor, the sexes are very much alike and normally indistinguishable in flight. Androconia are found only in some of the fritillaries, where they are usually concentrated in dark sex-brands along some of the veins in the centre of the fore-wings (see p. 293). This helps to distinguish the males, which are often also a little more brightly coloured than the female.

The eggs are generally barrel-shaped, with flat tops and prominent vertical ribbing. The larvae are smooth in the Purple Emperor and other *Apatura* species and also in the Two-tailed Pasha, but the majority of nymphalid caterpillars bear an assortment of branching spines. As you would expect from the numerous habitats occupied by these butterflies – which include woodlands, gardens, and open grassland – the caterpillars use a very wide range of food-plants, from lofty elms to violets and other low-growing herbs. Stinging nettle, which is used by no other butterfly family, is the sole food-plant of several common species.

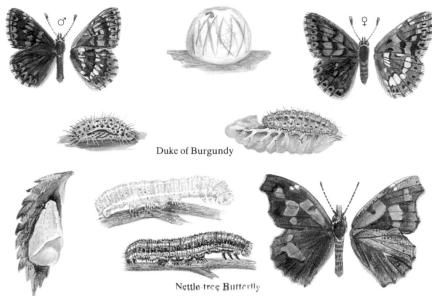

Duke of Burgundy

Nettle tree Butterfly

The pupa is suspended and has two prominent horns at the head end and often several other spiky points. It is often gilded with golden patches and the word chrysalis was originally coined for pupae of this type (from the Greek, *chrysos* meaning gold).

There are about 70 species in Europe, of which 16 breed in the British Isles – including the Red Admiral and Painted Lady. Many nymphalids are great migrants and several other species, including the Queen of Spain Fritillary, are occasional visitors from the continent.

TWO-TAILED PASHA *Charaxes jasius*. An unmistakable butterfly: the only European species with two tails. HAB scrubby places, especially near coasts. ALT sl–500. FLIGHT 5–10: 2 broods: fast-flying and not easily approached. FP strawberry tree. EGG 5–9: solitary on fp. LARVA 1–12: very well camouflaged. PUPA 4–9: suspended. WINTER larva. NOTES Very fond of ripe fruit, often visiting orchards; also frequents fig trees in autumn. STATUS LP; Greece. SEE ALSO p. 228, 229, 250, 251, 259, 286.

Two-tailed Pasha

Purple Emperor

Lesser Purple Emperor

f. *clytie* ♂

▲PURPLE EMPEROR *Apatura iris*. ♂ ups show purple or bluish iridescence only at certain angles: ♀ has no iridescence. HAB mature woodlands. ALT sl–1000. FLIGHT 7–8: usually around tall oaks and other trees. FP sallows. EGG 7–8: solitary on upper leaf surfaces. LARVA 8–6: greyish brown when young but bright green after hibernation: always superbly camouflaged. PUPA 6–7: leaf-like and suspended from fp. WINTER hibernating larva on twig of fp. STATUS E; Holland: V; in many other areas. LP; W. Germany, Hungary, Liech., Poland, and Switzerland. SEE ALSO p. 19, 21, 220, 221, 228, 229, 244, 258, 259, 288, 306.

LESSER PURPLE EMPEROR *Apatura ilia*. Like the Purple Emperor but black spot in s2 of upf is ringed with orange: antennal tip brown (not black as in *iris*). HAB light woodland. ALT sl–1000. FLIGHT 5–9: 1–2 broods. FP willows and poplars, especially aspen. EGG 6–10: solitary on upper leaf surfaces. LARVA 1–12: brown before hibernation, green afterwards. PUPA 4–9: suspended. WINTER small hibernating larva on a twig. VAR pale areas of ups often yellow (f. *clytie*). In northern Spain the wings are darker with a very bold white stripe. STATUS E; Lux.: V; elsewhere. LP; W. Germany, Greece, Hungary, Liech., Poland, Switz.

FREYER'S PURPLE EMPEROR *Apatura metis*. Like *A. ilia* f. *clytie* but with a broader orange band near edge of upf: no black pd spots on uph. HAB light woodland. ALT sl–1000. FLIGHT 5–8: 2 broods. FP willows. EGG ? LARVA ? PUPA ? WINTER ? STATUS V. LP; Hungary.

Purple Emperor

Lesser Purple Emperor

Freyer's Purple Emperor

Poplar Admiral

POPLAR ADMIRAL *Limenitis populi*. Ups like ♀ Purple Emperor, but with an orange sub-marginal band on uph: uns unmistakable with its blue border. HAB lightly wooded areas, especially near rivers: very local. ALT sl–1600. FLIGHT 6–7. FP aspen and other poplars. EGG 6–8: solitary on upper leaf surface. LARVA 8–5: brownish when young. PUPA 5–6: yellow with dark markings and partly concealed in a curled leaf. WINTER small larva in rolled dead leaf. VAR white bands are occasionally missing from ♂ ups. STATUS E; Denmark, Hungary, Lux.. V; elsewhere. LP; W. Germany, Hungary. SEE ALSO p. 239.

▲WHITE ADMIRAL *Limenitis camilla*. Ups velvety black at first, but rapidly becoming brownish: unh grey at base and with two rows of black dots on brown pd area. HAB woodland. ALT sl–1500. FLIGHT 6–8: often glides for long distances 2–3m above the ground. FP honeysuckle. EGG 6–8: solitary on upper leaf surfaces. LARVA 7–5: spiny brown before hibernation, becoming green afterwards. PUPA 5–6: like a shrivelled leaf hanging from twig. WINTER small larva hibernating in folded leaf. VAR melanic individuals with little or no white occur occasionally. STATUS E; Sweden (extinct?). R; Lux. LP; W. Germany. SEE ALSO p. 22, 207, 213, 216, 220, 221, 236, 238, 239, 244, 260.

SOUTHERN WHITE ADMIRAL *Limenitis reducta*. Like White Admiral, but upf has a prominent white spot in the cell: unh silvery at base and with only one row of black pd spots in a grey band. HAB light woodland and scrub. ALT sl–1500. FLIGHT 5–9: 1–3 broods. FP honeysuckle. EGG 5–10: solitary on upper leaf surfaces. LARVA 1–12. PUPA 4–9: grey with silvery markings and hanging like a crumpled leaf. WINTER hibernating larva. STATUS E; Lux. (extinct?). V; W. Germany, Hungary. LP; W. Germany.

COMMON GLIDER *Neptis sappho*. Uph has two white bands. HAB lowland woods: very local. ALT sl–500? FLIGHT 5–9: 2 broods. FP spring pea. EGG 5–9. LARVA 1–12. PUPA 4–8. WINTER nearly fully grown larva. STATUS E; Czech., Greece. V; elsewhere. SEE ALSO p. 260.

HUNGARIAN GLIDER *Neptis rivularis*. Resembles White Admiral, but unh has no grey or silver. HAB open woodland. ALT sl–1500. FLIGHT 6–9: 2 broods. FP *Spiraea* spp. EGG 6–9. LARVA 1–12. PUPA 5–8. WINTER larva. STATUS V; Czech., Hungary. SEE ALSO p. 260.

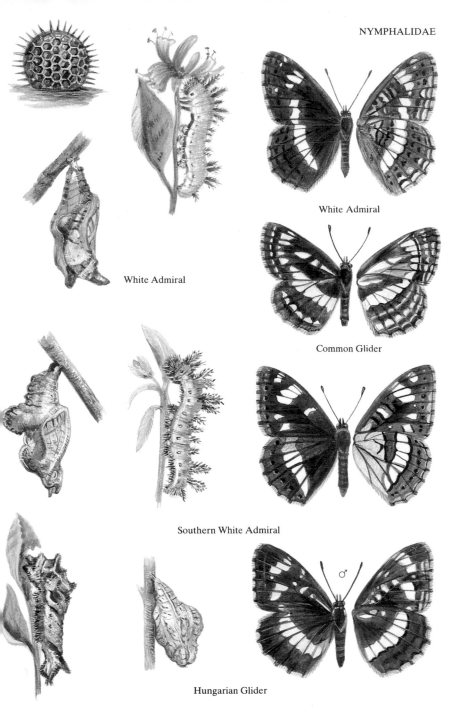

White Admiral

White Admiral

Common Glider

Southern White Admiral

♂

Hungarian Glider

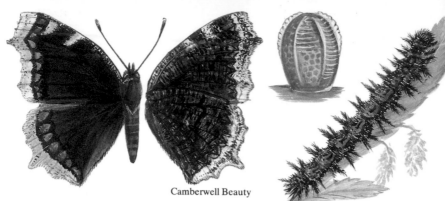

Camberwell Beauty

△**CAMBERWELL BEAUTY** *Nymphalis antiopa*. Pattern is unmistakable, although wing margins become white after hibernation. HAB open woods and scrub, mainly in upland areas. ALT sl–2500. FLIGHT 6–8 and again 3–4 after hibernation. FP sallow, birch, and other trees. EGG 3–4: clustered on twigs. LARVA 4–7: in a communal web until fully grown, but spinning a fresh web after each moult. PUPA 5–8: brown with black and orange markings and suspended on fp. WINTER adult. NOTES The English name commemorates the fact that the first recorded British specimen was found in Camberwell. Merely a vagrant to B. STATUS E; Holland, Lux. V; Austria, Belgium, Czech., W. Germany. LP; Belgium, W. Germany, Hungary, Switzerland. SEE ALSO p. 204, 217, 244, 251, 268, 272, 273.

△ ? **LARGE TORTOISESHELL** *Nymphalis polychloros*. Uph lacks dark basal patch and dark border has sharply defined inner margin: hair on legs is black. HAB light woodland, especially the forest edge. ALT sl–2000. FLIGHT 6–8 and again 2–4 after hibernation. FP elms and various other deciduous trees. EGG 3–5: clustered around twigs. LARVA 4–6: gregarious, spending early instars in communal webs. PUPA 6–7: hanging like a withered leaf, often with metallic spots. WINTER adult. STATUS E; Holland. V; Czech., W. Germany: R; Denmark. LP; W. Germany, Switzerland. Possibly extinct as a resident in B, although vagrants arrive in most years. SEE ALSO p. 213, 217, 234, 238, 304.

YELLOW-LEGGED TORTOISESHELL *Nymphalis xanthomelas*. Like Large Tortoiseshell, but uph has less distinct inner margin to black border: hair on legs is yellowish brown. HAB woodland edges, especially near water. ALT sl–600? FLIGHT 6–9 and again 3–4 after hibernation. FP deciduous trees, especially willows and elms. EGG 4–5: batched on twigs. LARVA 5–6: gregarious when young but solitary later. PUPA 6–7: very like Large Tortoiseshell but often darker. WINTER adult. STATUS E; Greece, Hungary. V; elsewhere. LP; W. Germany, Hungary.

FALSE COMMA *Nymphalis vau-album*. Resembles Large Tortoiseshell but with a prominent white spot near the front of each wing on ups: outer edge of fw deeply indented. HAB woodland margins and surrounding grassland: never far from trees: local. ALT sl–500? FLIGHT 7–9 and again 3–5 after hibernation. FP deciduous trees, especially willows. EGG 4–5. LARVA 5–6. PUPA 6–7. WINTER adult. NOTES Migrations to Baltic coasts are sporadic. STATUS E. LP; W. Germany, Hungary. SEE ALSO p. 304.

▲**PEACOCK** *Inachis io*. Wing pattern is unmistakable. HAB flowery places, including gardens. ALT sl–2000. FLIGHT 7–9 and 3–5 after hibernation. FP common nettle. EGG 4–5: in large batches under the leaves. LARVA 5–7: gregarious until ready to pupate. PUPA 6–7: golden green or occasionally dark brown: suspended from fp or neighbouring plant. WINTER adult, often in buildings. STATUS LP; Hungary, Switzerland. SEE ALSO p. 22, 204, 206, 217, 245, 251, 252, 266, 270, 271, 272, 273, 275, 286–7, 301, 309, 312.

Camberwell Beauty

Large Tortoiseshell

Yellow-legged Tortoiseshell

Large Tortoiseshell

Yellow-legged Tortoiseshell

False Comma

Peacock

Red Admiral

▲**RED ADMIRAL** *Vanessa atalanta*. Wing pattern is unmistakable. HAB flowery places, including gardens. ALT sl–2000. FLIGHT 5–10: usually in 2 broods, and also in early spring in the south after a short hibernation. FP common nettle: occasionally hop. EGG 3–9: solitary on upper surface of leaf. LARVA 4–10: normally concealed in folded leaf. PUPA 5–10: dark grey with golden spines: suspended, usually inside last larval shelter. WINTER adult: few, if any survive the winter in B. NOTES Flight is normally fast and 'fidgety'; the insect is very fond of ripe fruit. STATUS LP; Hungary, Switzerland. SEE ALSO p. 216, 238, 251, 259, 264, 265, 287, 289, 290, 298, 300, 301, 306, 307, 308.

▲**PAINTED LADY** *Cynthia cardui*. Cannot be confused with any other European butterfly: the American Painted Lady (*C. virginiensis*), which turns up very occasionally in SW, is similar but unh has just two very large ocelli. HAB flowery places of all kinds, including gardens and roadsides. ALT sl–2500. FLIGHT 4–10: 2 broods: fast-flying with much gliding. FP thistles and, less often, stinging nettle and mallows. EGG 4–10: solitary on upper leaf surface. LARVA 4–10: usually in a tent of leaves and silk. PUPA 5–10: pink and gold and usually hanging inside a shelter of silk, with or without protective leaves. WINTER unable to survive European winters, except possibly in southern Spain and Malta. NOTES Continuously brooded in N. Africa, from where it migrates northwards in spring and summer. STATUS Common in S, but numbers fluctuate markedly from year to year further N. SEE ALSO p. 216, 239, 242, 243, 248, 251, 253, 264, 265, 266, 267, 308.

▲**SMALL TORTOISESHELL** *Aglais urticae*. Uph has extensive black basal patch. HAB flowery places of all kinds. ALT sl–2500; higher on migration. FLIGHT 3–10: 1–3 broods. FP common nettle and small nettle. EGG 5–8: in batches of up to 100 near top of fp. LARVA 5–9: clustered in silken tents at first but separating when half grown. PUPA 6–10: suspended from fp. WINTER adult, often in buildings. VAR *A. u. ichnusa* of Corsica and Sardinia is brighter, without obvious black spots in hind part of upf. STATUS One of the commonest garden butterflies. SEE ALSO p. 23, 25, 204, 205, 206, 217, 237, 239, 242, 245, 248, 251, 253, 260, 266, 272, 276, 287, 299, 301.

▲**COMMA** *Polygonia c-album*. A distinct white C-shaped mark on unh. HAB woodland margins, gardens, hedgerows, and other flowery places. ALT sl–2000. FLIGHT 3–9: 2 broods, the second one over-wintering and appearing again in the spring. FP stinging nettle, elm, hop. EGG 4–8: solitary or in small groups on margin of upper surface of leaf. LARVA 5–9: resembles a bird dropping and can thus sit freely exposed on top of leaf. PUPA 6–9: brown with silvery spots and suspended from fp. WINTER adult. VAR 1st brood consists partly of f. *hutchinsoni*, which is much paler than the 2nd (hibernating) generation. STATUS Generally common in most parts of its range, but rather local in northern areas, where it occurs mainly as a migrant. V: Holland. R; Denmark. LP; W. Germany. One of the few British butterflies to have increased its range in the 20th Century. SEE ALSO p. 25, 229, 243, 244, 251, 262, 274, 300, 307.

Painted Lady

ichnusa

Small Tortoiseshell

Small Tortoiseshell

Comma

Comma   f. *hutchinsoni*

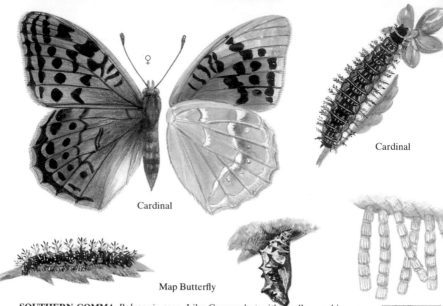

Cardinal

♀

Cardinal

Map Butterfly

SOUTHERN COMMA *Polygonia egea*. Like Comma but with smaller markings on ups and only a faint white v- or y-shaped mark on unh. HAB hot, dry hillsides and other rocky places. ALT sl–1700. FLIGHT 3–9: 2 broods, the second of which hibernates and flies again in the spring. FP pellitory of the wall and, occasionally, stinging nettle and various trees. EGG 3–7: solitary or in small groups. LARVA 4–8. PUPA 4–5 and 8–9: brownish yellow and rather spiny and suspended from rocks or plants. WINTER adult. VAR 1st brood (f. *j-album*) paler than 2nd brood as in the Comma. STATUS Not uncommon.

MAP BUTTERFLY *Araschnia levana*. Marbled uns with prominent white veins unmistakable in both generations. HAB lightly wooded areas and other rough ground. ALT sl–1000. FLIGHT 4–9: 2 broods which differ markedly from each other. FP stinging nettle. EGG 4–9: laid in strings which resemble catkins of fp. LARVA 5–9: gregarious on fp. PUPA 9–7: green, often with silvery spots: suspended on fp. WINTER pupa. VAR very marked seasonal polyphenism, with 1st brood (f. *levana*) fritillary-like and 2nd brood (f. *prorsa*) resembling a small White Admiral: ♀ *prorsa* has orange pd stripe on uph. STATUS Generally common. SEE ALSO p. 25, 210, 300.

CARDINAL *Pandoriana pandora*. Rosy red lower half and green apex of unf: ups with greenish suffusion in both sexes: silver stripes on unh best seen in ♀. HAB flowery meadows and woodland margins. ALT sl–2200. FLIGHT 5–7. FP wild pansy and other *Viola* spp. EGG 6–8: solitary on fp or nearby vegetation. LARVA 7–5: nocturnal. PUPA 5–6: brown or grey with gold spots and suspended amongst low vegetation. WINTER small larva. STATUS E & LP; Hungary.

▲**SILVER-WASHED FRITILLARY** *Argynnis paphia*. Unf ground colour pale orange throughout: unh largely green with silver stripes and a purplish border. HAB woodland rides and clearings. ALT sl–1500. FLIGHT 5–8. FP violets. EGG 6–8: solitary in bark crevices and amongst mosses up to 2m high on tree trunks. LARVA 8–5: hibernates at egg site as soon as it hatches and is active only 3–5. PUPA 5–7: suspended in low vegetation and beautifully camouflaged. WINTER 1st-instar larva, occasionally remaining inside the egg-shell. VAR a proportion of ♀♀ (up to 15% in some areas) are f. *valezina*, with extensive greenish suffusion. *A. p. immaculata* of Corsica and Sardinia has a golden sheen and much reduced markings on unh. STATUS E; Holland. V; Finland. R; Denmark. LP; W. Germany. SEE ALSO p. 22, 25, 203, 211, 216, 221, 239, 244, 251, 261, 283, 289, 290, 292–3, 298, 299.

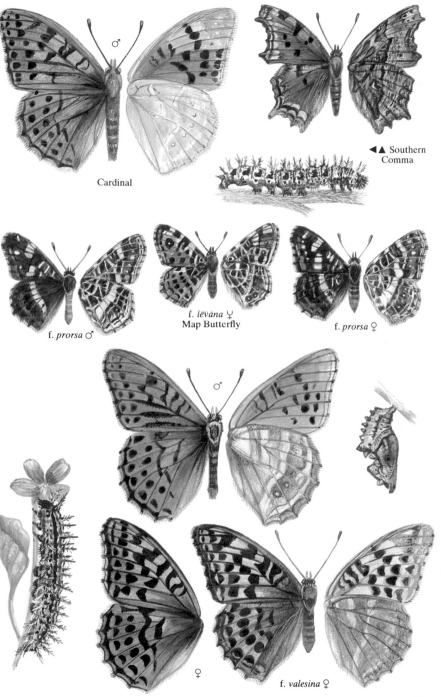

Cardinal

◀▲ Southern
Comma

f. *prorsa* ♂

f. *levana* ♀
Map Butterfly

f. *prorsa* ♀

♀

f. *valesina* ♀

Silver-washed Fritillary

Pallas's Fritillary   Dark Green Fritillary

PALLAS'S FRITILLARY *Argyronome laodice*. Unh light green basally and purplish brown in outer half: ♂ upf lacks the small white mark near the apex. HAB damp woodland clearings. ALT ? lowland. FLIGHT 7–8. FP marsh violet and, less often, other *Viola* spp. EGG 7–9. LARVA 9–6. PUPA 6–7. WINTER 1st-instar larva. STATUS E; Czech. V; elsewhere. LP; Hungary.

▲**DARK GREEN FRITILLARY** *Mesoacidalia aglaja*. Unh largely green and straw-coloured, with all spots silver: unf has silver marginal spots, at least near apex. HAB flower-rich, unimproved grasslands and heaths, including coastal cliffs and dunes. ALT sl–2500. FLIGHT 6–8. FP violets. EGG 6–8: solitary on fp vegetation and leaf litter. LARVA 8–6: hibernates soon after hatching and does not become active until spring. PUPA 5–7: suspended in a shelter of leaves spun together with silk. WINTER 1st-instar larva. VAR ups often with dark suffusion, especially in north and in ♀: spots vary in size. STATUS V; Holland. LP; W. Germany. SEE ALSO p. 221, 242, 243.

▲**HIGH BROWN FRITILLARY** *Fabriciana adippe*. Ups like Dark Green Fritillary but unh is usually less green and has a row of brown pd spots with silver pupils: unf usually lacks silver spots on outer margin: uph has a fringe of long hairs on vein 7. HAB woodland clearings and flowery meadows in wooded country, often in uplands. ALT sl–2000. FLIGHT 6–8. FP violets. EGG 6–3: solitary on or near fp. LARVA 2–5: feeding by day on leaves and, in early stages, on flowers. PUPA 4–6: resembling a shrivelled leaf and suspended amongst vegetation: often surrounded by leaves drawn together with silk. WINTER egg. VAR f. *cleodoxa*, which lacks silver on uns, occurs occasionally in north, becoming more common in south and replacing the normal form altogether in Greece (where it can thus be regarded as a sub-species): *F. a. chlorodippe* from Iberia has very green unh and a green tip with silver spots on unf. f. *cleodippe* of N. Spain has greenish unh, but no silver spots. STATUS V; Belgium, B, Lux. LP; W. Germany. SEE ALSO p. 208, 243.

NIOBE FRITILLARY *Fabriciana niobe*. Very similar to High Brown Fritillary but unh has strong black veins: size varies, and often much larger than shown here. HAB flowery meadows, especially in uplands. ALT sl–1900. FLIGHT 6–7. FP violets and occasionally plantains. EGG 6–8: solitary on fp. LARVA 7–5. PUPA 4–6: suspended amongst vegetation. WINTER larva, sometimes remaining in egg-shell in N. VAR both sexes occur in two forms: f. *niobe* with silver spots on unh, and f. *eris* without. f. *eris* is generally the commoner of the two and is the only form known from Iberia. ♂ sex brands vary in their development and may be absent in parts of Spain. STATUS E; Lux. V; Belgium. LP; Belgium, W. Germany.

CORSICAN FRITILLARY *Fabriciana elisa*. Like a small Niobe Fritillary but with smaller spots on ups and more small silver spots on unh. HAB maquis and open woods. ALT 1000–1500. FLIGHT 6–7. FP violets. EGG 6–8: solitary on fp. LARVA 7–5. PUPA 5–6: suspended amongst vegetation. WINTER larva. NOTES Possibly a sub-species of the Niobe Fritillary. STATUS V.

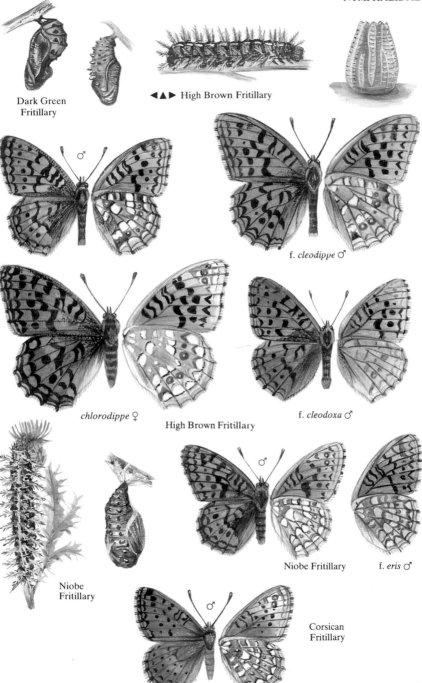

Dark Green
Fritillary

◄▲► High Brown Fritillary

f. *cleodippe* ♂

chlorodippe ♀

High Brown Fritillary

f. *cleodoxa* ♂

Niobe
Fritillary

Niobe Fritillary

f. *eris* ♂

Corsican
Fritillary

89

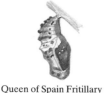

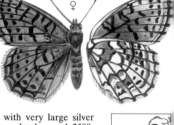

Queen of Spain Fritillary

Twin-spot
Fritillary

△**QUEEN OF SPAIN FRITILLARY** *Issoria lathonia*. Unh with very large silver spots: outer margin of fw slightly concave. HAB flower-rich grassland. ALT sl–2500. FLIGHT 2–10: 2+ broods. FP violets. EGG 3–9: solitary on fp. LARVA 1–12: dormant in winter. PUPA 1–12: suspended from vegetation and strongly resembling a bird dropping as a result of its white 'saddle'. WINTER resting larva or pupa: possibly also as egg and adult. NOTES A great migrant, but a rare visitor to B. STATUS V; Holland. LP; W. Germany. SEE ALSO p. 262, 268, 271.

TWIN-SPOT FRITILLARY *Brenthis hecate*. Two complete rows of small black spots in outer part of wings on both ups and uns. HAB rough, flowery hillsides: local. ALT 600–1500. FLIGHT 5–6. FP *Dorycnium* and related legumes. EGG 5–6. LARVA 1–12. PUPA 4–5. WINTER hibernating larva. STATUS E; Czech. V; elsewhere.

MARBLED FRITILLARY *Brenthis daphne*. Pd spots of upf very unequal in size: unh mottled lilac and brown in outer half. HAB sunny, flower-rich valleys and hillsides. ALT sl–1900. FLIGHT 6–8. FP violets, bramble, and other *Rubus* spp. EGG 6–9: solitary on fp. LARVA 7–5. PUPA 5–6: yellowish or grey with red and gold spots and suspended from fp. WINTER larva. NOTES Adults particularly fond of bramble flowers. STATUS E & LP; W. Germany.

LESSER MARBLED FRITILLARY *Brenthis ino*. Like Marbled Fritillary but a little smaller and pd spots of upf more uniform in size: ups with continuous black margins: unh less violet in Marbled Fritillary, with base of s4 yellow (mostly brown in Marbled Fritillary). HAB Damp, flowery grassland. ALT sl–1600. FLIGHT 6–8. FP meadowsweet, great burnet, raspberry, and other rosaceous plants. EGG 6–8. LARVA 7–4: nocturnal and very secretive. PUPA 4–7: yellowish brown with yellow spikes. WINTER larva. STATUS V; W. Germany. LP; W. Germany and Hungary. Declining everywhere through land drainage. SEE ALSO p. 304.

SHEPHERD'S FRITILLARY *Boloria pales*. Discal spots of upf rather square: basal and discal areas of unh generally deep red: a prominent yellow patch at extremity of s3. HAB mountain slopes, usually above the tree line. ALT >1500. FLIGHT 6–8. FP violets. EGG 6–9: solitary on fp. LARVA 8–5. PUPA 5–6: suspended from fp. WINTER larva. VAR generally paler in south (*B. p. palustris*), and with less black on uph, especially in Spain (*B. p. pyrenesmiscens*). STATUS V; Balkans, Czech., Poland. R; Rumania. LP; W. Germany and Greece.

MOUNTAIN FRITILLARY *Boloria napaea*. Like Shepherd's Fritillary but upf markings are linear and pd spots usually form a thin zig-zag line. HAB mountain slopes, usually near the tree line. ALT sl (Scand.)–3000. FLIGHT 7–8. FP Alpine bistort and violets. EGG 7–9: solitary on fp. LARVA 1–12: often 2-year life cycle. PUPA 5–7: suspended on fp. WINTER larva (once or twice). VAR most Scandinavian specimens are rather small (f. *frigida*). NOTES Not easily distinguished from Shepherd's Fritillary in the field, but ♂ genitalia are slightly different. STATUS LP; W. Germany.

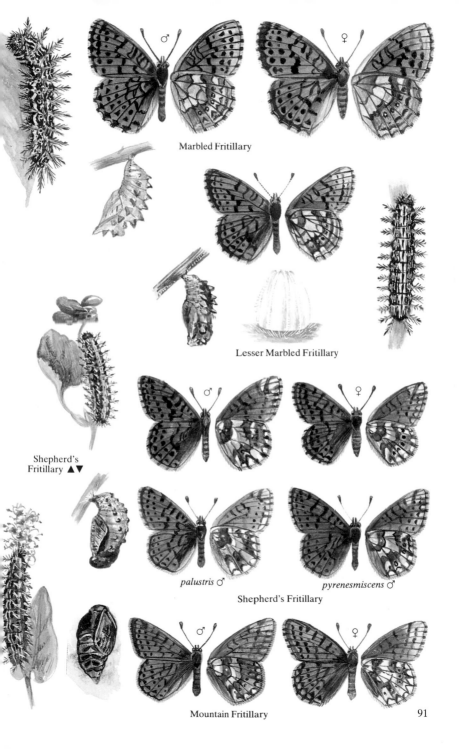

Marbled Fritillary

Lesser Marbled Fritillary

Shepherd's
Fritillary ▲▼

palustris ♂   *pyrenesmiscens* ♂

Shepherd's Fritillary

Mountain Fritillary

Cranberry Fritillary

CRANBERRY FRITILLARY *Boloria aquilonaris*. Basal and discal spots of upf prominent and often v-shaped, especially in s1b: uns like Shepherd's Fritillary but unf more heavily spotted and unh without prominent yellow patch. HAB bogs and wet heaths. ALT sl–1800. FLIGHT 6–7. FP cranberry. EGG 6–8: solitary. LARVA 1–12: often 2-year life cycle. PUPA 5–7: suspended close to ground. WINTER hibernating larva, often inside stems of fp. VAR f. *alethea*, from certain lowland areas in southern parts of the range, is larger than the typical form. STATUS E. LP; Belgium, France, W. Germany. SEE ALSO p. 304, 305.

BALKAN FRITILLARY *Boloria graeca*. Like Shepherd's Fritillary but unf spotting is heavier and more complete: pd spots of unh generally large and white-centred. HAB alpine meadows. ALT >1500. FLIGHT 7–8. FP ? EGG ? LARVA ? PUPA ? WINTER ? VAR Alpine specimens (*B. g. tendensis*) are slightly smaller and paler than Balkan ones, with greener unh. STATUS R; Bulgaria, Italy. LP; Greece.

BOG FRITILLARY *Proclossiana eunomia*. Pd spots of unh in the form of clear black rings filled with white or yellow. HAB bogs and other wet, grassy places. ALT sl–1500. FLIGHT 5–7. FP common bistort, cranberry, and other plants. EGG 5–8. LARVA 1–12: often 2-year life cycle. PUPA 4–6: grey with silvery spots. WINTER larva (once or twice). VAR *P. e. ossiana* from moors and bogs of Scandinavia has silver or white discal and marginal spots on unh: *P. e. eunomia* from more southerly areas has bright yellow spots. STATUS E. LP; France, W. Germany. SEE ALSO p. 304, 305.

▲**PEARL-BORDERED FRITILLARY** *Clossiana euphrosyne*. Unh largely sandy but discal band yellow with a large central silver spot: marginal spots of unh all silver. HAB woodland margins and clearings, meadows, and heathland: especially fond of bugle flowers. ALT sl–2000. FLIGHT 4–8: 1–2 broods, but 2nd well developed only in the south. FP violets. EGG 5–8: solitary or paired on or near fp. LARVA 1–12. PUPA 5–8: suspended from fp. WINTER larva, concealed in rolled leaf. VAR ♀ smaller and darker in north and on high mountains (f. *fingal*). NOTES Larva likes to bask in spring sunshine, as do those of many other fritillaries. STATUS R; Ireland and Lux. LP; W. Germany. SEE ALSO p. 23, 221, 304.

TITANIA'S FRITILLARY *Clossiana titania*. Unh pd spots usually linked to marginal chevrons: ♀ paler, often with a greenish tinge on unh. HAB light woodland and clearings. ALT 1200–2000. FLIGHT 6–7. FP violets and bistorts. EGG 6–7. LARVA 7–5. PUPA 4–6: grey with black and white markings. WINTER larva. VAR unh has a strong purple tinge in Alpine areas (*C. t. cyparis*). STATUS V; Finland.

▲**SMALL PEARL-BORDERED FRITILLARY** *Clossiana selene*. Like Pearl-bordered Fritillary but discal band of unh is usually either all silver or all yellow. HAB damp woodland and clearings, grassland, and heathland. ALT sl–1800. FLIGHT 5–8: 1–2 broods. FP violets. EGG 5–8: solitary on or near fp. LARVA 6–4: hides at base of fp and comes up only briefly to feed: does not bask like many other fritillaries. PUPA 4–7: decorated with metallic spots and suspended from fp. WINTER larva. VAR discal band of unh may be yellow with 3 silver spots; f. *hela* from northern areas has extensive black patch on uph. STATUS V; Holland: R; Lux. LP; W. Germany.

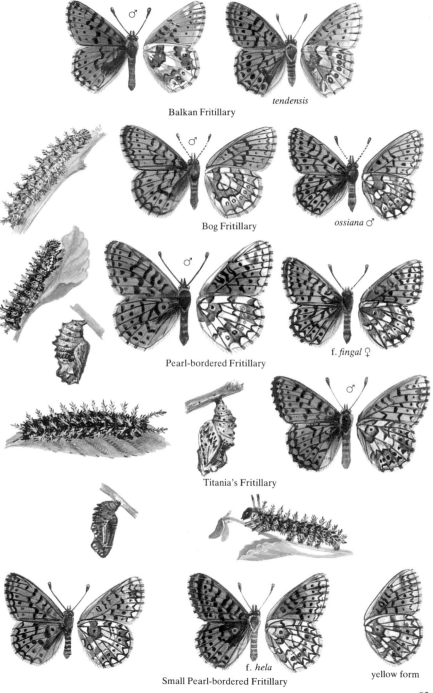

tendensis

Balkan Fritillary

Bog Fritillary

ossiana ♂

Pearl-bordered Fritillary

f. *fingal* ♀

Titania's Fritillary

f. *hela*

Small Pearl-bordered Fritillary

yellow form

ARCTIC FRITILLARY *Clossiana chariclea*. Discal spots of upf fused into a continuous band: discal band of unh usually silver and very conspicuous. HAB tundra. ALT sl–1400. FLIGHT 6–8. FP violets? and cassiope? EGG ? LARVA ? PUPA ? WINTER ? STATUS R; Norway. SEE ALSO p. 222, 242, 247.

FREIJA'S FRITILLARY *Clossiana freija*. Discal spots of upf joined to form a thick zig-zag band: unh has a prominent zig-zag band in discal area. HAB moorland and tundra. ALT sl–1000, but usually at low levels. FLIGHT 5–7. FP cloudberry and bog bilberry. EGG 6–7. LARVA 7–5: black with long brown hairs at first, bearing orange spikes after 1st moult. PUPA 5–7. WINTER larva. STATUS ?

WEAVER'S FRITILLARY *Clossiana dia*. One of the smallest fritillaries, with hw sharply angled at apex: unh purplish brown with 3 prominent silver spots in discal row and with well-marked pd spots. HAB light woodland and scrub, mainly in the hills. ALT sl–1000. FLIGHT 4–10: 2–3 broods. FP violets, *Rubus* spp, and other low-growing plants. EGG 4–9: solitary on fp. LARVA 1–12. PUPA 4–9: brown with black dots and suspended low down on fp. WINTER larva. NOTES Also known as the Violet Fritillary. STATUS V; Lux. R; Greece, Lith. LP; W. Germany, Greece.

POLAR FRITILLARY *Clossiana polaris*. Unh with a white spot next to each dark pd spot and with many other white spots. HAB tundra slopes: local. ALT sl–1000. FLIGHT 6–7: swift and erratic. FP mountain avens. EGG ? LARVA ? PUPA ? WINTER ? NOTES Similar to Weaver's Fritillary, but ranges do not overlap. STATUS R; Norway. SEE ALSO p. 222, 309.

THOR'S FRITILLARY *Clossiana thore*. Discal band of unh pale yellow and very prominent: metallic grey marginal spots on unh: ♀ ups with less black suffusion. HAB wooded areas in uplands. ALT sl–1700. FLIGHT 6–7. FP violets. EGG 6–7. LARVA 1–12: 2-year life-cycle. PUPA 5–6. WINTER larva (twice). VAR *C. t. borealis* of Scandinavia is much paler than Alpine race (*C. t. thore*): Finnish race (*C. t. carelia*) is somewhat intermediate between the other two sub-species, generally pale but with a wide black border on uph. STATUS V; Italy. R; W. Germany, Norway. LP; W. Germany.

FRIGGA'S FRITILLARY *Clossiana frigga*. Unh has conspicuous white marks in front half, but no white marginal spots. HAB damp moors and bogs. ALT sl–500. FLIGHT 6–7. FP cloudberry. EGG 6–7. LARVA 7–5: olive green at first, becoming brown with branched black spikes later. PUPA 5–6. WINTER larva. STATUS E; Lith.

DUSKY-WINGED FRITILLARY *Clossiana improba*. Coloration unlike any other fritillary: unh has pronounced white costal margin. HAB dry upland slopes: very local. ALT 400–1100. FLIGHT 7. FP Alpine bistort and dwarf willow? EGG 7–8. LARVA 1–12: 2-year life cycle. PUPA 5–7. WINTER larva (twice). STATUS R; Finland, Norway.

▲**GLANVILLE FRITILLARY** *Melitaea cinxia*. Uph has 5 black spots in orange sub-marginal band: unh sub-marginal band has a distinctly scalloped inner margin. HAB flowery fields and hillsides. ALT sl–2500. FLIGHT 4–9: 1–2 broods. FP plantains and, occasionally, knapweed. EGG 5–9: yellow and batched on fp. LARVA 1–12: gregarious on silken webs for much of life, often forming black swarms on vegetation: solitary later and resembling plantain head when mature. PUPA 4–8: suspended amongst vegetation or in rocky crevices and very well camouflaged: occasionally under stones. WINTER hibernating larvae in dense silken nest. VAR density of black pattern varies, often very heavy at high altitudes. STATUS V; Belgium, W. Germany, Holland. R; Austria, B, Lux. LP; Belgium, W. Germany. SEE ALSO p. 217, 229.

FREYER'S FRITILLARY *Melitaea arduinna*. Very like Glanville Fritillary but sub-marginal band of unh is not scalloped on inner margin: black marginal lunules are linked into a continuous line. HAB flowery mountain slopes: local. ALT >1200. FLIGHT 5–6. FP ? EGG ? LARVA ? PUPA ? WINTER ? STATUS V; Greece.

Polar Fritillary

Arctic Fritillary

Freija's Fritillary

Weaver's Fritillary

♂

borealis ♂
Thor's Fritillary

Dusky-winged Fritillary

Freyer's Fritillary

Frigga's Fritillary

Glanville Fritillary

95

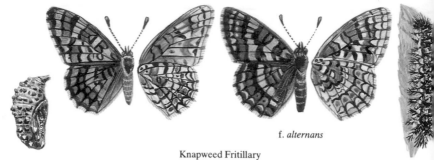

f. *alternans*

Knapweed Fritillary

KNAPWEED FRITILLARY *Melitaea phoebe*. Like Glanville Fritillary but without black spots on uph: unh has clear orange spots in yellow sub-marginal band: upf has marginal lunule in s3 much bigger than the others. HAB flowery fields and hillsides. ALT sl–2000. FLIGHT 4–9: 1–3 broods. FP knapweeds and occasionally plantains. EGG 5–9: batched on fp. LARVA 1–12: gregarious in silken nests until final instar. PUPA 4–8: grey with black and red spots and suspended from fp. WINTER larva in silken nests. VAR 3rd brood in S often very small and pale (f. *pauper*): black markings often larger and orange often deeper in S Alps, producing a very contrasting pattern (f. *alternans*), although this may fade a little after death. STATUS E; Lux. (extinct?). V; Belgium. R; Austria, W. Germany. LP; W. Germany.

AETHERIE FRITILLARY *Melitaea aetherie*. Like Knapweed Fritillary but uph lacks a well defined orange sub-marginal band: unf discal spots often very small. HAB flowery fields and light woodland: local. ALT sl–500. FLIGHT 4–5. FP knapweeds. EGG ? LARVA ? PUPA ? WINTER ? STATUS ?

SPOTTED FRITILLARY *Melitaea didyma*. An extremely variable species, but normally recognised by the clear orange sub-marginal band of unh: marginal spots of unh usually rounded or semi-circular, not triangular. HAB flowery fields and hillsides. ALT sl–1800. FLIGHT 5–9: 1–3 broods. FP plantains, toadflaxes, and speedwells. EGG 6–9: batched on fp. LARVA 1–12: gregarious in silken shelters in early stages. PUPA 4–9: green with black and orange markings and suspended from fp. WINTER larvae in silken shelters. VAR ♀ is often heavily dusted with grey in the mountains (*M. d. meridionalis*): ups markings much reduced in Iberia (*M. d. occidentalis*) and 3rd brood insects often very small (f. *dalmatina*). NOTES The sub-species grade into each other, with numerous intermediate forms. The species is not easy to separate from the Lesser Spotted Fritillary, although the latter is absent from most of France. Male genitalia differ, and there are also subtle differences in venation. STATUS E; Lux: R; Austria, Belgium, Lith. LP; W. Germany. SEE ALSO p. 229, 246, 301, 304.

LESSER SPOTTED FRITILLARY *Melitaea fascelis*. Very like Spotted Fritillary but generally a little smaller: unh marginal spots clearly triangular. HAB rough, flowery places, often in uplands. ALT sl–1500. FLIGHT 5–8: 2 broods. FP mulleins. EGG ? LARVA ? PUPA ? WINTER ? VAR black markings are small and incomplete in Iberia (*M. t. ignasti*), giving the insect a much more distinctly spotted appearance. A very large form occurs in some Balkan mountains. STATUS V.

FALSE HEATH FRITILLARY *Melitaea diamina*. Ups generally very dark, especially on uph: sub-marginal band of unh contains a row of pale spots, each with a small, dark mark beyond it: unh edged with yellow or orange between two thin but distinct black lines. HAB damp grassland, especially with scattered trees. ALT sl–2000. FLIGHT 5–8 in 1–2 broods. FP plantains, cow-wheat, speedwells, and other low-growing plants. EGG 6–8: batched on fp. LARVA 1–12: gregarious when young. PUPA 5–7: suspended from fp. WINTER gregarious larvae in silken shelter (the larvae separate after hibernation). VAR often smaller in mountain areas: in the mountains of N. Spain ups lack the dark suffusion and the pale spots in sub-marginal band of unh may be missing (*M. d. vernetensis*), but wide, dark margins of ups will distinguish it from most forms of the Heath Fritillary. STATUS E; Denmark & Lux. V; Finland. LP; W. Germany.

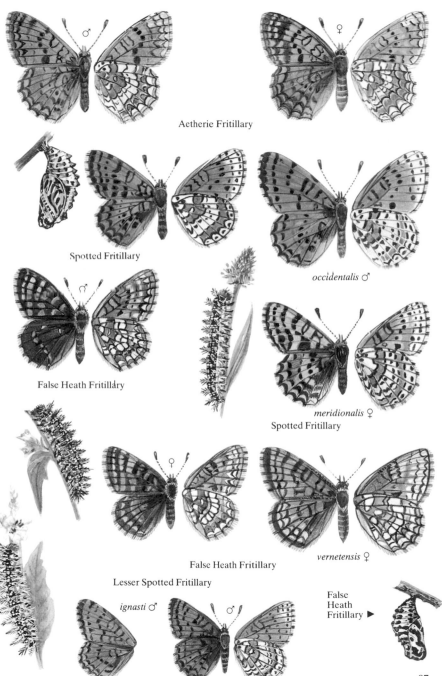

Aetherie Fritillary

Spotted Fritillary

occidentalis ♂

False Heath Fritillary

meridionalis ♀
Spotted Fritillary

False Heath Fritillary

vernetensis ♀

Lesser Spotted Fritillary

ignasti ♂

False
Heath
Fritillary ▶

97

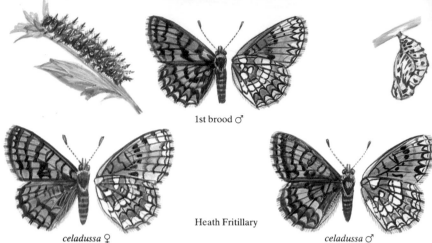

1st brood ♂

Heath Fritillary

celadussa ♀   *celadussa* ♂

▲**HEATH FRITILLARY** *Mellicta athalia*. An extremely variable species but usually distinguished from similar species by the heavy black inner borders to the sub-marginal lunules in s2 and sometimes s3 of unf. HAB flowery fields, open woods, and woodland margins. ALT sl–2000. FLIGHT 5–9 in 1–3 broods. FP common cow-wheat and ribwort plantain, occasionally on germander speedwell and foxglove. EGG 5–9: batched under old leaves near the fp. LARVA 1–12: in small groups in silken shelters when young, but separating later and basking openly on vegetation. PUPA 5–9: suspended from dead leaves and very well camouflaged. WINTER hibernating larvae in silken shelters. VAR rather more brightly marked in SW (*M. a. celadussa*): small in far north (*M. a. norvegica*) and also in late broods in south: border of uph very broad in Balkans (*M. a. boris*), and uph may be largely brown in mountains in this area (f. *satyra*): the latter resembles the False Heath Fritillary but has no dark spots in sub-marginal band of unh. NOTES Variability makes the Heath Fritillary difficult to identify in many areas other than by the absence of the diagnostic features of the other species, although the genitalia are quite different in the various *Mellicta* species. STATUS V; B & Holland: R; Lux. LP; France, W. Germany & B. SEE ALSO p. 213, 245, 305, 306, 311, 312.

PROVENÇAL FRITILLARY *Mellicta deione*. Like Heath Fritillary but inner black borders of marginal lunules in s2 and s3 of unf are generally faint or absent: discal spot in s1b of upf often dumb-bell shaped. HAB flowery fields and hillsides, usually in mountains. ALT sl–1500. FLIGHT 5–9: 1–2 broods. FP toadflaxes and related plants. EGG 6–9. LARVA 1–12. PUPA 4–8. WINTER larva. VAR pale marginal lunules of uph ± obliterated by dark borders in alpine regions (*M. d. berisalii*): *M. d. rosinae* from southern Portugal has darker and more uniform ground colour on ups, and unf has conspicuous black borders to marginal lunules, but Heath Fritillary does not occur here and there is no confusion. STATUS E; Italy & Switzerland. V; elsewhere.

GRISON'S FRITILLARY *Mellicta varia*. Small, with a black basal streak in s1b of unf: discal spot in s1b of upf often dumb-bell shaped but with outer edge always vertical. HAB montane grassland. ALT usually >1800. FLIGHT 6–8. FP gentians, plantains, and other low-growing plants. EGG 7–9. LARVA 1–12. PUPA 6–8. WINTER larva. VAR often much darker at higher altitudes: f. *piana* is a rather large form occurring at lower altitudes in Maritime Alps. It is very similar to the Meadow Fritillary but vertical outer edge of the 'dumb bell' will always distinguish it. STATUS ?

MEADOW FRITILLARY *Mellicta parthenoides*. Like Grison's Fritillary but black discal spot in s1b is an oblique dash. HAB mountain foothills, especially where damp. ALT 500–2100, but usually below 1000. FLIGHT 5–9: 1–2 broods. FP plantains, cow-wheat, and other plants. EGG 5–9. LARVA 1–12. PUPA 4–8: grey with a black and white pattern and suspended from fp. WINTER larva. VAR *M. p. plena* flies up to 2100m in Pyrenees and is darker with more complete markings. NOTES Overlaps with Grison's Fritillary only in SW Alps, where Grison's generally flies at much higher altitudes. STATUS R; Italy. LP; W. Germany.

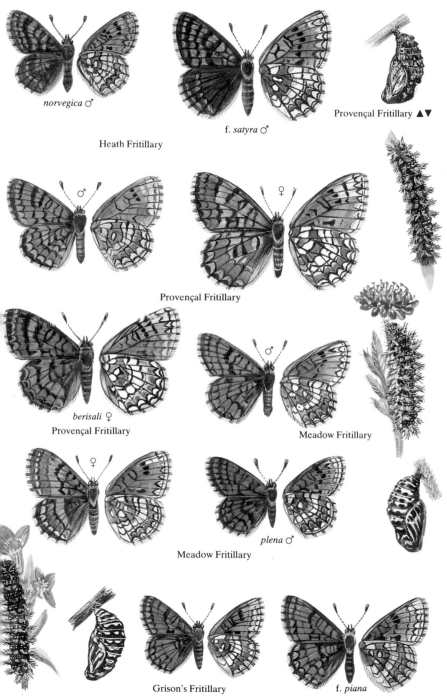

norvegica ♂

Heath Fritillary

f. *satyra* ♂

Provençal Fritillary ▲▼

♂

♀

Provençal Fritillary

berisali ♀
Provençal Fritillary

♂

Meadow Fritillary

♀

Meadow Fritillary

plena ♂

Grison's Fritillary

f. *piana*

99

Nickerl's Fritillary

NICKERL'S FRITILLARY *Mellicta aurelia*. Like Grison's Fritillary in size but black markings on ups are more complete: pale discal band of unh is narrower, especially in ♂. HAB flowery fields and slopes, including heaths and moors. ALT sl–1500. FLIGHT 6–7. FP plantains, cow-wheat, and speedwells. EGG 6–8: batched on fp. LARVA 7–5: gregarious in early stages. PUPA 4–6: suspended from fp. WINTER hibernating larva. NOTES Examination of genitalia is necessary for accurate separation from related species. STATUS V; Belgium & Lux. R; Lith. LP; W. Germany.

ASSMANN'S FRITILLARY *Mellicta britomartis*. Like Nickerl's Fritillary and Meadow Fritillary but ups fringes are usually darker: outer border of unh much darker than adjacent lunules. HAB flowery heaths and grasslands. ALT sl–1000. FLIGHT 5–8 in 1–2 broods. FP plantains and speedwells. EGG 5–9: batched under leaves. LARVA 1–12: gregarious in dense web when young. PUPA 4–8. WINTER larvae: gregarious in web. NOTES Examination of genitalia is necessary for accurate determination. Does not overlap with Meadow Fritillary. STATUS E; Italy. V; elsewhere.

LITTLE FRITILLARY *Mellicta asteria*. Very small and dark: unh with a single black marginal line. HAB mountain slopes. ALT >2000. FLIGHT 7–8. FP various alpines. EGG 7–9. LARVA 1–12. PUPA 6–7. WINTER larva. STATUS R; Italy.

SCARCE FRITILLARY *Hypodryas maturna*. Upf has pale spots in pd area near costa: margins of uns deep orange: sub-marginal lunules of unf irregular and largest in s2 and s3. HAB light woodland, especially in valleys: very local. ALT sl–1000. FLIGHT 5–7. FP ash, poplar, and beech in summer: plantains and other low-growing plants in spring after hibernation. EGG 5–7: batched on trees. LARVA 6–4: gregarious on trees until after hibernation, but then becoming solitary. PUPA 4–6: suspended from tree trunks or undersides of stones. WINTER hibernating larvae (gregarious in cluster of fallen leaves). STATUS E. LP; W. Germany. SEE ALSO p. 304, 305.

ASIAN FRITILLARY *Hypodryas intermedia*. Like Scarce Fritillary but without pale spots at front of upf: unf lunules regular: pale discal band of unh encloses a thin black line. HAB light mountain woodland, especially in clearings. ALT 1600–1800. FLIGHT 6–7. FP plantains, cow-wheat, and speedwells. EGG 6–7: in irregular heap. LARVA 1–12: 2-year life cycle. PUPA 5–6: suspended amongst fp. WINTER larva (twice). STATUS R.

CYNTHIA'S FRITILLARY *Hypodryas cynthia*. ♂ easily identified by white patches: ♀ like Asian Fritillary but discal band of unh has no black line in it: orange pd band of hw contains black dots on both surfaces. HAB montane scrub and grassland. ALT 500–2500. FLIGHT 5–8. FP plantains and lady's mantles. EGG 6–7: batched haphazardly on fp. LARVA 1–12: gregarious clearly banded with yellow. PUPA 5–7: greyish with black and yellow spots and suspended from fp. WINTER hibernating larvae in silken web. VAR at high levels, especially in SW Alps, the brick colour of ♂ is largely overlaid by black, producing a startling black and white pattern (*H. c. alpicola*). STATUS LP; W. Germany.

LAPLAND FRITILLARY *Hypodryas iduna*. The cream, orange and dark brown or black pattern of ups, together with the orange margins of uns, readily distinguish this species: there is nothing else like it in the far north: the Marsh Fritillary is similar but uns margins are yellow. HAB damp moors and light woodland near tree line: local. ALT *c*. 600. FLIGHT 6–7. FP speedwells, plantains and *Vaccinium* spp. EGG 6–8: in small batches on fp. LARVA 7–5: gregarious in web. PUPA 5–7. WINTER hibernating larvae in web. STATUS Locally common.

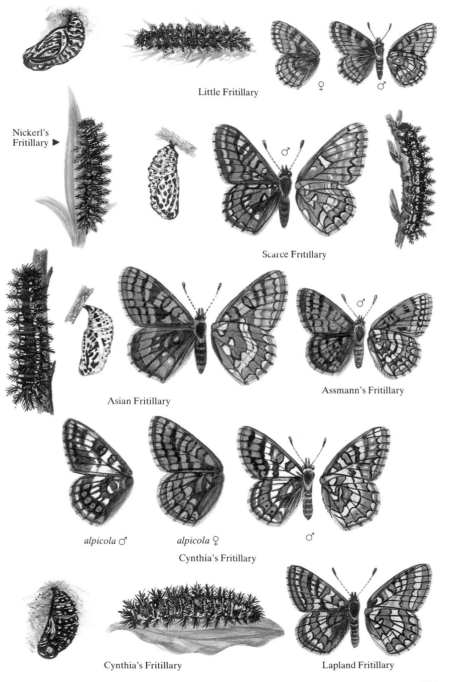

Little Fritillary

♀   ♂

Nickerl's
Fritillary ▶

Scarce Fritillary

♂

Asian Fritillary

Assmann's Fritillary

♂

alpicola ♂   *alpicola* ♀   ♂

Cynthia's Fritillary

Cynthia's Fritillary   Lapland Fritillary

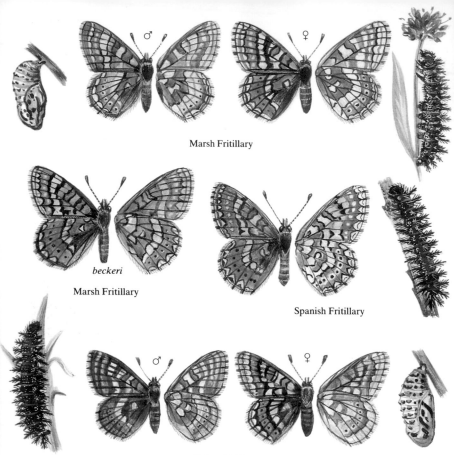

Marsh Fritillary

beckeri

Marsh Fritillary

Spanish Fritillary

Alpine Fritillary

▲MARSH FRITILLARY *Eurodryas aurinia*. Black dots prominent in orange pd band on both surfaces of hw: unf usually lacks any obvious black lines in discal area: uns margins yellow. HAB bogs, moors and open grassland, both wet and dry. ALT sl–1500. FLIGHT 4–7. FP devil's-bit scabious, plantains, and assorted other plants: honeysuckle in Iberia. EGG 5–7: piled up on leaves: yellow at first, becoming red later. LARVA 6–4: gregarious in silken tents for much of the time but becoming solitary towards maturity. PUPA 4–5: hanging in dense vegetation. WINTER hibernating larvae, in silken shelters. VAR larger and redder in Iberia, sometimes without any yellow spots (*E. a. beckeri*). STATUS E; Holland, Hungary & Poland. V; elsewhere, largely through drainage and improvement of grasslands. LP; Holland, Hungary, W. Germany and N. Ireland. SEE ALSO p. 217, 226, 227.

ALPINE FRITILLARY *Eurodryas debilis*. Like a small, dark Marsh Fritillary and sometimes regarded as a sub-species of that butterfly. HAB montane grassland. ALT generally >2000. FLIGHT 6–8. FP viscid primrose and perhaps gentians. EGG 6–8. LARVA 1–12: 2-year life cycle. PUPA 5–7. WINTER larva (twice). STATUS ?

SPANISH FRITILLARY *Eurodryas desfontainii*. Like a Marsh Fritillary but ups much brighter and unf with prominent black lines. HAB sunny hillsides. ALT *c.* 1000. FLIGHT 5–6. FP knapweeds and scabious. EGG ? LARVA ? PUPA ? WINTER larva? STATUS R.

FAMILY SATYRIDAE – THE BROWNS

Sometimes treated as a sub-family of the Nymphalidae, this is a large group of predominantly brown butterflies in which there are just four walking legs in both sexes. The front legs have been reduced to short, hairy 'brushes'. The antennal club is often poorly developed and is not usually sharply separated from the rest of the antenna. Wingspans range from about 25mm to 80mm in the European species and, with very few exceptions, the outer margins of the wings carry a number of prominent eye-spots on both upper and lower surfaces (see p. 274). A number of veins are distinctly swollen near the base of the forewing. The sexes often differ, especially in the extent of the paler markings on the wings, and the males of several species carry dark sex brands in the centre of the fore-wing. The androconia or scent scales are long and tapering and end in tufts of microscopic filaments. Flight is weak in most species and the butterflies spend a lot of time resting on the ground or vegetation.

The eggs are usually barrel-shaped or slightly conical and delicately ribbed. The larvae, which all feed on grasses or sedges, are green or brown and they taper at each end. They are usually clothed with short hairs and they all bear a short forked 'tail' at the rear. Most species spend the winter in the larval stage. The pupae show none of the spiny projections that adorn the nymphalid pupae and are usually suspended from the food-plants by the tail-end, although some lie freely at the base of the food-plants.

There are more than 1,500 species in the family, of which just over 100 occur in Europe. Eleven species breed in the British Isles, including several very common species such as the Meadow Brown. Nearly all are grassland butterflies, although some prefer the shadier conditions of woodland rides and clearings. Many species live in the Alps, where each usually has a very restricted distribution.

▲**MARBLED WHITE** *Melanargia galathea*. Upf cell has no black bar across it, although it has a heavy black patch at the apex: unh ocelli are in a greyish brown band. HAB rough, flowery grassland. ALT sl–2000. FLIGHT 6–7. FP red fescue and other grasses. EGG 7–8: scattered freely over habitat. LARVA 7–5: hibernating as soon as it hatches and not feeding until spring: largely nocturnal. PUPA 5–7: in soil or leaf litter. WINTER 1st-instar larva. VAR black markings often more extensive, especially in mountains and S.E. (f. *procida*). ♀ unh sometimes unmarked in S; all wing markings much reduced in Iberia and SW France (*M. g. lachesis*). STATUS LP; W. Germany. SEE ALSO p. 202, 203, 206, 211, 246, 247, 268, 282.

Marbled White   *lachesis*

f. *procida*

British race
(*semele*)

cadmus ♀

cadmus ♂

Grayling

▲**GRAYLING** *Hipparchia semele*. Uph has distinctly separate orange triangular patches in submarginal band: ♂ has prominent dark sex brand in centre of upf. HAB heaths and rough grassland. ALT sl–2000. FLIGHT 6–9. FP assorted grasses, mostly fine-leaved species. EGG 6–9: solitary on leaf blades. LARVA 1–12: largely nocturnal. PUPA 5–7: in silk-lined chamber under plant debris. WINTER larva. VAR specimens from B and neighbouring parts of NW Europe are much smaller than those from more southerly areas (*H. s. cadmus*). NOTES Adult spends most of its time, well camouflaged, on the ground and, like its relatives, never opens its wings at rest. STATUS E; Lux. V & LP; W. Germany. SEE ALSO p. 234, 274, 275, 285, 289, 291–292.

SOUTHERN GRAYLING *Hipparchia aristaeus*. Very like southern races of Grayling but with much more extensive orange patches on ups: genitalia are also distinct. HAB rough and stony grassland and heaths. ALT sl–1200. FLIGHT 6–7. FP various grasses. EGG ? LARVA ? PUPA ? WINTER ? VAR ocellus in s2 of upf may be vestigial: ups with a variable amount of brown suffusion in Greece (*H. a. senthes*). STATUS R; Bulgaria & Italy. LP; Greece.

TREE GRAYLING *Neohipparchia statilinus*. Ups ocelli usually blind, but small white spots present in s2 and s3, especially noticeable in ♀: outer margin of hw slightly scalloped. HAB heaths, scrub, and light woodland on warm and well-drained sites, often resting on tree trunks. ALT sl–1500. FLIGHT 7–9. FP various grasses. EGG 7–9: solitary on fp. LARVA 9–6: feeding mainly by night. PUPA 5–7: among debris on ground. WINTER larva. VAR unh pattern is variable and sometimes almost unmarked brown or grey: the butterflies tend to be much larger in south, especially in Iberia. STATUS E; Belgium, Czech., W. Germany (extinct?), Holland & Poland. Still common in S of range. LP; W. Germany.

FREYER'S GRAYLING *Neohipparchia fatua*. Like Tree Grayling but considerably larger and ♀ ups with more pale markings: hw more strongly scalloped. HAB light woodland in hills, especially near coasts: local. ALT sl–1000, but usually below 500. FLIGHT 7–8. FP various grasses. EGG ? LARVA ? PUPA ? WINTER ? STATUS V; Bulgaria.

Southern Grayling

Tree Grayling

Tree Grayling

Freyer's Grayling

Freyer's Grayling

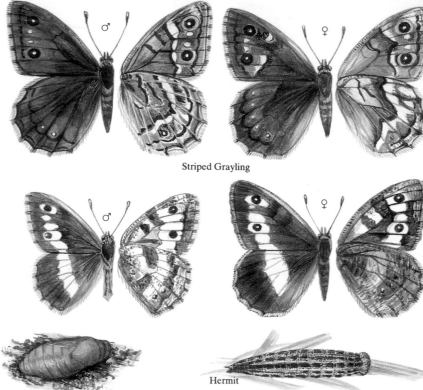

Striped Grayling

Hermit

STRIPED GRAYLING *Pseudotergumia fidia*. Conspicuous sharply-angled black lines on unh are characteristic. HAB stony ground and light woodland, mainly in hills. ALT sl–1800, usually above 1000. FLIGHT 7–8. FP various grasses. EGG 7–8. LARVA 8–5. PUPA 5–7. WINTER larva. STATUS R; Italy.

HERMIT *Chazara briseis*. Costa of upf distinctly pale: upf with 2 ocelli, often blind in ♂. HAB dry, stony grassland. ALT sl–2000. FLIGHT 6–8. FP various grasses, especially blue moor-grass and fescues. EGG 7–9: solitary. LARVA 9–6: feeding mainly at night. PUPA 5–6: among grass roots just below ground. WINTER larva. VAR size is variable, and so is pattern of unh: ♀ occasionally has white areas replaced by buff. STATUS E; Belgium, Lux. (extinct?) & Poland. V & LP; W. Germany.

SOUTHERN HERMIT *Chazara prieuri*. Like Hermit but ♂ upf has buff patch in cell: no white mark just below front ocellus: white pd band of uph does not reach costa: unh has prominent black arrow heads in outer region. HAB stony mountain slopes: local. ALT *c*. 1000. FLIGHT 6–7. FP grasses. EGG ? LARVA ? PUPA ? WINTER ? VAR ♀ dimorphic, with white often replaced by buff (f. *uhagonis*). STATUS ?

WHITE-BANDED GRAYLING *Pseudochazara anthelea*. Resembles Hermit but upf ocelli are larger (with or without pupils) and ♂ has prominent sex brand inside the cell: uph has small ocellus in a slightly orange area at rear of white band. HAB stony hillsides. ALT sl–1800. FLIGHT 6–9. FP grasses. EGG ? LARVA ? PUPA ? WINTER ? STATUS ?

NEVADA GRAYLING *Pseudochazara hippolyte*. Like Grayling but with more extensive pale areas on upf and with whiter chequered fringes: unf has grey basal area. HAB stony mountainsides. ALT 1400–3000. FLIGHT 6–7. FP grasses. EGG ? LARVA ? PUPA ? WINTER ? STATUS ?

110

Striped Grayling larva

f. *uhagonis* ♀

♂ ♀

Southern Hermit

♂ ♀

White-banded Grayling

Nevada Grayling

SATYRIDAE

Brown's Grayling

Pseudochazara orestes

Macedonian Grayling

BROWN'S GRAYLING *Pseudochazara amymone*. Two small white spots between the ocelli on both upf and unf: unchequered margins: scalloped hw. HAB rough, grassy places. ALT 200–700. FLIGHT 7–8. FP grasses. EGG ? LARVA ? PUPA ? WINTER ? STATUS ?

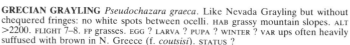

GRECIAN GRAYLING *Pseudochazara graeca*. Like Nevada Grayling but without chequered fringes: no white spots between ocelli. HAB grassy mountain slopes. ALT >2200. FLIGHT 7–8. FP grasses. EGG ? LARVA ? PUPA ? WINTER ? VAR ups often heavily suffused with brown in N. Greece (f. *coutsisi*). STATUS ?

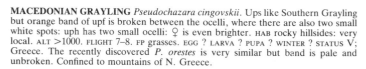

MACEDONIAN GRAYLING *Pseudochazara cingovskii*. Ups like Southern Grayling but orange band of upf is broken between the ocelli, where there are also two small white spots: uph has two small ocelli: ♀ is even brighter. HAB rocky hillsides: very local. ALT >1000. FLIGHT 7–8. FP grasses. EGG ? LARVA ? PUPA ? WINTER ? STATUS V; Greece. The recently discovered *P. orestes* is very similar but band is pale and unbroken. Confined to mountains of N. Greece.

GREY ASIAN GRAYLING *Pseudochazara geyeri*. Unh with a prominent sub-marginal arc of arrow heads: ♀ ups have heavier black markings. HAB dry hillsides. ALT 1200–2000. FLIGHT 7–8. FP grasses. EGG ? LARVA ? PUPA ? WINTER ? STATUS ?

NORSE GRAYLING *Oeneis norna*. Ocelli on fw, together with a prominent white pd band on unh distinguish this from other northern graylings. HAB moorland. ALT sl–300. FLIGHT 7. FP various grasses and sedges. EGG 7–8. LARVA 1–12, with a 2-year life cycle. PUPA 5–7. WINTER hibernating larva (twice). VAR ocelli vary in number and may be blind or not. NOTES This and the other *Oeneis* species are typical of the far north and high altitudes further south. The antennae are relatively short and the basal wing veins are hardly or not at all swollen. STATUS ?

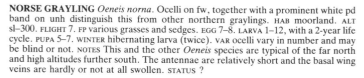

ARCTIC GRAYLING *Oeneis bore*. No ocelli: thinly and loosely scaled, becoming very worn-looking after a short while. HAB stony hillsides, especially around summits: very local. ALT sl–700. FLIGHT 6–7. FP sheep's fescue and other fine grasses. EGG 6–7. LARVA 1–12: 2-year life cycle: only in sheltered spots. PUPA 5–6: green and yellow with darker markings: amongst litter on ground. WINTER larva (twice). NOTES See Norse Grayling. STATUS ? SEE ALSO p. 247.

ALPINE GRAYLING *Oeneis glacialis*. ♂ unh has conspicuous white-lined veins, also present in ♀, but less obvious because of paler ground colour: ♀ ups unmistakable. HAB rocky slopes near the tree line. ALT 1600–3000. FLIGHT 6–8. FP sheep's fescue grass. EGG 6–9: solitary. LARVA 1–12: 2-year life cycle at higher altitudes: nocturnal. PUPA 5–6: buried in debris and soil. WINTER larva (twice at higher altitudes). NOTES ♂ unlikely to be confused with other alpine butterflies because of narrow fw and lack of swollen veins (see Norse Grayling). STATUS V. LP; W. Germany.

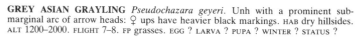

Grecian Grayling

f. *coutsisi* ♂

Norse Grayling

Arctic Grayling

Alpine Grayling

Grey Asian Grayling

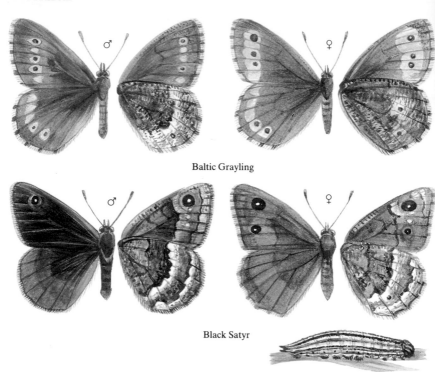

Baltic Grayling

Black Satyr

BALTIC GRAYLING *Oeneis jutta*. Ups with ocelli (usually blind) in yellow patches. HAB moorland and light pine woods, mainly in wet places. ALT lowland. FLIGHT 5–7. FP assorted grasses. EGG 5–8. LARVA 1–12. PUPA 4–6. WINTER larva (twice). VAR yellow patches on ups vary from several small spots (most ♂♂) to a complete band (most ♀♀). NOTES See Norse Grayling. STATUS E; Poland & Lith. SEE ALSO p. 222.

BLACK SATYR *Satyrus actaea*. Unh has two white bands, although these vary in development: ♂ upf has a single ocellus, but ♀ generally has two. HAB dry hillsides: local. ALT 1000–2000. FLIGHT 6–8. FP various grasses, especially bromes. EGG 7–9: solitary. LARVA 9–6: nocturnal. PUPA 6–7: suspended from fp. WINTER larva, active in all but coldest weather. VAR ♀ ups often has extensive yellowish patch around ocelli on upf. STATUS R; Italy (occurring only in extreme W).

GREAT SOOTY SATYR *Satyrus ferula*. Like Black Satyr but unh has less obvious white lines: ♂ is blacker and both sexes have two ocelli on upf. HAB rocky hillsides: local. ALT sl–2000. FLIGHT 6–8. FP fine grasses, especially fescues. EGG 7–9: solitary. LARVA 9–6: nocturnal. PUPA 6–7: suspended. WINTER larva, active for much of the time. VAR the one or two white spots between the ocelli of upf vary in size and may be absent. STATUS R; Spain (only in Pyrenees).

DRYAD *Minois dryas*. Like Great Sooty Satyr but with blue pupils to ocelli: hind wing scalloped. HAB lightly wooded slopes and grassland: usually in dry places but also in fens in S. Germany: local. ALT sl–1500. FLIGHT 7–9. FP purple moor-grass and other grasses. EGG 7–10: solitary on fp. LARVA 9–6: nocturnal. PUPA 6–7: brown and grey amongst debris on the ground. WINTER larva, active other than in coldest weather. NOTES A rather bouncy, although weak up and down flight. STATUS E; Lux. (extinct?) & Poland. LP; W. Germany.

Great Sooty Satyr

Dryad

Great Banded Grayling

False Grayling

Great Banded Grayling

False Grayling

GREAT BANDED GRAYLING *Brintesia circe*. Like Woodland Grayling but blacker and with a much cleaner white stripe: only one ocellus (usually blind) on upf: like White Admiral in flight, but uns totally different. HAB grassy places and light woodland: often basks on tree trunks and rocks and also on roads. ALT sl–1800. FLIGHT 6–8. FP assorted tall grasses. EGG 6–9: solitary. LARVA 9–6: nocturnal. PUPA 5–6: brown with yellow spots and suspended from fp. WINTER larva. NOTES Flight often with long, graceful glides. STATUS E; Lux. R & LP; W. Germany. SEE ALSO p. 000.

FALSE GRAYLING *Arethusana arethusa*. A single blind ocellus on upf, although ♀ sometimes has a small black spot further back: veins of unh often lined with white, especially in south-west. HAB dry heaths and rough grassland. ALT sl–1800. FLIGHT 7–9. FP various grasses, especially fescues. EGG 7–9: solitary. LARVA 8–6. PUPA 5–7: brown and hard to find in debris on ground. WINTER larva. VAR a very variable species, generally more brightly marked in western Europe (*A. a. dentata*) and especially so on uns in S. Spain (*A. a. boabdil*). STATUS E & LP; W. Germany. R; Belgium (extreme south only).

The *Erebia* species, nearly all of which possess ocelli at least in spaces 4 & 5 of upf, are found mainly in upland and northern areas. Separation of some of the species is difficult without examination of the male genitalia.

ARRAN BROWN *Erebia ligea*. The clear white stripe on unh will normally identify this species: ♂ has a slender black sex brand on upf. HAB heaths, rough grassland, and light woodland. ALT sl–1500: usually above 500 in southern areas. FLIGHT 6–8. FP various grasses. EGG 7–8: solitary on fp. LARVA 1–12, often with 2-year life cycle: nocturnal. PUPA 5–7: on or just under the ground or leaf litter. WINTER larva (twice), first winter may be passed as fully-formed larva inside the egg. VAR smaller in far north (*E. l. dovrensis*), with much-reduced white markings on unh and often with blind ocelli. NOTES Despite its common name, the species has not been recorded from Scotland with any certainty. STATUS V; Greece. R; Belgium. LP; Belgium, W. Germany & Greece.

boabdil ♂   False Grayling   *dentata* ♀

dovrensis ♂   Arran Brown

Large Ringlet

ocellaris ♂   *adyte* ♂

LARGE RINGLET *Erebia euryale.* Ups like Arran Brown but ♂ lacks sex brand: unh lacks the vivid white stripe, although ♀ usually has a pale band. HAB grassland and light woodland in uplands. ALT 1000–2000. FLIGHT 7–8. FP various grasses. EGG 7–9: solitary on fp. LARVA 1–12: two-year cycle. PUPA 6–7: dull yellow and formed on the ground at the base of the turf. WINTER larva (twice). VAR the orange bands of ups are much reduced in the Dolomites and neighbouring parts of the Alps (*E. e. ocellaris*): ocelli of ups usually blind in ♂, but clearly pupilled in southern and western Alps (*E. e. adyte*), where ♀ may have yellow or grey band on unh. STATUS V; Greece. LP; W. Germany.

ERIPHYLE RINGLET *Erebia eriphyle.* Unf has distinct red flush extending over most of wing, although somewhat less prominent in ♀: orange spots on unh never contain black dots: always at least one orange spot on uph, in s4. HAB rough mountain slopes: very local. ALT 1200–2000. FLIGHT 7. FP various grasses. EGG 7–8. LARVA 8–5. PUPA 5–7. WINTER larva. VAR orange spotting variable, better developed in east of range (*E. e. tristis*). STATUS V. LP; W. Germany.

YELLOW-SPOTTED RINGLET *Erebia manto.* Orange band of upf generally wider in s4 & s5 than elsewhere (sometimes present only in these two spaces): ♀ unh has irregular yellowish bands without black dots. HAB montane grassland. ALT 900–2100. FLIGHT 6–8. FP various grasses. EGG 6–8. LARVA 7–4. PUPA 4–7: yellow with black markings: in leaf litter. WINTER larva. VAR extremely variable, especially regarding the extent of the orange bands and their black dots: both sexes are almost unmarked in Pyrenees (*E. m. constans*): ♀ unh often has white bands in Vosges (f. *bubastis*): small and dark with reduced markings in high Alps (*E. m. pyrrhula*). STATUS E; Poland. LP; W. Germany.

WHITE SPECK RINGLET *Erebia claudinia.* Unh has a regular sub-marginal row of tiny white dots: ♂ uph has two or three similar white dots, while ♀ uph has five: only ♀ has twin ocelli on fw. HAB montane grassland: very local. ALT >1800. FLIGHT 7. FP various grasses, especially Alpine hair-grass. EGG ? LARVA ? PUPA ? WINTER ? STATUS R; Austria.

adyte ♀ yellow band   *adyte* ♀ grey band

Large Ringlet

tristis ♂   *tristis* ♀

Eriphyle Ringlet

constans ♂

Yellow-spotted Ringlet

pyrrhula ♂

f. *bubastis* ♀
Yellow-spotted Ringlet

White Speck Ringlet

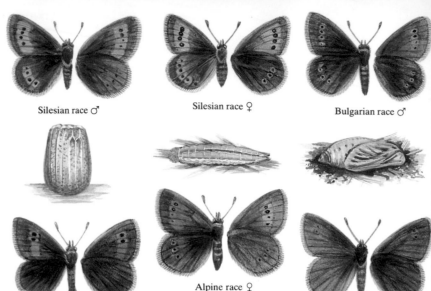

Silesian race ♂

Silesian race ♀

Bulgarian race ♂

Alpine race ♀

Alpine race ♂

Mountain Ringlet

f. *nelamus*

▲**MOUNTAIN RINGLET** *Erebia epiphron*. Orange bands of ups rather shiny: usually four un-pupilled black spots on upf and three on uph, although ♀ sometimes has pupilled spots: pale markings of ♂ tend to be less clearly defined than in ♀. HAB mountains and moorland, and also woodland clearings in uplands. ALT 500–3000: occasionally as low as 200 in Scotland. FLIGHT 6–8. FP mat grass and various other grasses. EGG 7–8: solitary at base of fp. LARVA 7–5: nocturnal. PUPA 5–7: pale green in a loose cocoon at base of fp. WINTER small larva. VAR a very variable species, usually darker and with less orange in the north and high altitudes: spotting virtually absent in f. *nelamus* from E. Alps. STATUS E; Eire (extinct?), W. Germany & Poland. R; B. LP; W. Germany. SEE ALSO pp. 249, 269.

YELLOW-BANDED RINGLET *Erebia flavofasciata*. Unh has a clear and regular yellow band: HAB rocky montane grassland: very local. ALT >2000. FLIGHT 6–7. FP sheep's fescue and other fine grasses. EGG 7–8. LARVA 1–12. PUPA 5–6. WINTER larva. VAR yellow band is somewhat narrower in E. Switzerland (f. *thiemei*). STATUS V.

BLIND RINGLET *Erebia pharte*. Orange bands or spots entirely without black dots on both surfaces: ♀ a little paler, with yellow markings. HAB damp montane grassland. ALT >1600. FLIGHT 7–9. FP various grasses. EGG 8–9. LARVA 8–5. PUPA 5–8. WINTER larva. VAR size varies greatly, with specimens from above 2000m very small and hardly marked (*E. p. phartina*): wing markings brightest in eastern and northern parts of the range (*E. p. eupompa*). STATUS E; Poland. V; Czech. LP; W. Germany.

RÄTZER'S RINGLET *Erebia christi*. Like Mountain Ringlet but unh has a greyish outer region, with or without black spots, and black spots on ups are usually much smaller: orange band on uph of ♂ is of constant width. HAB rocky and grassy slopes in mountains: very local. ALT 1500–1800. FLIGHT 6–7. FP grasses, especially sheep's fescue. EGG ? LARVA ? PUPA? WINTER? STATUS V. LP; Switz. with all butterfly collecting prohibited in the Laggintal area around its home. SEE ALSO p. 310.

LESSER MOUNTAIN RINGLET *Erebia melampus*. Like Mountain Ringlet, but generally with only two or three black dots on upf and with more obvious orange markings on unh: spot in s3 of unh is slightly nearer the margin than the others, forming an irregular curve. HAB alpine grassland. ALT >1000. FLIGHT 6–7. FP various grasses, especially meadow grasses (*Poa* spp.). EGG 6–8. LARVA 7–4. PUPA 4–6: on the ground. WINTER larva. VAR generally smaller at highest altitudes: upf sometimes has extra black spots. STATUS V; Hungary. LP; W. Germany.

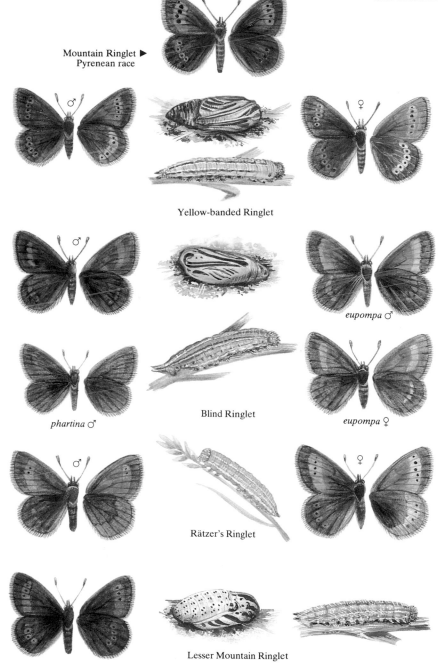

Mountain Ringlet ▶
Pyrenean race

♂

Yellow-banded Ringlet

♂

eupompa ♂

phartina ♂

Blind Ringlet

eupompa ♀

♂

Rätzer's Ringlet

♀

Lesser Mountain Ringlet

121

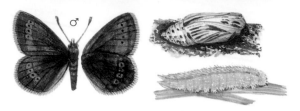

Scotch Argus

Sudetan Ringlet

SUDETEN RINGLET *Erebia sudetica*. Like Lesser Mountain Ringlet but unh has 4–6 orange spots in a smooth curve. HAB light woodland and clearings in mountains. ALT generally 1000–1200. FLIGHT 6–8. FP grasses. EGG 7–8. LARVA 8–6. PUPA 5–7. WINTER larva. VAR orange markings are brighter and larger in eastern parts of the range, especially on hw. STATUS E; Poland. V or R; elsewhere.

▲SCOTCH ARGUS *Erebia aethiops*. The pale greyish ♂ or yellowish ♀ pd band on unh, enclosing three or four tiny white dots, distinguishes this from several similar species. HAB damp grassland, often among trees: generally in uplands, but sometimes also on coastal dunes. ALT sl–2000, mainly 300–1500. FLIGHT 7–9. FP grasses especially blue moor grass. EGG 8–9: solitary and deep down in grass tussocks. LARVA 8–6: crepuscular. PUPA 6–8: enclosed in a flimsy cocoon just under the ground or in leaf litter. WINTER small larva. VAR size is very variable, with Scottish individuals (f. *caledonia*) often rather small: ♀ unh sometimes has pale lilac pd bands (f. *violacea*). STATUS E; Lux. V; Belgium. LP; Belgium & W. Germany.

DE PRUNNER'S RINGLET *Erebia triaria*. Uns very dark, especially in ♂ one small ocellus nearly always present in front of the two main ones: pd band of upf somewhat paler in ♀. HAB montane grassland, often near tree line: very local. ALT 1000–2100. FLIGHT 4–7. FP various grasses. EGG 4–7. LARVA 1–12. PUPA 3–6. WINTER larva. VAR pale bands often yellowish in Spain and with smaller ocelli (*E. t. hispanica*). NOTES Difficult to distinguish from Piedmont Ringlet, but the latter has more obvious ocelli on unh and ♂ genitalia are very different. STATUS LP; Greece. Most common in Spain.

LAPLAND RINGLET *Erebia embla*. Ocelli distinctly yellow-ringed: ocelli of uph always blind: costa of unh has a small pale mark: ♀ is paler overall. HAB bogs, moors and light woodland: local. ALT sl–500. FLIGHT 5–7. FP tufted hair grass and various sedges. EGG ? LARVA ? PUPA ? WINTER ? VAR ocelli of upf commonly blind. STATUS ?

ARCTIC RINGLET *Erebia disa*. Unmarked uph distinguishes this from all other *Erebia* spp. in far north. HAB moors and bogs, usually at higher altitudes than Lapland Ringlet: local. ALT >500. FLIGHT 6–7. FP grasses. EGG 6–7. LARVA 1–12: 2-year life cycle. PUPA 4–6. WINTER larva (twice). STATUS Not uncommon where it does occur.

WOODLAND RINGLET *Erebia medusa*. Unh uniformly brown with four or five pupilled ocelli: upf often has only the three main ocelli, in spaces 2, 4, and 5: orange or yellow pd band of upf usually broken along vein 3 in ♂: tip of antenna brown: ♀ generally a little brighter than ♂. HAB moors, damp grassland and open woods. ALT sl (in N)–2500. FLIGHT 5–7. FP wood millet, hairy finger grass and various other grasses. EGG 6–8: solitary on fp. LARVA 1–12: often taking two years to mature at high altitudes and latitudes: nocturnal. PUPA 5–6: amongst leaf litter on the ground. WINTER larva (sometimes twice). VAR pd bands are very yellow in eastern areas (*E. m. psodea*): insects from high levels in SE Alps are small and have reduced markings (*E. m. hippomedusa*): the three sub-species grade into each other and are part of a cline. NOTES This is one of the few *Erebia* spp. regularly found in the lowlands. It is easily confused with Bright-eyed Ringlet, but the latter has a black antennal tip. See also Almond-eyed Ringlet. STATUS R; Lux. LP; W. Germany.

ARCTIC WOODLAND RINGLET *Erebia polaris*. Like Woodland Ringlet from high altitude but unh has a faint pd band, best seen in ♀: unlike any other species in far north. HAB light woodland. ALT sl–300. FLIGHT 6–7. FP assorted grasses. EGG 6–7. LARVA 1–12: 2-year life cycle. PUPA 5–7. WINTER larva (twice). VAR ocelli vary in number, often more in ♀. NOTES Sometimes regarded as a sub-species of Woodland Ringlet. STATUS R; Norway.

Scottish race ♂

Scotch Argus

Scottish race ♀

Scotch Argus

Lapland Ringlet

De Prunner's Ringlet

Arctic Woodland Ringlet

Arctic Ringlet

Woodland Ringlet

hippomedusa ♂

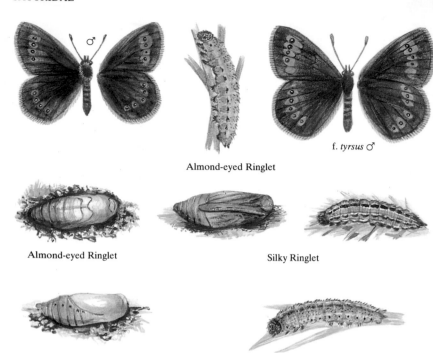

f. *tyrsus* ♂

Almond-eyed Ringlet

Almond-eyed Ringlet

Silky Ringlet

Sooty Ringlet

ALMOND-EYED RINGLET *Erebia alberganus*. Orange spots are clearly oval (almond-shaped): ocelli of ups contain minute white pupils: ♀ is similar but with paler uns. HAB alpine grassland. ALT 900–2100. FLIGHT 6–8. FP fescues and other fine-leaved grasses. EGG 7–8. LARVA 8–5. PUPA 5–7: yellow and brown in a flimsy cocoon. WINTER larva. VAR some specimens in W. Alps are large, with large orange spots (f. *tyrsus*): at high altitudes in N. Alps many specimens are small, with reduced markings (f. *caradjae*): in parts of Bulgaria *E. a. phorcys* is large, with white spots on unh. NOTES Can be confused with Woodland Ringlet when orange spots are not well marked, but ♂ genitalia are distinct. STATUS V; Spain (recently discovered). SEE ALSO p. 273, 288.

SOOTY RINGLET *Erebia pluto*. ♂ usually velvety black, unmarked or with very small pupilled ocelli: ♀ paler, with broad chestnut flash on unf: unh usually unmarked in both sexes. HAB mountain scree. ALT usually above 2000. FLIGHT 6–8. FP meadow grasses. EGG 7–8. LARVA 7–4. PUPA 4–7. WINTER larva. VAR ♂ ups dark brown in Swiss Alps and both sexes with orange pd band on upf (*E. p. oreas*): *E. p. alecto* from Bavaria and E. Alps has 2 small ocelli on upf. f. *velocissima* from E. Switzerland has larger ocelli and more of them, including some on unh. STATUS LP; W. Germany (found only in Bavarian Alps).

SILKY RINGLET *Erebia gorge*. Ups shiny all over, with gleaming orange patches with or without ocelli: unf largely orange: unh usually has a prominent discal band, darker than the rest of the wing and with wavy edges. HAB scree and rocky slopes in mountains. ALT >2000. FLIGHT 6–8. FP various grasses. EGG 6–9. LARVA 7–4. PUPA 4–7. WINTER small larva. VAR very variable species: ocelli totally absent in most specimens from Basses Alpes (*E. g. erynis*): in parts of the Pyrenees hw has three or four prominent ocelli (*E. g. ramondi*): *E. g. triopes* from Swiss Alps is like *E. g. ramondi* but has extra ocelli on fw. STATUS E; Poland. LP; W. Germany.

f. *velocissima* ♀

oreas ♂

oreas ♀

alecto ♂

alecto ♀

Sooty Ringlet

triopes ♂

erynis ♂

ramondi ♂

Silky Ringlet

ramondi ♀

False Mnestra Ringlet

Mnestra Ringlet   Swiss Brassy Ringlet   Common Brassy Ringlet

FALSE MNESTRA RINGLET *Erebia aethiopella*. Like Silky Ringlet but pd band of uph tapers towards rear: ♂ has a more prominent sex brand on upf. HAB montane grassland: very local. ALT >1800. FLIGHT 6–7. FP grasses. EGG ? LARVA ? PUPA ? WINTER ? VAR Bulgarian specimens (*E. a. rhodopensis*) are larger and usually have more ocelli on ups. STATUS R; Italy. LP; Bulgaria.

MNESTRA'S RINGLET *Erebia mnestra*. Like False Mnestra Ringlet and some forms of Silky Ringlet, but pd band of uph is clearly truncated near middle of wing: ♂ rarely has any ocelli and unh is unmarked. HAB montane grassland: local. ALT >2000. FLIGHT 7–8. FP grasses. EGG 7–9. LARVA 1–12: 2-year life cycle. PUPA 6–7. WINTER larva (twice). VAR ♂ sometimes has very small ocelli on ups: ♀ uph with or without ocelli. STATUS Uncommon.

GAVARNIE RINGLET *Erebia gorgone*. Like Silky Ringlet but less shiny and almost always with three ocelli on upf: veins of unh lined with white, especially in ♀. HAB montane grassland. ALT >1500. FLIGHT 7–8. FP various grasses. EGG ? LARVA ? PUPA ? WINTER ? VAR unh ocelli often absent (never very conspicuous). STATUS R; France.

SPRING RINGLET *Erebia epistygne*. Yellowish pd area and cell of upf are diagnostic. HAB rough grassland and woodland edges. ALT 400–2300. FLIGHT 3–6. FP fescues and other fine-leaved grasses. EGG ? LARVA ? PUPA ? WINTER ? VAR smaller at high altitudes in parts of Spain. STATUS R; Spain.

BRASSY RINGLETS The following six species all fly at high altitude and, with the exception of the Ottoman Brassy Ringlet, all are confined to Europe. Identification is often difficult unless the exact source of the specimen is known, for no two species occupy exactly the same area: where their ranges overlap the species occupy different altitudes. The male genitalia will usually separate the species quite easily if necessary.

SWISS BRASSY RINGLET *Erebia tyndarus*. Wings rather short: upf with small ocelli and a clearly tapering orange pd band: uph usually unmarked, but sometimes with very small ocelli. HAB montane grassland. ALT 1800–2500. FLIGHT 7–8. FP mat grass. EGG 7–8. LARVA 8–5. PUPA 5–7. WINTER larva. VAR ocelli often absent from upf. STATUS R; Austria.

COMMON BRASSY RINGLET *Erebia cassioides*. Orange patch on upf rarely reaches back beyond vein 3 and does not extend into cell: three obvious ocelli on uph. HAB montane grassland. ALT 1700–2000. FLIGHT 6–8. FP mat grass. EGG 6–8. LARVA 7–4. PUPA 4–7. WINTER larva. VAR rather small in central Pyrenees: unf distinctly yellowish in Spain and Massif Central of France (*E. c. arvernensis*). NOTES More southerly distribution than Swiss Brassy Ringlet. STATUS LP; Greece.

SPANISH BRASSY RINGLET *Erebia hispania*. Fw bands distinctly yellowish on both surfaces, tapering strongly towards the rear on upf: apical ocelli strongly oblique: ♀ paler. HAB rocky and grassy slopes. ALT 1500–2500. FLIGHT 6–7. FP fescues and other fine-leaved grasses. EGG ? LARVA ? PUPA ? WINTER ? VAR pd ocelli of uph well developed in Pyrenees (*E. h. rondoui*), but virtually absent in southern Spain (*E. h. hispana*), especially in ♀. STATUS V.

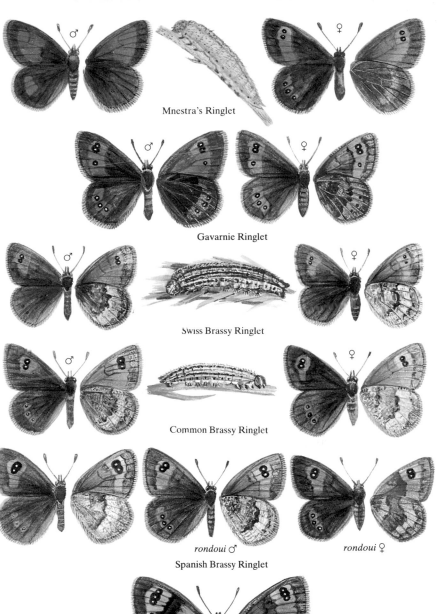

Mnestra's Ringlet

Gavarnie Ringlet

Swiss Brassy Ringlet

Common Brassy Ringlet

rondoui ♂

rondoui ♀

Spanish Brassy Ringlet

Spring Ringlet

Balkan race ♂

De Lesse's Brassy Ringlet · Ottoman Brassy Ringlet

DE LESSE'S BRASSY RINGLET *Erebia nivalis*. Like Swiss Brassy Ringlet but orange patch on upf extends into the cell: uph with or without orange spots: uph of ♂ lacks ocelli, but these may be present in ♀: unh is bright bluish grey when fresh. HAB montane grassland. ALT >2100. FLIGHT 6–8. FP mat grass. EGG 7–9. LARVA 1–12: 2-year life cycle. PUPA 5–7. WINTER larva (twice). NOTES Where the range overlaps with that of the Common Brassy Ringlet, De Lesse's Brassy Ringlet normally flies some 300m higher than its congener. The range in Austria is well to the east of the Swiss Brassy Ringlet. STATUS Quite common in the east of its range.

LORKOVIC'S BRASSY RINGLET *Erebia calcaria*. Rather short wings with much reduced orange markings: unh has a yellowish tinge in ♀. HAB montane grassland. ALT 1500–1600. FLIGHT 7–8. FP fescues? EGG ? LARVA ? PUPA ? WINTER ? var ocelli are often absent from uph. NOTES Only member of this group in its area. STATUS V.

OTTOMAN BRASSY RINGLET *Erebia ottomana*. Like Common Brassy Ringlet but generally larger and unh rather greyer in ♂: ♀ uns much yellower, especially in France. HAB montane grassland: local. ALT >1200. FLIGHT 7. FP grasses. EGG ? LARVA ? PUPA ? WINTER ? VAR size varies a good deal: ocelli commonly absent from unh. NOTES Where the range overlaps with that of the Common Brassy Ringlet the latter usually flies somewhat higher and a little later. STATUS V; Italy. R; elsewhere. LP; Greece.

WATER RINGLET *Erebia pronoe*. ♂ unh has a clear violet tinge: ♀ unh is paler, greyish or yellowish brown with a clearly defined brown border: often resembles Scotch Argus but has no white dots in pd band of unh. HAB damp mountainsides, especially amongst trees. ALT 1000–2000. FLIGHT 7–9. FP various grasses, especially meadow grasses (*Poa* spp.). EGG 7–9. LARVA 8–5. PUPA 4–7: yellow and brown. WINTER small larva. VAR orange markings much reduced in western Alps and ♂ usually lacks ocelli in this region (*E. p. vergy*). STATUS E; Poland. V; Czech. LP; W. Germany.

BLACK RINGLET *Erebia melas*. The two very black apical ocelli are usually the only obvious markings on ups, apart from the orange patch around them in ♀: ♂ could be mistaken for Sooty Ringlet, but latter has much smaller ocelli and range differs. HAB rocky slopes in mountains. ALT <2200. FLIGHT 7–8. FP grasses. EGG ? LARVA ? PUPA ? WINTER ? VAR more brightly marked in east of range, where ♂ has clear orange around ocelli and ♀ has all ocelli larger. NOTES No other similar ringlet lives in SE Europe. STATUS LP; Greece.

LEFÈBVRE'S RINGLET *Erebia lefebvrei*. ♂ is generally easily identified by the conspicuous ocelli close to the margin of uph: ♀ is like Piedmont Ringlet but lacks pale band on unh. HAB mountain scree. ALT generally >1800. FLIGHT 6–8. FP fescues and other fine-leaved grasses. EGG 6–8. LARVA 7–4. PUPA 4–7. WINTER larva. VAR amount of orange varies and is much reduced in E Pyrenees: *E. l. astur* from Cantabrian Mountains has no orange at all and ocelli are also much reduced in both sexes. NOTES *E. l. astur* resembles Black Ringlet and Sooty Ringlet, but neither of these lives in SW. STATUS ?

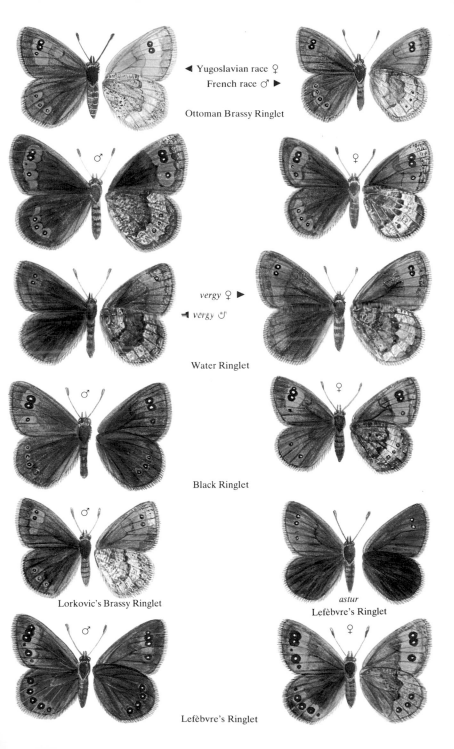

◀ Yugoslavian race ♀
French race ♂ ▶

Ottoman Brassy Ringlet

vergy ♀ ▶
◀ *vergy* ♂

Water Ringlet

Black Ringlet

Lorkovic's Brassy Ringlet

astur
Lefèbvre's Ringlet

Lefèbvre's Ringlet

Larche Ringlet

Styrian Ringlet

◀ Stygian Ringlet ▶

LARCHE RINGLET *Erebia scipio*. Largely orange unf together with unmarked brown unh (♂) and largely unmarked grey unh (♀) are characteristic. HAB rocky slopes in lime-rich areas: local and becoming rare. ALT 1500–2500. FLIGHT 6–8. FP grasses. EGG ? LARVA ? PUPA ? WINTER ? VAR ♂ occasionally has additional ocelli like ♀. NOTES Range centred on Col de Larche. STATUS V; Italy. R; elsewhere.

STYRIAN RINGLET *Erebia styria*. Dark border of unf tapers away towards anal angle: orange patches of ups heavily dusted with brown, especially in ♂: hw has a somewhat wavy margin in ♀. HAB stony mountainsides. ALT 800–1500. FLIGHT 7–9. FP blue moor-grass and other grasses. EGG ? LARVA ? PUPA ? WINTER ? VAR markings are much reduced in some places, especially at altitude (f. *morula*). STATUS R; Italy.

STYGIAN RINGLET *Erebia styx*. Often like Styrian Ringlet but brown border of unf is of constant width: orange bands on ups are brighter and not broken into spots on uph of ♂: can be confused with Water Ringlet, but latter has less orange on ♂ unf and a better defined brown margin to unh. HAB steep rocky slopes on mountains. ALT 800–2000. FLIGHT 7–9. FP various grasses. EGG 7–9. LARVA 1–12: 2-year life cycle. PUPA 6–7. WINTER larva (twice). VAR considerable variation in brightness of orange patches and ocelli: unh rarely has ocelli in north of range: *E. s. trentae*, from SE parts of range, has ocelli on unh of both sexes, but especially prominent in ♀. STATUS ?

MARBLED RINGLET *Erebia montana*. Very like Stygian Ringlet but mottled unh with its prominent white band will usually identify the Marbled Ringlet: unh veins often lined with white: ♀ hw and fw margins clearly chequered. HAB rocky slopes in mountains. ALT 1500–2200, but occasionally lower. FLIGHT 7–9. FP various grasses. EGG 7–9. LARVA 1–12. PUPA 6–8. WINTER larva. VAR unh veins less obviously white in E Alps. STATUS ?

ZAPATER'S RINGLET *Erebia zapateri*. Pale orange patch on upf together with lack of ocelli on uph are characteristic. HAB light pine woodland and scrubby grassland. ALT 1000–2000. FLIGHT 7–8. FP fescues and other fine-leaved grasses. EGG ? LARVA ? PUPA ? WINTER ? VAR vestigial ocelli occasionally present on uph of ♀. STATUS ?

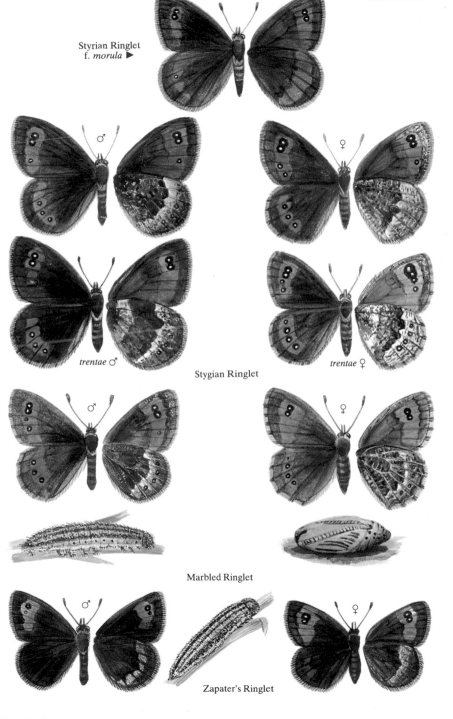

SATYRIDAE

Styrian Ringlet
f. *morula* ▶

trentae ♂   *trentae* ♀

Stygian Ringlet

Marbled Ringlet

Zapater's Ringlet

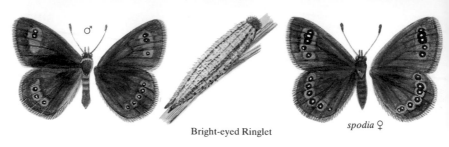

♂

Bright-eyed Ringlet

spodia ♀

Bright-eyed Ringlet

Piedmont Ringlet

AUTUMN RINGLET *Erebia neoridas*. Orange band of upf tapers strongly towards the back, while that of unf is abruptly truncated, particularly obvious in ♂. HAB rough grassland on mountains. ALT 300–1500. FLIGHT 8–9: rather later than most other *Erebia* spp. FP *Panicum sanguinalis* and other grasses. EGG ? LARVA ? PUPA ? WINTER ? VAR smaller and without ocelli on uph in C Italy (*E. n. sibyllina*). STATUS ?

BRIGHT-EYED RINGLET *Erebia oeme*. Ocelli with very bright pupils, especially in ♀: ♀ unh has ocelli in yellowish band: apex of antenna black (brown in the rather similar Woodland Ringlet). HAB damp grassland and light woodland. ALT 1200–1700, usually above 1500. FLIGHT 6–7. FP woodrush and fescue grasses. EGG 6–7. LARVA 7–4. PUPA 4–6. WINTER larva. VAR *E. o. spodia*, from E parts of range has larger and brighter markings in both sexes: markings almost absent in N Switzerland and Bavaria (*E. o. lugens*). STATUS V; Greece. LP; W. Germany.

PIEDMONT RINGLET *Erebia meolans*. The very dark unf with its clear, bright orange patch distinguishes this from most other superficially similar species: ocelli of unh lack clear orange rings in ♂: most like De Prunner's Ringlet but ♂ genitalia are very different and ocelli of unh are much less obvious in De Prunner's Ringlet. HAB grassy slopes and scree. ALT 1500–2000. FLIGHT 6–8. FP fescues and other fine-leaved grasses. EGG 6–8. LARVA 7–4. PUPA 4–7. WINTER larva. VAR size varies, with largest individuals in Spain (*E. m. bejarensis*): markings reduced in northern parts of range (*E. m. valesiaca*). STATUS LP; W. Germany.

CHAPMAN'S RINGLET *Erebia palarica*. Like Piedmont Ringlet but larger, the largest *Erebia* sp. in Europe: unh mottled grey: ♀ ups paler, with yellower bands. HAB rocky slopes. ALT 1000–1800. FLIGHT 6–7. FP fescues. EGG ? LARVA ? PUPA ? WINTER ? STATUS V.

DEWY RINGLET *Erebia pandrose*. Four blind black spots on both surfaces of fw, together with greyish unh, separate this from all other *Erebia* spp. HAB montane slopes and tundra. ALT sl(N)–3000. FLIGHT 6–8. FP fescues and other fine-leaved grasses. EGG 6–8. LARVA 7–5. PUPA 4–7: formed on surface of ground. WINTER larva. VAR black spots sometimes missing from ups: unh has a dark brown discal band in parts of Carpathians (f. *roberti*). STATUS E; Poland.

FALSE DEWY RINGLET *Erebia sthennyo*. Like Dewy Ringlet but with less orange on fw and with pd spots nearer to margin: unf has only two black spots. HAB montane pastures. ALT >1900. FLIGHT 6–7. FP fescues and other fine grasses. EGG ? LARVA ? PUPA ? WINTER ? NOTES ♂ genitalia are clearly different from those of Dewy Ringlet. STATUS R.

DALMATIAN RINGLET *Proterebia phegea*. Colour and arrangement of ocelli are characteristic: ♀ ocelli are larger. HAB rough coastal grassland. ALT sl. FLIGHT 5. FP grasses. EGG ? LARVA ? PUPA ? WINTER ? STATUS E. SEE ALSO p. 304.

Piedmont Ringlet

valesiaca ♂
Piedmont Ringlet

Autumn Ringlet

Chapman's Ringlet

Autumn Ringlet

f. *roberti* ♀

Dewy Ringlet

◀ False Dewy Ringlet

Dalmatian Ringlet ▶

133

Meadow Brown

hispulla ♀

▲**MEADOW BROWN** *Maniola jurtina*. Upf has a single apical ocellus, sometimes blind in ♂, but usually with one white pupil: ♂ has prominent sex brand on upf. HAB grassy places of all kinds: woodlands in S. Europe. ALT sl–2000. FLIGHT 5–9. FP meadow grasses (*Poa* spp.) and other grasses with medium-width blades. EGG 7–9: solitary on grasses but often dropped by ♀ when perched. LARVA 1–12: nocturnal. PUPA 5–7: suspended from vegetation. WINTER small larva. VAR there is considerable variation in the extent of the orange flush: *M. j. hispulla* from B, western France, Iberia, most Mediterranean islands, and S. Italy usually has orange on upf of ♂ and extensive orange on ♀, with brightest specimens in W. Scotland. This race could be a separate species. STATUS One of the commonest European butterflies, but *M. j. hispulla* is vulnerable in Malta. SEE ALSO p. 23, 206, 220, 251, 274, 282, 308.

SARDINIAN MEADOW BROWN *Maniola nurag*. Like Meadow Brown, but smaller and uph always has an orange patch in both sexes: sex brand very conspicuous on ♂ upf. HAB scrubby places: local. ALT sl–1500. FLIGHT 6–7. FP various grasses. EGG ? LARVA ? PUPA ? WINTER ? STATUS R.

DUSKY MEADOW BROWN *Hyponephele lycaon*. Like Meadow Brown but unh more uniform and without black dots: ♂ sex brand relatively narrow: ♀ upf always with two ocelli, usually blind. HAB dry grassy places. ALT sl–1800. FLIGHT 6–8. FP meadow grasses (*Poa* spp.) and other grasses. EGG 6–9: solitary on fp. LARVA 7–5. PUPA 5–6: brown or green with paler markings and suspended from fp. WINTER small larva. VAR amount of orange varies and ♂ occasionally has a small ocellus in s2 of upf. STATUS E; Finland (extinct?). V & LP; W. Germany.

ORIENTAL MEADOW BROWN *Hyponephele lupina*. ♂ like Dusky Meadow Brown but with a broader and less well defined sex brand: ♀ upf browner than Dusky Meadow Brown: hw more deeply scalloped in both sexes. HAB scrubby, south-facing hillsides, mainly on limestone: local. ALT <2000, but usually in lowlands. FLIGHT 6–8. FP various grasses. EGG 7–8. LARVA 8–5. PUPA 4–7. WINTER larva. VAR very large in Sicily and SE, where ♂ ups are largely golden (*H. l. rhamnusia*): golden suffusion absent from ♂ in Iberia, where ♀ uph is also very dark (*H. l. mauretanica*). STATUS ?

▲**RINGLET** *Aphantopus hyperantus*. Very dark ups and yellow-ringed ocelli on uns are characteristic: ♀ ups often a little paler, as are those of older individuals. HAB hedgerows and woodland rides and margins, especially in damp places. ALT sl–1500. FLIGHT 6–8. FP various grasses. EGG 7–8: scattered freely over grasses by flying ♀. LARVA 8–5: mainly nocturnal. PUPA 5–7: wrapped in flimsy cocoon at base of fp. WINTER small larva. NOTES Adult is very fond of bramble blossom. STATUS Generally common. SEE ALSO p. 202, 245, 251, 268, 292. 308

Sardinian Meadow Brown

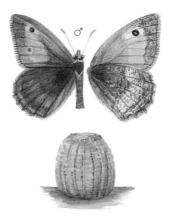

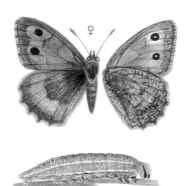

Dusky Meadow Brown

Oriental Meadow Brown

Ringlet

Gatekeeper

▲**GATEKEEPER** *Pyronia tithonus*. A single apical ocellus with two pupils: ♂ has a prominent sex brand: unh pattern readily distinguishes this species from the meadow browns. HAB hedgerows and woodland rides and margins. ALT sl–1000, but most common in lowlands. FLIGHT 7–9. FP various fine-leaved grasses. EGG 7–9: solitary on fp. LARVA 8–6: green or brown and largely nocturnal. PUPA 6–8: suspended from grasses and other low vegetation. VAR ♂ upf occasionally has additional ocelli: very occasionally apical ocellus has only one pupil. NOTES Adult is very fond of bramble blossom and also marjoram flowers. The species is also known as the Hedge Brown. STATUS R & LP; W. Germany. SEE ALSO p. 11, 20, 251, 302.

SOUTHERN GATEKEEPER *Pyronia cecilia*. Like Gatekeeper but unh is greyer and hw lacks ocelli on both surfaces: ♂ sex brand is crossed by pale veins. HAB dry, scrubby areas. ALT sl–1500. FLIGHT 5–8: 2 broods. FP various fine-leaved grasses, especially tufted hair grass. EGG 5–8. LARVA 1–12. PUPA 4–8: greyish brown with black spots and suspended from fp. WINTER larva. STATUS Generally common.

SPANISH GATEKEEPER *Pyronia bathseba*. Like Gatekeeper but unh has a prominent cream or yellow stripe: small ocelli are prominent on uph. HAB rough grassland and scrub: also in light woodland. ALT sl–1000. FLIGHT 5–8: 2 broods. FP various grasses, especially *Brachypodium* spp. EGG 5–8. LARVA 1–12. PUPA 4–7. WINTER larva. VAR specimens from southern half of the range have narrower stripe on unh: ♀♀ always larger than ♂♂. STATUS Generally common.

▲**LARGE HEATH** *Coenonympha tullia*. Ups heavily dusted with grey: margins of ups often wide, but not sharply defined: uns always with some irregular white striping. HAB bogs, moors, and damp grassland. ALT sl–2500. FLIGHT 6–8. FP various grasses and sedges, including cotton grass. EGG 7–8: large; laid singly on fp. LARVA 7–5: largely nocturnal. PUPA 5–7: suspended from vegetation. WINTER small larva. VAR a very variable species, forming several complex clines within the various sub-species. Ocelli are much reduced or absent in northern parts of the range, including Scotland (*C. t. scotica*) and Fennoscandia. Specimens are very small in far north (*C. t. demophile*), while *C. t. lorkovici* from N Yugoslavia is as large as a Meadow Brown. NOTES Like other *Coenonympha* spp. the butterfly never opens its wings at rest. STATUS V. LP; France, W. Germany, Hungary & N. Ireland. SEE ALSO p. 262.

BALKAN HEATH *Coenonympha rhodopensis*. Like Large Heath but slightly smaller and with no pale stripes on uns, just a small white spot on unh. HAB montane grassland. ALT 1000–2100, but rarely below about 1500. FLIGHT 6–7. FP grasses and sedges. EGG ? LARVA ? PUPA ? WINTER ? VAR ocelli of unh vary in number, but always well developed in Italy. NOTES Never opens its wings at rest. STATUS V; Greece.

▲**SMALL HEATH** *Coenonympha pamphilus*. Ups generally unmarked except for a small apical ocellus and the narrow, but distinct greyish border: uns markings sometimes show through to ups. HAB grassy places of all kinds. ALT sl–2000. FLIGHT 4–10 in 1–3 broods. FP various grasses, especially fescues and bents. EGG 5–9: solitary on grasses. LARVA 1–12: active by day. PUPA 4–9: suspended from grasses. WINTER larva, in various stages. VAR often brighter and more strongly marked in southern parts of the range, especially in summer broods (f. *lyllus*): *C. p. thyrsis* from Crete has well-marked ocelli on unh. It is possible that *C. pamphilus* is actually an aggregate of several distinct species. NOTES In central and southern regions summer larvae include quick-developers, which produce another brood of adults in the same year, and slow-developers which hibernate as large larvae and produce adults in spring. Autumn larvae hibernate when small and produce adults in mid-season. It never opens its wings at rest. STATUS One of the commonest European butterflies, but V; Malta. LP; W. Germany. SEE ALSO p. 206, 242.

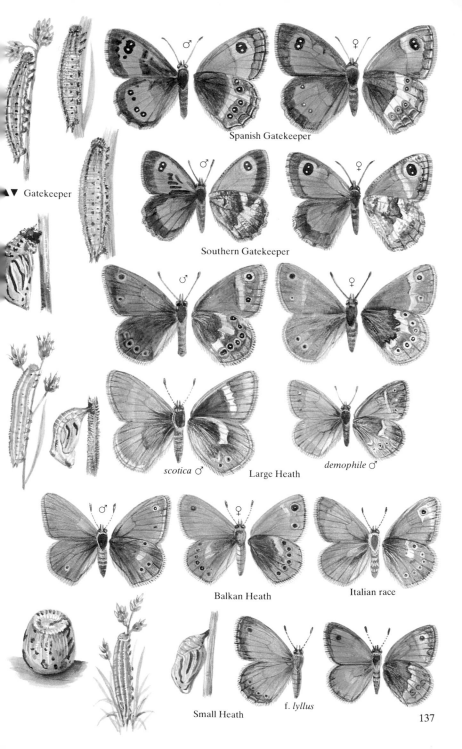

Gatekeeper

Spanish Gatekeeper

♂ ♀

Southern Gatekeeper

♂ ♀

♂ ♀

scotica ♂   Large Heath   *demophile* ♂

♂ ♀

Balkan Heath   Italian race

Small Heath   f. *lyllus*

137

CORSICAN HEATH *Coenonympha corinna*. Ups very bright, with a very dark border on upf: unh has an irregular yellow band: ocelli of unh very small and often missing. HAB grassy places. ALT sl–1500. FLIGHT 5–10 in several broods. FP various grasses and sedges. EGG 5–10. LARVA 1–12. PUPA 4–9: reddish grey with white markings. WINTER larva. STATUS R; Italy (Sardinia).

ELBAN HEATH *Coenonympha elbana*. Like Corsican Heath but uph has ocelli and unh has a more regular yellow band and prominent ocelli. HAB grassland. ALT sl–500. FLIGHT 6–9. FP grasses. EGG ? LARVA ? PUPA ? WINTER ? STATUS ?

DUSKY HEATH *Coenonympha dorus*. Ocelli of hw form a curved row which is convex internally (curving away from the wing margin) on both surfaces. HAB rough, dry grassland. ALT sl–2000. FLIGHT 6–7. FP fescues, bents, and other fine-leaved grasses. EGG 6–8: solitary on fp. LARVA 7–5. PUPA 5–6: suspended from grasses. WINTER larva. VAR extent of orange varies on ups: *C. d. bieli* from N Iberia has little or no orange on uph. STATUS Generally common.

PEARLY HEATH *Coenonympha arcania*. Unh has a conspicuous white band and a prominent sub-marginal ocellus just internal to it at the front of the wing: a silvery or lead-coloured sub-marginal line runs round uns. HAB grassland and light woodland, especially in the hills. ALT sl–2000. FLIGHT 6–7: occasionally with partial 2nd brood in 9 in S. FP various grasses, especially melicks. EGG 6–10: solitary on fp. LARVA 7–5. PUPA 5–8: green or brown and suspended from fp. WINTER larva. VAR uph may have an orange sub-marginal band. STATUS E; Denmark, Holland & Norway. LP; W. Germany.

ALPINE HEATH *Coenonympha gardetta*. Like Pearly Heath but all ocelli on unh are enclosed within the white band and they are not ringed with yellow. HAB montane grassland. ALT 1500–2300. FLIGHT 6–9. FP various grasses. EGG 7–9. LARVA 1–12. PUPA 6–8. WINTER larva. VAR ocelli often larger at lower altitudes in S Alps (f. *macrophthalmica*): ♂ may lack orange on ups at highest altitudes. STATUS ?

DARWIN'S HEATH *Coenonympha darwiniana*. Intermediate between Pearly Heath and Alpine Heath: unh ocelli usually prominent and ringed with yellow, but front one (in s6) is enclosed in the white band. HAB alpine meadows. ALT 1000–1500. FLIGHT 6–8. FP grasses. EGG 7–9. LARVA 1–12. PUPA 5–7. WINTER ? NOTES Also called Simplon Heath, this species is probably a hybrid of the Pearly and Alpine Heaths. STATUS ?

RUSSIAN HEATH *Coenonympha leander*. Unf bright orange with no grey at apex: unh has prominent yellow-ringed ocelli just inside a bright orange band: apical ocellus of upf variably developed and often obscured. HAB rough grassland, usually in uplands: local. ALT sl–2000. FLIGHT 5–6. FP various grasses. EGG ? LARVA ? PUPA ? WINTER ? VAR yellow rings of ocelli on unh fuse to form a pale band in W Greece and parts of Yugoslavia (*C. l. orientalis*). STATUS R & LP; Greece, but *C. l. orientalis* is vulnerable.

CHESTNUT HEATH *Coenonympha glycerion*. Like Russian Heath but upf has no apical ocellus and unf has a greyish apex: also resembles Alpine Heath, but unh ocelli are ringed with yellow and white band is much smaller, sometimes just a patch in s4. HAB grassy places, usually in uplands: local. ALT sl–2000. FLIGHT 6–7. FP various grasses, especially false brome. EGG 6–8: solitary on fp. LARVA 7–5. PUPA 5–6: green with white spots and suspended from grasses. WINTER larva. VAR *C. g. iphioides* from N. Spain is larger, with more prominent ocelli on unh and with more orange on ♂ upf. NOTES *C. g. iphioides* is sometimes regarded as a separate species. STATUS R; Belgium. LP; Belgium & W. Germany.

Chestnut Heath

Pearly Heath

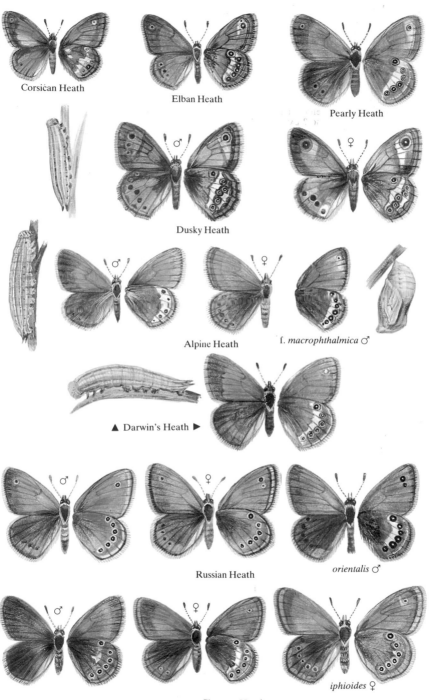

Corsican Heath

Elban Heath

Pearly Heath

Dusky Heath ♂

♀

Alpine Heath ♂ ♀

f. *macrophthalmica* ♂

▲ Darwin's Heath ▶

Russian Heath ♂ ♀

orientalis ♂

Chestnut Heath ♂ ♀

iphioides ♀

139

FALSE RINGLET *Coenonympha oedippus*. Like Ringlet but smaller and with no obvious ocelli on ups: unh has a distinct orange border: unf ocelli are most common in ♀. HAB bogs and other damp grassy places, and occasionally in open woodland: very local. ALT sl–1000. FLIGHT 6–7. FP grasses, sedges, and yellow iris. EGG 6–7. LARVA 7–5. PUPA 5–6: olive green with paler spots and suspended from fp. WINTER larva. VAR ocelli vary in size and may be much reduced in eastern areas (f. *hungarica*). STATUS LP & E: declining everywhere and the most endangered of all European butterflies. France, W. Germany (extinct?), Hungary.

SCARCE HEATH *Coenonympha hero*. Uns coloration is unmistakable: ♀ is paler, with more prominent ocelli on ups, including an apical one on upf. HAB damp moors and grassland, and also in dry open woodland. ALT sl–500. FLIGHT 5–7. FP lyme grass, wood barley, and other grasses. EGG 6–7: solitary on fp. LARVA 7–5. PUPA 4–6: suspended from grasses. WINTER larva. STATUS E; Belgium, Czech., Denmark, E. Germany and Lux.: declining and vulnerable elsewhere. LP; Belgium and W. Germany. SEE ALSO p. 304.

▲**SPECKLED WOOD** *Pararge aegeria*. Cream and brown coloration of northern race is unmistakable: southern race resembles Wall Brown but strongly scalloped hw and lack of obvious ocelli on unh readily distinguish it. HAB woodland rides and clearings, often in quite dense shade. ALT sl–1200. FLIGHT 3–10: single-brooded in N, but with 2 or 3 overlapping broods elsewhere. FP various grasses. EGG 4–9: solitary on fp: always in a shady spot. LARVA 1–12: grass coloured, but with a jet black head in 1st-instar. PUPA 6–3: green to brown and suspended from fp. WINTER larva or pupa: always pupa in monovoltine populations in N. VAR *P. a. tircis* from the northern and eastern parts of the range (including B), has cream spots: *P. a. aegeria* from south-western areas has orange spots, but the two grade into each other along a line from Brittany to Greece. Individuals passing the winter as larvae tend to be bigger and darker than those over-wintering as pupae and have smaller spots. NOTES This is the only British butterfly to over-winter in both larval and pupal stages. Rarely seen at flowers, the adult feeds mainly on honeydew. STATUS R; Lith. SEE ALSO p. 207, 222, 233, 245, 283–286, 288, 301, 302.

▲**WALL BROWN** *Lasiommata megera*. Superficially like a fritillary, but easily distinguished by its eye-spots: resembles southern race of Speckled Wood, but the orange is more extensive and hw is less scalloped: unh has prominent ocelli: ♂ has prominent sex brand on upf. HAB rough, grassy places, with areas of bare ground: sometimes in gardens. ALT sl–2200. FLIGHT 3–10 in 2–3 broods. FP cocksfoot, Yorkshire fog, and other coarse grasses. EGG 5–10: solitary or in small groups on fp, usually around the edges of bare patches: green at first, becoming pearly-white later. LARVA 1–12: mainly nocturnal. PUPA 3–9: suspended amongst grasses and very well camouflaged. WINTER larva, often feeding when the weather is not too cold. VAR *L. m. paramegaera* from Corsica and Sardinia has few or no pd streaks on ups. NOTES Adult enjoys sunbathing on bare patches or short grass, sitting with wings open and rarely flying far when disturbed. Supposedly named for its liking for walls, where it often basks, but the name could come from the brick-like colour and pattern of upf. STATUS LP; W. Germany & Switzerland. SEE ALSO p. 220, 251, 288, 292.

LARGE WALL BROWN *Lasiommata maera*. Like a very dark Wall Brown but fw has only one cross-bar in cell, best seen on unf. HAB rough, grassy places and open woodland, usually in uplands. ALT sl–2000. FLIGHT 5–9 in 1–2 broods. FP various grasses, especially wood barley and meadow grasses. EGG 5–10. LARVA 1–12. PUPA 4–9: green or brown and suspended low down in vegetation or even under rocks. WINTER larva. VAR summer broods generally smaller and with more extensive orange: *L. m. adrasta* from southern parts of the range is much more orange and more like Wall Brown, especially ♀, but somewhat larger than Wall Brown: rather small in Scandinavia. STATUS E; Lux. LP; W. Germany.

Scarce Heath

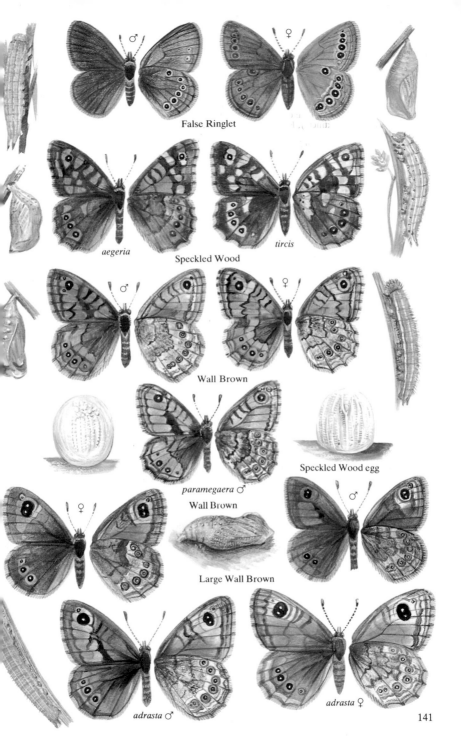

False Ringlet

aegeria　　*tircis*

Speckled Wood

Wall Brown

paramegaera ♂

Wall Brown

Speckled Wood egg

Large Wall Brown

adrasta ♂　　　*adrasta* ♀

141

SATYRIDAE

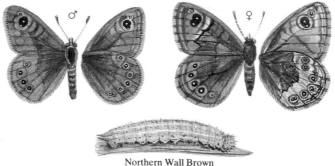

Northern Wall Brown

NORTHERN WALL BROWN *Lasiommata petropolitana*. Like Large Wall Brown but fw has two cross-bars in cell: uph has a dark line across the centre, although this is often indistinct. HAB light coniferous woodland: on mountains in S of range. ALT sl–2000. FLIGHT 5–7, occasionally with a partial 2nd brood 8–9 in S. FP fescues and other grasses. EGG 5–7 and occasionally 9–10. LARVA 6–4. PUPA 8–6. WINTER pupa in northern areas, but probably mainly as larva in S & C. STATUS E; W. Germany. LP; W. Germany and Greece.

WOODLAND BROWN *Lopinga achine*. Pattern of large, blind ocelli on ups is unmistakable. HAB shady woodlands: local. ALT sl–1000. FLIGHT 6–8. FP various grasses, especially false brome and tor grass, and sedges. EGG 6–8. LARVA 7–5. PUPA 5–7: green with white spots and stripes. WINTER larva. STATUS E; Belgium, Czech. W. Germany, & Lux. (extinct?). V; elsewhere. LP; W. Germany & Sweden.

LATTICE BROWN *Kirinia roxelana*. Superficially like some of the graylings, but easily distinguished by large ocelli on unh: ♂ fw rather narrow and distorted by sex brand. HAB scrubby grassland. ALT sl–1400. FLIGHT 5–9. FP meadow grasses (*Poa* spp.) and other grasses. EGG ? LARVA ? PUPA ? WINTER ? NOTES Reluctant to fly. STATUS ?

LESSER LATTICE BROWN *Kirinia climene*. Like Lattice Brown but uns much paler, especially in ♂, and with much smaller ocelli: ♂ fw lacks sex brand. HAB rough grassland. ALT ? FLIGHT 6–7. FP ? EGG ? LARVA ? PUPA ? WINTER ? STATUS Generally thought to be a vagrant from Asia, but now believed to be established in NE Greece.

FAMILY DANAIDAE – THE MONARCH
The only European member of this family is the colourful Monarch, and until recently even this was only a sporadic visitor from the Canaries or from North America. It is now established, somewhat precariously, in southern Spain. There are just four walking legs, with the front legs much reduced in both sexes. The family is thus commonly treated as a sub-family of the Nymphalidae. The antennal club is slender and the male has a small sex brand on the hind wing. He also possesses 'hair-pencils' which are everted from his abdomen during mating (see p. 290). The bold colours warn of a disagreeable taste, which is coupled with an unpleasant odour. Flight is swift and powerful.

The egg is conical and strongly ribbed and the boldly marked larva has a pair of whip-like filaments on the thorax and a shorter pair on the 8th abdominal segment. The pupa is short and plump, without sharp angles, and is suspended from the tail end.

△**MONARCH** *Danaus plexippus*. Pattern is unmistakable: ♀ is slightly paler. HAB flowery places, including gardens. ALT sl–1000, but higher on migration. FLIGHT 4–10, but most immigrants arrive in late summer. FP milkweeds (*Asclepias* spp.) EGG 5–7: solitary on fp. LARVA 5–8. PUPA 6–9: suspended from fp. WINTER adult. NOTES This butterfly cannot normally breed in Europe as the food-plants do not exist in the wild, but has recently established itself on cultivated plants in Spain. STATUS ? SEE ALSO p. 13, 14, 205, 230, 290, 294.

Woodland Brown

Lattice Brown

Lesser Lattice Brown

Monarch

143

FAMILY HESPERIIDAE – THE SKIPPERS

The skippers are named for the swift, darting flight that takes them from flower to flower on a whirring blur of wings. This is totally different from the fluttering flight of most other butterflies and rapid changes of direction make the skippers very difficult to follow in flight. They are all small butterflies but, compared with other families, most of them have distinctly plump, moth-like bodies. The head is as wide or wider than the thorax and the antennae are widely separated at the base. They are strongly curved or hooked at the tip and commonly end in a point.

All six legs are fully functional in both sexes, with the front tibia nearly always bearing a prominent epiphysis. The forewings are quite narrow and in the males of several species they bear a prominent dark sex brand. In many other species, including the Dingy Skipper and the Grizzled Skipper and its numerous relatives, the androconia are borne in a narrow groove on the front edge of each forewing. The androconia are always elongate and, under high magnification, most of them appear like tiny strings of beads. The wing veins all spring from the base of the wing or from the cell and do not branch. All the European skippers are brown, orange, or grey with white spots.

The resting positions of the skippers are unusual among butterflies. Although most species close their wings vertically over the body at night and in cold or dull weather, when feeding or sunbathing they commonly hold their hind-wings flat with the fore-wings partly closed above them. This is particularly true of the golden skippers of the sub-family Hesperiinae. The Dingy Skipper and the grizzled skippers usually bask with their wings almost flat, and the Dingy Skipper actually goes to sleep with its wings wrapped around its body, just like a moth.

The eggs are either lozenge-shaped, as in the Small Skipper and other *Thymelicus* species, or domed like tiny pudding basins. Some are ornamented, while others are plain. The caterpillars are mostly green and slightly downy and they taper at both ends. The head is relatively large and globular and is accentuated by the fact that the first thoracic segment is much narrower than the rest and forms a distinct 'neck'. Grasses are the food-plants of the larvae of the Hesperiinae, but the other skipper larvae use a variety of low-growing herbs. Most of the caterpillars spin leaves together to form shelters, sometimes feeding inside them and sometimes using them just for resting. They pupate in flimsy cocoons, either on the ground or spun amongst the leaves of the food-plant, and in view of the sturdy adult body the pupa is remarkably slender.

There are about 40 species in Europe, of which just eight are resident in the British Isles. Only the Dingy Skipper occurs in Ireland. All the species inhabit grassy habitats.

▲**GRIZZLED SKIPPER** *Pyrgus malvae*. The clear row of white sub-marginal spots on upf together with large white discal spot on uph distinguishes this from other similar *Pyrgus* spp. with brownish unh. HAB flower-rich grassland. ALT sl–2000. FLIGHT 4–8: 1–2 broods. FP wild strawberry, cinquefoils, and other low-growing herbs, especially rosaceous spp. EGG 5–8: solitary on fp. LARVA 6–10: rests in loose tent formed by drawing leaves together with silk. PUPA 7–5: in loose cocoon at base of fp. WINTER pupa. STATUS LP; W. Germany. SEE ALSO p. 216.

LARGE GRIZZLED SKIPPER *Pyrgus alveus*. White discal band of unh is usually complete and much wider at front than behind. HAB open flowery places, especially in uplands. ALT sl–2000, but rarely below 1000. FLIGHT 5–9: single extended emergence. FP cinquefoil, bramble, and other rosaceous plants: also rockrose and milkwort. EGG 6–8 (6–4 in Scandinavia): solitary on fp. LARVA 7–5: largely nocturnal. PUPA 5–8: dark brown in a flimsy cocoon amongst leaf litter. WINTER larva, but egg in Scandinavia. VAR *P. a. centralhispaniae* from SW Europe and Italy has rather more distinct white markings on uph. NOTES Separated with certainty from several similar species only by examining the male genitalia. STATUS E; Lux. R; Greece. LP; W. Germany.

OBERTHUR'S GRIZZLED SKIPPER *Pyrgus armoricanus*. Like Large Grizzled Skipper but generally smaller: usually with better developed markings on uph, although Large Grizzled Skipper is well-marked in SW Europe. HAB dry, flowery places with scrub. ALT <1900, but usually a lowland species. FLIGHT 5–10: 1–3 broods, but usually 2 broods, 5–6 and 8–9, either side of peak emergence of Large Grizzled Skipper. FP cinquefoils and wild strawberry. EGG 5–10: solitary on fp. LARVA 1–12, in shelter of spun leaves. PUPA 4–9: concealed in leaf sheath of fp. WINTER larva. VAR larger in S, with uph markings better developed. NOTES Flight periods and altitude may help to separate this species from Large Grizzled Skipper. STATUS E; Lux. R; Austria, Denmark & W. Germany. LP; Belgium & W. Germany.

FOULQUIER'S GRIZZLED SKIPPER *Pyrgus foulquieri.* Very like Large Grizzled Skipper but hw has more white on both surfaces: separated with certainty only by looking at ♂ genitalia. HAB flowery places in mountains. ALT <2000. FLIGHT 7–8. FP ? EGG ? LARVA ? PUPA ? WINTER ? VAR *P. f. picenus* of C. Italy is slightly smaller and unh is rather yellow. STATUS ?

WARREN'S GRIZZLED SKIPPER *Pyrgus warrenensis.* Small and with very few markings on ups. HAB montane grassland: very local. ALT >1800. FLIGHT 7–8. FP ? EGG ? LARVA ? PUPA ? WINTER ? STATUS ?

OLIVE SKIPPER *Pyrgus serratulae.* Like Large Grizzled Skipper but unh generally brown or yellowish and discal band incomplete. HAB flowery grassland, usually in uplands. ALT <2400, but rarely below 1000. FLIGHT 6–8. FP cinquefoils and lady's mantles. EGG 6–8. LARVA 7–5. PUPA 5–7. WINTER larva. VAR often larger, with better marked unh in southern areas, especially SE (*P. s. major*). STATUS E; Lux. V; Lith. LP; W. Germany.

CARLINE SKIPPER *Pyrgus carlinae.* Like Olive Skipper but over much of the range (*P. c. cirsii*) uph is more heavily patterned and unf has a large rectangular white spot: unh often rather red. HAB flowery hillsides. ALT sl–2400, but *P. c. cirsii* flies mainly in lowlands and rarely reaches 1500. FLIGHT 7–8. FP cinquefoils. EGG 7–8. LARVA 8–6. PUPA 6–7. WINTER larva, often dormant for 9 months. VAR *P. c. carlinae* of Alps flies at above 1600 and has very few markings on uph: cell spot of unf is crescent-shaped. NOTES The two sub-species are sometimes treated as distinct species. STATUS *P. c. cirsii* is R & LP; W. Germany.

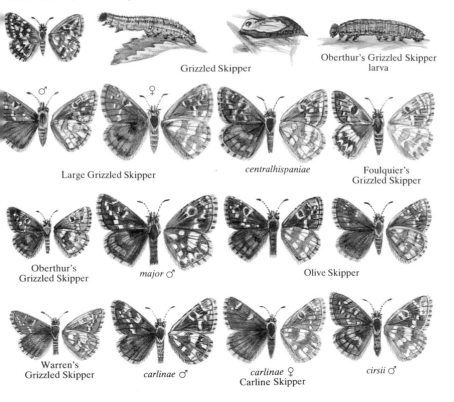

Grizzled Skipper

Oberthur's Grizzled Skipper larva

♂ ♀

Large Grizzled Skipper

centralhispaniae

Foulquier's Grizzled Skipper

Oberthur's Grizzled Skipper

major ♂

Olive Skipper

Warren's Grizzled Skipper

carlinae ♂

carlinae ♀
Carline Skipper

cirsii ♂

ROSY GRIZZLED SKIPPER *Pyrgus onopordi*. Like Carline Skipper but usually distinguished from this and most other *Pyrgus* spp. by the large white spot on the front edge of uph, although this spot is occasionally indistinct. HAB dry, flower-rich grassland. ALT sl–1500. FLIGHT 4–9 in 2 broods. FP *Malope malacoides* – a type of mallow. EGG 4–9. LARVA 1–12. PUPA 3–8. WINTER larva. STATUS ?

SANDY GRIZZLED SKIPPER *Pyrgus cinarae*. ♂ upf has a prominent ± rectangular white cell spot: ♀ is paler and less well marked, very like Large Grizzled Skipper but with an incomplete discal band on unh. HAB dry grassy hillsides. ALT sl–1500. FLIGHT 6–7. FP ? EGG ? LARVA ? PUPA ? WINTER ? VAR unh is yellowish in Spain and ups also have yellowish flush (*P. c. clorinda*). STATUS V & LP; Greece. R; Spain.

YELLOW-BANDED SKIPPER *Pyrgus sidae*. Unh has bright yellow bands: uph has a clear row of white sub-marginal spots. HAB flowery grassland. ALT sl–1800. FLIGHT 5–7. FP various mallows. EGG 5–7. LARVA 6–4. PUPA 4–6. WINTER larva. VAR often somewhat smaller and with paler yellow bands in west of range. STATUS Common.

SAFFLOWER SKIPPER *Pyrgus carthami*. Like Large Grizzled Skipper but unh is greyish yellow with large white spots forming an almost complete border: uph has a distinct row of white sub-marginal spots. HAB open, flower-rich grassland. ALT sl–2200. FLIGHT 5–9 in one extended emergence. FP safflower, cinquefoils, and mallows. EGG 5–9. LARVA 6–4. PUPA 3–8. WINTER larva. VAR white spots often larger in S Spain. STATUS E; Lux. LP; W. Germany.

ALPINE GRIZZLED SKIPPER *Pyrgus andromedae*. Unh has a large discal spot and a prominent white streak and spot in slc: uph has three *small* white spots just below the end of the cell. HAB moors and mountainsides, especially near streams. ALT 500–2200, but rarely below 1500 in south of range. FLIGHT 5–8. FP mallows and lady's mantle. EGG ? LARVA ? PUPA ? WINTER ? STATUS R; Spain (Pyrenees only). LP; W. Germany.

DUSKY GRIZZLED SKIPPER *Pyrgus cacaliae*. Like Alpine Grizzled Skipper but less heavily spotted: spots of uns rather blurred. HAB montane grassland. ALT above 1600. FLIGHT 6–8. FP cinquefoils, coltsfoot and *Geum* spp. EGG ? LARVA ? PUPA ? WINTER ? STATUS V; Spain.

NORTHERN GRIZZLED SKIPPER *Pyrgus centaureae*. A conspicuous white mark at front of uph: unh heavily mottled with white and veins also lined with white: ups rather hairy. HAB bogs and tundra. ALT sl–1000. FLIGHT 6–7. FP cloudberry. EGG 6–8. LARVA ?: pale brown with a darker dorsal line. PUPA ? WINTER ? STATUS ?

RED-UNDERWING SKIPPER *Spialia sertorius*. Unh generally rust-red: ♂ lacks costal fold which is found in all *Pyrgus* and *Carcharodus* spp. HAB dry scrubby places. ALT sl–2200. FLIGHT 4–9: 1–2 broods. FP cinquefoils, bramble and various other rosaceous plants. EGG 4–9: solitary on fp. LARVA 1–12: largely nocturnal. PUPA 3–8: in leaf litter. WINTER larva. VAR very much smaller in Corsica and Sardinia (*S. s. therapne*): 2nd-brood insects tend to be smaller than 1st-brood everywhere. STATUS E; Holland. LP; W. Germany.

HUNGARIAN SKIPPER *Spialia orbifer*. Like Red-underwing Skipper but unh is less red, usually greenish brown: sub-marginal spots better developed on ups: round discal spot on unh distinguishes it from Olive Skipper and Carline Skipper, both of which also lack the sub-marginal spots on ups: ♂ lacks costal fold. HAB scrubby grassland, usually in uplands. ALT 600–2000. FLIGHT 4–9 in 2 broods. FP salad burnet. EGG ? LARVA ? PUPA ? WINTER ? NOTES Also known as Orbed Red-underwing Skipper. Overlaps with Red-underwing Skipper only in Hungary. STATUS ?

PERSIAN SKIPPER *Spialia phlomidis*. A large rectangular white spot in centre of uph: front margin of unh carries a broad white streak. HAB flower-rich, scrubby grassland: very local. ALT sl–1700. FLIGHT 6–7. FP *Phlomis* spp. (Labiatae). EGG ? LARVA ? PUPA ? WINTER ? STATUS R & LP; Greece.

TESSELLATED SKIPPER *Syrichtus tessellum*. Ups greyer than most similar skippers: a prominent oval white spot on front edge of uph: ♂ has a costal fold, as in all *Syrichtus* spp. HAB flower-rich grassland. ALT sl–1000. FLIGHT 5–6. FP *Phlomis tuberosa* EGG ? LARVA ? PUPA ? WINTER ? STATUS E & LP; Greece.

SPINOSE SKIPPER *Syrichtus cribrellum*. Like Tessellated Skipper but smaller and with prominent square white spot in centre of uph: upf has 2 pairs of small white spots in s1b near middle of hind margin. HAB dry grassland. ALT ? FLIGHT 5–6. FP cinquefoils. EGG ? LARVA ? PUPA ? WINTER ? STATUS E.

SAGE SKIPPER *Syrichtus proto*. Veins of unf largely white: unh with only vestigial marginal white spots: ♂ ups often clothed with yellowish hair. HAB dry grassy places. ALT sl–1200. FLIGHT 4–9 in 2–3 broods. FP *Phlomis* spp., sages, and other labiates. EGG 4–9. LARVA 1–12. PUPA 3–8. WINTER larva. VAR late broods may be smaller, with browner unh. STATUS V; France.

Rosy
Grizzled Skipper

Sandy Grizzled Skipper

Yellow-banded Skipper

Safflower Skipper

Alpine Grizzled Skipper

Dusky Grizzled Skipper

Northern Grizzled Skipper

Hungarian Skipper

Red Underwing Skipper

Persian Skipper

Tessellated Skipper

Spinose Skipper

Sage Skipper

MALLOW SKIPPER *Carcharodus alceae*. Hw clearly scalloped: fw has three tiny white sub-apical spots on both surfaces and a very narrow, transparent cell-spot. HAB dry grassland, especially in hills. ALT sl–1600. FLIGHT 4–9: 1–3 broods. FP mallows and related plants. EGG 5–9: solitary on fp. LARVA 1–12: largely nocturnal. PUPA 3–8: in leaf litter. WINTER larva. VAR 2nd & 3rd broods often paler, 3rd brood small and dark in far south. The smaller False Mallow Skipper (*C. tripolinus*) from Portugal and S. Spain can be distinguished only by examining the genitalia. STATUS V; Lux. R; Austria. LP; W. Germany.

MARBLED SKIPPER *Carcharodus lavatherae*. Arrow-shaped pd spots of uph and general pattern of upf readily distinguish this from other skippers. HAB dry, flowery places, usually in limestone uplands: very local. ALT sl–1800. FLIGHT 5–7. FP yellow woundwort. EGG 5–7. LARVA 6–4: living in a silken web on fp. PUPA 4–6: brown with bluish bloom. WINTER larva. STATUS R & LP; W. Germany.

SOUTHERN MARBLED SKIPPER *Carcharodus boeticus*. Unh has a prominent network of white bands and veins. HAB dry, flowery places, usually in uplands. ALT sl–1500. FLIGHT 5–10: 2–3 broods. FP horehounds. EGG 5–10. LARVA 1–12. PUPA 4–9. WINTER larva. STATUS ?

TUFTED MARBLED SKIPPER *Carcharodus flocciferus*. Like Southern Marbled Skipper but unh pattern is less distinct and uph has a more strongly marked pattern around the margin: ♂ has a conspicuous dark hair tuft at base of unf. HAB rough, flowery grassland, mainly in hills. ALT sl–2000. FLIGHT 5–8: 2 broods. FP horehounds and woundworts. EGG ? LARVA ? PUPA ? WINTER ? STATUS R; Austria, W. Germany & Greece. LP; W. Germany.

ORIENTAL MARBLED SKIPPER *Carcharodus orientalis*. Like Tufted Marbled Skipper but greyer, especially on unh, and lacking the elongate scalloping pattern around the margins. HAB hot, dry grasslands in uplands. ALT sl–1000, occasionally reaching 1800. FLIGHT 4–8: 2 broods. FP ? EGG ? LARVA ? PUPA ? WINTER ? NOTES Flies much lower than Tufted Marbled Skipper where the ranges overlap. STATUS ?

▲**DINGY SKIPPER** *Erynnis tages*. Colour pattern is unique: ♂ has costal fold. HAB flowery grassland. ALT sl–2000. FLIGHT 4–8: 1–2 broods. FP bird's-foot trefoil and other low-growing legumes. EGG 5–9: solitary on upper leaf surface. LARVA 1–12: hides in a shelter of leaves, as do the larvae of most skippers. PUPA 3–8: in the larval hibernation tent. WINTER fully-grown larva in a silken tent. VAR ups range from deep brown to almost grey: *E. t. baynesi* from Ireland has grey pattern on upf. NOTES Rests with wings wrapped around the body like a moth. Basks on ground with wings wide open and pressed against the earth. STATUS E; Holland. R; Lith. LP; N. Ireland. SEE ALSO p. 11, 234, 263.

INKY SKIPPER *Erynnis marloyi*. Like Dingy Skipper but uns very dark, with just a single white spot near tip of unf: ♂ lacks costal fold. HAB mountain scree and grassland. ALT up to 2000. FLIGHT 5–8: 2 broods? FP ? EGG ? LARVA ? PUPA ? WINTER ? STATUS R; Greece. SEE ALSO p. 263.

LARGE CHEQUERED SKIPPER *Heteropterus morpheus*. Wing pattern is unmistakable: ♀ has chequered fringes. HAB woodland clearings and open grassland, especially in damp areas. ALT sl–1000, but rare above 500. FLIGHT 6–8. FP purple moor-grass and other grasses, including large reeds. EGG 6–8: solitary on fp. LARVA 7–5: partly nocturnal: in tube of grass. PUPA 5–6: in leaf litter. WINTER larva. STATUS E; Czech., Denmark & Holland. V; elsewhere. LP; W. Germany.

▲**CHEQUERED SKIPPER** *Carterocephalus palaemon*. Wing pattern is unique: superficially like Duke of Burgundy, but shape is different and the skipper lacks white bands on unh. HAB woodland clearings and scrubby grassland. ALT sl–1500. FLIGHT 5–7. FP purple moor-grass and other grasses, especially bromes. EGG 6–7: solitary on grasses. LARVA 6–4: in a tube formed from a leaf-blade. PUPA 4–6: in a shelter of leaf blades. WINTER fully grown larva, hibernating in a shelter of leaf-blades and gradually turning from green to straw-coloured. STATUS V. Recently became extinct in England, but flourishing in parts of Scotland, where it was not discovered until 1942, and not in any apparent danger. LP; B. SEE ALSO p. 24, 305.

NORTHERN CHEQUERED SKIPPER *Carterocephalus silvicolus*. Like Chequered Skipper but much yellower, especially upf: two yellow spots close to front edge of uph. HAB light woodland, especially in damp areas. ALT <500. FLIGHT 6–7. FP dog's-tails, bromes, and other grasses. EGG 6–8. LARVA 7–5: in woven grass tube. PUPA 5–7: suspended from grass stalks. WINTER larva. STATUS E; Denmark. V & LP; W. Germany.

Oriental Marbled Skipper

Mallow Skipper

Tufted
Marbled Skipper

Southern
Marbled Skipper

Marbled Skipper

Dingy Skipper *haynesi*

Northern Chequered Skipper

Dingy Skipper

◀▲ Large Chequered Skipper

▼▼ Chequered Skipper

♀   ♂

Large Chequered Skipper

Chequered Skipper

Inky Skipper

149

▲LULWORTH SKIPPER *Thymelicus acteon*. Ups orange to brown: upf bears a ring of yellowish dots or streaks near apex (often rather obscure in ♂): ♂ has a prominent, but narrow black sex brand on upf: unh unmarked. HAB grassy places of all kinds. ALT sl–1700. FLIGHT 5–8. FP tor grass and other tall grasses, especially bromes, but only tor grass in B. EGG 6–9: in small clusters in old flower sheaths. LARVA 1–12: active only in spring and early summer as it goes into hibernation immediately on hatching and does not feed until following year: lives in a tube made by folding a leaf blade. PUPA 5–7: in a loose cocoon at base of fp. WINTER 1st-instar larva, in a flimsy cocoon spun close to the egg. VAR ups sometimes darker in Iberia. STATUS E; Holland. R; B, in the sense that it has a very restricted range; numbers are sometimes very high. SEE ALSO p. 24, 244, 247.

▲ESSEX SKIPPER *Thymelicus lineola*. Like Lulworth Skipper but lacks yellow spots on upf: underside of antennal tip is black: ♂ has a very slender and short sex brand running parallel to wing veins. HAB grassy places. ALT sl–2000. FLIGHT 5–8. FP various coarse grasses, including cocksfoot and creeping soft-grass. EGG 6–4: in linear clusters in flower sheaths of fp. LARVA 3–6: largely nocturnal, like other *Thymelicus* spp., and resting in a tube made by folding a grass blade. PUPA 5–7: in flimsy cocoon amongst grass blades. WINTER egg. VAR rather small in some southern areas. STATUS Generally common.

▲SMALL SKIPPER *Thymelicus sylvestris*. Very like Essex Skipper but underside of antennal club is orange: ♂ has a much thicker sex brand. HAB grassy places. ALT sl–2000. FLIGHT 5–8. FP various grasses, especially Yorkshire fog. EGG 6–8: in short linear clusters in leaf sheaths of fp. LARVA 1–12: active only in spring and early summer as it goes into hibernation immediately after hatching: it lives in a rolled-up leaf-blade and feeds by nibbling broad V-shaped notches in the blades, a feature shared with other *Thymelicus* spp. PUPA 4–7: in flimsy cocoon amongst the grasses. WINTER 1st-instar larva, clustered in minute silk cocoons where eggs were laid. VAR large and very bright individuals (f. *syriacus*) are common in south. STATUS Common. SEE ALSO p. 233, 262, 308.

▲SILVER-SPOTTED SKIPPER *Hesperia comma*. Uns greenish with silvery spots, especially unh: ♂ has a prominent black sex brand on upf. HAB grassy slopes on lime-rich soils – mainly in rough, grazed areas with areas of bare soil. ALT sl–2500. FLIGHT 6–8. FP sheep's fescue and other fine-leaved grasses. EGG 7–3: solitary on fp and looking like a miniature pudding basin. LARVA 3–7: largely nocturnal and concealed in a tent of grass and silk by day. PUPA 6–8: in a tough cocoon at base of fp. WINTER egg. VAR small and dark in far north. STATUS V; Holland. R; B. SEE ALSO p. 208, 246.

▲LARGE SKIPPER *Ochlodes venatus*. Like Silver-spotted Skipper, especially ♀, but unh is less green and has a less distinct pattern. HAB grassy places with flowers, including many roadsides. ALT sl–2500. FLIGHT 5–9: 1–3 broods (1 in B). FP cocksfoot and other coarse grasses. EGG 5–10: pearly white and solitary under leaf-blades. LARVA 1–12: largely nocturnal and living in a tube of grass and silk until nearly fully grown. PUPA 4–9: in a loose cocoon among the grasses. WINTER larva in a tent of grass and silk. VAR often smaller and darker in north of range and also at high altitude (f. *alpinus*). STATUS Generally common. SEE ALSO p. 247.

MEDITERRANEAN SKIPPER *Gegenes nostrodamus*. Shape and colour of wings, unmarked in ♂, are unmistakable. HAB dry, rocky places, usually near the coast: local. ALT sl–900. FLIGHT 5–10, commonest 8–9: ? broods. FP various grasses. EGG ? LARVA ? PUPA ? WINTER ? STATUS V; Italy. R; Greece & Spain. SEE ALSO p. 251.

PIGMY SKIPPER *Gegenes pumilio*. Like Mediterranean Skipper but smaller and ♂ is much darker than ♀: distinguished from Dingy Skipper by the very pointed wings. HAB dry, rocky places on coast. ALT sl–300. FLIGHT 4–10. FP various grasses. EGG ? LARVA ? PUPA ? WINTER ? NOTES Enjoys basking on bare ground in full sun. STATUS V; Malta. R; elsewhere. SEE ALSO p. 251.

ZELLER'S SKIPPER *Borbo borbonica*. Translucent spots on fw distinguish this from the two *Gegenes* spp.: ♀ has larger spots. HAB coastal cliffs and scrub. ALT sl–100. FLIGHT 9–10. FP various grasses. EGG ? LARVA ? PUPA ? WINTER ? NOTES Probably only an occasional immigrant from Africa. STATUS V.

◀◀▲ Lulworth Skipper

Lulworth Skipper

◀◀▲▲▲ Essex Skipper

Small ▲
Skipper ▶

Small Skipper   f. *syriacus* ♂

▲ Small
Skipper

Silver-spotted Skipper

◀▶
Silver-spotted
Skipper ▶

Large Skipper

◀▶
Large
Skipper
▼

Mediterranean Skipper

Pigmy Skipper

Zeller's Skipper

151

DAY-FLYING MOTHS

Diurnal moths belong to several different families and very often just a handful of species in a family fly by day (see p. 13). Only families in which all or a substantial proportion of species are diurnal are described on the following pages. Of these, only the burnets are likely to be confused with butterflies.

FAMILY MICROPTERIGIDAE These mini-moths, without any English name, are the most primitive of living Lepidoptera, retaining the biting mouth-parts of their ancestors and feeding on pollen instead of nectar. They have a sub-order to themselves – the Zeugloptera – and some entomologists favour giving them a whole order to themselves. Their wings are slender and clothed with shiny, metallic-looking scales. There is no frenulum, but the wings are lightly coupled with a jugum – a small flap on the rear of the fore-wing which rests on the front of the hind-wing where it is gripped by a patch of small spines. Wingspans rarely exceed 15mm and British species span no more than 11mm. The insects are most often seen on spring flowers. All prefer damp and slightly shaded places.

The larvae differ from other caterpillars in having eight pairs of prolegs – one on each of the first eight abdominal segments – and this is another reason for placing the insects in a separate order. They feed on leaf litter and probably on fungal hyphae as well, often going well below ground level in their search for tasty tit-bits. The pupa is enclosed in a tough silken cocoon amongst the leaf litter.

About 50 species (all *Micropterix* spp) occur in Europe, with just five in the British Isles.

▲*Micropterix aureatella*. 2 golden bands crossing purplish fw. HAB woods and moors. ALT sl–2000. FLIGHT 6–7. FP bilberry leaf litter. EGG 6–7: in leaf litter. LARVA ? PUPA ? WINTER ? NOTES Adults particularly attracted to sedge flowers. STATUS Generally common.

▲*Micropterix calthella*. Fw broadly purple at base and brassy elsewhere. HAB fens, damp woods, and other wet habitats. ALT sl–2000. FLIGHT 5–6. FP leaf litter and fungi associated with marsh marigold and other damp-loving plants. EGG ? LARVA ? PUPA ? WINTER ? NOTES Adults very fond of feeding in buttercups and marsh marigolds: also cling to pollen-clad spikes of sedges. STATUS Generally common.

▲*Micropterix mansuetella*. Black head together with broad purple band on fw and purple wing-tip distinguish this from several similar species. HAB fens and damp woods. ALT ? FLIGHT 5–6. FP leaf litter. EGG 5–7. LARVA ? PUPA ? WINTER ? NOTES Adults found mainly on sedge flowers. ♂ is very active in sunshine, but ♀ less so. STATUS ?

FAMILY ERIOCRANIIDAE This is another rather small family of diurnal moths in which front and hind wings are linked by a jugum instead of a frenulum. The forewings are mostly shiny gold or purple in colour. Jaws are still present, although very small and not used for feeding, and there is a short, but fully functional tongue or proboscis. The moths swarm in the spring sunshine, usually around the trees on which the larvae feed, and some are on the wing at night as well.

Eggs are laid inside plant tissues with the aid of a piercing ovipositor and the larvae are all legless leaf-miners, forming conspicuous blotches in the leaves of various trees. Pupation takes place in the soil in a tough, silken cocoon. In common with the pupae of several other groups of moths, it has large jaws which cut open the cocoon in due course and help the young moth to scramble up to the surface.

Only a few dozen species are known, with eight of them resident in the British Isles.

▲*Eriocrania unimaculella*. Solitary silvery spot at rear of plain reddish fw is characteristic (but worn specimens are easily confused with other species). HAB birch woods and scrub. ALT ? FLIGHT 3–4. FP birch. EGG 3–4: in birch buds. LARVA 4–5: in blotch mine on birch leaf. PUPA 6–3: in tough cocoon in ground. WINTER pupa. STATUS ?

▲*Eriocrania sparrmannella*. Fw golden, densely spotted with blue and purple. HAB birch woods and scrub. ALT ? FLIGHT 4–5. FP birch. EGG 5–6: in birch leaf. LARVA 6–8: in linear mine at first but later widening it to form a blotch mine. PUPA 8–5: in tough cocoon in ground. WINTER pupa. STATUS ?

▲*Eriocrania semipurpurella*. Long antennae, more than half as long as fw, distinguish this from other moths with a similar wing pattern: hw has a patch of hair-like scales in centre, revealing the membrane. HAB birch woods. ALT ? FLIGHT 3–4: night and day. FP birch. EGG 3–4: in leaf bud. LARVA 3–5: in blotch mine. PUPA 5–3: in tough cocoon in soil. WINTER pupa. NOTES One of the commonest members of the family, often swarming around birches in spring sunshine. Examination of genitalia is required for positive identification. STATUS Very common.

FAMILY INCURVARIIDAE This is a family of rather small moths. A frenulum is present, at least in the male. The proboscis is very short or rudimentary.

The majority of species fly by day, the most conspicuous being members of the sub-family Adelinae. These have extraordinarily long antennae – especially the males, which also have unusually large eyes. Males often swarm around trees and bushes in the spring sunshine, and also at dusk, but flight is relatively rather weak.

Eggs are inserted into plant tissues with a tough ovipositor. Some larvae are stem-borers, but others build portable cases with soil particles or fragments of the leaf litter on which they feed. There are no prolegs, and the stem-borers have no legs at all. Pupation takes place in the larval case or tunnel.

There are several hundred known species, with about 25 of them resident in the British Isles.

Nemophora scabiosella (see over for illustration). Golden patch towards tip of rich brown fw distinguishes this from related species: tegulae also golden. HAB damp grassland: local. ALT ? FLIGHT 6–8. FP scabious at first, and then leaf litter. EGG 6–8: on scabious flowers. LARVA 7–5: on flowers in 1st instar, then in a flat case in leaf litter. PUPA 5–7: in larval case. WINTER larva. STATUS ?

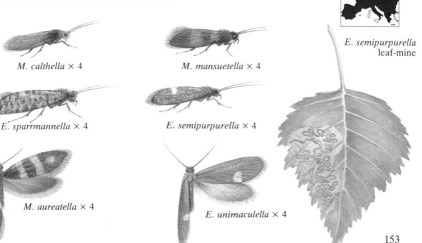

M. calthella × 4

M. mansuetella × 4

E. semipurpurella leaf-mine

E. sparrmannella × 4

E. semipurpurella × 4

M. aureatella × 4

E. unimaculella × 4

153

▲*Nemophora fasciella*. Deep purple band on fw is characteristic: tegulae golden green. HAB scrubby and waste places: local. ALT ? FLIGHT 6–7. FP black horehound and leaf litter. EGG 6–7: in flowers of fp. LARVA 7–5: feeding on seeds of fp at first and then on leaves and leaf litter: often gregarious in flat key-hole-shaped cases. PUPA 5–6: in larval case. WINTER larva. STATUS ?

▲*Nemophora degeerella*. Yellow head and yellow band on fw distinguish this from all related species. HAB damp woods and scrubby stream-sides. ALT ? FLIGHT 5–6: generally from late afternoon onwards. FP leaf litter, possibly nibbling flowers in 1st instar. EGG 5–7: in various flowers. LARVA 7–4: in flat pear-shaped case in leaf litter. PUPA 4–6: in larval case. WINTER larva. NOTES ♂ has longest antennae of any British butterfly or moth. STATUS Very common. SEE ALSO p. 288.

▲*Adela croesella*. Like *Nemophora degeerella* but smaller and with a dark head. HAB woodland edges and other areas of dense scrub, especially on limestone: local. ALT ? FLIGHT 5–7. FP privet and other shrubs at first, and then leaf litter. EGG 5–7: in flowers of shrubs. LARVA 6–4: on flowers and leaves at first and then in a flat case in leaf litter. PUPA 4–6: in larval case. WINTER larva. STATUS Uncommon.

▲*Adela fibulella*. Yellowish spot on fw: ♂ antennae only slightly longer than fw: ♀ antennae shorter than fw. HAB grassy places, including woodland rides and clearings. ALT ? FLIGHT 5–7. FP germander speedwell at first and then leaf litter. EGG 5–7: in flowers of fp. LARVA 6–4: in fruits of fp at first and then in flat case amongst leaf litter. PUPA 4–6: in larval case. WINTER larva. NOTES Smallest member of family. STATUS ?

▲*Adela reaumurella*. Purplish costa on otherwise uniformly golden green fw. HAB light deciduous woodland and scrub. ALT ? FLIGHT 4–6. FP leaf litter. EGG 4–6: on various plants. LARVA 6–3: falls from egg site immediately after hatching and lives in flat case of leaf fragments in leaf litter. PUPA 3–5: in larval case. WINTER larva. NOTES ♂♂ dance in clouds around trees and bushes in sunshine, their white antennae flashing as the moths rise and fall like miniature yo-yos. STATUS Very common. SEE ALSO p. 288.

FAMILY ZYGAENIDAE – THE BURNETS AND FORESTERS

Of all the day-flying moths, the burnets are the most likely to be confused with the butterflies – as a result of their bright colours and clubbed antennae. Their resting attitudes are very different from those of the butterflies, however, and the frenulum (see p. 11) clearly places them with the moths. Burnets (sub-family Zygaeninae) are mostly red and black, with a deep metallic green or bluish sheen on the black areas when fresh. Foresters (sub-family Procridinae) have bronzy green forewings and their antennae are lightly toothed or feathered, especially in the male.

The tongue is well developed. The forewings are relatively narrow and the insects seem to have trouble in getting their heavy bodies into the air. Although the wings beat rapidly, flight is slow and the moths seem to drift quietly from flower to flower. They are also rather sluggish when sitting on the flowers and they can be approached very easily and even picked up in the hand. This behaviour is, of course, linked to the insects' chemical defences and warning colours, for few natural predators would press home an attack on these foul-tasting, cyanide-containing moths. Many species are extraordinarily variable, with a host of geographical races (see p. 280), and it is extremely difficult to identify some of the more aberrant individuals. Only a few of the commoner races can be illustrated on the following pages.

The creamy white eggs are ovoid and of the flat type (see p. 206) and they are laid in batches on the food-plants – which include a wide variety of herbaceous plants and semi-shrubs, especially members of the pea family. The larvae are rather squat and generally yellowish with black spots or greenish black with yellow spots. They are somewhat 'warty', with tufts of fine, short hairs arising from each bump. Pupation among the burnets takes place in a papery cocoon, often attached to grass stems, and the pupa wriggles partly or completely out of this before the adult emerges. Foresters pupate in flimsy cocoons spun low down in the vegetation.

There are about 800 species in the family, of which some 60 occur in Europe. Some authorities recognise far more than this, but recent work has shown that many of the local 'species' are actually no more than geographical races of widely distributed types, and so the number of true species has been whittled down. Ten species – seven burnets and three foresters – occur in the British Isles. All inhabit rough, grassy places in sunny habitats.

Theresimima ampelophaga. Like a dark *Adscita* but with a narrower fw and with veins 9 & 10 stalked (no stalked veins in *Adscita* spp): antennae rather long, with strong feathering in ♂. HAB scrubby places, including vineyards. ALT ? FLIGHT 4–8: 2 broods: flies mainly at dusk. FP vines. EGG 5–9: green, in batches of 20–80. LARVA 1–12: ash grey with brown markings: gregarious when young. PUPA 3–7: in silken cocoon on leaves or stems of fp. WINTER larva. STATUS Often common enough for larvae to be injurious to shoots and leaves of vines.

Rhagades pruni. Resembles *Adscita* spp., but distinguished by having ♂ antennae pectinate right to the tip. Proboscis shorter than thorax. HAB scrubby grassland, woodland edges, and (in N) moorland: local. ALT ? FLIGHT 6–8. FP various shrubs, especially blackthorn and heather: also strawberry. EGG 6–8: orange-yellow, LARVA 1–12: flesh coloured with a black head. PUPA 5 7. WINTER larva. VAR fw often very blue: northern moors support the heather-feeding *R.p. callunae*—sometimes treated as a separate species—in which fw is almost all brown. STATUS ?

Adscita subsolana. Like Scarce Forester and *A. notata* but hw is less transparent and fw is bluer: head is smaller than in these other species and antennae of ♂ are stouter and more strongly toothed. HAB heath and moor: very local. ALT <2000 FLIGHT 5–8. FP knapweeds, thistles, and other grassland herbs. EGG 6–8. LARVA 7–4: yellowish with a black head. PUPA 4 7: in white or yellowish web in ground or leaf litter. WINTER larva. VAR brown patch often absent from fw. NOTES Forewing colour is not a reliable feature for identifying foresters. A given specimen can vary from golden green to blue according to the angle from which is is viewed. Dead specimens also vary according to treatment. STATUS ?

Adscita chloros. A small species, distinguished by the vivid blue-green head and thorax and base of fw: hw rather thinly scaled. HAB rough, dry grassland on sunny slopes: local. ALT <2000. FLIGHT 6–7. FP cornflower and other composites; also globularia. EGG 6–7. LARVA 7–4 PUPA 4 6. WINTER larva. VAR fw sometimes entirely bronze, especially in S. STATUS ?

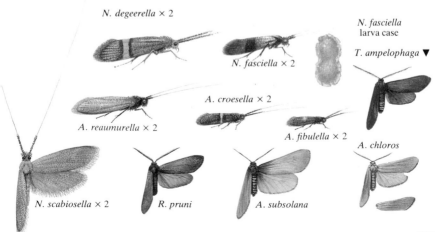

N. degeerella × 2

N. fasciella larva case

N. fasciella × 2

T. ampelophaga ▼

A. croesella × 2

A. reaumurella × 2

A. fibulella × 2

A. chloros

N. scabiosella × 2

R. pruni

A. subsolana

Adscita graeca. Like *A. chloros* but without the vivid blue-green on head, thorax, and fw base: fw generally darker and hw more densely scaled: antennae somewhat longer than in *A. chloros*: abdomen coppery at rear. HAB grassy places. ALT 1700. FLIGHT 5–7. FP ? EGG ? LARVA ? PUPA ? WINTER larva? STATUS ?

Adscita jordani. A small species with distinctly clubbed antennae. HAB sunny slopes, mainly in uplands. ALT <1800. FLIGHT 4–8. FP various low-growing herbs. EGG 5–8. LARVA 6–4. PUPA 4–7. WINTER larva. STATUS ?

Adscita notata. Like Scarce Forester, but abdomen is more slender and lacks the coppery sheen: antennae have shorter pectinations: wings seldom blue. HAB flowery grassland. ALT <2000. FLIGHT 4–7: often visits lights at night. FP scabious, knapweed, globularia, and other grassland plants. EGG 5–7: dirty yellow, becoming reddish just before hatching. LARVA 6–4: reddish grey and living as leaf miner throughout life. PUPA 3–6: in cocoon at base of fp. WINTER larva. STATUS ?

▲**FORESTER** *Adscita statices.* ♂ antennae thickened at apex, with 9–11 segments lacking pectinations: ♀ antennae weakly toothed and gradually thickened towards the tip: ♂ wingspan generally >25mm: ♀ wingspan generally >22mm. HAB rough grassland and woodland clearings: local. ALT sl–1500. FLIGHT 5–8. FP common sorrel. EGG 6–7: in short rows or irregular batches. LARVA 7–5: mining leaves at first and then nibbling lower leaves. PUPA 5–6: in tough cocoon under leaf. WINTER larva, in leaf litter. VAR fw golden to bluish green. NOTES Recent work has shown that in most parts of N & C this insect is represented by two biologically distinct forms – one flying 5–6 in damp grassland and the other 7–8 in dry habitats. It is likely that these two forms are distinct species. STATUS Generally common in suitable habitats.

▲**CISTUS FORESTER** *Adscita geryon.* Antennae thickened gradually towards tip: ♂ antenna with last 8–10 segments lacking pectinations: ♂ wingspan generally <25mm, ♀ wingspan <22mm. HAB dry grassland on limestone: local. ALT sl–1500. FLIGHT 5–8. FP common rockrose. EGG 5–7: yellow: solitary or in two short rows. LARVA 6–4: mining leaves at first and then stripping lower surfaces to form translucent windows. PUPA 4–6: in loose cocoon close to ground. WINTER larva. VAR fw ranges from golden green to bluish. NOTES Best separated from similar species by the genitalia. STATUS ?

▲**SCARCE FORESTER** *Adscita globulariae.* ♂ antennae tapered, with pectinations almost to tip: ♀ antennae of ± constant thickness. HAB limestone grassland: local. ALT sl–1800. FLIGHT 5–7. FP knapweeds. EGG 5–7: sometimes solitary but usually in short rows. LARVA 1–12: feeds by stripping lower surfaces from leaves to form translucent windows. PUPA 4–6: in double cocoon in ground or leaf litter. WINTER larva. NOTES Antennal structure readily distinguishes this from other British species. STATUS ?

Aglaope infausta. The rather translucent red and brown wings are diagnostic: antennae are pectinate in both sexes. HAB scrubby grassland: local. ALT sl–1500? FLIGHT 6–8. FP blackthorn, hawthorn, and other rosaceous shrubs. EGG 6–8: intense yellow and laid in batches of up to 400. LARVA 8–5: short and thick, bright yellow with whitish hair. PUPA 5–7: in elongate cocoon. WINTER larvae, in dense masses in fluffy nest. NOTES A tongueless species rarely seen on flowers. The larvae can be pests of rosaceous shrubs, especially almonds and plums.

Zygaena sedi. Spots sometimes separate, but more often fused in pairs to give three large white-edged spots on each fw, separated by translucent black bands: all spots often linked to form a branching pattern as in *Z. ignifera*, but that species has red abdominal band: collar black, often with whitish hairs. HAB coastal grassland. ALT sl–200? FLIGHT 5–7. FP ? EGG ? LARVA ? PUPA ? WINTER ? STATUS ?

Zygaena orana. Somewhat like a very small *Z. carniolica* but with virtually no pale collar and never with an abdominal belt: wing spots sometimes confluent. HAB dry grassland. ALT ? FLIGHT 5–6. FP assorted legumes, including *Hippocrepis* and *Lotus* spp. EGG 5–7. LARVA 6–4. PUPA 4–6. WINTER larva. NOTES Confined to Sardinia in Europe: widespread in N. Africa. STATUS ?

Zygaena carniolica. White collar and pale rings around red spots distinguish this from most other burnets: outer red spot always crescent-shaped: body with or without a red band. HAB scrubby places, usually in uplands: mainly on limestone. ALT 1000–2000. FLIGHT 6–8. FP bird's-foot trefoil, restharrow, and other small legumes. EGG 6–8. LARVA 1–12. PUPA 5–7. WINTER larva. VAR amount of white around red spots varies a good deal and is absent in *Z. c. berolensis*, which also lacks the pale collar: *Z. c. hedysari*, with no red belt, is common in Germany: *Z. c. diniensis* from Basses Alpes has a broad red belt: *Z. c. roccii* lacks the outermost spot and has a wide border to hw. STATUS Locally common, but rare in Spain and declining in many other areas through 'improvement' of grassland. LP; W. Germany.

Zygaena occitanica. Like *Z. carniolica* but smaller: outermost spot of fw generally plain white: abdomen always with a red belt. HAB sun-drenched flowery places. ALT sl–1600. FLIGHT 5–8. FP various low-growing legumes. EGG 6–8. LARVA 7–5. PUPA 4–7: in white or yellow cocoon. WINTER larva. VAR white rings may be missing from fw, or developed to such an extent that fw is largely white with red spots (*Z. o. vandalitia*): outer spot may be red and is sometimes missing. STATUS ?

Zygaena fausta. Red collar: red spots on fw always confluent and often more orange than in other burnets: hw also often very orange: the black is duller than in most burnets: white stripes on thorax, although these may not be obvious in worn specimens. HAB rough grassland on lime-rich soils, usually on warm slopes. ALT <1750. FLIGHT 7–8. FP crown vetches (*Coronilla* spp.) and other small legumes. EGG 7–8: in small groups under leaves. LARVA 9–6. PUPA 6–7. WINTER larva. VAR red abdominal band often absent, as in *Z. f. genevensis*: many small variations in wing pattern, with white edges to spots often absent. NOTES Red abdominal band always present in Spain, providing an easy distinction from *Z. hilaris* in that country. STATUS R; W. Germany: generally common further south. LP; W. Germany.

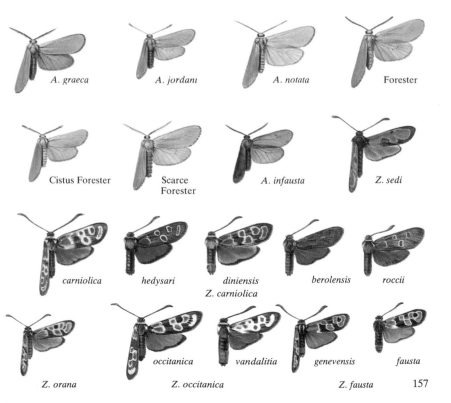

A. graeca   A. jordani   A. notata   Forester

Cistus Forester   Scarce Forester   A. infausta   Z. sedi

carniolica   hedysari   diniensis   berolensis   roccii
Z. carniolica

occitanica   vandalitia   genevensis   fausta

Z. orana   Z. occitanica   Z. fausta   157

Zygaena hilaris. Like *Z. fausta* but with a pale collar and no abdominal belt. HAB sun-drenched grassy slopes, especially with thyme. ALT sl–2000. FLIGHT 5–9: 2 broods. FP restharrows. EGG 6–9. LARVA 7–5: short and thick, with a brown head. PUPA 4–8: in wrinkled yellow or brown cocoon. WINTER larva. VAR fw has narrow pale borders to red spots in *Z. h. ononidis*: fw occasionally mainly red with small black spots. *Z. h. galliae* from S. France has yellowish white thoracic hair. STATUS ?

Zygaena oxytropis. Like 6-spot Burnet but smaller and with a more rounded fw: outer pair of spots on fw broadly united and middle pair sometimes united as well: hw border relatively broad. HAB flower-rich grassland. ALT ? FLIGHT 5–6. FP bird's-foot trefoil and other legumes. EGG 5–7. LARVA 7–4. PUPA 4–6. WINTER larva. VAR some specimens have red abdominal belt. STATUS ?

Zygaena rhadamanthus. Fw with 6 spots, all except the outermost with thick black inner and outer margins. HAB flower-rich grasslands. ALT sl–2000. FLIGHT 5–7. FP restharrows and other legumes. EGG 5–7. LARVA 7–5: greyish with a red collar and yellow and white stripes. PUPA 4–6: in oval white cocoon. WINTER larva. VAR a very variable species: *Z.r. aragonia* from Spain is very like *Z.r. rhadamanthus* but has a red belt: *Z.r. algarbiensis* from S. Portugal is very dark with almost black hw. STATUS LP; France.

Zygaena romeo. Fw normally with 5 elongate spots: all wings thinly scaled: antennae very long. HAB rough grassland. ALT <1500. FLIGHT 6–7. FP yellow vetchling, tuberous pea, and other legumes. EGG 6–8. LARVA 7–5. PUPA 4–6. WINTER larva. VAR fw spots often fuse to form a prominent red streak in basal half of wing. STATUS ?

Zygaena nevadensis. Rather small and transparent: wing pattern similar to that of *Z. romeo* but antennae much shorter. HAB upland grassland: local. ALT 500–2000. FLIGHT 6–7. FP trefoils. EGG 6–8. LARVA 8–5: golden yellow with black dots on the back. PUPA 4–6: in golden cocoon. WINTER larva. STATUS ?

Zygaena osterodensis. Rather like *Z. romeo* but fw has 3 streaks rather than streaks and spots: antennae thicken rather more gradually than in most burnets. HAB sunny woodlands and scrubby places: local. ALT <1500. FLIGHT 6–7. FP clovers, vetches and peas. EGG 6–8. LARVA 7–4. PUPA 4–6: in a rather shiny cocoon. WINTER larva. VAR *Z. o. schultei* has broader margins to both wings. STATUS LP; W. Germany.

▲**SCOTCH BURNET** *Zygaena exulans*. Wings thinly scaled, especially hw: anterior of 2 basal spots on fw extends as a streak as far as 2nd pair of spots: body abnormally hairy. HAB mountain slopes and tops: also on lowland moors in N. ALT sl–3000: rarely below 1800 on southern mountains. FLIGHT 6–8. FP crowberry and various ericaceous shrubs in northern parts of the range: polyphagous in S. EGG 7–8: in batches several layers deep. LARVA 1–12: 2-year life cycle at higher altitudes, including parts of Scotland. PUPA 4–7: in translucent cocoon low down in vegetation. WINTER larva (sometimes twice). VAR there are many sub-species, but the differences are generally minor: *Z. e. subochracea* is from Scotland and the north. NOTES Also called Mountain Burnet. STATUS Locally common on mountains on the continent. LP; W. Germany.

Zygaena anthyllidis. Like 6-spot Burnet but fw is paler and noticeably broader: abdomen has a slender red band: traces of a pale collar. HAB mountain slopes. ALT <2500. FLIGHT 7–8. FP clovers and other legumes. EGG 7–9. LARVA 8–5: yellow with black bands and a black head. PUPA 5–7: in white cocoon. WINTER larva. STATUS R.

▲**SLENDER SCOTCH BURNET** *Zygaena loti*. 2 outer spots on fw united to form a triangular or kidney-shaped blotch: basal spots often noticeably elongated and sometimes joined to central spots. HAB rough grassland, but restricted to coastal areas with heather and heath in B: generally on limestone elsewhere. ALT <2000. FLIGHT 6–7. FP mainly bird's-foot trefoil, but various other low-growing legumes on the continent. EGG 6–7: batched in a single layer. LARVA 7–5. PUPA 5–7: in shiny cocoon on ground at base of fp. WINTER larva. VAR many races are recognised: *Z. l. scotica* from Scotland is rather thinly scaled: *Z. l. miniacea* is bright, with a rather golden sheen on fw: some races, including the very dark *Z. l. osthelderi*, have just one small outer spot on fw. NOTES Flies somewhat faster than other burnets in Scotland. STATUS LP; W. Germany.

Zygaena ignifera. Red fw, with small black markings, together with extensive red ring near tip of abdomen, will distinguish this from most other burnets: *Z. laeta* is similar, but smaller and with red tegulae and more red on abdomen: *Z. laeta* also lives further east and the two species do not overlap. HAB flower-rich grassland. ALT <1800. FLIGHT 6–7. FP field eryngo and various legumes. EGG 6–8. LARVA 8–5: bluish green with white stripes. PUPA 4–6. WINTER larva. STATUS ?

Zygaena lavanduli. White collar and bluish-black hw readily distinguish this species in most areas. HAB flower-rich grassland ALT sl–1600. FLIGHT 4–6. FP *Dorycnium* spp., especially *D. suffruticosum*, and other legumes. EGG 5–7. LARVA 6–4: red underneath. PUPA 3–5: in white cocoon. WINTER larva. VAR some races, including *Z. l. consobrina* of S. France, have partly red hw. NOTES Adults tend to rest in head-down position and show less interest in flowers than most other burnets. STATUS ?

▲NEW FOREST BURNET *Zygaena viciae*. Fw has 5 spots, the outer one rounded or egg-shaped: anterior spot of the middle pair small and elongate: black of fw less dense than in some other burnets, but not translucent: antennae weakly clubbed. HAB dry grassland: confined to coasts in B. ALT sl–1000. FLIGHT 6–8. FP bird's-foot trefoil, meadow vetchling, and other legumes. EGG 7–8: batched in a single layer. LARVA 7–5, sometimes surviving until early 6. PUPA 5–7: in shiny yellow cocoon under leaf or on grass stem near ground. WINTER larva. VAR *Z. v. italica*, from Liguria, is very dark. NOTES No longer flies in New Forest. STATUS LP; B (Scotland only: *Z. v. argyllensis*) and W. Germany. SEE ALSO p. 304.

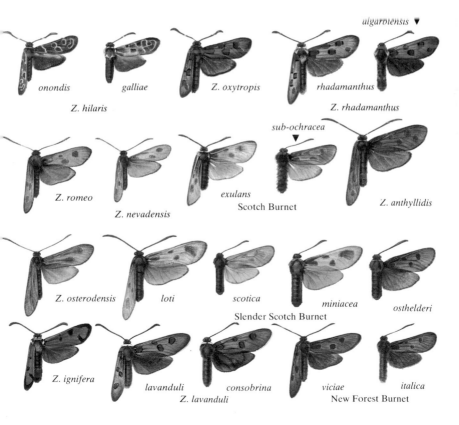

algarbiensis ▼

onondis *galliae* *Z. oxytropis* *rhadamanthus*

Z. hilaris *Z. rhadamanthus*

sub-ochracea ▼

Z. romeo *exulans* *Z. anthyllidis*

Z. nevadensis Scotch Burnet

Z. osterodensis *loti* *scotica* *miniacea* *osthelderi*

Slender Scotch Burnet

Z. ignifera *lavanduli* *consobrina* *viciae* *italica*

Z. lavanduli New Forest Burnet

Zygaena ephialtes. The most widespread sub-species *Z. e. peucedanoides*, from the northern parts of the range, is like the 6-spot Burnet but has a red abdominal band and broader borders on hw: outer spot on fw often very small and occasionally missing. HAB sunny hillsides and rough grassland, mainly on limestone: also in open woodland and woodland margins. ALT <1500. FLIGHT 6–9. FP crown vetch and related legumes. EGG 6–9. LARVA 1–12: some take 2 years to mature. PUPA 5–7: in a silvery cocoon on grass stalks. WINTER larva (sometimes twice). VAR *Z. e. ephialtes*, with most spots white and with black hw, occurs in several southern areas: in much of Italy and SE Europe the red is replaced by yellow (*Z. e. coronillae*): STATUS LP; W. Germany. SEE ALSO p. 280.

Zygaena transalpina. Like 6-spot Burnet but darker and with slightly smaller and more widely spaced spots: hw border generally rather broad. HAB sunny slopes in mountains: always on limestone: local. ALT 500–2000. FLIGHT 6–8. FP various low-growing legumes. EGG 6–8. LARVA 1–12: sometimes with a 2-year life cycle. PUPA 5–7. WINTER larva, sometimes twice. VAR *Z. t. sorrentina* is generally yellow, although some specimens are red: *Z. t. latina* from S Italy has black hw: *Z. t. collina* from C Italy has a very broad black border to hw: all races may have red replaced by yellow. STATUS LP; W. Germany.

▲**6-SPOT BURNET** *Zygaena filipendulae.* Fw has 6 plain red spots: hw border is narrow: no red abdominal band. HAB grassy places of all kinds, including waste land. ALT <2000. FLIGHT 6–8. FP bird's-foot trefoil and other low-growing legumes. EGG 7–8: in irregular mounds. LARVA 8–6. PUPA 5–8: in white to yellow papery cocoon on grass stem. WINTER larva. VAR two outer spots are often fused: red is occasionally replaced by yellow (f. *flava*): outer red spot is missing in most parts of Spain and sometimes in Italy (*Z. f. liguris*), making distinction from Narrow-bordered 5-spot Burnet difficult, although border of hw tends to be very broad in these varieties. STATUS LP; W. Germany. SEE ALSO p. 23, 299.

▲**5-SPOT BURNET** *Zygaena trifolii.* Like 6-spot Burnet but fw has only 5 red spots and hw has a broader margin: basal spots of fw ± equal: central pair of spots commonly joined. HAB grassland of all kinds, both damp and dry but most common in damp areas. ALT <2500. FLIGHT 5–8: one of the earliest burnets to appear. FP bird's-foot trefoil and greater bird's-foot trefoil, according to sub-sp. EGG 5–8: in an irregular, several-layered batch. LARVA 1–12: often with 2-year life cycle. PUPA 5–7: in bright yellow to greyish white cocoon, either high on grass or rush stems or low down in herbage according to race. WINTER larva (often twice). VAR a very variable species: central spots often separate. NOTES British specimens are *Z. t. decreta*, confined to damp moors and grassland, or the generally smaller and duller *Z. t. palustrella* found on dry chalk and limestone grassland. STATUS LP; W. Germany. SEE ALSO p. 277.

▲**NARROW-BORDERED 5-SPOT BURNET** *Zygaena lonicerae.* Like 5-spot Burnet but border of hw generally narrower and central spots of fw normally well separated: generally larger than 5-spot Burnet. HAB rough grassland of all kinds, including woodland clearings. ALT <2000. FLIGHT 6–8. FP meadow vetchling, red clover, and, less commonly, other legumes. EGG 7–8: in flat, single-layered sheets. LARVA 1–12: often with 2-year life cycle. PUPA 6–7: in pale, translucent cocoon high on herbage. WINTER larva. VAR less variable than 5-spot Burnet, but still with several ssp., some with linked central spots on fw and some with relatively broad border to hw, e.g. *Z. l. silana* from S. Italy: *Z. l. jocelynae* from Isle of Skye is rather large and hairy. STATUS LP; W. Germany.

Zygaena corsica. The smallest European burnet: fw with 5 glossy round spots on a greyish ground colour which sometimes has a golden sheen: collar generally of 2 white patches: tegulae with scattered white hairs: abdominal band clearly edged with white. HAB upland slopes. ALT <1500? FLIGHT 5–7. FP *Santolina* spp. (Compositae). EGG 6–8. LARVA 7–4. PUPA 4–6. WINTER larva. STATUS ?

Zygaena cynarae. Wings lightly scaled, pale and transparent with 5 spots: body ± hairless, with red abdominal ring more obvious on sides than on top. HAB damp meadows, scrubby hillsides, and woodland margins. ALT ? FLIGHT 6–8: FP *Peucedanum* spp. and other umbellifers. EGG 6–9. LARVA 8–6: greyish yellow on the sides and greenish on top. PUPA 5–7. WINTER larva. VAR abdominal band sometimes completely absent. STATUS LP; W. Germany.

Zygaena laeta. Very like *Z. ignifera*, but red collar and tegulae clearly distinguish it: ♂ abdomen almost entirely red. HAB rough grassland in warm places. ALT ? FLIGHT 7–8 FP field eryngo. EGG 7–8. LARVA 8–6: pale bluish green. PUPA 6–7: in shiny, yellowish cocoon. WINTER larva. STATUS Range contracting; already extinct in several areas. LP; W. Germany.

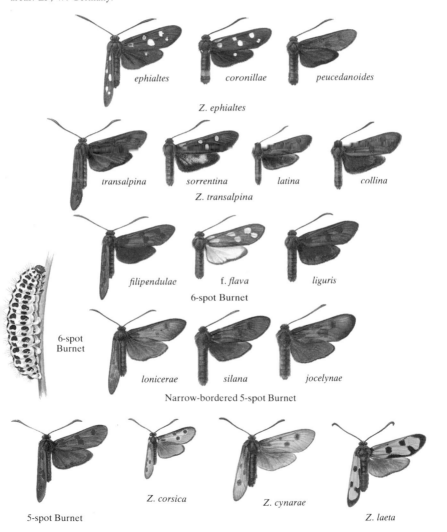

ephialtes   coronillae   peucedanoides

Z. ephialtes

transalpina   sorrentina   latina   collina

Z. transalpina

filipendulae   f. *flava*   liguris

6-spot Burnet

6-spot
Burnet

lonicerae   silana   jocelynae

Narrow-bordered 5-spot Burnet

Z. corsica   Z. cynarae

5-spot Burnet   Z. laeta

Zygaena brizae. A small, thinly scaled species with spots coalescing to form a forked red streak on fw: basal half of fw largely red: resembles Transparent Burnet, but is smaller and has broader black border on hw. HAB mountain slopes: local. ALT ? FLIGHT 5–7. FP creeping thistle and other composites. EGG 5–8. LARVA 7–5. PUPA 4–6: in silvery cocoon. WINTER larva. STATUS LP; France and W. Germany.

Zygaena punctum. Pattern like *Z. brizae* but with large red spot near tip of fw and a narrower border to hw: sides of thorax very grey. HAB warm, dry grassland. ALT <1700. FLIGHT 6–7. FP field eryngo. EGG 6–8: under leaves in groups of up to 30. LARVA 7–5: yellowish green with a black head and pale stripes. PUPA 5–7: in a whitish cocoon. WINTER larva. VAR *Z. p. italia* has more extensive red on fw. STATUS Locally common?

Zygaena sarpedon. Thinly scaled, with only 3 spots on each fw – generally forming 2 streaks and a spot or 2 spots and a streak: head and thorax black with whitish hair: always a prominent red abdominal band. HAB sunny grassland. ALT sl–2000. FLIGHT 6–8. FP field eryngo. EGG 6–9. LARVA 8–6. PUPA 5–7: in long, slender, brown cocoon. WINTER larva. VAR very variable but always with red abdominal band: *Z. s. vernetensis* from Balearics has black hw with red stripes: red sometimes absent from fw. STATUS ?

Zygaena contaminei. Like a small *Z. sarpedon*, but generally without a red belt on abdomen: antennae strongly clubbed. HAB dry and sunny upland grassland. ALT 1300–2000. FLIGHT 7–8. FP field eryngo. EGG 7–9. LARVA 8–5. PUPA 5–7: in long, slender cocoon. WINTER larva. STATUS ?

Zygaena rubicundus. Extensive red colour on fw separates this from other Italian species (but see *Z. erythrus*). HAB v. local. ALT ? FLIGHT 5–8. FP eryngos. EGG 6–8. LARVA 7–5. PUPA 4–6: in a long yellowish cocoon. WINTER larva. STATUS ?

Zygaena erythrus. Like *Z. rubicundus* but larger and with more black on fw: red forms three fairly distinct stripes or wedges: basal part of hind edge of fw is red. HAB ? ALT ? FLIGHT 5–7. FP field eryngo and wild thyme. EGG 6–8. LARVA 7–5. PUPA 4–6. WINTER larva. STATUS ?

▲**TRANSPARENT BURNET** *Zygaena purpuralis.* Wings thinly scaled and translucent: fw with 3 poorly separated longitudinal streaks, the longest of which bulges backwards at its outer end: could be confused with *Z. erythrus*, but hind edge of fw is entirely black. HAB grassy slopes in full sun. ALT <2000. FLIGHT 5–8. FP wild thyme. EGG 6–8: in an irregular batch of several layers. LARVA 7–5. PUPA 5–7: in shiny off-white cocoon concealed at ground level. WINTER larva. VAR size varies, but pattern is fairly stable: *Z. p. caledonensis* from Scotland tends to be smaller and blacker. STATUS LP; W. Germany.

Zygaena minos (Not illustrated). Visually indistinguishable from Transparent Burnet but genitalia and biology differ and the two are now regarded as distinct biological species. HAB ? ALT <2200. FLIGHT 6–8. FP burnet saxifrage (*Pimpinella* spp.). EGG 6–8. LARVA ? PUPA ? WINTER ? STATUS LP; W. Germany.

FAMILY LIMACODIDAE

▲**FESTOON** *Apoda limacodes.* 2 dark cross lines on fw, the outer one reaching the outer wing margin and sometimes appearing to bend sharply inwards again to reach the rear margin: ♀ is larger and paler. HAB deciduous woods with oak and beech. ALT ? FLIGHT 5–8: night and day. FP beech and oak. EGG 6–8: solitary under leaves: yellow at first, becoming grey. LARVA 1–12, active only 6–10: slug-like without prolegs, clinging tightly to leaves by silk and suction. PUPA 4–6: in reddish brown papery cocoon fixed to fallen leaf: cocoon has hinged lid at one end. WINTER fully grown larva in cocoon prepared for pupation. NOTES Seems to be more nocturnal now than in former times. Although resembling some small lasiocampids (p. 177), the venation and other features clearly link this family to the burnets. This and the Triangle are the only European members of the family.

▲**TRIANGLE** *Heterogenea asella.* Fw strongly triangular: wings held roofwise at rest. HAB deciduous woods. ALT ? FLIGHT 6–8: night and day. FP oak, beech, and several other trees. EGG 6–8: generally solitary on leaves. LARVA 1–12: active only 7–10. PUPA 5–7: in tough dark brown cocoon on leaf or twig. WINTER fully grown larva in silken cocoon ready for pupation. NOTES Appears to be more nocturnal now than in former times (see also Festoon).

FAMILY HETEROGYNIDAE

Heterogynis penella. ♂ thinly scaled and very like many of the bagworms (see below), but hind tibia has only one pair of spurs (2 in bagworms): radial veins of fw all spring directly from the cell without forking: black and yellow maggot-like ♀ never leaves her cocoon. HAB grassy and scrubby places. ALT ? FLIGHT 6–8 (♂♂ only). FP broom and other leguminous shrubs: also bramble. EGG 6–8: clustered in ♀ cocoon. LARVA 8–5: feeds on remains of mother's body before transferring to fp: rather shiny and with rings of tiny spines scattered over body. PUPA 5–7: in loose yellowish cocoon spun amongst herbage. WINTER larva, in a small globular web. NOTES The only European member of the family.

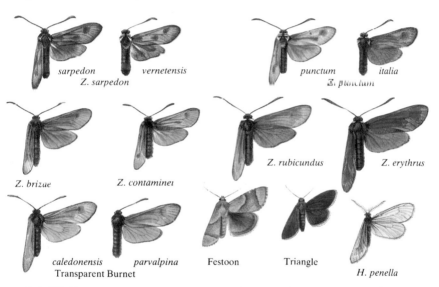

sarpedon   vernetensis   punctum   italia
Z. sarpedon   Z. punctum

Z. rubicundus   Z. erythrus

Z. brizae   Z. contaminei

caledonensis   parvalpina   Festoon   Triangle
Transparent Burnet   H. penella

FAMILY PSYCHIDAE – THE BAGWORMS

The members of this large family get their common name from the larval habit of constructing a portable case or bag in which it spends all or nearly all of the rest of its life. Pupation takes place in the case and, with a few exceptions, the females never leave it even when they are mature. Wings are normally found only in males and they are thinly scaled and always of a sombre colour – brown or black in most species. A frenulum is present. The tongue is minute and non-functional, so no food is taken in the adult stage and the latter is very short, often just a few hours for the male. Many males fly rapidly in the sunshine and some are strictly nocturnal, but the majority are on the wing just after daybreak or just before sunset and, for present purposes, are not considered to be day-flying. Only a few species have winged females, and this sex very often lacks legs and antennae as well. Some crawl on to the outside of the larval bag, but others remain imprisoned in it for life, sometimes as much as two weeks. The males find them by scent and mate with the enclosed females by thrusting their extensible abdomens deep into the bags, but several species can lay fertile eggs without mating. The eggs are laid on or in the female's bag, except by those few species with winged females.

As soon as it hatches, the young larva begins to make its own case, starting with a silken tube. It gradually adds plant fragments or other debris to the outside and ends up with a remarkably well camouflaged home. Each species works to its own design and uses characteristic materials, so it is often possible to recognise a species just from its case. When active, the front end of the larva protrudes from the case and clings to the food-plant with its thoracic legs. The rear end of the case is normally closed with silk, although this is opened periodically to eject droppings. When moulting and hibernating, the larva withdraws right into its bag and fixes the front end to a suitable surface with silk. It does the same thing when ready to pupate, often choosing a rock or a tree trunk at this time. Before turning into the chrysalis, however, the larva turns round in its case and faces the rear end ready for emergence. In many species the pupa protrudes from the case before the adult emerges.

The bagworms are related to the clothes moths and, more distantly, to the burnets. There are more than 1,000 known species, of which some 200 live in Europe. Eighteen species occur in the British Isles.

Melasaina ciliaris. ♂ and ♀ fully winged, with fw rather narrow: HAB montane scrub and grassland. ALT upland. FLIGHT 7–8, usually 10–15.00hrs. FP low-growing plants and dead leaves. EGG 7–9: solitary on vegetation. LARVA 1–12: 2 or 3-year life cycle: in cylindrical case up to 40mm long and covered with sand grains. PUPA 4–8: pupates in larval case immediately after larval hibernation. WINTER larva in ground or attached to rocks (twice or three times). STATUS ?

▲*Epichnopterix plumella*. Antennae with very long 'feathers': only 8 veins arise from fw cell, which also has an accessory cell at its outer end: wings are clothed with fine, hair-like scales which fade from black to brown after death. HAB moors and grassland: local. ALT ? FLIGHT 4–6: usually from about 10–15.00hrs. FP grasses. EGG 5–7: inside pupal skin. LARVA 7–4: reddish with a black head (like all *Epichnopterix* spp.), in case coated with grass blades. PUPA 4–5: in case attached to grass stem. WINTER larva. STATUS ?

Epichnopterix sieboldi. Like *E. plumella* but redder and less densely scaled. HAB montane pastures. ALT ? FLIGHT 3–5: from about 10–15.00hrs. FP ? EGG ? LARVA like that of *E. plumella* but in a somewhat shorter sac. PUPA ? WINTER ? STATUS ?

▲*Whittleia retiella*. Easily identified by wing pattern, produced by hair-like scales. HAB saltmarshes: local. FLIGHT 5–6. FP common salt-marsh grass and other coastal grasses. EGG 5–7: in pupal skin. LARVA 8–4: in case decorated with grass fragments, some much longer than the tube itself. PUPA 4–6: in case fixed to grass: ♂ case often right at base, but ♀ case usually higher. WINTER larva. STATUS ?

Oreopsyche plumifera. Very like *O. angustella* but with matt wings. HAB grassy places, generally in hilly areas. ALT <1500. FLIGHT 2–7, following closely the melting of the snow: always in sunshine. FP various low-growing plants, especially grasses. EGG ? LARVA in case of dried plant fragments. PUPA ? WINTER pupa. STATUS Common.

Oreopsyche angustella. Hw very narrow: fw glossy. HAB heaths, moors, and open woodland: very local. FLIGHT 6–7: mainly from 10–15.00 hrs. FP heather. EGG 6–8. LARVA 7–5: sac short and slender. PUPA 5–7. WINTER larva. STATUS ?

Oreopsyche albida. Conspicuous white hair on wings and body readily identify: HAB grassy and scrubby places. FLIGHT 4–5: mainly from 10–15.00 hrs. FP low-growing grasses and occasionally on shrubs, including gorse. EGG ? LARVA ?: case clothed with moss, but gorse fragments are used in SW. PUPA ? WINTER ? VAR Some populations have darker hair on the body and are sometimes as separate species. STATUS ?

▲*Acanthopsyche atra*. Front tibia has a very long spur: veins 1a and 1b of fw are fused near base, but then separate again and reach the margin independently: body clothed with long black hair. HAB heaths and moors: local, especially in B. ALT sl–2000. FLIGHT 5–6: mainly in afternoon, but some populations also fly in the evening. FP grasses and sallows. EGG 5–7: in pupal skin. LARVA 1–12: individuals mature in 1 or 2 years: in cylindrical case clothed with grass or heather fragments. PUPA 4–6. WINTER larva (sometimes twice). STATUS ?

Leptopterix plumistrella. Wings dark brown and hardly translucent. HAB montane slopes. ALT >2000. FLIGHT 7. mainly from 10–15.00hrs. FP ? EGG ? LARVA ?: sac coated with sand grains and, at the rear, with grass fragments: sometimes entirely coated with grass. PUPA ? WINTER ? STATUS ?

Canephora unicolor. Broad and very dark brown wings distinguish this from most other species: fw strongly pointed. HAB warm, sandy places. ALT sl–2000. FLIGHT 6–8: afternoon or evening, according to locality. FP grasses, broom, and possibly other legumes. EGG 6–8. LARVA 7–5: deep yellow with brown head and thorax: ♂ case is decorated with relatively broad leaf fragments, while ♀ case is covered with more slender fragments. PUPA 5–6. WINTER larva. NOTES The largest European bagworm. STATUS Locally common.

FAMILY TINEIDAE

Euplocamus anthracinalis. Pattern is unmistakable. HAB light deciduous forest, especially in damp places. ALT ? FLIGHT 5–8 in one prolonged emergence. FP bracket fungi growing on various trees. EGG 5–9. LARVA 1–12. PUPA 4–7. WINTER larva. STATUS ?

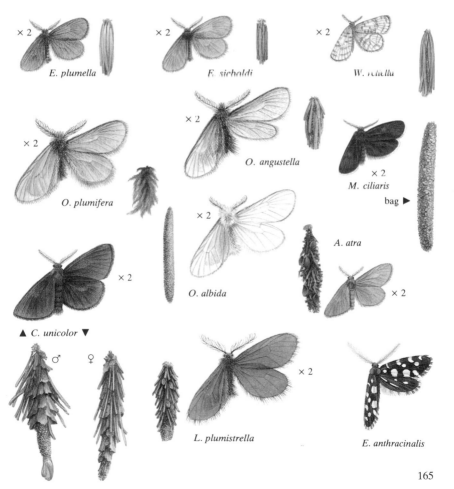

E. plumella

E. sicholdi

W. rebella

×2 *O. plumifera*

×2 *O. angustella*

×2 *M. ciliaris*

bag ▶

×2 *O. albida*

A. atra

▲ *C. unicolor* ▼

♂ ♀

L. plumistrella ×2

E. anthracinalis

165

FAMILY SESIIDAE – THE CLEARWINGS

This is a large family in which, after the first flight, the wings lose nearly all their scales and become largely transparent. The forewings are very narrow and are linked to the hind wings by two independent systems. A frenulum is present (see p. 11), but the wings are also connected by a unique system of folds. The hind margin of the forewing turns down and hooks over an upward fold on the front margin of the hind wing. Curved, interlocking spines hold the joint firmly together and are reminiscent of the minute hooks that link the wings of bees and wasps – which the clearwings mimic very effectively in both appearance and behaviour (see p. 278). The antennae are often dilated towards the tip, although not really clubbed, and those of the males are usually somewhat feathery or toothed. A tongue is present in some species and absent in others. The abdomen, commonly banded with yellow or orange, ends in a conspicuous tuft of scales.

The moths are of small to medium size – up to about 50mm across the wings in the European species – and they fly rapidly in the sunshine, often with a clear hum or buzzing sound. Much time is spent resting on the vegetation, with the wings partly open or folded neatly along the sides of the body like those of the wasps.

The eggs are dark and flat and are commonly laid in bark crevices. The caterpillars are white or cream, usually with a tough brownish head, and they feed in the wood of trees and shrubs and in the roots of certain herbaceous plants. They often indicate their presence by throwing out large quantities of frass and wood fragments. Pupation takes place in the larval tunnel after the caterpillar has sealed the opening. The spiky pupa then breaks through the wafer-thin covering before the adult emerges. Empty pupal skins can often be seen protruding from the food-plants.

There are about 1,000 known species, with 15 in the British Isles, but only six in Ireland.

Zenodoxus tineiformis. Wings very narrow, fully scaled and dusted with yellow on dark background: rear of head yellow: tibiae with tufts of yellow hair: proboscis absent. HAB dry scrubby areas. ALT ? FLIGHT 4–8. FP *Echium* spp. EGG ? LARVA in stems of fp. PUPA ? WINTER ? STATUS ?

Pennisetia hylaeiformis. Fw heavily scaled, with posterior transparent area much nearer the wing base than the anterior transparent area: ♂ has 4 broad yellow bands on abdomen. HAB woods and gardens. ALT ? FLIGHT 6–9. FP raspberry, both wild and cultivated, and less commonly bramble. EGG 6–9: laid or dropped freely on ground near fp. LARVA 8–5: in roots of fp. PUPA 5–8: naked in lower part of stem of fp. WINTER larva. STATUS ?

Sesia melanocephala. Blue-black body with yellow borders to tegulae: proboscis much reduced. HAB damp woodland: very local. ALT ? FLIGHT 6–7. FP aspen, especially old trees. EGG 6–9: in bark crevices on or near dead branches. LARVA 1–12: 2-year life cycle: bone-coloured with a yellow last segment and usually feeding in dead branches. PUPA 4–7: naked: sometimes in dead small branches but more often in neighbouring part of trunk. WINTER larva (twice). STATUS ?

▲**HORNET MOTH** *Sesia apiformis.* Head and front half of tegulae yellow: patches of brown scales often in all 3 clear areas of fw: legs brown. HAB damp woodland. ALT ? FLIGHT 6–8: often rests on poplar trunks in morning: egg-laying ♀♀ often fly around the trees in afternoon. FP poplars, especially black poplar. EGG 6–8: dark red and very small: solitary or in small batches in bark crevices. LARVA 1–12: 2 or 3 year life cycle: in roots and trunks of poplars. PUPA 4–7: in cocoon close to surface. WINTER larva (at least twice): fully grown larva hibernates in cocoon before pupating in spring. VAR wing membrane occasionally coffee coloured in Alps (ab. *brunnea*). Abdomen sometimes completely black in eastern areas (ab. *tenebrioniformis*). NOTES A remarkable mimic of the hornet. Emergence holes of adult *c*. 8mm in diameter. STATUS Locally common. SEE ALSO p. 278, 281.

▲**LUNAR HORNET MOTH** *Sesia bembeciformis.* Head black with a yellow collar: prominent orange hairs on hind leg. HAB damp woodland. ALT ? FLIGHT 6–8: often sits on willow trunks in morning. FP willows. EGG 6–8: reddish brown and laid in loose batches on bark. LARVA 1–12: 2-year life cycle: 1st year is spent just under the bark and position is marked by ejection of coarse frass. PUPA 5–6: pale brown and in a cocoon re-inforced with wood chips. WINTER larva (twice). NOTES Adult emergence holes *c*. 8mm in diameter. STATUS Generally common.

▲**DUSKY CLEARWING** *Paranthrene tabaniformis*. Fw almost completely clothed with brown scales, leaving just 2 small 'windows' at base: head black: 3 yellow abdominal bands in ♀, 4 in ♂. HAB damp woodland. ALT ? FLIGHT 5–7: most often seen resting on foliage. FP poplars, willows, and also sea buckthorn. EGG 5–7: on leaf bases or in bark crevices. LARVA 1–12: 2-year life cycle: young larva lives externally in silken web, but tunnels into wood before winter. PUPA 4–6: pale brown: naked in chamber in outer part of larval tunnel. WINTER larva (twice). VAR *P. t. rhingiaeformis*, which replaces nominate ssp. in S, has paler fw and yellow or brown antennae: abdomen has much more yellow. It flies 5–9. Sometimes regarded as a separate species. NOTES Tunnelling induces formation of pear-shaped galls on twigs in spring. A pest of poplar plantations in parts of S & C. STATUS Locally common.

▲**CURRANT CLEARWING** *Synanthedon tipuliformis*. Head black with a ring of yellow at the rear: inner margin of tegula yellow: outer margin of fw dusted yellow: ♀ abdomen has only 3 yellow rings. HAB woods and gardens, wherever there are currants. ALT ? FLIGHT 5–7: most obvious in afternoon, basking on leaves of fp. FP black and red currants. EGG 5–7: dark brown: solitary in leaf axils or in cut ends of twigs. LARVA 7–4: in large and small branches. PUPA 4–6. WINTER larva. NOTES As in all members of the genus, the posterior transparent area of fw clearly reaches the transverse black spot. STATUS Locally common. SEE ALSO p. 252.

▲**SALLOW CLEARWING** *Synanthedon flaviventris*. Very like Currant Clearwing but head has no yellow at rear and tegulae are entirely black: segments 2–6 of abdomen yellow underneath. HAB damp woodland. ALT ? FLIGHT 6–7. FP willows. EGG 6–8: solitary in leaf axils on fine twigs. LARVA 1–12: 2-year life cycle: causes pear-shaped swellings on twigs in 2nd year. PUPA 4–6: in chamber just above larval swelling. WINTER larva (twice). STATUS Locally common.

Z. tineiformis

♀

P. hylaeiformis

S. melanocephala

Hornet Moth

Lunar Hornet Moth

rhingiaeformis ▶

Dusky Clearwing

Currant Clearwing

Sallow
Clearwing

167

Synanthedon cephiformis. Like Currant Clearwing but with yellow hairs on metathorax: anal brush all yellow in ♀, largely black in ♂ but always with some yellow in central area. HAB coniferous woodland. ALT ? FLIGHT 5–8. FP fir, spruce, and larch. EGG 6–9. LARVA 1–12: 2-year life cycle: gregarious in galls caused by fungal infection of twigs. PUPA 4–6: in larval tunnel just under bark. WINTER larva (twice). STATUS ?

Synanthedon conopiformis. Like Currant Clearwing but with rich brown patches at tip of fw and yellow patch on rear of thorax: anal tuft blue-black in both sexes. HAB open oak woods and parkland: needs plenty of sunshine. ALT ? FLIGHT 5–9. FP oak. EGG 5–9. LARVA 1–12: 2-year life cycle: under bark of diseased twigs and also in cankerous swellings, making remarkably large tunnels for its size. PUPA 4–7: in a cocoon decorated with frass and wood shavings. WINTER larva (twice). STATUS ?

▲**YELLOW-LEGGED CLEARWING** *Synanthedon vespiformis.* Mid and hind tibiae bright yellow with a broad black band: transverse bar of fw largely orange: tegulae with a thin yellow inner border: anal tuft black on top in ♂ and largely yellow in ♀. HAB mixed oak woods, in sunny clearings. ALT ? FLIGHT 5–8. FP oak: occasionally also beech, birch, and sweet chestnut. EGG 5–8: in bark crevices on stumps and lower parts of trunks. LARVA 7–5 in most places but 1–12, with 2-year life cycle, in N: almost always in stumps. PUPA 4–8: in hard brown cocoon just under bark. WINTER larva (twice in N). VAR front and outer margin of fw occasionally deep orange (ab. *rufomarginata*). STATUS Quite common where oaks have been felled.

▲**ORANGE-TAILED CLEARWING** *Synanthedon andrenaeformis.* Generally identified by deep orange-yellow rear half of anal tuft: head and antennae completely black: ♂ abdomen strongly compressed from side to side towards the rear. HAB sunny woodland edges and scrub-covered hillsides. ALT ? FLIGHT 5–7. FP wayfaring tree and, less often, guelder rose. EGG 5–7: in bark crevices. LARVA 1–12: 2 or 3-year life cycle: in stems up to 2.5cm thick. PUPA 4–6: near bottom of larval tunnel, which bends sharply towards surface. WINTER larva (2–3 times). NOTES Adults rarely seen, for they prefer to rest high in the trees. STATUS Generally common.

▲**RED-TIPPED CLEARWING** *Synanthedon formicaeformis.* Red-tipped fw and red abdominal belt. HAB damp woods, fens, and other marshy places. ALT ? FLIGHT 5–8: fond of raspberry flowers. FP willows, especially osier. EGG 5–8: solitary or in small groups in bark crevices. LARVA 7–5: in stumps and trunks, usually close to bark. PUPA 4–7: in silk-lined chamber. WINTER larva. NOTES May cause galls when tunnelling in young twigs, especially on goat willow. STATUS Not uncommon at flowers in suitable habitats.

▲**WHITE-BARRED CLEARWING** *Synanthedon spheciformis.* A single pale abdominal belt: head completely black, but antennae have white band near tip: anal tuft all black on top. HAB heaths, riversides, and damp woods. ALT ? FLIGHT 5–7. FP alder and birch. EGG 5–8: in ground at base of fp. LARVA 1–12: 2-year life cycle (sometimes possibly 3 years): rather pink: in stumps, trunks, and roots. PUPA 4–6: in chamber lined with silk and chewed wood. WINTER larva (2-3 times): often in roots at this time. NOTES 5mm emergence holes usually near base of tree. STATUS Locally common.

▲**WELSH CLEARWING** *Synanthedon scoliaeformis.* Like White-barred Clearwing but abdomen has 2 pale belts and anal tuft is brown or orange: ♀ is much larger than ♂, with a brighter anal tuft and with antennae distinctly yellow towards the tip. HAB heaths and birchwoods: very local. ALT ? FLIGHT 6–7. FP birch. EGG 6–8: solitary in bark crevices and old emergence holes low down on the trunks. LARVA 1–12: 2- or 3-year life cycle: tunnels just below bark. PUPA 5–6: in rough cylindrical cocoon made of silk and wood shavings. WINTER larva (2 or 3 times). NOTES Named because first British specimens were found in Wales, but it has not been found there for many years. STATUS ?

▲**RED-BELTED CLEARWING** *Synanthedon myopaeformis*. Red abdominal belt, black legs and pure black wing margins: a bright orange streak on side of thorax, just under wing base. HAB woods and orchards: also in gardens with apple trees. ALT ? FLIGHT 5–8. FP apple and some other rosaceous trees, usually old plants. EGG 5–7: olive green: in bark crevices. LARVA 7–5: tunnels under loose bark and especially in cankerous tissues of older trees. PUPA 4–7: in cylindrical cocoon reinforced with bark fragments: usually just under bark. WINTER larva. STATUS Quite common around old apple trees, flying rapidly in sunshine. SEE ALSO p. 252.

▲**LARGE RED-BELTED CLEARWING** *Synanthedon culiciformis*. Like Red-belted Clearwing but generally a little larger and with a prominent red suffusion at base of fw: tarsi largely yellow. HAB heaths and birch woods with plenty of sunshine. ALT ? FLIGHT 5–7. FP birch and occasionally alder. EGG 6–8: pale brown: in cracks and crevices, more often in stumps than in complete trees. LARVA 6–4, possibly 1–12 in N with 2- year life cycle: most common in stumps. PUPA 4–6: in cocoon coated with wood shavings. WINTER hibernating larva. VAR red areas sometimes replaced by yellow. NOTES A 1-year life cycle is normal in most areas, but there may be a 2-year cycle in at least some parts of N. STATUS One of the commonest clearwings in N.

Synanthedon stomoxiformis. Like Large Red-belted Clearwing but fw not red at base: inner border of tegulae red: abdominal belt more extensive, running along sides to some extent. HAB woodland margins and scrub. ALT ? FLIGHT 5–8. FP medlar. EGG ? LARVA ?: in trunk of fp. PUPA ? WINTER ? STATUS ?

S. cephiformis

S. conopiformis

Yellow-legged Clearwing ♂ ♀

Orange-tailed Clearwing

Red-tipped Clearwing

White-barred Clearwing

Welsh Clearwing

Red-belted Clearwing

Large Red-belted Clearwing

S. stomoxiformis

169

▲**SIX-BELTED CLEARWING** *Bembecia scopigera*. Like Yellow-legged Clearwing but posterior transparent area of fw is largely obliterated and does not usually reach the transverse spot: a clear orange streak along hind edge of fw: abdomen has 6 yellow bands in ♂ but only 5 in ♀. HAB rough grassy places on chalk and limestone. ALT ? FLIGHT 6–9. FP bird's-foot trefoil, kidney vetch, and other legumes. EGG 6–8: black: solitary or in small clusters, usually on leaves. LARVA 1–12: sometimes completely enclosed in roots but more often in a deep groove and covered with frass and chewed root fragments. PUPA 5–7: in silk-lined larval tunnel or in a specially constructed silken tube running from root to surface. WINTER larva. STATUS ?

▲**FIERY CLEARWING** *Bembecia chrysidiformis*. Brilliant orange-red scales along rear edge of fw and also around outer transparent area: posterior transparent area largely obliterated: tibiae bright orange. HAB rough hillsides and disturbed areas, especially sea cliffs and quarries: very local. ALT ? FLIGHT 6–7. FP docks and sorrels. EGG 6–7: black with a violet sheen. LARVA 1–12: 2-year life cycle: in stout roots. PUPA 5–6: low down in stem or in a tough silken tube on the ground. WINTER larva (twice). STATUS E; B, where it occurs only on a few cliffs in SE England.

Bembecia megillaeformis. Like Six-belted Clearwing but with fewer yellow belts – none on segments 3 & 5: anal tuft all black: antennae uniformly black on upper surface in both sexes. HAB sunny slopes. ALT ? FLIGHT 6–8. FP dyer's greenweed. EGG 6–8. LARVA ?: in roots of fp. PUPA ? WINTER ? STATUS ?

▲**THRIFT CLEARWING** *Bembecia muscaeformis*. No trace of red on wings: posterior transparent area of fw obliterated, leaving just a single triangular clear patch in basal half of wing: abdomen with indistinct white bands: ♀ antenna has a sub-apical white patch. HAB rocky coasts: also some upland regions inland on the continent. ALT ? FLIGHT 6–8. FP thrift. EGG 6–8: black: in soil near roots. LARVA 7–5: in roots at first, but later concealed in clumps of fp, often in silken tube. PUPA 5–7: in silken tube in fp clump. WINTER larva. NOTES Adults fond of thyme flowers. STATUS ?

Chaemaesphecia empiformis. A rather variable species: top of head orange: thorax has a yellow stripe in the centre and tegulae have yellow inner borders: fw bluish black with yellow streaks in outer region. HAB rough sunny slopes. ALT ? FLIGHT 5–9: occasionally nocturnal. FP spurges: possibly also rosebay willowherb. EGG 5–9: rich brown and glued lightly to base of fp. LARVA 1–12: in roots and rhizomes. PUPA 4–7: in silk-lined cell in roots or rhizomes. WINTER larva. STATUS The commonest member of this large root-feeding genus, which differs from *Synanthedon* in having veins 10 & 11 of fw converging towards the margin (parallel in *Synanthedon*).

Chamaesphecia colpiformis. A rather pale species: tibiae pale, with dark ring just before apex: tarsi pale brown. HAB dry grassland. ALT ? FLIGHT 6–8. FP ? EGG ? LARVA ? PUPA ? WINTER ? STATUS ?

Chamaesphecia annellata. Prominent pale yellow flashes on tegulae: a whitish ring around the eye: 4 yellowish abdominal rings in ♂, but only 3 in ♀: anal tuft with just 2 pale yellow stripes in ♀. HAB rough grassland and waste places. ALT ? FLIGHT 6–7. FP horehound. EGG 7–9. LARVA 1–12: in roots. PUPA 4–7. WINTER larva. STATUS ?

Chamaesphecia doryliformis. Rear of head, inner edge of tegulae, mid and hind tibiae are all yellow in ♂ and red in ♀: ♀ larger than ♂. HAB flowery grassland. ALT ? FLIGHT 5–7. FP sorrel. EGG 5–8. LARVA 8–4: in roots. PUPA 4–6. WINTER larva. NOTES Adults fond of feeding at thistles. ♀♀ rarely seen.

Chamaesphecia chalcidiformis. Mid and hind tibiae with vermillion hair tufts: no obvious pale belts on abdomen, although there are patches of greenish scales. ALT ? FLIGHT 5–8. FP sage and other labiates. EGG 6–8. LARVA 1–12: in roots of fp. PUPA 4–7. WINTER larva. VAR *C. c. schmidtiiformis* from SE has brilliant red scales on wings. NOTES Smallest of the red-winged spp. STATUS ?

FAMILY COCHYLIDAE – This family, with about 50 British species, is very closely related to the Tortricidae (p. 172) and can be distinguished with certainty only by looking at the forewing venation.

▲*Aethes tesserana*. Yellow and brown spotting is unlike that of any other day-flying species. HAB rough grassland and waste places, especially on limestone. ALT ? FLIGHT 5–8. FP oxtongues and other composites. EGG 6–9. LARVA 9–4: in roots of fp. PUPA 5–6: in larval chamber. WINTER larva. VAR spotting varies and fw is sometimes brown with just yellow spots on front margin. STATUS ?

▲*Aethes rutilana*. Brilliant fw pattern is unmistakable. HAB juniper scrub on chalk and limestone: local. ALT ? FLIGHT 7–8: usually very low over ground. FP juniper. EGG 6–7: solitary on leaf stalks. PUPA 9–6: web of silk and frass reveals position. PUPA 7: in flimsy cocoon amongst leaves. WINTER larva in silken tube. STATUS declining in many places, especially in B, through loss of juniper.

▲*Cochylis roseana*. Fw rose-pink and yellow, with a dark median band in rear half only: marginal cilia with a dark line running through them. HAB rough grassland and waste places. ALT ? FLIGHT 5–8: mainly after noon. FP teasel: occasionally daisies (*Aster* spp.) on continent. EGG 7–8: solitary in seed heads of fp. LARVA 8–5: chews through seeds, making silken tunnel as it goes. PUPA 5–7: in tough cocoon in seed heads. WINTER larva. STATUS ?

Six-belted Clearwing

Fiery Clearwing

B. megillaeformis

Thrift Clearwing

C. empiformis

C. colpiformis

C. annellata

C. doryliformis

C. chalcidiformis

A. tesserana × 2½

A. rutilana × 2½

C. roseana × 2½

171

FAMILY TORTRICIDAE   This is a large family of rather small moths with more or less rectangular forewings. The wings are held roofwise over the body at rest, giving the moths a triangular appearance when seen from above. Greys and browns are the main colours and the moths are often very well camouflaged. Many resemble birds' droppings and others are hard to distinguish from leaf fragments. Most are nocturnal, although many, including the abundant Greek Oak Tortrix, are easily disturbed by day. The eggs are rather flat, and scale-like, and laid singly or in small groups. The larvae are slender and have few hairs and many live as leaf-miners or in rolled-up leaves, from which they often fall on silken threads when disturbed. Pupation takes place in a cocoon formed at the larval feeding site and the pupa protrudes from the cocoon before the adult emerges. There are about 500 European species, just over 300 of them British.

▲*Archips podana*. One of several rather similar moths, but generally identified by the orange outer half of hw – especially prominent in ♀: ♂ generally smaller and with less pointed wings. HAB woods, orchards, gardens, and other places with trees and bushes. ALT ? FLIGHT 6–8: night and day. FP polyphagous on trees and shrubs. EGG 6–8: in batches of 50–100 on leaves: well camouflaged under a waxy green coating. LARVA 7–5: often makes shelter by spinning leaves or flowers together: may also nibble fruit in autumn: attacks buds in spring. PUPA 6–7: in larval shelter. WINTER larva in silken shelter on bark. VAR depth of brown colour of fw varies. NOTES One of several moths resembling leaf fragments when resting. STATUS Generally common.

▲*Cacaecimorpha pronubana*. Bright orange hw distinguishes this from several similar moths: ♂ has less pointed fw and a narrow black margin to hw. HAB scrubby places, including hedgerows and gardens. ALT ? FLIGHT 5–11 in 2 overlapping broods. FP polyphagous, mainly on shrubs. EGG 5–10: in small batches on uppersides of leaves. LARVA all year. PUPA 4–10: in folded leaves. WINTER larva in various stages. STATUS ?

▲*Paraclepsis cinctana*. Fw pattern is characteristic. HAB dry grassland, including coastal cliffs and dunes. ALT ? FLIGHT 6–7. FP various legumes, both shrubs and herbs. EGG 7–8. LARVA 9–6: in silken tube on fp. PUPA 5–7. WINTER larva. NOTES Appears very white on the wing: resembles bird dropping when resting on grass. STATUS ?

▲*Philedone gerningana*. Male fw unmistakable, with a very straight boundary between the yellow and brown: ♀ has less contrast, but readily identified by the strong brown diagonal bar. HAB heaths and grasslands, mainly in uplands. ALT ? FLIGHT 6–9. FP various low-growing plants. EGG 6–4. LARVA 4–6: in leaves or flower heads bound up with silk. PUPA 6–8: in larval home. WINTER egg. STATUS ?

▲*Philedonides lunana*. Strong diagonal brown bar, with grey or white on each side, characterises ♂ fw: ♀ is like *Paraclepsis cinctana* but has an additional brown bar on fw and hw is much greyer: ♂ antennae feathered and have tufts of long cilia. HAB heaths and moors, generally in uplands but also on some coastal sandhills: local. ALT ? FLIGHT 3–5. FP heathers and various other low-growing shrubs and herbs: sometimes on young conifers. EGG 3–5: in small batches on leaves and covered with a sticky yellow secretion. LARVA 5–6: in folded leaves and flower heads. PUPA 6–3: spun up in leaves and debris. WINTER pupa. NOTES Generally only ♂♂ diurnal. STATUS ?

▲*Ditula angustoriana*. Mottled, carpet-like pattern of fw together with rounded wing-tips and dark brown hw are characteristic. HAB woodland margins, hedgerows, orchards, and gardens. ALT ? FLIGHT 6–7: night and day. FP a wide range of trees. EGG 6–8: yellow and batched on leaves. LARVA 8–5: on leaves and fruit in autumn and on buds and flowers in spring. PUPA 5–6: spun amongst leaves or debris. WINTER larva: in silken case fixed to twigs. NOTES Mostly ♂♂ fly by day. STATUS Very common in both town and country.

▲*Pseudargyrotoza conwagana.* Prominent yellow blotch on rear edge of fw, combined with a general dusting of shiny yellow scales. HAB woods and scrub: sometimes in gardens. ALT ? FLIGHT 5–7. FP ash, privet, and lilac. EGG 6–8. LARVA 8–10: in fruit and seeds of fp. PUPA 10–5: in white cocoons in leaf litter. WINTER pupa. STATUS Generally common wherever food-plants grow.

▲*Tortricodes alternella* Pale band on fw generally well marked, with sharply angled inner margin and oblique, wavy outer margin. HAB open woodland. ALT ? FLIGHT 2–4: one of the earliest moths to appear in spring: ♀♀ do not fly readily. FP oak, hazel, hawthorn, and various other trees. EGG 3–5. LARVA 4–7: in folded leaf or leaves. PUPA 7–3: in tough cocoon in leaf litter. WINTER pupa. STATUS ?

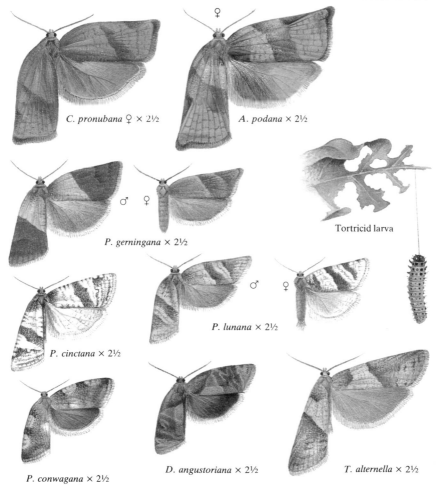

C. pronubana ♀ × 2½

♀

A. podana × 2½

♂ ♀

P. gerningana × 2½

Tortricid larva

P. cinctana × 2½

♂ ♀

P. lunana × 2½

P. conwagana × 2½

D. angustoriana × 2½

T. alternella × 2½

▲*Olethreutes cespitana*. One of several fairly similar species, but differing from most in the very strong, blunt tooth projecting from outer margin of the dark median band of fw – although this is not always as clear as illustrated. HAB rough, dry grassland, including coastal dunes: local. ALT ? FLIGHT 6–8. FP many low-growing plants, including thrift and wild thyme. EGG 6–8. LARVA 7–5: in silken tube on fp. PUPA 5–6. WINTER larva. STATUS ?

▲*Olethreutes arcuella*. Fw pattern, with eye-like marking, is unique. HAB deciduous woods and heathland, especially with oaks. ALT ? FLIGHT 5–8. FP dead and decaying leaves of all kinds. EGG 6–8. LARVA 8–4: in leaf litter. PUPA 4–5: in leaf litter. WINTER larva. VAR fw ground colour ranges from golden to deep orange. NOTES One of few moths whose larvae feed on dead leaves instead of living ones. STATUS Generally common, especially in warmer habitats.

▲*Lobesia littoralis*. Fw very narrow, with a dark quadrangular blotch near base of rear margin: usually 3 prominent black dots on outer part of front edge. HAB coastal cliffs and saltmarshes: also in some inland gardens where fp is grown. ALT Generally near sl. FLIGHT 6–10: 2 broods. FP thrift. EGG 6–4. LARVA 4–8: sometimes amongst leaves, but generally in flowers and seed heads. PUPA 5–9: in sturdy cocoon on fp. WINTER egg. VAR reduction of black on fw is quite common: pale areas are very white in N. STATUS ?

▲*Epinotia nemorivaga*. Like *Olethreutes cespitana*, but smaller and without the prominent tooth on median band. HAB upland moors: also in coastal areas in N: local. ALT ? FLIGHT 6–7. FP bearberry. EGG 6–9. LARVA 9–5: excavating deep channels in leaves, the latter being spun into clusters in spring. PUPA 5–6: generally in an excavated leaf. WINTER larva. STATUS ?

▲*Epiblema farfarae*. White blotch on rear of fw usually without any dark markings: apical third of fw distinctly paler than the rest. HAB rough grassland and waste places. ALT ? FLIGHT 5–6. FP coltsfoot, winter heliotrope, and burdock. EGG 5–7. LARVA 7–4: deep pink or red: tunnelling in roots at first but moving up into flower stems in spring. PUPA 4–5: in silken shelter amongst roots. WINTER larva. STATUS Locally common.

▲*Cydia compositella*. White patch at rear of fw composed of 4 parallel stripes: ♀ hw brownish grey. HAB grassy places with clovers. ALT ? FLIGHT 5–8: 2 broods. FP clovers and, less often other legumes. EGG 5–9: solitary on leaves. LARVA 6–4: 1st brood feed in stems, 2nd brood on terminal leaves, flowers, and seed pods: becomes deep red when mature. PUPA 4–7: in pale cocoon in leaf litter. WINTER larva. STATUS Generally common.

▲*Cydia lunulana*. Curved white mark on fw not dilated at tip (see below): ♀ darker, with no white on hw. HAB rough grassland and hedgerows, mainly in uplands. ALT ? FLIGHT 5–6. FP peas and vetches, including cultivated forms. EGG 5–6. LARVA 6–4: deep yellow: tunnels in leaves and stems at first and then moves into pods. PUPA 3–5: in tough cocoon in leaf litter. WINTER fully grown larva in cocoon prepared for pupation. NOTES *C. orobana* is very similar but has broader wings and white patch is slightly dilated at tip and flies 6–7. STATUS ?

▲**PEA MOTH** *Cydia nigricana*. Fw has fine stripes along front edge: hw distinctly edged with white. HAB fields and gardens, wherever wild or cultivated peas grow. ALT ? FLIGHT 5–9: 1 or 2 overlapping broods. FP wild and cultivated peas and vetches. EGG 5–9: singly or in small groups on leaves and young pods. LARVA 6–4: feeds on seeds in pods, moving from seed to seed and producing much frass. PUPA 5–7: in tough cocoon in soil. WINTER fully grown larva in cocoon deep in soil. STATUS A common and often serious pest of field and garden peas.

▲*Cydia aurana*. Fw pattern is unique. HAB light woodland, hedges, gardens, and waste land. ALT ? FLIGHT 6–7: very fast. FP hogweed. EGG 6–7. LARVA 7–5: feeds on fruits which it spins together with silk. PUPA 5–6: in cocoon in soil. WINTER fully grown larva in cocoon prepared for hibernation. STATUS ?

▲*Dichrorampha alpinana*. Golden blotch almost diamond-shaped (distinctly elongate in the closely related *D. flavidorsana*). HAB rough grassland and waste land. ALT ? FLIGHT 6–8. FP oxeye daisy. EGG 6–8. LARVA 8–6: in roots of fp. PUPA 5–7: in cocoon fixed to roots. WINTER larva. STATUS Locally common.

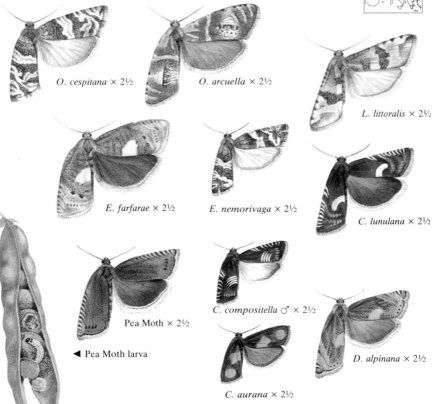

O. cespitana × 2½

O. arcuella × 2½

L. littoralis × 2½

E. farfarae × 2½

E. nemorivaga × 2½

C. lunulana × 2½

Pea Moth × 2½

C. compositella ♂ × 2½

◀ Pea Moth larva

C. aurana × 2½

D. alpinana × 2½

FAMILY PYRALIDAE – This is a huge family of small to medium-sized moths with relatively long, thin legs. Most are nocturnal or crepuscular, and when at rest their wings may be held well out to the sides or else swept back around the body. The front of the abdomen bears an 'ear-drum' on each side – not too difficult to see in a captured specimen – and this will distinguish the pyralids from most other small moths. Some of the larger species may be confused with the geometer moths (see p. 180), which also have abdominal ear-drums, but the hind wing venation is quite different. The larvae are slender, with scattered bristles and they often live in rolled-up leaves or silken tubes. They can wriggle backwards and forwards at high speed when disturbed. Several species are serious pests of growing and stored food crops. Most species pupate in a flimsy cocoon, but the pupa does not protrude from the cocoon when it is time for the adult to emerge.

Over 300 species live in Europe. About 200 are found regularly in the British Isles, but about 60 of these are aliens living in warehouses and other buildings. The best known pyralids are probably the little grass moths – nocturnal species that rest on grass stems by day but are easily disturbed by anyone walking through the grass.

▲*Pyrausta sanguinalis*. Fw coloration is unique among day-flying pyralids. HAB dry grassy places, including coastal dunes: very local. ALT ? FLIGHT 5–8: 2 broods: night and day. FP wild thyme and other labiates. EGG 5–9. LARVA 6–4: in silken shelter amongst flowers at first, but moving to leaf litter when fully grown. PUPA 4–8: in tough cocoon on or under ground. WINTER fully-grown larva in tough cocoon, ready for pupation. VAR relative amounts of red and yellow vary. STATUS Locally common.

▲*Pyrausta cingulata*. Strong, almost straight white band on each wing distinguishes this from most other moths. HAB limestone grassland and coastal sandhills: local. ALT ? FLIGHT 5–8: 2 broods: occasionally at night. FP wild thyme and some other labiates, including *Salvia* spp. EGG 5–8. LARVA 6–4: in silken shelter on underside of lower leaves. PUPA 4–8: in papery cocoon amongst leaf litter. WINTER fully grown larva in cocoon prepared for pupation. STATUS ?

▲*Pyrausta nigrata*. Like *P. cingulata* but with more angled white lines and with additional white spots. HAB rough grassland. ALT ? FLIGHT 5–10: 2 broods. FP wild thyme, marjoram, and other labiates: also woodruff. EGG 5–10. LARVA 6–4: in flimsy web under lower leaves, usually making translucent windows and complete holes in the leaves. PUPA 4–9: in coarse silk cocoon at base of fp. WINTER fully-grown larva. STATUS ?

▲*Pyrausta aurata*. Dark patch at base of hw bears no spots. HAB rough grassland, especially on limestone and often near water. ALT ? FLIGHT 4–9: 2 overlapping broods: night and day. FP marjoram, mint, and other labiates. EGG 4–9. LARVA 5–3: feeds under leaves at first and then in flimsy web among flowers. PUPA 4–8: in cocoon among flowers. WINTER fully grown larva in cocoon among flowers. VAR amount of gold on fw varies, often reduced to just one small spot and making the moth like Small Yellow Underwing (p. 196). STATUS Locally common.

▲*Pyrausta purpuralis*. Like *P. aurata* but generally with more gold on fw and always with a white spot in dark basal area of hw. HAB grassland and scrub, especially on limestone. ALT ? FLIGHT 4–9: 2 broods: night and day. FP thyme and other labiates. EGG 4–9. LARVA 5–3: between leaves spun together with silk. PUPA 3–8. WINTER fully grown larva? VAR 2nd brood insects tend to be larger and brighter. NOTES *P. ostrinalis*, often confused with *purpuralis*, has paler yellow spots on fw and *unh* has 2 pale bands instead of 1. STATUS Generally common.

▲*Anania funebris*. Yellowish hairs on sides of thorax distinguish this from the few similarly patterned species. HAB rough grassland and woodland margins, especially on limestone: local. ALT ? FLIGHT 5–8: 1 or 2 broods. FP golden rod and broom. EGG 5–8. LARVA 6–9: on flowers at first, moving later to lower leaves and living in flimsy web on the underside. PUPA 4–8: in a yellowish cocoon. WINTER fully grown larva, in cocoon spun ready for pupation in spring. VAR the small white dot in centre of fw is often absent, especially in E: all spots are much enlarged in parts of Ireland. NOTES Flight is usually low over vegetation, with a distinctly swirling motion. STATUS Locally common.

▲*Synaphe punctalis*. Rather long-legged and with long palps: narrow-winged ♀ is easily identified: ♂ colour varies, but there is usually a row of tiny white dots along front edge of fw. HAB damp grassland, especially on coast. ALT ? FLIGHT 5–8: night and day. FP mosses. EGG 5–8. LARVA 1–12: in silken tunnels among mosses. PUPA 4–7: in pale cocoon on vegetation, rather like a miniature burnet cocoon. WINTER larva. NOTES Mainly ♂ diurnal: small-winged ♀ flies little. STATUS Locally common.

FAMILY THYRIDIDAE

Thyris fenestrella. Translucent 'windows' on each wing: abruptly narrowed abdomen. HAB hedgerows, river banks, and woodland margins with a good mixture of light and shade. ALT sl–500? FLIGHT 5–8. FP traveller's-joy. EGG 5–8. LARVA 7–9. PUPA 9–6. WINTER pupa. VAR 'windows' larger in northern parts of range: amount of orange or gold dusting varies, producing wing colours from golden brown to almost black. NOTES The only member of its family in Europe, it darts rapidly over the vegetation, occasionally visiting umbellifers and elder flowers but spending most of its time basking on leaves with wings partly raised. This family has been suggested as an ancestor for the butterflies. STATUS Locally common, especially in S.

FAMILY LEMONIIDAE

Lemonia dumi. Superficially like small ♂ Oak Eggar, but wings are narrower and generally darker: discal spot of fw is yellow, not white: yellow base to fw is characteristic. HAB bogs and damp meadows, especially in wooded regions. ALT sl–1500. FLIGHT 9–11. FP various low-growing composites. EGG 9–5. LARVA 4–7. PUPA 7–9. WINTER egg. NOTES ♂ flies rapidly in sunshine from mid-morning to mid-afternoon, when ♀ takes over. Sometimes included in Lasiocampidae. STATUS LP; Austria, W. Germany, and Lux.

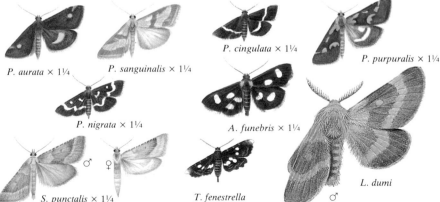

P. aurata × 1¼   *P. sanguinalis* × 1¼   *P. cingulata* × 1¼   *P. purpuralis* × 1¼

P. nigrata × 1¼   *A. funebris* × 1¼

S. punctalis × 1¼   *T. fenestrella*   *L. dumi* ♂

FAMILY LASIOCAMPIDAE – EGGARS

The eggars are mostly large, brown moths with no frenulum. The wings are linked simply by a large overlap. Females are always considerably larger than males. The moths are mostly nocturnal, but the males of a few species fly by day, usually with a very fast and erratic flight as they search for the resting females. Eggs are often scattered freely over the vegetation, but some species lay their eggs in neat batches. The larvae are stout and hairy and those of several species live gregariously in silken tents. Pupation takes place in a strong silken cocoon attached to the vegetation. About 25 species live in Europe, 11 of them in the British Isles.

▲**OAK EGGAR** *Lasiocampa quercus quercus*. Fw and hw alike, apart from white discal spot on fw. HAB open woodland, heaths, grassland, and hedgerows. ALT sl–1500. FLIGHT 7–8. FP bramble and a wide range of other shrubs and trees. EGG 7–9: dropped freely over vegetation. LARVA 8–6. PUPA 5–7: in large cocoon on or at base fp. WINTER small larva. VAR see Northern Eggar. NOTES Only ♂ diurnal, flying rapidly in search of resting ♀: latter is orange-yellow and much larger. STATUS Common. LP; Austria and Lux.

▲**NORTHERN EGGAR** *Lasiocampa quercus callunae*. Like Oak Eggar but yellow band of fw turns outwards at rear margin. HAB heaths and moors. ALT sl–1500. FLIGHT 5–6. FP heathers and bilberry. EGG 5–6: dropped freely over vegetation. LARVA 1–12: 2-year life-cycle: indistinguishable from Oak Eggar. PUPA 9–6: in cocoon like Oak Eggar. WINTER 1st winter as small larva: 2nd winter as pupa. VAR a melanic form (f. *olivacea*) occurs in N, including N. Britain. NOTES Only ♂ diurnal. Although now recognised as a ssp. of Oak Eggar, its different habits and habitats have led to the retention of the separate vernacular name. STATUS LP; Lux., where whole family is protected.

▲**GRASS EGGAR** *Lasiocampa trifolii*. Hw almost unmarked, but otherwise like a pale Oak Eggar. HAB heaths and grassy places: mainly coastal in B. ALT ? FLIGHT 7–9. FP bramble, broom, clover, and many other plants. EGG 7–4: scattered freely over vegetation. LARVA 3–6. PUPA 6–7: in brown cocoon at base fp. WINTER egg. VAR yellowish in some coastal areas: often very dark in N. NOTES Only ♂ diurnal: ♀ larger and pa. ¯ STATUS local, but not rare in suitable habitats. LP; Austria and Lux.

▲**FOX MOTH** *Macrothylacia rubi*. Like Grass Eggar but fw has 2 pale bands. HAB heaths and grassy and scrubby places. ALT sl–1800. FLIGHT 5–7. FP bramble, heather, and many other low shrubs. EGG 5–7: in cylindrical batches on stems. LARVA 6–4: often basks in spring sunshine, but does not feed after hibernation. PUPA 4–6: in a tough, tubular cocoon at base of fp. WINTER fully grown larva, hibernating in leaf litter. NOTES Only ♂ diurnal, usually flying after noon. ♀ is larger and greyer. STATUS Common and often abundant. LP; Austria and Lux.

FAMILY SATURNIIDAE–EMPEROR MOTHS
This family contains some of the world's largest insects – the giant silkmoths of India and the Far East. All are stoutly-built moths without probosci and the males have extremely large and complex antennae (see p. 256) with which they can detect females several kilometres away. The five European species all have prominent eye-spots on their wings. Only two of these species are diurnal, and even then only the males fly by day. Eggs are laid in batches on the food-plants and the larvae usually go through a marked colour change as they grow up. Pupation takes place in tough, oval cocoons with a parchment-like inner lining. The silk is very coarse in the European species.

▲**EMPEROR MOTH** *Saturnia pavonia*. Prominent eye-spot on both upper and lower surface of each wing: Giant Peacock Moth is similar but about twice as big and nocturnal. HAB heaths, moors, and all open and lightly wooded areas. ALT sl–2000. FLIGHT 4–6. FP blackthorn, bramble, heather, and many other shrubs. EGG 4–6: in cylindrical clusters on twigs. LARVA 5–7: black with orange spots at first, becoming green later. PUPA 7–5: in a tough brown cocoon on fp. WINTER pupa. NOTES Only ♂ diurnal, with fast, erratic flight in search of ♀: usually flies after noon: ♀ is greyish. *S. spini* of E Europe is very similar, but both sexes are greyish and nocturnal. STATUS Generally common. LP; Austria, W. Germany, Liech. and Lux. SEE ALSO p. 248–250, 255, 257, 276, 283, 295.

TAU EMPEROR *Aglia tau*. Usually distinguished from Emperor by yellow wings: no eye-spot on unh, just a white T-shaped mark. HAB deciduous woods, especially with beech. ALT sl–1600. FLIGHT 3–6. FP beech, birch, oak, and various other deciduous trees. EGG 3–6. LARVA 4–8: carries fine red spines in early instars. PUPA 7–5: in a tough cocoon of silk and leaves. WINTER pupa. VAR dark brown or almost black forms are not uncommon and can be confused with Emperor. NOTES Only ♂ diurnal, with a fast, erratic flight in morning sunshine. STATUS Generally common. LP; Austria, W. Germany, and Lux. SEE ALSO p. 232.

Oak Eggar larva

Oak Eggar

Northern Eggar

young larva

Grass Eggar

Emperor Moth

Fox Moth

Tau Emperor

FAMILY ENDROMIDAE

▲**KENTISH GLORY** *Endromis versicolora*. Fw pattern, with irregular outer cross line and triangular white spots near apex, is unmistakable, although ground colour varies. HAB birch woods and birch-clad heaths and moors: only in mountains in S. ALT sl–2000. FLIGHT 3–5. FP birch: occasionally alder and other trees. EGG 3–5: in rows on twigs. LARVA 5–7: black at first and then green, just like curled birch leaves: gregarious when young. PUPA 7–4: in coarse cocoon in leaf litter or just under soil. WINTER pupa. VAR fw somewhat darker in N. NOTES Only ♂ diurnal, flying very rapidly in sunshine from mid-morning to mid-afternoon. Also flies by night in warm weather. STATUS Locally common, but R; B (Scotland only). LP; W. Germany. SEE ALSO p. 229.

FAMILY DREPANIDAE

▲**BARRED HOOKTIP** *Drepana cultraria*. Hooked wing-tips, together with a darker brown stripe through each wing: usually a single indistinct discal spot on fw. HAB beech woods. ALT sl–1000. FLIGHT 4–8: 1–2 broods: night and day. FP beech and possibly oak. EGG 4–8. LARVA 6–9. PUPA 7–5: in flimsy cocoon in folded leaves. WINTER pupa. NOTES Generally only ♂ diurnal, flying around trees in sunshine. ♀ is a little larger and paler, without feathery antennae. STATUS Locally common.

FAMILY GEOMETRIDAE – GEOMETER MOTHS This is a large family of generally rather flimsy moths which normally rest with their wings well out to the sides of the body and flattened against the surface – often producing exceedingly good camouflage. Ear-drums at the front of the abdomen distinguish the geometers from nearly all other moths apart from the pyralids (see p. 176). Most are nocturnal or crepuscular. The eggs are of the flat type (see p. 206) and are often rather box-like. The larvae are the familiar loopers and are slim, with little or no hair and with only two pairs of prolegs, including the claspers at the rear. They loop along in a very characteristic way, stretching forward and then arching their bodies upwards in a loop as they bring the rear end up to the front legs. Many are extremely twig-like when at rest. Pupation takes place in the ground or in a cocoon on the food-plant. There are about 800 European species, of which just over 300 reside in the British Isles.

▲**ORANGE UNDERWING** *Archiearis parthenias*. Fw usually well marked with pale patches in both sexes: unh has a clearly broken dark border: ♂ antennae finely toothed. HAB woods and heaths with birch trees. ALT ? FLIGHT 3–4, mostly high up around trees: ♀ flies little. FP birch. EGG 3–4: on catkins of fp. LARVA 4–5: in catkins at first and then on leaves, usually concealed between 2 leaves spun together. PUPA 6–3: in dead wood or bark. WINTER pupa. STATUS LP; W. Germany.

▲**LIGHT ORANGE UNDERWING** *Archiearis notha*. Very like Orange Underwing but slightly smaller and fw less mottled, especially in ♂: unh has a complete dark border: ♂ antennae feathered. HAB heaths and light woodlands with aspen. ALT ? FLIGHT 3–5: around tree tops, mostly ♂♂. FP aspen and occasionally birch and sallow. EGG 3–5. LARVA 5–7: usually concealed between 2 leaves spun together. PUPA 6–3, often 1–12: in soft wood and bark. WINTER pupa. NOTES May spend two or three years in pupal stage. STATUS LP; W. Germany.

Archiearis puella. Like the last 2 species, but paler and with yellow pattern on hw: fw fringes not chequered. HAB light woodland. ALT ? FLIGHT 3–5. FP aspen and white poplar. EGG 3–5. LARVA 5–6. PUPA 6–4. WINTER pupa. STATUS LP; W. Germany.

▲**SLENDER STRIPED RUFOUS** *Coenocalpe lapidata*. Pointed fw, especially in ♀ crossed by several fine lines, together with lightly scalloped margin of hw, distinguishes this species. HAB upland moors and grasslands. ALT >100. FLIGHT 9–10. FP grasses? EGG 9–5. LARVA 4–8. PUPA 7–9. WINTER egg. STATUS Locally common.

▲**ARGENT AND SABLE** *Rheumaptera hastata*. Distinguished from superficially similar species by white diamond-shaped spot in dark border of each wing. HAB birch woods and birch-dotted moorland. ALT ? FLIGHT 5–7. FP birch, bilberry and various other shrubs. EGG 5–7: in small, loose clusters on leaves. LARVA 6–8: concealed between leaves spun together. PUPA 8–5. WINTER pupa. VAR central black stripe often reduced: *R. h. nigrescens* of northern moors is small and resembles Small Argent and Sable – a mainly nocturnal species with an unbroken black band across centre of fw. STATUS Locally common.

▲**CHIMNEY SWEEPER** *Odezia atrata*. Sooty wings with white-tipped tw. HAB grasslands, both damp and dry: local. ALT <2000. FLIGHT 5–7. FP pignut and other small umbellifers (flowers). EGG 6–4. LARVA 4–6. PUPA 5–6. WINTER egg. STATUS Locally common.

▲**HEATH RIVULET** *Perizoma minorata*. Fw pattern, with wavy white line in dark border, does not occur in other species of similar size. HAB upland moors and pastures: local. ALT ? FLIGHT 7–8. FP eyebright (seeds). EGG 7–8: in flowers of fp. LARVA 8–9: in fruiting heads. PUPA 9–7. WINTER pupa. VAR British specimens (*P. m. ericetata*) are smaller and darker. STATUS Locally common.

Kentish Glory

Orange Underwing larva

Barred Hooktip

Barred Hooktip larva

Light Orange Underwing

A. puella

Orange Underwing

Slender Striped Rufous

Argent and Sable

Chimney Sweeper

Heath Rivulet

GEOMETRIDAE

▲**DRAB LOOPER** *Minoa murinata*. Like a small and very pale Chimney Sweeper: wings silky and completely unmarked, fading with age and losing the sheen. HAB woodland paths and clearings. ALT ? FLIGHT 4–8: 1–2 broods. FP wood spurge. EGG 5–8. LARVA 6–9. PUPA 1–12. WINTER pupa. STATUS Locally common.

▲**LATTICED HEATH** *Semiothisa clathrata*. Chequered pattern of black on white or cream background is quite distinctive: ♂ antennae not feathery. HAB grassy places, including woodland clearings and wasteland. ALT ? FLIGHT 4–9: 1–2 broods: night and day. FP clovers and other legumes. EGG 5–8. LARVA 5–10. PUPA 1–12. WINTER pupa. VAR *S. c. hugginsi* from Ireland has a pure white background: melanic individuals, with just a few white spots, are not uncommon. STATUS Generally common.

▲**NETTED MOUNTAIN MOTH** *Semiothisa carbonaria*. Like a small, dark Latticed Heath but with a whiter ground colour and without the black veins forming the clear chequered pattern: central band on hw is sharply angled in middle. HAB mountain and moorland: very local. ALT ? FLIGHT 4–7. FP bearberry: occasionally birch and sallow and other shrubs. EGG 5–7. LARVA 6–8: nocturnal. PUPA 8–5: amongst leaf litter. WINTER pupa. STATUS E; W. Germany. R: Britain. LP; W. Germany.

▲**RANNOCH LOOPER** *Semiothisa brunneata*. Cross-lines of fw almost straight, without jagged teeth. HAB moors and open woodland, usually in uplands. ALT ? FLIGHT 6–8. FP bilberry: sometimes willow and other low-growing shrubs. EGG 6–9: sometimes over-wintering until 4. LARVA 8–5. PUPA 4–7. WINTER egg or 1st-instar larva: sometimes pupa, which may remain dormant for several years. NOTES Only ♂ normally diurnal: ♀ is darker, with more obvious cross-lines. STATUS Locally common.

FROSTED YELLOW *Isturgia limbaria*. Coloration is unique. HAB heaths and wasteland. ALT ? FLIGHT 4–8: 2 broods. FP broom. EGG 4–9. LARVA 5–10. PUPA 1–12: often for 2+years. WINTER pupa. STATUS Extinct in B since early 20th Century: locally common on continent.

▲**LITTLE THORN** *Cepphis advenaria*. Irregular wing margins make this unlikely to be confused with any other moth of its size. HAB moors, bogs, and open woods: local. ALT ? FLIGHT 5–7. FP bilberry, strawberry, bramble? and cow-wheat. EGG 5–7. LARVA 7–8. PUPA 8–5. WINTER pupa. STATUS Locally common.

▲**SPECKLED YELLOW** *Pseudopanthera macularia*. Coloration is unmistakable. HAB open woods and scrub. ALT sl–2000. FLIGHT 4–7. FP wood sage, mint and other labiates. EGG 4–7. LARVA 5–8. PUPA 8–5. WINTER pupa. VAR degree of spotting varies, with spots often joined into bands or irregular blotches: sometimes reduced to one or two spots on each wing. STATUS Generally common.

▲**COMMON HEATH** *Ematurga atomaria*. Like both Latticed Heath and Netted Mountain Moth but the 2 central bands of fw converge and often join before reaching hind margin: wings never have true chequered pattern: ♂ antennae strongly feathered. HAB heaths, moors, grassland, and open woodland. ALT ? FLIGHT 4–9: 1–2 broods. FP heathers and other low-growing plants, especially legumes. EGG 4–9. LARVA 5–10. PUPA 1–12. WINTER pupa. VAR rather small in the north. NOTES Mainly ♂♂ are diurnal: ♀ is paler and largely nocturnal. STATUS Common.

▲**BLACK MOUNTAIN MOTH** *Psodos coracina*. Superficially like Netted Mountain Moth, but stouter and with a broad black band across fw, best seen in ♀. HAB montane scree and moor. ALT >600. FLIGHT 6–7. FP crowberry. EGG 6–8. LARVA 1–12: 2-year life cycle. PUPA 4–6. WINTER larva (×2). STATUS R; B. SEE ALSO p. 250.

Psodos quadrifaria. An unmistakable species. HAB mountain slopes. FLIGHT 6–7. FP assorted low-growing herbs and shrubs. EGG 6–8. LARVA 7–4. PUPA 4–6. WINTER larva. STATUS ?

Drab Looper	Latticed Heath	Netted Mountain Moth

Rannoch Looper	Frosted Yellow	Common Heath larva

Little Thorn		Common Heath

Speckled Yellow	*P. quadrifaria*	Black Mountain Moth

Psodos canaliculata. Dark brown to black, but always with some white pattern. HAB montane pastures and scree. ALT ? FLIGHT 7–8. FP polyphagous on low-growing herbs. EGG 7–9. LARVA 8–5. PUPA 5–7. WINTER larva. VAR often more heavily patterned in eastern areas. STATUS ?

Psodos alpinata. Like Chimney Sweeper but without white wing-tips. HAB montane pastures and scree, up to snow-line. ALT <3000. FLIGHT 6–8. FP polyphagous on low-growing herbs. EGG 6–9. LARVA 8–4. PUPA 4–7. WINTER larva. STATUS One of the commonest moths on high mountains.

Psodos alticolaria. Wing pattern is characteristic, with white bands on uns even more pronounced than on ups. HAB montane scree and grassland. ALT 2000–3000. FLIGHT 7–8: only in sunshine. FP lichens. EGG 7–9. LARVA 8–5. PUPA 5–7. WINTER larva. STATUS Generally common in suitable habitats.

▲**BLACK-VEINED MOTH** *Siona lineata*. Unmistakable pattern. HAB grassy places, especially in uplands on continent: local. ALT sl–1500. FLIGHT 5–7. FP tor grass and ? other grasses. EGG 5–7. LARVA 6–4. PUPA 4–6. WINTER larva. STATUS E; Britain.

Euranthis plumistraria. Pattern is unmistakable. ♀ is generally smaller and lacks feathered antennae. HAB grassy places: local, especially in northern parts of range. ALT ? FLIGHT 3–4, 8–9: 2nd brood much less numerous than 1st. FP *Dorycnium* spp. and possibly other small legumes. EGG 3–5, 8–9. LARVA 4–10: smooth, yellowish brown with dark lines on the back. PUPA 10–8. WINTER pupa. STATUS ?

Crocota lutearia. An unmistakable moth: ♀ is slightly smaller. HAB montane grassland. ALT >1000. FLIGHT 5–7. FP polyphagous on low-growing plants. EGG 5–8. LARVA 7–5. PUPA 3–6. WINTER larva. VAR a black discal dot is often present on all wings. STATUS ?

FAMILY SPHINGIDAE – HAWKMOTHS
The hawkmoths are stout-bodied, fast-flying moths with relatively narrow forewings. The wings are usually held flat at rest and swept back like arrowheads. Only five of the European species are diurnal, including the transparent-winged bee hawkmoths which have a remarkable similarity to bumble bees. Most species have long tongues and commonly feed while hovering in front of flowers. The eggs are oval, with the micropyle at one end (see p. 206), and they are generally green and shiny. They are laid singly or in small groups. The larvae nearly all have a curved horn at the rear, although its function is unknown. Most are well camouflaged by diagonal stripes which break up their outlines. Pupation takes place in an underground chamber. There are 23 European species, including several which are summer visitors from Africa. Only nine are permanent residents of the British Isles.

▲**BROAD-BORDERED BEE HAWKMOTH** *Hemaris fuciformis*. Wings largely transparent, with broad chestnut borders and a dark discal spot on fw. HAB sunny flower-rich spots in woodland rides and clearings: also in other grassy and scrubby places, including railway cuttings and alpine meadows. ALT sl–2000. FLIGHT 4–7: sometimes partial 2nd brood in late summer in S or in very hot years. FP honeysuckle, snowberry, and bedstraws. EGG 4–8: solitary on underside of leaf: shiny green and somewhat rounder than most hawkmoth eggs. LARVA 6–8. PUPA 8–6: in a flimsy cocoon just under the soil. WINTER pupa. NOTES Wings fully scaled until first flight. A splendid bumble bee mimic, although flight is faster and more darting than that of a bumble bee. Hovers to feed at flowers. Very fond of bugle flowers. STATUS Declining in many places. LP; Austria, E. Germany, W. Germany, Lux. & Switz. SEE ALSO p. 18, 278, 279.

▲**NARROW-BORDERED BEE HAWKMOTH** *Hemaris tityus*. Like Broad-bordered Bee Hawkmoth but wing borders are blacker and narrower, especially on hw: fw lacks prominent discal spot. HAB woodland rides and clearings and other scrubby and grassy places with flowers and sunshine: also on bogs, moors, and mountain pastures. ALT sl–2000. FLIGHT 4–6. FP various kinds of scabious, but mainly devil's-bit scabious. EGG 5–6: solitary under leaf: smooth and oval like most hawkmoth eggs. LARVA 6–8. PUPA 8–5: in a rather stout cocoon just under the soil. WINTER pupa. NOTES Wings fully scaled until first flight. Very fond of bugle flowers. Flight behaviour like Broad-bordered Bee Hawkmoth. STATUS Rather local and becoming rare in many places. LP; Austria, E. Germany, W. Germany, Lux. & Switz. SEE ALSO p. 13, 278.

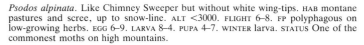

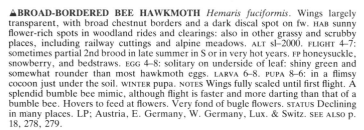

▲**HUMMING-BIRD HAWKMOTH** *Macroglossum stellatarum*. Colour is unmistakable, although normally seen only as a brown blur as it hovers at flowers. HAB flowery places. ALT sl–2500. FLIGHT 1–12: 2 broods: dormant in coldest weather. FP bedstraws. EGG 5–9: solitary: round and shiny green. LARVA 6–10: green or brown. PUPA 7–5: in a loose cocoon on ground. WINTER pupa or adult, but neither stage can survive N winters. NOTES Hums as it hovers. Permanent resident only in S, but a strong migrant, spreading to limits of vegetation in summer. Adult sleeps in crevices in winter in S. STATUS Generally common, but numbers migrating northwards vary from year to year. LP; Austria, E. Germany, Lux. & Switz. SEE ALSO p. 14, 200, 203, 240, 252, 253, 261, 266.

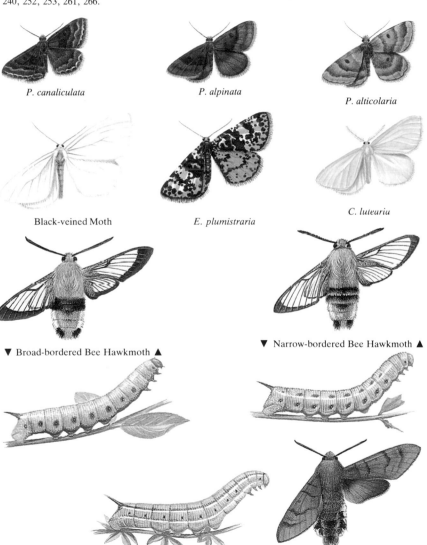

P. canaliculata

P. alpinata

P. alticolaria

Black-veined Moth

E. plumistraria

C. lutearia

▼ Broad-bordered Bee Hawkmoth ▲

▼ Narrow-bordered Bee Hawkmoth ▲

Hemaris croatica. Yellow and red fw is unmistakable. HAB dry, flower-rich grassland, mainly in mountains. ALT sl–1500. FLIGHT 5–9: 2 broods. FP scabious. EGG 5–9. LARVA 6–10. PUPA 7–5. WINTER pupa. NOTES Darts rapidly flower to flower like Humming-bird Hawkmoth. Very fond of thistles. STATUS R.

Proserpinus proserpina. Bright yellow hw, with broad dark border: 'ragged' margin to fw. HAB sunny slopes and woodland clearings, especially near water: sometimes in parks and gardens. ALT sl–1500. FLIGHT 5–6. FP willowherbs and evening primrose. EGG 5–7: solitary or in small groups. LARVA 6–8: no horn: shiny eye-spot at rear gives a snake-like appearance, especially as larva often rests with its head down. PUPA 8–5: in a shallow chamber in the ground. WINTER pupa. VAR fw often brownish. STATUS R. and apparently declining in C. LP; Austria, E. Germany, W. Germany, Hungary & Switz. SEE ALSO p. 232.

FAMILY LYMANTRIIDAE – TUSSOCKS AND VAPOURERS   The moths in this family are mostly rather sombre species. Only a few fly by day, and among these it is only the males that are diurnal, using their feathery antennae to search out the resting females. Many of the latter are unable to fly, and those of the vapourers are completely wingless. The proboscis is absent in all species, so the adults do not feed at all. Eggs are laid in batches and usually covered with hairs from the female's abdomen. The larvae are generally very hairy, often sporting brightly coloured tufts or tussocks, but the hairs can be extremely irritating and the larvae should be handled with care. Most of them feed on trees and shrubs. Pupation takes place in a loose silken cocoon which incorporates a lot of the larval hairs. The family contains over 2000 species, but only 17 of these live in Europe – 11 of them in the British Isles.

Penthophora morio. ♂ like some bagworm moths (p. 163), but distinguished from most by its larger size and also by the venation, with no vein running through the cell: ♀ has much reduced wings. HAB dry grassy places: very local. ALT ? FLIGHT 4–8: 1–2 broods. FP various grasses. EGG 5–8. LARVA 6–4. PUPA 3–8: in silken cocoon. WINTER larva: hibernating in grass tufts: also pupa in S. NOTES Only ♂ can fly, usually on sunny mornings. STATUS Locally common and occasionally damaging grassland. LP; W. Germany.

▲VAPOURER *Orgyia antiqua.* Comma-shaped mark at rear of fw. HAB wherever there are trees and shrubs. ALT sl–2000, FLIGHT 6–10: 1–3 broods. FP almost any deciduous tree or shrub. EGG 6–4: in a large batch on ♀ cocoon. LARVA 3–9. PUPA 5–10: in a cocoon attached to twigs or bark. WINTER egg. NOTES ♀ is wingless and moves no further than the outside of her cocoon. ♂ has a darting zig-zag flight, often along hedgerows. STATUS Common and often a pest in orchards and town parks and streets. SEE ALSO p. 230, 252, 253, 283.

▲SCARCE VAPOURER *Orgyia recens.* Very like Vapourer, but generally more heavily marked and with white spots at apex of fw – sometimes joined to tornal spot by a white line. HAB deciduous woods. ALT sl–2000. FLIGHT 6–10: 2 broods. FP willows and various other deciduous trees. EGG 6–10: in large batch on ♀ cocoon. LARVA 1–12. PUPA 5–10: in a tough cocoon on or under fp. WINTER small larva. NOTES ♂ flies erratically in sunshine, and also at night in warm weather. ♀ is wingless. STATUS Locally common, but declining in Britain and some other places. V; Britain. LP; W. Germany.

Orgyia ericae. Like Vapourer, but smaller and generally much paler with a very small white spot on fw. HAB heath and moor. ALT ? FLIGHT 7–9. FP heaths, dwarf willow and other low-growing shrubs. EGG 7–5. LARVA 5–7. PUPA 6–8: in yellowish grey cocoon. WINTER egg. NOTES ♀ is wingless. STATUS Locally common in N. V. & LP; W. Germany.

GYPSY MOTH *Lymantria dispar*. Strongly toothed cross-lines on fw distinguish ♂ from other superficially similar moths. HAB woods and parks. ALT sl–1500? FLIGHT 6–8. FP numerous deciduous trees and shrubs and some conifers. EGG 7–4: batched on bark and covered with yellow hairs from ♀ body. LARVA 3–7. PUPA 6–7: in a flimsy cocoon amongst leaves. WINTER egg. NOTES ♀ is much larger and creamy white with black and grey markings like ♂: she cannot fly. STATUS Generally common and a serious forest pest in many places. Extinct in B since early 20th Century.

FAMILY ARCTIIDAE – TIGERS, ERMINES, AND FOOTMEN   The members of this large family fall into two very distinct groups – the sturdy tigers and ermines on the one hand and the delicate footmen on the other. The tiger moths include several brightly coloured day-flying species that are unlikely to be confused with any other groups. The footmen, most of which are nocturnal, are a rather varied group and are sometimes mistaken for geometers or even grass moths (see p. 176), but the day-flying species are fairly easy to identify by their wing patterns. The eggs are hemispherical and smooth and are usually laid in batches. The larvae are mostly rather hairy, those of the tigers and ermines feeding on various low-growing herbs

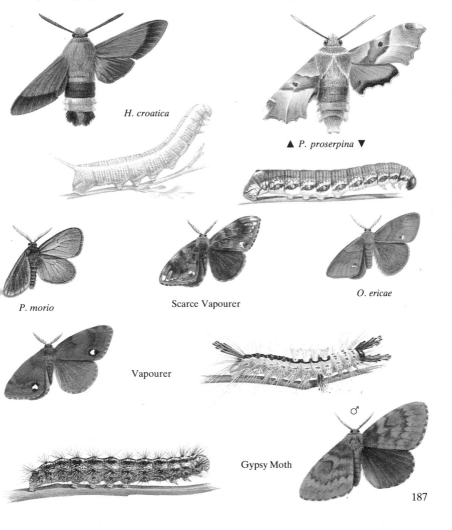

H. croatica

▲ *P. proserpina* ▼

P. morio

Scarce Vapourer

O. ericae

Vapourer

♂

Gypsy Moth

while those of the footmen feed mainly on lichens. Pupation takes place among the vegetation or leaf litter in a flimsy cocoon which incorporates many of the larval hairs. Of the 10,000 or so known species, only about 80 live in Europe and only 30 of these are resident in the British Isles.

FEATHERED FOOTMAN *Spiris striata*. Prominent black fw veins distinguish ♂: ♀ has black only on outer extremities of veins and lacks feathery antennae. HAB woodland clearings, heaths, and dry grassy slopes. ALT ? FLIGHT 5–8. FP a wide range of herbs. EGG 6–8. LARVA 7–5: gregarious when young. PUPA 4–7: in a flimsy cocoon. WINTER small larvae, hibernating in a communal web. VAR hw is sometimes completely brown apart from the yellow fringe. STATUS Locally common, especially in S. LP; Austria, E. Germany, W. Germany & Lux.

▲**SPECKLED FOOTMAN** *Coscinia cribraria*. Fw dirty white with a variable amount of black in the form of longitudinal streaks and cross bands composed of numerous black dots. HAB dry heaths and open woodland with heather. ALT ? FLIGHT 5–8. FP dandelions, grasses and other low-growing herbs. EGG 6–8: batched on heather, although larvae rarely eat this. LARVA 8–6. PUPA 4–7: in a flimsy cocoon amongst herbage. WINTER larva. VAR fw is almost pure white in *C. c. arenaria*, which is common on continent. NOTES Mainly nocturnal, but flies weakly when disturbed by day. STATUS V. LP; Austria, E. Germany, W. Germany, Hungary & Lux.

Ocnogyna parasita. Distinctly elongate fw spots of ♂, often ringed with white, readily distinguish this related (often nocturnal) species: ♀ wings much reduced. HAB uplands and high mountains. ALT <3000? FLIGHT 2–5: rather rapid. (♂♂ only). FP grasses and other low-growing plants, including nettles and plantains. EGG 3–5. LARVA 5–6. PUPA 6–4: in grey cocoon. WINTER pupa. STATUS ?

△**CRIMSON SPECKLED** *Utetheisa pulchella*. Fw unmistakable. HAB scrub and grassland. ALT ? FLIGHT 4–10: 2–3 broods. FP various low-growing herbs, including borage and forget-me-not. EGG 4–9: batched on fp. LARVA 1–12. PUPA 4–9: in a thin cocoon on fp or in leaf litter. WINTER larva: active in warm weather in S, but hibernating in northern parts of winter range. NOTES Resident only in S, migrating northwards each spring and summer and most common in northern areas in autumn. A rare visitor to B. Unable to survive winters north of the Alps. STATUS LP; Austria, E. Germany & Lux.

▲**RED-NECKED FOOTMAN** *Atolmis rubricollis*. Velvety black wings and red collar (patagia) are characteristic. HAB damp woodland, especially with conifers, and heather-clad moors. ALT sl–2000. FLIGHT 5–8, by night and day, but especially in evening. FP tree-trunk lichens and algae. EGG 6–8: creamy white and batched on trunks. LARVA 7–10: very well camouflaged on lichens. PUPA 9–7: in a silken cocoon in a bark crevice or in leaf litter. WINTER pupa. NOTES Usually flies high up around trees in woodland. STATUS Locally common. LP; Austria & Lux.

▲**DEW MOTH** *Setina irrorella*. Fw thinly scaled, with 3 cross bands of small black dots. HAB upland areas, mainly on chalk and limestone: mainly coastal in B. ALT sl–1800. FLIGHT 6–8: night and day. FP lichens on rocks. EGG 7–8: batched on lichens. LARVA 8–5: hibernates soon after hatching in 8. PUPA 5–7: in a flimsy cocoon in a crevice. WINTER 1st-instar larva. NOTES Only ♂ diurnal. ♀ is smaller and redder. STATUS LP; Austria & Lux.

▲**FOUR-SPOTTED FOOTMAN** *Lithosia quadra*. ♂ identified by bluish-black streak on basal part of fw costa: ♀ readily identified by the 2 large spots on each fw. HAB mature woodland. ALT sl–1000. FLIGHT 7–9: night and day. FP tree-trunk lichens. EGG 7–9: batched on trunk: green at first, becoming brown. LARVA 9–7. PUPA 5–8: in a loose cocoon on trunk. WINTER 1st-instar larva, hibernating amongst lichens. NOTES A strong migrant, often arriving in B in numbers from the continent. STATUS LP; Austria & Lux.

Cycnia luctuosa. Heavy spotting distinguishes ♂ from most similar species: ♀ resembles Muslin Moth but is somewhat darker. HAB warm grassy slopes, including coastal cliffs and the lower slopes of mountains. ALT sl–2000. FLIGHT 4–9: 1–2 broods. FP polyphagous on low-growing plants. EGG ? LARVA ? PUPA ? WINTER ? NOTES Only ♂ flies by day. STATUS ?

▲**MUSLIN MOTH** *Diaphora mendica.* ♀ wings thinly scaled, white with small black dots: abdomen white. HAB rough grassland, open woodland, hedgerows and gardens. ALT sl–1500? FLIGHT 5–7. FP a wide range of low-growing herbs. EGG 5–7: batched on fp, often in rows. LARVA 6–9. PUPA 8–5: in a thick cocoon in leaf litter. WINTER pupa. NOTES Only ♀ diurnal. ♂ is generally brown. STATUS LP; Austria, E. Germany & Lux.

▲**CLOUDED BUFF** *Diacrisia sannio.* ♂ fw is unmistakable. HAB heaths, moors, and, less often, grassland. ALT sl–2500. FLIGHT 4–8: generally 2 broods although 1 in B (6–7). FP polyphagous on low-growing herbs. EGG 4–9: shiny white and batched on fp. LARVA 1–12. PUPA 3–8: in a flimsy cocoon in leaf litter. WINTER small larva. VAR hw often entirely grey. NOTES Only ♂ diurnal: ♀ is smaller and largely orange. STATUS Locally common. LP; Austria, E. Germany & Lux.

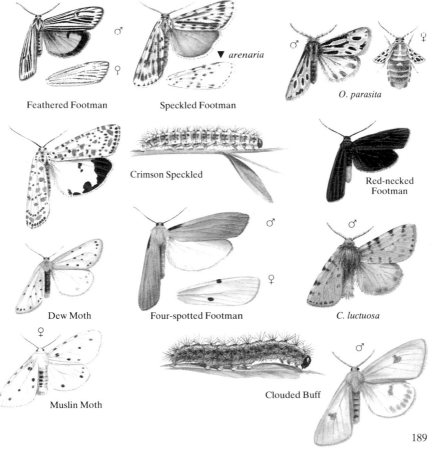

Feathered Footman

Speckled Footman

▼ *arenaria*

O. parasita

Crimson Speckled

Red-necked Footman

Dew Moth

Four-spotted Footman

C. luctuosa

Muslin Moth

Clouded Buff

Hyphoraia aulica. Rich brown fw with cream or beige spots distinguishes this from several similar species. HAB sunny heaths and dry grasslands, especially on sand. ALT ? FLIGHT 5–7: occasionally partial 2nd brood later. FP polyphagous on low-growing herbs. EGG 5–8: batched on fp. LARVA 7–4. PUPA 4–6. WINTER half-grown larva. VAR much variation in extent of pattern on both wings. NOTES Only ♂ is diurnal, flying very fast over vegetation, usually in morning. STATUS V. Recently extinct in several areas. LP; Austria, E. Germany, W. Germany & Lux.

▲**WOOD TIGER** *Parasemia plantaginis.* Fw black with variable yellow or white pattern, but always with yellow or orange spots along the front edge. HAB heaths, grassland and open woodland, especially in damp areas. ALT sl–3000+. FLIGHT 5–7, fast and low in sunshine. FP polyphagous on low-growing plants. EGG 5–7: in small batches. LARVA 7–5. PUPA 4–6: in a cocoon amongst leaves. WINTER half-grown larva. VAR colour and pattern vary considerably: at high altitudes and in northern areas white replaces yellow in ♂: ♀ hw is often quite red. NOTES ♀ generally flies only in afternoon and evening. STATUS Locally common, but declining in many areas. LP; Austria, E. Germany, W. Germany & Lux.

Grammia quenselii. Like Wood Tiger but fw is more obviously striped. HAB tundra and alpine screes and meadows. ALT sl(N)–2600. FLIGHT 6–8. FP various low-growing herbs, including grasses. EGG ? LARVA 1–12: 2-year life cycle. PUPA 5–7. WINTER larva (twice). STATUS R. and local. LP; Austria.

Holoarctia cervini. Like Wood Tiger but fw pattern is more reticulate and hw only weakly patterned. HAB mountain slopes. ALT 2500–3300. FLIGHT 6–9. FP polyphagous on low-growing plants. EGG 6–9. LARVA 1–12: 2-year life cycle. PUPA 5–8. WINTER larva (twice). NOTES Only ♂♂ fly regularly: ♀♀ are sluggish and spend most of their time under rocks or in crevices. STATUS ?

Rhyparia purpurata. Yellow fw and red hw will always distinguish this moth, although the spot pattern varies and the spots may run together. HAB dry sunny heaths and grassland, and also woodland clearings. ALT ? FLIGHT 6–7: sometimes 2nd brood in S (9). FP bramble, bedstraws and many other low-growing herbs and shrubs. EGG 6–8. LARVA 7–5. PUPA 4–6. WINTER almost fully grown larva. NOTES Only ♂ diurnal. STATUS Locally common in S. R; W. Germany and other northern areas. LP; Austria, E. Germany, W. Germany & Lux.

Ammobiota festiva. Black tip to abdomen, especially noticeable in ♀, distinguishes this from other superficially similar tiger moths: fw generally more obviously banded than in other species. HAB warm dry grassland and scrub, usually on limestone. ALT ? FLIGHT 5–6. FP polyphagous on low-growing herbs. EGG 5–7. LARVA 6–4: often basks in spring sunshine, but does not feed in spring. PUPA 4–5. WINTER fully grown larva: pupates without feeding after hibernation. VAR northern specimens are often rather pale – grey and pink instead of brown and red. STATUS R in northern parts of range and becoming scarce in other places: recently extinct in some places. LP; Austria, E. Germany, W. Germany, Hungary & Lux.

▲**SCARLET TIGER** *Callimorpha dominula.* Fw bluish black, with variable spotting but always with an oval or cream spot near base of hind margin: hw generally scarlet. HAB fens, damp woods and other wet places. ALT sl–2000. FLIGHT 6–8. FP a wide range of low-growing herbs and shrubs. EGG 6–8: shiny cream and in batches. LARVA 7–5. PUPA 4–6: in flimsy cocoon in leaf litter. WINTER small larva. VAR hw sometimes yellow. STATUS Local and becoming rare through drainage of many habitats. LP; Austria, E. Germany, W. Germany & Lux.

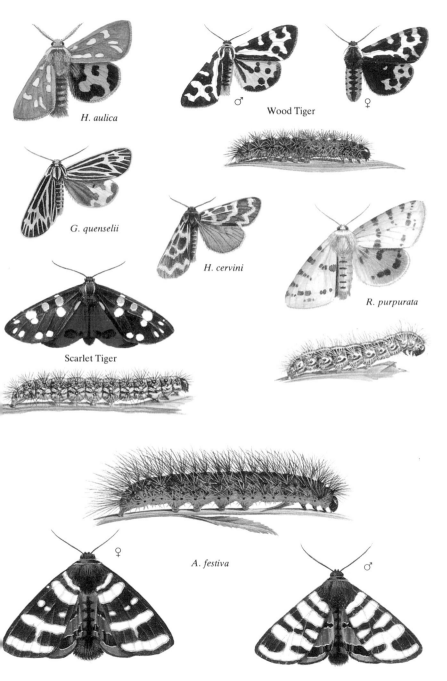

H. aulica

Wood Tiger

♂

♀

G. quenselii

H. cervini

R. purpurata

Scarlet Tiger

♀

A. festiva

♂

▲**JERSEY TIGER** *Euplagia quadripunctaria*. Fw pattern, with a pale V in outer half and a pale stripe along rear edge, is unlike that of any other tiger moth. HAB hot, stony places, including open woodland: usually on limestone and near water: often on coasts. ALT sl–1500 (in Alpine valleys). FLIGHT 6–9. FP dandelions and many other low-growing herbs. EGG 6–8: batched: yellow at first, becoming violet. LARVA 7–5. PUPA 5–7: in flimsy cocoon in leaf litter. WINTER small larva. VAR hw ranges from red to bright yellow. NOTES In the hotter parts of Europe the moth aestivates, often in huge numbers in light woodland. The Valley of Butterflies on Rhodes is a famous example. STATUS Locally common in S, rarer in N. LP; Austria, E. Germany, W. Germany & Lux. SEE ALSO p. 13, 277.

Pericallia matronula. Fw pattern is unmistakable, although spot sizes vary. HAB open woodland. ALT ? FLIGHT 5–7: night and day. FP various herbs and shrubs. EGG 5–8. LARVA 1–12: 2-year life cycle. PUPA 4–6. WINTER larva (×2). NOTES Only ♂ diurnal. ♀ is large and clumsy and rarely flies. STATUS R. and local everywhere; probably E., at least in western parts of its range. LP; Austria, France, E. Germany, W. Germany & Hungary.

▲**CINNABAR** *Tyria jacobaeae*. Fw pattern unmistakable. HAB grassy places, but absent from heaviest soils where larva cannot burrow to pupate: mainly coastal in N. ALT sl–1600. FLIGHT 5–8: largely nocturnal but commonly flutters weakly by day. FP ragwort. EGG 5–8: bright yellow and batched under leaves. LARVA 7–9: protected by striking warning colours. PUPA 8–6: in flimsy cocoon just below soil or in leaf litter. WINTER pupa. NOTES A useful control agent against ragwort in pastures. STATUS Generally common. LP; Austria, E. Germany, W. Germany & Lux. SEE ALSO p. 230, 231, 277, 280.

FAMILY CTENUCHIDAE Several members of this family resemble burnet moths in both appearance and behaviour, and some enter mimicry rings with them (see p. 280), but they have no clubbed antennae and are actually more closely related to the tiger moths of the family Arctiidae (see p. 187). They are sometimes included in that family. Their hairy larvae are very like those of some tiger moths. Most of the 2,000 or so species in the family are tropical insects, often with brilliant colours and atrocious smells to match. Nearly all fly by day, employing a slow, drifting motion very much like that of the burnets. The half dozen or so species found in southern Europe flourish in a wide range of sunny and flowery habitats, including gardens. The *Syntomis* species are all much alike but have been shown to be distinct by biochemical studies. The insects are not found in the British Isles.

NINE-SPOTTED *Syntomis phegea*. Hw has 1 or 2 small basal spots and a larger one beyond them, although basal spots of ♀ may be quite large and may run together. HAB sunny valleys and other flowery places: local. ALT <2000. FLIGHT 5–8. FP plantains, dandelions and other herbs, including grasses. EGG 6–8: in large batches. LARVA 7–5: gregarious. PUPA 5–6: in silken cocoon on ground. WINTER larvae in communal web under stones. STATUS Locally common on southern slopes of Alps and further S: rare north of Alps. LP: W. Germany. SEE ALSO p. 280.

Syntomis marjana. Like *S. phegea* but hw has a large inner spot and a smaller one beyond it: anterior of the 3 outer spots on fw usually smaller than the other 2. HAB flowery places, mainly on limestone and especially near water. ALT sl–1500. FLIGHT 4–7. FP various low-growing herbs. EGG 4–6. LARVA ? PUPA ? WINTER ? STATUS ?

Syntomis albionica. Like *S. marjana* but generally smaller: anterior spot on outer part of fw is ± equal to the other 2 spots (smaller in *marjana*). HAB dry, rocky places with plenty of flowers: usually on calcareous soils. ALT 800–1300. FLIGHT 5–6. FP various legumes? EGG ? LARVA ? PUPA ? WINTER ? NOTES Range does not overlap with that of *S. marjana*. Adult is very fond of thistles. STATUS ?

Syntomis ragazzi. Like *S. marjana* but outer spot of hw is very small or absent: hindmost of 3 outer spots on fw is the smallest. HAB montane grassland and deciduous woodland (probably two separate races). ALT 300–2000. FLIGHT 6–7: about a month later than *S. phegea* where the two overlap. FP polyphagous. EGG ? LARVA ? PUPA ? WINTER ? STATUS ?

Dysauxes ancilla. Fw has 2 or 3 white spots near outer edge: hw ± uniformly brown. HAB dry, open woodland. ALT ? FLIGHT 6–9: 1–2 broods: occasionally by night. FP mosses, lichens, various low-growing composites and plantains. EGG 7–9. LARVA 7–5. PUPA 5–9. WINTER small larva. VAR front spot on fw is often very small and sometimes absent. STATUS Rare north of Alps. LP; W. Germany.

Dysauxes punctata. Like *D. ancilla* but with additional white spots in middle of fw. HAB dry woods and hillsides. ALT <1700. FLIGHT 6–9: 2 broods. FP lichens and various low-growing herbs, especially their flowers. EGG 6–9. LARVA ? PUPA ? WINTER ? VAR f. *servula* of some southern areas is devoid of spots. *D. p. famula* has yellower fw, with indistinct spots, and largely translucent hw. *D. p. hyalina* has very dark fw and almost transparent hw. NOTES ssp *famula* and *hyalina* are often treated as distinct species. Both are southern, but there is little information on their exact ranges. STATUS ?

Jersey Tiger

▼ *P. matronula*

▲▼ Cinnabar

S. marjana

▼▲ Nine-spotted

S. albionica

S. ragazzi

D. punctata

D. ancilla

FAMILY NOCTUIDAE   This is one of the largest families of the Lepidoptera, with more than 25,000 known species. Most are fairly stout moths and the great majority are nocturnal. A proboscis is nearly always present and the male antennae are never strongly feathered, but otherwise the adults are not markedly different from the tussock moths (see p. 186). The sexes are much alike. The forewings are generally brown or greyish and the hindwings are generally drab as well, although they are brightly coloured in the yellow underwings and some others. The forewings usually have three prominent spots or stigmata – the orbicular near the centre, the kidney-shaped reniform just beyond it, and the elongate claviform below it – although all or any may be missing. The form of the stigmata plays an important role in the identification of the moths. The wings are sometimes held flat over the body at rest, but the majority of species hold their wings in a roof-wise fashion.

The eggs are generally hemispherical, with the micropyle at the top, and they are often delicately ribbed. The larvae are rather fleshy, usually with few hairs, and most have five pairs of prolegs, including the claspers at the rear. The Silver Y and its relatives, however, have only three pairs of prolegs, and some species have three pairs in the early instars and five pairs later in their lives. Pupation takes place in the ground or in flimsy cocoons on the vegetation. Over 1200 species live in Europe, of which just over 300 are resident in the British Isles.

▲**NORTHERN RUSTIC** *Standfussiana lucernea*. Fw has 2 wavy black cross-lines clearly edged with fawn: stigmata rarely obvious: uns strongly barred. HAB coastal cliffs and mountains. ALT sl–3000. FLIGHT 6–10: night and day. FP various grasses and other low-growing herbs. EGG 7–10. LARVA 1–12. PUPA 4–9. WINTER larva. VAR darker, sometimes almost black, in Shetland and other northern areas. NOTES Flies at high speed on sunny afternoons, but evening flight is slower. STATUS LP; W. Germany.

▲**BEAUTIFUL YELLOW UNDERWING** *Anarta myrtilli*. Reddish tinge to fw, together with banded abdomen, separates this from similar species. HAB heaths and moors. ALT sl–2000. FLIGHT 4–8: 1–2 broods. FP heathers. EGG 4–9: solitary or paired. LARVA 4–10: very well camouflaged on heather shoots. PUPA 1–12: in a tough cocoon on or just under soil. WINTER pupa: sometimes, possibly, as larva. NOTES Skims fast and low over vegetation in sunshine. STATUS LP; W. Germany & Hungary.

▲**SMALL DARK YELLOW UNDERWING** *Anarta cordigera*. Like Beautiful Yellow Underwing but fw lacks red and has a large white reniform stigma: no pale bands on abdomen. HAB heaths, bogs, and mountain slopes. ALT sl–2000. FLIGHT 5–7: very fast. FP bearberry. EGG 5–7: solitary. LARVA 6–8: nocturnal. PUPA 7–5: in a rather long and slender cocoon at base of fp. WINTER pupa. STATUS R; Britain. LP; W. Germany. SEE ALSO p. 250.

▲**BROAD-BORDERED WHITE UNDERWING** *Anarta melanopa*. Black-bordered white hw is characteristic, although fw colour and pattern vary a good deal. HAB mountain and moorland. ALT sl–2500. FLIGHT 5–7: very fast. FP bilberry, crowberry, and related heathland shrubs. EGG 5–6: solitary or paired. LARVA 6–8: nocturnal. PUPA 8–5: in a cocoon in moss or leaf litter. WINTER pupa. STATUS ?

▲**THE SILURIAN** *Eriopygodes imbecilla*. White reniform stigma on fw and uniformly brown hw distinguish this from several similar brown noctuids. HAB bogs and damp grassland in uplands: very local. ALT <2000. FLIGHT 6–7: usually after noon. FP bedstraws and other low-growing herbs. EGG 6–7: red and white. LARVA 7–5. PUPA 4–6: subterranean. WINTER larva. STATUS R; B. LP; W. Germany.

ANTLER MOTH *Cerapteryx graminis*. Fw bears pale branching pattern reminis-cent of a deer's antler: ♀ is much larger than ♂ and somewhat paler. HAB moors and grassland, most commonly on acidic soil. ALT sl–2000. FLIGHT 6–9: night and day. FP mat grass and other coarse grasses: also rushes. EGG 6–3: scattered freely by ♀ in flight. LARVA 3–6: largely nocturnal. PUPA 5–8: in oval chamber in soil. WINTER egg. VAR 'antler' mark is often reduced to just the central stem. STATUS Very common, the larvae often causing much damage to grassland.

LEAST MINOR *Photedes captiuncula*. Shiny wings and distinct pattern make this small moth easily recognisable in most areas (see below). HAB upland and coastal grassland, especially on limestone: very local. ALT sl–2000? FLIGHT 5–8. FP glaucous sedge. EGG 6–8. LARVA 7–5: usually inside shoots of fp. PUPA 4–6: in a flimsy cocoon on ground. WINTER larva. VAR outer part of fw is noticeably pink in Ireland (*P. c. tincta*). British race (*P. c. expolita*) is much less strongly marked. ♀♀ of all races are more strongly marked than ♂♂. NOTES It is mainly the ♂♂ that fly by day, usually after noon and following a very erratic course. STATUS R; B.

HAWORTH'S MINOR *Celaena haworthii*. Large white reniform stigma, usually with a prominent white vein below it: veins usually noticeably white in outer part of fw. HAB moors, fens and wet heaths. ALT sl–? FLIGHT 8–9. FP cotton grass and various rushes. EGG 8–4, but some may hatch in autumn. LARVA 4–7: inside fp stem. PUPA 7–8: in flimsy cocoon at base of fp. WINTER egg, or possibly larva. VAR fenland insects often paler and larger than moorland ones. NOTES Generally only ♂♂ fly by day – usually in afternoon sun. STATUS Local, but not rare in suitable habitats. LP; W. Germany.

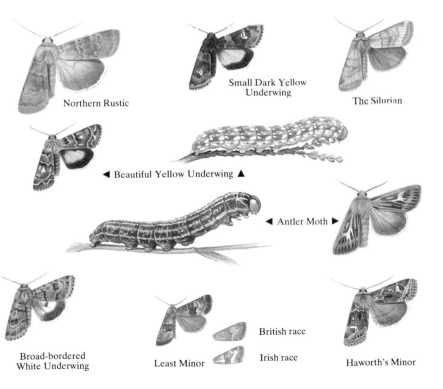

Northern Rustic

Small Dark Yellow Underwing

The Silurian

◀ Beautiful Yellow Underwing ▲

◀ Antler Moth ▶

Broad-bordered White Underwing

Least Minor

British race

Irish race

Haworth's Minor

GOLDWING *Synthymia fixa.* Fw pattern, with straight white sub-marginal line, distinguishes this from other species with yellow hw: ♀ fw is browner. HAB dry hillsides. ALT ? FLIGHT 3–5. FP pitch trefoil. EGG ? LARVA ? PUPA ? WINTER ? STATUS ?

▲**SMALL YELLOW UNDERWING** *Panemeria tenebrata.* Like Beautiful Yellow Underwing, but smaller and with plainer fw: hw has large brown patch at base. HAB flowery grasslands and woods. ALT sl–1600. FLIGHT 4–6. FP mouse-ears. EGG 5–6: solitary in flowers. LARVA 6–7: striped white and dark green in early stages. PUPA 7–5: in tight cocoon in soil. WINTER pupa. VAR fw often redder: hw sometimes all brown. NOTES Not closely related to the other other yellow underwings. STATUS Locally common.

PEASE BLOSSOM *Periphanes delphinii.* Fw unmistakable. HAB flowery places, including gardens and wasteland. ALT ? FLIGHT 5–6. FP larkspur and monkshood. EGG 6–7. LARVA 7–8. PUPA 8–5: deep in soil. WINTER pupa. STATUS Once widespread, but range has contracted sharply in 20th Century: now rare to N & W of Alps. LP; W. Germany.

▲**MARBLED CLOVER** *Heliothis viriplaca.* Discal band of fw is broad and extends outwards to form a rectangular patch at rear. HAB flowery places, including wasteland and coastal dunes. ALT ? FLIGHT 5–9: 2 broods. FP polyphagous on herbaceous plants. EGG 5–9. LARVA 6–10: feeding on flowers and developing fruits. PUPA 7–5: in flimsy cocoon on or just under soil. WINTER pupa. NOTES Continental specimens often migrate to B. STATUS Declining, probably due to more intensive grassland management, but still locally common in S. R; Britain.

▲**SHOULDER-STRIPED CLOVER** *Heliothis maritima.* Very like Marbled Clover but dark band of fw extends noticeably towards base at the rear: usually a dark streak at base of fw. HAB damp heaths and grasslands and coastal saltmarshes. ALT ? FLIGHT 5–9: 1–2 broods. FP heaths and other low-growing plants. EGG 5–9. LARVA 5–10. PUPA 1–12: in flimsy cocoon. WINTER pupa. VAR basal streak often missing from fw in SE. NOTES British race confined to heathland. STATUS R; Britain. LP; W. Germany.

△**BORDERED STRAW** *Heliothis peltigera.* Superficially like Marbled Clover but fw lacks a complete dark discal band and hw lacks dark basal patch. HAB flowery places. ALT ? FLIGHT 3–10: several broods. FP polyphagous: especially fond of garden marigolds. EGG 3–10. LARVA 3–10. PUPA 1–12. WINTER pupa. VAR fw colour ranges from pale straw to rich brown: hw sometimes entirely grey. NOTES A notable migrant, with erratic movements to N in summer. Larvae often found in B, but producing adults only in exceptionally good summers. STATUS Common.

△**SPOTTED CLOVER** *Protoschinia scutosa.* Blotched fw and narrow pd line of hw are characteristic. HAB grassy places everywhere. ALT ? FLIGHT 5–8: 2 broods. FP various herbs, especially field wormwood and goosefoots. EGG 5–9. LARVA 6–10: usually in flowers. PUPA 7–5. WINTER pupa. NOTES Resident in S & E, migrating northwards each year and sometimes establishing itself for a few years well outside its normal range: rare visitor to B. STATUS ?

▲**SPOTTED SULPHUR** *Emmelia trabealis.* Fw pattern is unmistakable. HAB grassy heaths and other rough grassland: very local. ALT ? FLIGHT 5–8: 2 broods: mainly towards evening. FP field bindweed. EGG 5–8. LARVA 6–9: often in flowers and developing fruits. PUPA 1–12: in flimsy cocoon amongst grasses. WINTER pupa. STATUS Declining in many areas through loss of habitat. E. and possibly extinct in B.

PALE SHOULDER *Acontia lucida*. White base of fw distinguishes this from other similar moths. HAB flowery places, especially clover fields. ALT ? FLIGHT 5–8: 2 broods: in hot sunshine. FP bindweeds, mallows, and other herbs. EGG 5–8. LARVA 6–9. PUPA 7–5. WINTER pupa. NOTES Resident in much of S & C, with sporadic northward migration in summer. Not recorded in B since 19th Century. STATUS ?

△**DEWICK'S PLUSIA** *Macdunnoughia confusa*. Solid silvery white streak on reddish brown fw distinguishes this from related moths. HAB flowery places. ALT sl–1200. FLIGHT 5–10: 2 broods: night and day. FP various herbs, especially yarrow and chamomile. EGG 5–9. LARVA 1–12. PUPA 4–9. WINTER larva. NOTES An eastern species which has spread rapidly across western Europe in 20th Century. Now well established in SW, from where it migrates northward each summer. Sporadic visitor to B. STATUS ?

▲**SILVER Y** *Autographa gamma*. Silvery Y-shaped mark on greyish or purplish fw: a dark stripe runs from apex towards the Y. HAB flowery places. ALT sl–2500. FLIGHT 4–11 (1–12 in parts of S): 2+ broods: night and day: usually seen only as a grey blur at flowers by day. FP polyphagous on low-growing herbs. EGG 4–10: solitary or in small groups: white at first, becoming green. LARVA 1–12: pale to very dark green (almost black) and, like other members of its group, with just 3 pairs of prolegs. PUPA 3–10: in flimsy cocoon amongst leaves. WINTER larva: also as adult in far S. VAR Late insects often darker than spring ones: the Y is often broken into a V and a dot. NOTES A great migrant. Resident in S and perhaps in a few lowland areas of C, but spreading all over Europe in summer. Some return movement in autumn. STATUS Abundant everywhere in summer. Larvae often damage brassicas and other crops. SEE ALSO p. 202, 227, 252, 253, 266.

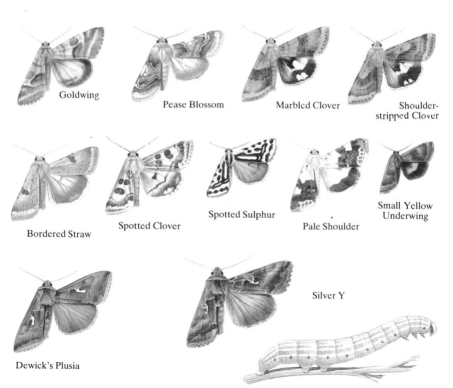

Goldwing

Pease Blossom

Marbled Clover

Shoulder-stripped Clover

Bordered Straw

Spotted Clover

Spotted Sulphur

Pale Shoulder

Small Yellow Underwing

Dewick's Plusia

Silver Y

▲**SCARCE SILVER Y** *Syngrapha interrogationis*. Like Silver Y but Y-shaped mark usually broken and indistinct: central area of fw rather black: fore and mid tibiae spined. HAB mountain and moorland. ALT sl–2500. FLIGHT 6–8: night and day: fast and low over vegetation. FP heather and bilberry. EGG 6–8. LARVA 1–12. PUPA 5–7: in pale cocoon at base of fp. WINTER small larva. NOTES Migratory, with continental specimens often arriving in B. STATUS LP; W. Germany.

Syngrapha devergens. Like Silver Y but fw greyer and with clear white border: discal area bordered by clear white lines: fore and mid tibiae spined. HAB alpine meadows. ALT <3000. FLIGHT 7–8. FP various herbs. EGG 7–8. LARVA 1–12: 2-year life cycle. PUPA 5–6: under stones. WINTER larva (twice). STATUS Not common.

Syngrapha microgamma. Rather like *S. devergens* but hw border is broader and there is a dark spot near front of hw: rectangular brown patch of fw longer than in related spp: arms of Y strongly divergent and stem often missing, leaving a silvery crescent. HAB moors and mountains. FLIGHT 5–7 in sunshine. FP dwarf sallows. EGG 5–8. LARVA 7–5: violet brown with pale brown head and yellow lateral lines. PUPA 4–6. WINTER larva. STATUS Not rare, but populations fluctuate markedly.

Syngrapha ain. Like *S. devergens* but larger and with much broader border to hw: outer margin of fw is much blacker. HAB montane larch woods. ALT <2200. FLIGHT 7–8. FP larch needles. EGG 7–8. LARVA 8–5: mostly hibernating. PUPA 5–7: in a brownish cocoon. WINTER small larva. STATUS Locally common.

Caloplusia hockenwarthi. Very like *S. devergens* but silvery streak on Y is more slender and sits on a velvety brown patch: hw largely orange with a thin, wavy submarginal band (thick in *devergens*). HAB flowery mountain slopes around the tree line. ALT <2500. FLIGHT 6–8. FP umbellifers and plantains. EGG 6–8. LARVA 1–12: 2-year life cycle. PUPA 5–7. WINTER larva (twice). STATUS Not rare.

▲**MOTHER SHIPTON** *Callistege mi*. Fw pattern, said to resemble witch-like profile of the legendary Mother Shipton, is characteristic. HAB grassy and scrubby places. ALT sl–1700. FLIGHT 5–9: 1–2 broods. FP clover and other legumes. EGG 5–9. LARVA 6–10. PUPA 7–5. WINTER pupa. NOTES Rarely feeds and not normally attracted to flowers. STATUS Generally common.

▲**BURNET COMPANION** *Euclidia glyphica*. Like Mother Shipton, especially in flight, but fw is much browner and lacks the deeply lobed pd line: hw largely orange. HAB grassy places, especially on calcareous soils: often flies with Mother Shipton and with burnet moths. ALT sl–2000. FLIGHT 4–8: 1–2 broods. FP clovers and other legumes. EGG 4–8: batched on leaves. LARVA 5–9: nocturnal. PUPA 1–12: in cocoon in or on soil under fp. WINTER pupa. STATUS Generally common.

▲**FOUR-SPOTTED** *Tyta luctuosa*. Superficially like Pale Shoulder, especially in flight, but easily distinguished by black patch at base of each wing. HAB rough, flower-rich grassland, especially on limestone. ALT ? FLIGHT 5–8: 1–2 broods. FP field bindweed. EGG 5–8: solitary on stems and buds. LARVA 6–9: 3 pairs of prolegs at first, but 5 pairs in final instar. PUPA 1–12: in sturdy cocoon just under soil. WINTER pupa. STATUS Declining in many areas. V; Britain.

Euclidia triquetra. Fw pattern unmistakable. HAB dry grasslands, mainly in uplands. FLIGHT 5–8: 2 broods. 2nd brood generally only partial. FP bird's-foot trefoil and other low-growing legumes. EGG 5–8. LARVA 6–10. PUPA 1–12. WINTER pupa. STATUS ?

Aedia funesta. Superficially like Four-Spotted but larger and without black patch at base of hw. HAB damp woods and grassland. ALT ? FLIGHT 6–7. FP bindweeds. EGG 6–7. LARVA 7–5. PUPA 5–6. WINTER larva. STATUS LP; W. Germany.

▲**SMALL PURPLE-BARRED** *Phytometra viridaria.* Pink or purple cross lines are characteristic. HAB heaths and grasslands: local. ALT sl–2000. FLIGHT 4–8: 1–2 broods. FP milkworts and louseworts. EGG 4–8: solitary or in small groups. LARVA 5–9: nocturnal on leaves and flowers. PUPA 1–12: in sturdy cocoon among leaves or leaf litter. WINTER pupa. VAR purplish cross lines are often more slender, especially in B, and occasionally absent. STATUS Generally common, but local in N.

▲**STRAW DOT** *Rivula sericealis.* Reniform stigma of 2 conspicuous dots on a greyish patch. HAB damp heaths and grasslands and also in damp woodland. ALT sl–1700. FLIGHT 5–10: 2–3 broods: night and day. FP tor grass, false brome grass, and other coarse grasses. EGG 5–10: in batches. LARVA 1–12. PUPA 4–9: green and concealed in a folded leaf blade. WINTER hibernating larva, attached to silken pad on a leaf blade. VAR fw colour ranges from straw to deep yellow. NOTES Tends to be more diurnal on continent than in B. STATUS Generally common.

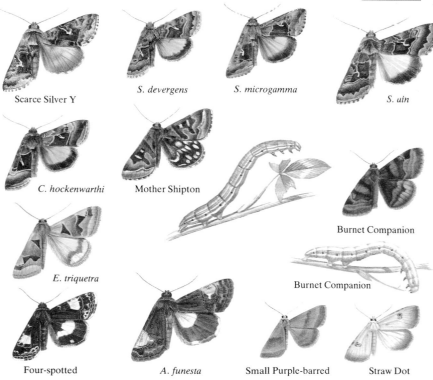

Scarce Silver Y

S. devergens

S. microgamma

S. uin

C. hockenwarthi

Mother Shipton

Burnet Companion

E. triquetra

Burnet Companion

Four-spotted

A. funesta

Small Purple-barred

Straw Dot

From Egg to Adult

EGGS AND EGG LAYING

All butterflies and moths begin their lives as eggs and they have to look after themselves right from the outset. The female is usually considerate enough to lay her eggs on or near suitable food-plants, but this is normally the limit of her maternal care. Only in one species – the tropical nymphalid *Hypolimnas antilope* – does she hang about to look after her eggs and perhaps ward off potential predators and parasites. But laying her eggs on the right kind of food-plant for the resulting caterpillars is a start, for which the youngsters should be grateful, and this seems as good a place as any at which to begin the description of the life cycle of butterflies and moths.

CHOOSING THE FOOD-PLANT

Selecting the right food-plant from a forest of green leaves might seem a rather daunting prospect for humans, but we have not been programmed for the job. The butterflies have, and natural selection over countless generations has endowed them with some incredibly sensitive detectors which ensure that very few eggs get laid in the wrong place.

It was once thought that adult females remember the food plants on which they grew up and seek out the same species when ready to lay their own eggs. This might be so in some instances, but it is certainly not the whole story. Consider the Holly Blue: the summer butterflies grow up on holly as a rule, but when laying their own eggs they seek out the flower buds of the ivy. Memory clearly plays no part here and, as with most butterflies and moths, it is instinctive behaviour – just as much a part of an animal's make-up as its shape and colour – that leads it to the correct food-plant.

Assuming that the gravid female,

itching to get on with her egg-laying, finds herself in a suitable habitat (see p. 242), she may rely on colours to guide her in the early stages of her search for suitable food-plants. The Large White certainly uses colour, and experiments have shown that she is attracted to certain shades of bluish green – just the colours found in a cabbage patch. The day-flying Hummingbird Hawkmoth also responds to colour – bright greens in this instance – when searching for the bedstraws on which to lay its eggs, and such visual searching is likely to be found in all day-flying Lepidoptera.

Smell does not seem to be important in the initial stages of the search, but certainly comes into play as the insects get closer to the plants. Scents may then combine with more detailed visual clues, such as leaf-shape, to tell the insects whether or not to bother with a particular plant.

But even if it looks and smells right, a plant might not be right for egg-laying and the butterfly or moth must make sure by further examination. Antennae, palps, mouth-parts, ovipositor, and even the feet are used, picking up subtle chemical clues and also paying close attention to the texture of leaves and their water content. Healthy, succulent leaves are necessary for a caterpillar's well-being and it would not have much to thank its mother for if she started it off on a dead or withered leaf: the leaf might even fall before the egg hatches, and that is bad news for a tiny caterpillar that needs to start feeding very soon after hatching. Young caterpillars normally cannot move very far and they are thus utterly dependent for their survival on the mother's skill at picking out the right spot.

A female butterfly searching for the ideal spot for her eggs has quivering

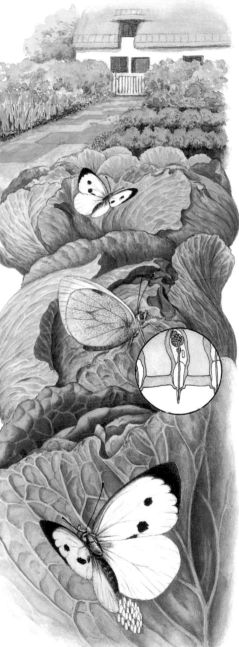

The Large White lays her eggs in batches, after making sure that the plant is suitable with the aid of chemical receptors in her feet

antennae and bends over to tap the leaves as she 'sniffs' them. Her tongue may also shoot out to 'taste' the leaves, but the most important chemical sensors are often on the feet and the butterfly will often 'stamp' on the leaves to decide whether they really are suitable for her offspring. Minute spines on her feet puncture the leaf surfaces and release the chemicals that stimulate the sense organs. This stamping, often known as drumming, may also provide some physical assessment of the leaf texture. The Large White has sensory equipment on all its feet and, as long as one foot is intact, the butterfly can lay its eggs on any suitable plant. Removal of all six feet, however, prevents the butterfly from laying any eggs, because it just does not get the right signals. Some butterflies carry their sensors only on their front feet, and then removal of just these two feet prevents egg-laying.

When stamping occurs it usually indicates that the plant is at least in the right family, as the butterfly will not bother with stamping unless its antennae have already picked up favourable signals.

Egg-laying butterflies clearly pick up lots of chemical signals from the vegetation, and egg-laying in most species may depend on getting just the right mixture of these signals. On the other hand, there are some species, such as the economically important and hence intensively studied Large White, that rely on just a single substance to trigger off egg-laying. The Large White's feet carry receptors which respond only to the mustard oils found in cabbages and other brassicas. Unless the butterfly can detect these compounds it will not begin laying, but if the compounds are present and other conditions are acceptable the eggs will be deposited. The Large White can even be persuaded to lay on green paper that has been treated with a solution of mustard oils, and in theory it should be possible to divert at least some of the butterflies from your cabbage patch by spraying neighbouring non-cabbage plants with the material.

Eggs may be laid on these plants, but the resulting caterpillars will be unable to feed there and will perish. Some success has been reported in this sphere through spraying the neighbouring plants with liquidised cabbage leaves, but it seems unlikely that this simple method will provide any real control of the cabbage whites: the mustard oils might attract the butterflies, but damaged cabbage leaves tend to deter them from laying (see below) and they are unlikely to be fooled into laying all their eggs on these unsuitable plants.

Most butterfly species, whether relying on a single substance or a complex mixture of signals to trigger egg-laying, use a rather limited range of food-plants – usually limited to just one family and very often to a single genus – because unrelated plants usually contain a wide range of chemicals and give totally different signals to the investigating butterflies. But there are exceptions. The cultivated nasturtium, for example, contains almost identical mustard oils to those found in cabbages and is regularly used by both Large and Small Whites, although it is quite unrelated to the cabbage tribe.

But egg-laying is not entirely about finding the right chemical signals and then dumping the eggs. In many instances the absence of inhibitory signals is just as important to the female butterfly as the presence of stimulatory substances. The Large White, for example, tends not to lay on plants, however suitable in other respects, if they already carry eggs or larvae. Both sight and smell are involved here, with the smell of the nibbled leaves being the main factor repelling the butterflies from plants already bearing caterpillars. Such behaviour clearly helps to reduce competition between caterpillars, so mutilation of a leaf or two of a brassica plant may also reduce infestation.

Sticking small clumps of artificial eggs to the leaves might also help, for experiments suggest that butterflies do move away when they see other egg batches on the cabbage leaves.

Marbled Whites scatter eggs over grassland

The Orange-tip also tends to avoid laying on plants that already carry its bright orange eggs – a wise move, for the caterpillars of this species are infamous cannibals. It is interesting to note here that some tropical plants have actually evolved their own fake eggs, small swellings on the leaves and stalks, that apparently deter a number of egg-laying butterflies.

For polyphagous species, whose larvae can feed happily on a wide range of food-plants, it is likely that the absence of inhibitory substances in the leaves is a more important stimulus to egg-laying than the presence of any specific trigger. These species can then lay their eggs on a wide variety of plants, all of which lack the inhibitor. Polyphagy is not common among butterflies, but is very common among moths – including the day-flying Silver Y. Several moths actually scatter their eggs from the air, but the only European butterflies to broadcast their eggs are the Marbled Whites (*Melanargia spp.*) and the Ringlet. The larvae of these species feed on a range of grasses and, as long as the egg-laying females stay over the grass, the larvae will survive. There is little point in the Marbled White gluing its eggs to the grasses, for the larva wanders away and hibernates as soon as it hatches and it does not feed until the following spring.

GETTING IT WRONG

Butterflies occasionally make mistakes in their egg-laying despite their innate programming, but the commonest 'mistake' is probably more to do with the unavailability of the food-plant than with making a wrong choice. For example, some butterflies may be 'taken short' and have to drop their eggs on any plant when the weather is not good enough for them to fly and search for the right plants. The same thing may happen when they are confined in captivity without the right food-plant, but in fact most butterflies prefer to re-absorb their eggs rather than lay them on unsuitable plants. Moths tend to be less fussy and many will lay almost anywhere when they get desperate. The Hummingbird Hawkmoth, for example, if given free access to food-plants, will approach and settle only on the correct plants at first. But if it is prevented from laying eggs on these plants – by disturbance every time it is about to lay – it will start approaching other plants of the right colour and eventually lay its eggs on them, even though these plants are unsuitable for the larvae. Comfortable once more, the moth will ignore the unsuitable plants and seek out the correct plants again. Many moths will even lay eggs when confined in small boxes without any kind of vegetation.

Many 'mistakes', however, are nothing of the kind. Even if the chosen site seems totally unsuitable to us, further study usually shows that the butterfly knows what it is doing. The Silver-Washed Fritillary, for example, lays its eggs on tree trunks. But, as the caterpillars go into hibernation immediately after hatching and without feeding, the tree trunk with its numerous cosy crevices is not such a bad place after all, even if it can mean a bit of a walk for the caterpillars in the spring.

The first of the Small Heath's eggs are generally larger than the last

Moths will lay their eggs in captivity without any food-plant

HOW MANY EGGS?

Butterflies lay anything from a few dozen to a few hundred eggs. Species like the Marbled White, that scatter their eggs freely over the vegetation, tend to produce more eggs than those that glue their eggs carefully to their specific food-plants, but there is also considerable variation in the numbers of eggs produced by females of a single species. Large females have a greater egg-laying potential than smaller individuals, and this can usually be traced back to better food supplies in the larval state. There is also a temperature effect in some species. Caterpillars of the Small White reared at low temperatures produce larger adults than those reared at high temperatures, and more eggs are laid by these larger individuals. This temperature effect may explain the small size of third-brood butterflies reared at the end of a hot summer, although the effect might not be a direct one. It is possible that the small size results from relatively dry food eaten by the larvae in late summer.

There is also some variation in the size of the eggs within a species, with eggs laid towards the end of an adult's life often being noticeably smaller than earlier ones. This seems to be as a result of the quality of the adult's food. It is known that some nectars are richer in nitrates than others, and butterflies having access to such nectars tend to produce full-sized eggs throughout their lives. Those denied such nutritious meals produce smaller eggs in later life. There is, however, no evidence to suggest that small eggs

Small White

Brown Hairstreak

Large White

Peacock

Emperor Moth

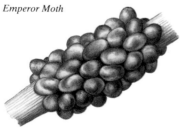

Butterfly and moth eggs may be laid singly, or in small or large batches

are in any way inferior to large ones or that caterpillars hatching from small eggs are any less successful in later life.

So why do the butterflies not lay small eggs right from the start? In theory this would be a good idea, for it would allow the butterflies to increase egg production and have more offspring. But the actual number of eggs produced in the female's body is not the only factor involved here. Finding suitable sites and the actual process of egg-laying take a good deal of time and a butterfly simply may not have time in its short life to lay more than a certain number of eggs. Overcast and windy weather keeps the insects inactive and, although a butterfly may live for several weeks, relatively little of this time can be spent in egg-laying. There is, therefore, nothing to be gained by producing larger numbers of eggs and evolution has not proceeded very far down this particular avenue. As it is, many females still die with some of their eggs unlaid.

CLUSTERED OR SINGLE?

If time is a major factor in finding the right food-plants and laying the eggs it would seem sensible for the butterflies to lay a lot of eggs together once they have found suitable sites, but relatively few species actually behave in this way. The majority of our butterflies deposit their eggs singly or in small groups. Of the 59 species that breed regularly in Britain, only six lay their eggs in large clusters. They are the Peacock, the Small Tortoiseshell, three fritillaries, and our old friend (and enemy) the Large White. A few more batch-layers occur on the continent, including the Camberwell Beauty and the Black-Veined White, but they are still heavily outnumbered by those species that lay their eggs singly or in small batches. The advantages of the latter method must be considerable, but the butterflies have not yet revealed them to us and we can only guess at the relative importance of the many factors involved.

Eggs laid singly are usually cryptically coloured and hard to discover, and therefore less likely to be destroyed by predators and parasites. Being spaced out, the resulting caterpillars also compete less with each other, and this spacing is particularly important for cannibalistic species like the Orange-tip. But perhaps an even greater advantage stems from the fact that the egg-laying female does not hang about for long in any one place and is thus less at risk from predators than an insect that spends a lot of time in one spot.

So how do the batch-layers survive? Most batch-laying species are well camouflaged on the underside or, like the Large White, unpalatable to predators. They are thus able to sit and pump out eggs for some time in one place without fear of detection or predation. This might also explain the greater proportion of moths that lay their eggs in large batches: being nocturnal, they are far less at risk from predators when sitting on the vegetation than the day-flying butterflies. The day-flying burnet moths get away with batch-laying because of their foul tastes and warning colours (see p. 277).

But all the adult protection in the world would be useless if the egg batches were then destroyed *en bloc*, and we find that batched eggs usually have some fairly efficient protection of their own. Merely by existing in groups, especially if they are heaped on top of each other as they are in some burnet moths and a few butterflies, they can reduce the number affected by parasites because the little parasites (see p. 209) cannot reach

into the centre of the clusters. Predators might be expected to gobble up complete batches – and they sometimes do – but it is likely that the eggs of many cluster-laying species are unpalatable and that, having tried a couple at the edge, a predator leaves the rest of the batch alone. Batched eggs are often brightly coloured as well, serving to warn predators of their unpalatability, although not all enemies are deterred by this; a number of bird species will eat the bright yellow eggs of the Large White. Distasteful or even poisonous compounds in the eggs may act against parasites as well as predators, although undoubted toxins have so far been found in only very few butterfly eggs – including those of the Monarch, which actually lays its eggs singly!

Caterpillars emerging from batched or clustered eggs generally stay together, at least during the first two or three instars, and, like the eggs, they are often unpalatable and brightly coloured. Many are clothed with long hairs, which irritate predators and actually prevent small parasites from getting at the body. Many also live in silken tents as extra protection against their enemies.

KEEPING TO THE EDGE

It has often been observed that butterflies prefer to lay their eggs on the edges of food-plant clumps rather than distributing them evenly all over the plants. This phenomenon, known as the edge effect, has been noticed in both cluster-layers, like the Small Tortoiseshell, and species laying their eggs singly, like the Orange-tip. Many

The graph shows that the number of Small Tortoiseshell eggs are much higher around the edges of nettle patches than in the centre

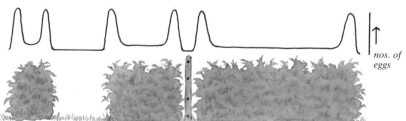

nos. of eggs

investigations have been carried out on this behaviour, but there still is not any really good explanation of why the butterflies do it. The favoured explanation is that butterflies are more ready to lay eggs after a flight, so they start laying as soon as they meet a new clump of food-plant and automatically deposit most of their eggs near the edge. But things are not quite as simple as this and several factors are known to be involved in the edge effect.

More eggs should be laid in the outer region of a large clump because, for example, the area within 15cm of the edge of the circular patch 45cm in diameter is five times the size of the area within 15cm of the centre. But field observations show that far more eggs are laid in the outer ring than could be expected from simple random distribution. In one investigation with Small Tortoiseshells about 66% of all egg batches were laid right at the margins of the nettle clumps.

Egg-laying Small Tortoiseshells are also attracted to internal margins, such as those created where fences run through the centre of nettle patches, and several other butterflies are known to favour similar landmarks when seeking egg-laying sites.

It is clear that different species choose marginal plants for different reasons, although we do not always know what these reasons may be. The Orange-tip goes for the larger plants, whereas the stage of growth – and hence the quality of the leaves – and the amount of light and shade are important to many butterflies. It is well known, for example, that butterflies prefer to lay their eggs in the sunshine, and this should be kept in mind when planning a butterfly garden (see p. 253). Nettles might grow well enough in a shady corner but they will not attract the egg-laying butterflies. To be of use the nettle bed must be in the sun for at least part of the day.

THE EGG

A butterfly's egg is enclosed in a tough, waterproof coat and it has a small depression on the upper surface. A powerful microscope may reveal a delicate, flower-like pattern around the depression and, at the bottom of the hollow, one or more minute perforations known as micropyles. These are the holes through which sperm enters to fertilise the egg, and they also enable the developing embryo to breathe although there are commonly breathing pores elsewhere on the egg-shell as well.

Butterfly eggs range from skittle-shaped, as in the whites, through a range of miniature domes and barrels, to the flattened button-like eggs laid by many of the blues and some of the skippers. Apart from a few skipper eggs, they are all circular in cross section and the shape is fairly constant within each family.

Moth eggs are equally variable: commonly hemispherical, but often oval or rectangular and box-like. Some moths lay extremely flat, scale-like eggs. Whereas the butterfly egg is always 'upright', with the micropyle at the top, moth eggs commonly have the micropyle at one end and are then described as 'flat' – even when distinctly oval in shape!

There is also a great variation in the size of butterfly eggs, often quite independent of the size of the adult insects. Species with adults of similar proportions may lay eggs of widely different sizes. The Meadow Brown, for example, lays an egg resembling a tiny truncated acorn, about 0.5mm high and about the same in diameter. The related and similar sized Marbled White lays a spherical egg about 1mm in diameter, while the much larger Peacock lays a barrel-shaped egg only 0.8mm high. The Small Heath, one of our smallest butterflies, lays an acorn-shaped egg about 0.7mm high. There is also a certain amount of variation in

Butterfly eggs display a wide range of colours and shapes

egg size within a species, with older individuals tending to lay slightly smaller eggs (see p. 203).

When looked at under higher magnification the surface of some insect eggs is seen to be exquisitely sculptured. Some of the most elaborate designs are found on the eggs of various blues and also on some nymphalid eggs, such as those of the White Admiral. The cut-glass delicacy of these eggs, described by Edward Newman more than a century ago as '*a thousand times more delicate and fine than any human hand could execute*', is truly one of nature's marvels. At the other end of the scale, some of the more primitive moths lay eggs without any trace of ornamentation, and this is one reason for placing the butterflies fairly high up on the scale of lepidopteran evolution. There are, however, some moth families that produce both plain and sculptured eggs, so we should not place too much emphasis on this feature until we understand its significance. The spinier eggs may provide some protection from parasites (see p. 209).

The scanning electron microscope has revealed even finer details on the egg-shell, with the most amazing patterns of pores and pimples on and between the ridges of many eggs. This microscopic pattern has been shown to be concerned with getting oxygen into the eggs, especially when they are immersed in water after heavy rain.

High magnification reveals the intricate structure of a lycaenid egg

EGG COLOUR

Butterfly eggs are usually rather pale when first laid, but they colour up quite rapidly – often within twelve hours. Most adopt cryptic hues of brown or green and blend effectively with their surroundings, but there are some that advertise their presence with bright colours. The eggs of the Large White come into this category, and so do those of the Orange-tip (see p. 202). Some eggs, especially the larger ones, develop disruptive colour patterns which break up their outlines and make them difficult to pick out against their natural backgrounds. This trick is found mainly among the moths, but is also employed by some swallowtails. The eggs of the Common Swallowtail, for example, develop irregular brown bands to break up their outlines (see p. 26).

Another trick, used by the Puss Moth and several other species, is the development of a small dark spot at the top of the egg. Resembling an exit hole, this tricks some birds into thinking that the caterpillar has already left and that there is no point in having a go at the egg.

Further colour changes may occur during the development of the eggs. These may be true changes in the colour of the egg-shells, but are more often associated with what is going on inside the eggs. In these cases the colours are actually those of the caterpillars inside the thin and largely transparent shells. The eggs of the Duke of Burgundy, for example, are pearly white at first, but become criss-crossed with slender brown lines just before hatching – the lines being the larval hairs showing through the shell. The Speckled Wood egg is also pearly at first, and then gets a dark 'lid' which is actually the black head capsule of the young larva inside. Many eggs take on a purplish or leaden colour shortly before they hatch.

INSIDE THE EGG

Although the eggs are normally laid very soon after fertilisation, it may be quite some time before development starts. But when they do start things happen very quickly. The clear fluid that fills the newly laid egg thickens to a soup – more like a custard in the yellow eggs of the Large White and some other species – and the larva gradually begins to take shape as cells multiply in the fluid. A simple tube develops and forms a ring just inside the shell. Legs soon develop. They face outwards at first, but then the embryonic caterpillar gets restless and wriggles about until its legs face inwards. The young caterpillar, still forming a ring, can be seen quite clearly in some of the thinner-shelled eggs, especially when the ocelli develop and form dark patches on the face. The caterpillar eventually fills the whole egg and is then ready to hatch.

Embryonic development may take only a few days during the summer and caterpillars of the Small Dusty Wave moth have been known to hatch only two days after the eggs were laid. Between ten and thirty days is, however, usual for most butterflies apart from those that spend the winter in the egg stage. These may take 300 days to hatch, spending the winter in a state of arrested development known as diapause. This can occur at any stage of development but for a given species it usually occurs at a fixed point each year. Many over-wintering eggs remain in the initial clear fluid stage throughout the winter and do not begin their development until the spring. On the other hand, there are species that complete their embryonic development in late summer or autumn and then go into diapause as fully formed caterpillars still inside their egg shells. Examples include the Silver-spotted Skipper, the Apollo, the High Brown Fritillary, and the Black Hairstreak. Relatively few species pass the winter in an intermediate stage of embryonic development.

The overwintering eggs have nothing to fear from the weather. Their tissues contain small amounts of glycerol, alcohol, and other substances which act like anti-freeze to lower the freezing point of the body fluids and protect the tissues from all but the severest of winters.

Diapause may occur at any stage of the butterfly's life cycle and is not confined to the eggs, but related groups tend to use the same stage for diapause. Most members of the swallowtail family (Papilionidae) diapause as pupae, but the apollos diapause in the egg stage. The whites (Pieridae) generally diapause as pupae, but the clouded yellows do it as larvae. Most browns (Satyridae) diapause as larvae, and so do most members of the Nymphalidae, although some of the latter pass the winter as hibernating adults. The blues and their relatives (Lycaenidae) and the skippers (Hesperiidae) mostly pass the winter as diapausing larvae, but they also include species that overwinter as eggs or pupae. Butterflies with an egg diapause are nearly all single-brooded (see p. 22).

Although it is often thought of simply as a way of overcoming cold or other unfavourable conditions, diapause has another very important function – that of synchronising the appearance of the insects with each other and with their food-plants. It ensures that the eggs hatch when the food-plants become available and, when it occurs at later stages of the life cycle, it ensures that the adults are all around at the same time and can find mates without any trouble.

The onset of diapause is occasionally brought about by adverse conditions, but this could be too late to enable an insect to survive those conditions and preparations for diapause usually begin long before the bad weather starts. The number of hours of daylight is of over-riding importance in preparing the insects for winter diapause or hibernation (see p. 220). Diapause in some eggs is initiated by the reduced hours of daylight experienced by the egg-laying females in late summer and autumn, and can be prevented by keeping the adults in artificial daylight for 15 hours or more each day. But most of our butterflies that pass the winter as eggs have an obligate diapause, with development being arrested regardless of the environmental conditions.

The ending or breaking of diapause is occasionally a spontaneous action, but it usually depends on prolonged exposure to cold, followed by the rising temperatures of spring. It is this factor that ensures that the eggs do not hatch before the leaves of the food-plant appear. Many amateur butterfly breeders fail to appreciate the importance of low temperatures to their livestock and are disappointed to find that many eggs do not hatch in the spring when they have been kept in the house. Diapausing eggs should be kept in the shed, or even in the fridge, for the winter. Refrigerated eggs should be brought out when the buds start to burst in the spring.

THE ENEMIES OF EGGS

Butterfly eggs are attacked by a wide range of both predators and parasites. The predators include numerous birds, beetles, earwigs, bush-crickets, ants, wasps, bugs, and harvestmen. Mites are important predators in some places, piercing the egg and sucking out the nutritious contents. But it is the parasites that grow up inside the eggs that are the most interesting, not least because of their own complex life cycles.

Obviously an insect that grows up inside the egg of a butterfly is going to be very small, and these egg parasites do include some of the smallest of all insects – the fairy flies of the family Mymaridae. These are not true flies but, like most other egg-parasites, mini-relatives of the ichneumons that parasitise so many caterpillars (see p. 223). Their bodies are often no more than 0.5mm long and their feathery wings rarely span more than 2mm. Most are yellow or black. The females pierce the egg shells and lay one or more eggs inside. The resulting grubs feed on the contents of the egg and pupate therein when ready. Adult parasites emerge in due course and

The parasitic fairy fly cannot reach the eggs in the centre of the irregular pile of Peacock butterfly eggs

adult

a

b

c

Trichogramma *developing in small moth eggs (a) are smaller than those reared in large eggs (b) while males developing in alder fly eggs (c) are wingless*

seek out more butterfly or moth eggs. They usually produce several generations in a year and, because they are not particularly fussy about the host species, they can usually find suitable eggs quite easily. Fairy flies pass the winter either in diapause inside the host egg or as hibernating adults.

The family Trichogrammatidae is related to the fairy flies and its members attack butterfly eggs in much the same way, although the adults are much stouter than the fairy flies and have much broader wings. They are very catholic in their choice of host egg, but generally go for the largest eggs available. Parasites growing up in large eggs are much bigger than those emerging from small eggs, and there may be other differences as well. An extreme example is afforded by *Trichogramma semblidis*, which does not even confine itself to the eggs of Lepidoptera. When reared in the eggs of various moths, the male parasites are fully winged, but when reared in alder fly eggs (order Neuroptera) they are wingless. Like the fairy flies, the trichogrammatids are well able to synchronise their activities with those of the host species, producing several generations in a year and going into a long diapause when they find themselves in diapausing eggs in the autumn.

While exploring the host eggs the adult egg parasite often leaves a scent trail which tells other females that the eggs are already occupied – a neat way of ensuring that the eggs are not over-populated, for this would inevitably lead to starvation of most, if not all of the young parasites.

Despite all the predators and parasites eager to destroy them, plenty of butterfly eggs survive and it seems that in Europe they are more at risk from the physical environment than from any of their enemies. We have seen that they are not harmed by the cold, but many undoubtedly succumb

during winter flooding. A much higher proportion of eggs is lost to enemies, especially parasites, in the tropics, where about 90% are destroyed in this way.

PROTECTING THE EGGS

We have already seen that many butterfly and moth eggs are protected from predators by camouflage or by warning coloration, but the butterflies also get up to other tricks to ensure that at least some of their eggs survive. Our European fauna cannot match the range of cunning devices found in the tropics, but there are still some interesting examples. The Map Butterfly is one of those species that lays its eggs in clusters, but it does not just dump them in a heap: it glues them into neat little chains which greatly resemble the catkins of the stinging nettles on which they are laid, and the camouflage fools many birds as well as many entomologists.

But visual camouflage is no use against the parasites, which seek out the eggs by smell. As we have seen, some eggs contain anti-parasite materials that prevent the growth of the parasite grubs, and it is quite possible that some eggs also give off scents which actually deter the parasites from laying. Several of the European butterflies, notably some of the skippers and lycaenids, coat their eggs with scales from the tip of the abdomen. The Sloe Hairstreak, the female of which has a prominent tuft of black scales on her abdomen, is a particularly good example. The scales do not actually conceal the eggs like the large tufts of hair-like scales used by some moths, but it is possible that they form an effective barrier against the tiny egg parasites. The scales are also thought to emit a scent which deters these parasites. Among the lycaenids, however, the scales may actually play a more important role in larval nutrition. In those species that coat their eggs with scales the emerging larvae eat their egg shells completely, whereas the others normally nibble just a small exit hole and then move on to the vegetation.

Chain of Map butterfly eggs and a Sloe Hairstreak egg with scales

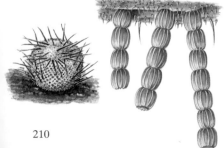

THE CATERPILLAR

The caterpillars of butterflies and moths have no special egg-breaking apparatus such as is found in the youngsters of most other insects and they have to bite their way out of their egg-shells when they are ready. Their jaws, although tiny, are well able to cope with this task and many are not content with just chewing an escape hatch. Many species eat the whole shell when they have struggled out of it, and they may well obtain vital minerals or symbiotic bacteria in this way. The larvae of quite a number of species die if they are not allowed to eat their egg-shells after hatching.

When they first leave their eggs, butterfly caterpillars nearly all look alike; pale green or cream and with a similar arrangement of pimples and bristles when examined under a lens. This is not really surprising, because this first instar is simply a continuation of the embryonic stage; the caterpillar does not change its form or appearance when it leaves the egg. Except in those species like the Marbled White and the Silver-washed Fritillary that go into hibernation without feeding, this 'embryonic instar' does not last for long. The young caterpillar is already a remarkable eating machine with a considerable appetite and it puts on weight rapidly. Within a few days it is ready for its first moult. This is when the specific characteristics begin to appear in most caterpillars, although the larvae of the swallowtails and some other butterflies are quite distinct from the outset.

THE CATERPILLAR BODY

A caterpillar is basically a flexible tube with a relatively tough, globular head at the front and a number of short legs strung out along the body. The latter is composed of 13 rings or segments, although not all are clearly visible, and it may be clothed to a greater or lesser extent with hairs or bristles. It is designed purely for eating and growing. Most caterpillars are clearly cylindrical, although slightly flattened on the lower surface, and their shape is maintained largely by the pressure of the fluids inside. But there are a number of departures from this familiar shape, especially among caterpillars of the family Lycaenidae. This family includes the blues and their relatives, whose larvae are rather dumpy creatures with very short legs that are normally hidden under the body. Many look more like slugs or woodlice than caterpillars. The Duke of Burgundy larva has a similar shape, as do the larvae of the burnet moths.

The head consists of six tiny segments, but these are distinguishable only in the very early stages of embryonic growth and by the time the caterpillar chews its way out of its egg-shell they have become intimately welded together to form a more or less spherical, horny capsule. It is, however, possible to distinguish two hemispheres, one on each side, and the triangular frons between them at the front. Each hemisphere or cheek

The parts of a caterpillar

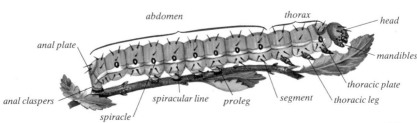

anal plate — abdomen — thorax — head

anal claspers — spiracular line — proleg — segment — mandibles — thoracic plate — thoracic leg

spiracle

211

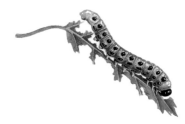

Sawfly caterpillars are very similar to butterfly caterpillars, but have more than five sets of prolegs

usually carries six simple eyes or stemmata, arranged in a circular or horseshoe-shaped cluster. Carried very low down on each side, these eyes are unlikely to be able to detect much more than light and shade and perhaps slight movements in the immediate vicinity. There is no trace of the compound eyes found in the adult butterflies.

Just in front of each cluster of eyes there is a very short antenna. Little more than a bristle with a fleshy base, it is nevertheless well supplied with sensory receptors and undoubtedly plays a part in determining the acceptability of food.

The jaws or mandibles, attached just under the front of the head, are more or less square horny plates with toothed inner edges. A feeding caterpillar, seen from the front, shows how the jaws chomp their way through the leaves like a pair of pinking shears. Just below the jaws are two fleshy, carrot-shaped maxillae, whose sensory bristles play a major role in tasting the leaves. The maxillae also help to hold the leaves in the right position for the jaws to get to work on them. Finally, below and between the maxillae and forming the floor of the chomping area, is the labium or lower lip. Its function is largely sensory, but its front edge carries the spinneret, through which the caterpillar spins its strands of multi-purpose silk. The glands that produce the silk are highly modified salivary glands, forming long tubes that lie close to the food canal. Each caterpillar has two of these glands, and in caterpillars that use a lot of silk they occupy a considerable part of the body.

The ornamentation of the body segments may change as the caterpillar gets older especially between the first and second instars (see p. 211). but otherwise remains pretty constant for each species. Each segment commonly has a number of tubercles on its back and sides, and the exact arrangement of these tubercles may be of use in distinguishing closely related species. The tubercles generally bear bristles or tufts of hair, and are themselves branched and spiky in the caterpillars of the tortoiseshells and most other nymphalids. In addition, the body often carries finer hairs, scattered all over the surface and forming a velvety coat. This is well developed in the caterpillars of many of the whites (Pieridae) and browns (Satyridae). Many moth larvae are clothed with long hairs, which may completely hide the body.

The first three segments of the body form the thorax, although this region is not as clearly separated from the rest of the body as it is in the adult insect. The three segments are generally much alike, although in some skippers the first segment – the prothorax – is more slender than the others and forms a fairly obvious 'neck'. Some burrowing caterpillars also have a tough, protective plate on the first thoracic segment, but this is not found in any of the European butterfly larvae. Lycaenid caterpillars have a rather swollen prothorax, into which the head can be withdrawn when necessary (see p. 219)

Each thoracic segment carries a pair of legs corresponding to the six legs of the adult butterfly, although the larval legs are considerably smaller and simpler in construction. They are not able to carry the body, and this function has been taken over by the abdominal prolegs. The thoracic legs play only a minor part in walking, except in the caterpillars of the looper moths (family Geometridae), and in many caterpillars their job seems to be to grab leaves and to hold them firmly while the jaws get to work.

The ten abdominal segments are very like those of the thorax except that they have no true legs. Stumpy prolegs are borne on the third, fourth, fifth, sixth, and tenth segments, those of the last segment being slightly different in shape and known as claspers. This arrangement holds good for all the European butterflies and most of the European moths, although some of the prolegs are missing in some moth groups: the geometers or loopers, for example, have prolegs only on the sixth and tenth segments, while the caterpillars of the Silver Y and its relatives have prolegs on the fifth, sixth, and tenth segments. Apart from the miniscule larvae of the micropterigids, which have eight pairs of prolegs (see p. 152), caterpillars with more than five pairs of prolegs are sawfly larvae, not butterfly or moth.

The prolegs are soft and fleshy but quite unlike the true legs, but remarkably well built for their job. They are partly telescopic, being extended and contracted by muscular action. The feet are equipped with flanges or circular pads bearing numerous microscopic hooks, which give the caterpillar an excellent grip. The skippers, which are not closely related to the other butterfly families, have an almost complete circle of hooks on each proleg. The rest of the butterflies, together with most of the larger moths, have just a row of hooks along the inner margin of the foot flange. When walking, the typical caterpillar extends each pair of prolegs in turn and ensures that each pair regains a good grip before lifting the next two – often a rather slow, but safe, process.

The last three segments of the abdomen are somewhat modified in shape, with the eighth and ninth often distinctly wedge-shaped. The tenth segment appears to consist of little more than the claspers and three fleshy flaps surrounding the anus. Satyrid caterpillars can be recognised as such because the last segment is drawn out to form two short tails, but in general European butterfly larvae are much more conservative in appearance than those of many moth groups. Their claspers do not form whip-like tails as they do in the caterpillars of the Puss Moth and various other species, nor do they have the bizarre horns and other fleshy outgrowths that are so common in moth larvae. European butterfly caterpillars do not even have long fur.

Caterpillar segments showing various kinds of ornamentation

Black-veined White

Large Tortoiseshell

White Admiral

Heath Fritillary

Buff Ermine

BREATHING THROUGH HOLES

Caterpillars, in common with the adult butterflies and moths and all other insects, breathe by means of tracheae – fine tubes that spread through the body and carry air to all parts. The tubes link up and open to the outside air through small pores which are generally located low down on each side of the body. These pores are called spiracles and there are nine pairs of them – one on the prothorax and one on each of the first eight abdominal segments. They are quite easy to see on the less hairy or spiky larvae, often being ringed with black or white and commonly linked by a pale line along the side of the body. The first and last spiracles tend to be a bit larger than the rest because they serve a larger region of the body. A powerful microscope will show that the spiracular opening is covered by a mesh of feathery outgrowths from the rim. These allow free passage of air, but keep out dust and also reduce water loss. The entrance to the tracheae can be completely closed by muscles at the inner end of the spiracular chamber. This happens mainly in dry weather and prevents desiccation of the caterpillar, but the spiracles have to open periodically to let in fresh air and to release the accumulated carbon dioxide.

Tracheal respiration depends mainly on simple diffusion of air along the tubes, although some of the more active insects can pump air in and out to some extent by muscular action.

The air-breathing system of a caterpillar

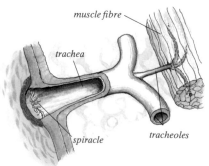

muscle fibre

trachea

spiracle

tracheoles

But even then the system is efficient only over short distances, and this is one of the reasons why insects are all rather small. Very rarely is any part of the body more than about a centimetre from the surface: even butterflies and moths with wing-spans of 30cm do not have bodies much more than the size of a man'a finger.

GROWTH AND MOULTING

Although the caterpillar body is flexible, this is due mainly to the soft inter-segmental membranes. The outer coat or cuticle has only limited elasticity and cannot grow with the caterpillar. It must be changed from time to time as the caterpillar gets bigger. This skin-changing, known as moulting or ecdysis, takes about two days for most species, but the exact time depends on the stage of growth – large caterpillars take longer than small ones – and also on the weather. Low temperatures slow down the process, as they do all metabolic activities.

When the caterpillar feels its skin getting uncomfortably tight it seeks a moulting site on its food-plant. This is usually well concealed for, during moulting, the caterpillar is completely defenceless. It spins a silken pad in its chosen retreat and, clinging firmly with its prolegs, becomes quiescent for a day or so. The first visible change is a swelling behind the head, caused by the development of a new and larger head capsule under the skin. The old head capsule gradually comes to resemble a pimple stuck on the front. Meanwhile, other important changes are taking place inside the body. Glands in the prothorax secrete the hormone ecdysone, also known as the moulting hormone, which causes the epidermal cells just under the cuticle to multiply rapidly. The layer of epidermal cells becomes wrinkled and folded as it grows in its confined space and it gradually becomes detached from the overlying cuticle. The inner layers of the latter are gradually digested by enzymes and the products are taken back into the body for recycling.

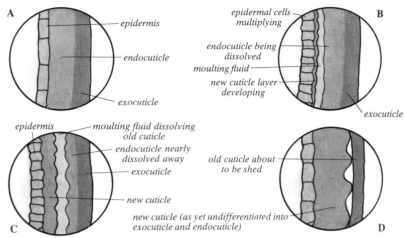

A — epidermis, endocuticle, exocuticle

B — epidermal cells multiplying, endocuticle being dissolved, moulting fluid, new cuticle layer developing, exocuticle

C — epidermis, moulting fluid dissolving old cuticle, endocuticle nearly dissolved away, exocuticle, new cuticle

D — old cuticle about to be shed, new cuticle (as yet undifferentiated into exocuticle and endocuticle)

Changes in the cuticle and epidermis during the moulting cycle

Meanwhile, the epidermal cells are secreting a new cuticle, which follows the folds and creases of the cells themselves. When this new cuticle is complete the caterpillar swallows air and pumps itself up to such an extent that the old coat, now very thin and brittle, bursts. The caterpillar now struggles out of the old coat, which crumples up like a concertina and is known as the exuvia. But things are not yet plain sailing: the new coat is still very soft and the caterpillar cannot move until the coat has hardened. Nor can it eat until its re-covered jaws have hardened. The drying and hardening processes take a few hours, and then the caterpillar gets rid of the excess air to make room for growth. The new coat is still wrinkled, but it is gradually 'ironed out' during the next round of eating, which often begins with the consumption of the cast skin. But the head capsule cannot stretch and remains the same size from one moult until the next. It looks rather too big for the freshly-moulted larva, but as the next moult approaches it begins to look decidedly small for the body.

The stage of development between one moult and the next is called an instar, and a newly-hatched caterpillar is said to be in its first instar. Most butterfly and moth species have five

larval instars – and therefore five moults – but some species have only three or four and a few have as many as eight. The number is generally constant for each species under normal conditions, although some double-brooded species that hibernate as larvae may have an extra instar in the over-wintering generation. The moult following the final larval instar reveals the pupa or chrysalis (see p. 234).

FEEDING HABITS

As we have already seen, a caterpillar's first meal is often its own egg-shell, but from then on most caterpillars rely entirely on plants for food. Butterfly larvae feed mainly on leaves, although other green parts are eaten by some species. The Orange-tip caterpillar, for example, feeds mainly on the young seed capsules of its food plants, while the early instars of many of the blues feed on flowers. The food-plants utilized by butterfly larvae are virtually all flowering plants. Ferns and mosses are never used and, apart from a few non-European hairstreaks, no butterfly uses conifers as food-plants, although the adult Green Hairstreak is strongly attracted to young pine shoots in the spring. Moth larvae go in for a much

*White Admiral
on honeysuckle*

*Silver-washed
Fritillary on violet*

Feeding damage by caterpillars

wider range of food-plants, with a lot using conifers and quite a number using lichens, although there are still not many on ferns and mosses. They also make use of more parts of the food-plant, with many living on roots and many more tunnelling inside the stems. Some even burrow into the trunks of trees.

Newly-hatched leaf-feeding caterpillars generally start by scraping the surface with their jaws, and this often leads to the appearance of small holes in the leaves, but before long the caterpillars begin to carve out slices from the leaves as they munch their way in from the margins. Although the caterpillars themselves are often very well camouflaged, it is quite easy to track them down by looking for the chewed leaves, and, of course, the tell-tale droppings scattered beneath the plants. Some species have their own special ways of attacking leaves, and it is then possible to say what kind of caterpillar is or has been at work without actually seeing it. The White Admiral is a good example. Before hibernation, the young caterpillars attack the distal parts of the honeysuckle leaves leaving the mid-ribs sticking out like spines. After hibernation, the caterpillars prefer to munch the basal parts of the leaves first and gradually work their way up to the tip. Leaves are often abandoned half-way, with the upper part left flapping like a tiny green flag.

The Silver-washed Fritillary larva, together with several other violet-feeding species, also betrays its activity by leaving characteristic feeding marks, for it tends to nibble only the lower lobes of the violet leaves and this damage is easy to spot.

The larvae of many small moths feed entirely within the leaf, tunelling between the upper and lower surfaces and producing characteristic 'mines' in the form of twisting channels or extensive blotches.

A few larvae feed all round the clock, but the majority have definite feeding times. Most butterfly larvae feed by day, although those of the browns (Satyridae) feed mainly at night, and so do some of the skipper larvae. The latter commonly spend the day in tubular retreats which they make by drawing grass blades together with silk. They also have a remarkable piece of apparatus to ensure that their homes are not fouled by their droppings, or frass. The device consists of a minute comb on the underside of the flap that overhangs the anus. When about to pass a pellet of frass, the caterpillar wriggles backwards so that its rear end pokes out of the bottom end of the tube. The pellet is then passed, but instead of falling directly under the tube it is held by the teeth of the comb. The comb then flicks up with considerable force and throws the pellet as much as a metre away from the tube. The caterpillar is not just being house-proud: there is some evidence that parasites track down their hosts by the odour of their droppings, so the further away the better!

Several other kinds of caterpillar construct shelters by drawing leaf blades together with silk, sometimes using them purely for resting but often feeding inside them as well. The Red Admiral larva, for example, folds a nettle leaf to form a pouch and then feeds inside it, literally eating itself out of house and home and having to make a new shelter after a few days. The Painted Lady caterpillar behaves in a similar way on thistles and nettles and the ruins of its abandoned dwellings can sometimes be found scattered all over the plants. The Grizzled Skipper larva makes itself a neat home by drawing the leaflets of bird's-foot trefoil together and binding them with silk to form a pouch. These shelters may protect the occupants from parasites and also from some predators, but they often make them more conspicuous to us.

Some gregarious larvae make large silken tents or webs on their food-plants, although none of our butterfly larvae constructs anything quite like the tents of the Pine Processionary Moth larvae which are abundant on pine trees in many parts of southern and central Europe. As far as butter-flies are concerned, the most exten-sive feeding webs are those of the tree-feeding Camberwell Beauty and Large Tortoiseshell larvae. These caterpillars spew out silk wherever they go, draping it over whole bran-ches and forming secure shelters under which they can feed without fear of being blown away by the wind. Peacock and Small Tortoiseshell lar-vae make much flimsier shelters in the nettles, and the Small Tortoiseshell caterpillars actually leave their com-munal homes after the fourth moult and live independently. Peacock lar-vae remain gregarious until they are fully grown, although as they get bigger their writhing black bodies are far more conspicuous than the silk threads they spin.

Larvae of the Black-veined White, the Marsh Fritillary, and the Glanville Fritillary all live gregariously in com-pact feeding webs when young and they all hibernate, when still quite small, in specially reinforced webs. The Black-veined White larvae aban-don their tents after hibernation, but the fritillary larvae extend theirs and use them as sleeping and resting quarters. They often sunbathe on the outside of the web, a habit that is especially prominent in the Marsh Fritillary. Emerging from hibernation early in March, the caterpillars wan-der off to feed but they return to bask in dense clusters on the web in sunny weather. Even when the air tempera-ture is low, their black bodies absorb the sun's radiant heat very efficiently and measurements have shown that their body temperature can rise to as much as 30°C above that of the surrounding air. Having warmed up, the dense clusters also stay warm much longer than a solitary caterpillar would do. The high body temperature speeds up the digestion and assimila-tion of food, and thereby speeds up growth and development at what is often a rather cold time of year. The caterpillars gradually disperse after the fourth moult and feed singly until ready to pupate.

Carnivores and cannibals

As we shall see on p. 218, the caterpillars of the Large Blue and a few related butterflies adopt a carni-vorous diet in their later stages, but there are quite a number of tropical lycaenids whose larvae are almost entirely carnivorous throughout their lives. They eat an assortment of aphids, scale insects, and other small bugs, often washed down with the honeydew that these insects exude.

Apart from the Large Blue and its relatives, however, there are no regu-lar carnivores among the European butterflies and moths, but sporadic cannibalism is quite common. We have already seen (p. 202) that the Orange-tip larvae are notorious can-nibals, and we shall meet the habit in first-instar Large Blue larvae (see p. 219). It is also prevalent among the larvae of the Green Hairstreak and the White-letter Hairstreak and several other lycaenids, including the Common Blue. Swallowtail larvae will also attack each other. Moulting larvae and freshly-formed pupae are especially at risk, but it is likely that such cannibalism is far less common in the wild, where fresh vegetation is always available, than in captive col-onies where most of the observations have been made. The caterpillars of the browns and skippers never seem to turn to cannibalism, and very few European nymphalids are known to indulge in the habit, even when over-crowded.

CATERPILLARS AND ANTS

It is well known that the caterpillars of many butterflies, belonging to several different families, form close associa-tions with ants, but it is the blues of the family Lycaenidae that have evolved this relationship to the high-est degree and have also been most intensively studied. It is probable that most of the lycaenids, apart from those living at high altitude or in the far north, have some kind of association with ants. The relationship is always based on the production by the caterpillar of a sugary secretion – hereafter called nectar – which is attractive to and probably nutritionally valuable to the ants. The larvae also produce scents or pheromones that calm the aggressive tendencies of the ants.

The nectar is produced in a gland, Newcomer's Organ, in the seventh abdominal segment of the caterpillar and is exuded through a slit on the top of that segment following prolonged stimulation by an attendant ant.

Two major theories have been put forward to explain the association between the caterpillars and the ants. One is that because they forage in the same places the caterpillars have to placate the carnivorous tendencies of the ants, and the other is that the association developed because the ants provide protection from parasites and other enemies. Experiments with a number of non-European lycaenids have shown that larvae reared without ants certainly suffer more parasitism, but the role of defender could well have developed from an initial appeasement relationship. Investigations with *Glaucopsyche lygdamus* larvae in North America suggest that they release alarm pheromones when approached by parasites and that the ants immediately come to the rescue by attacking the parasites. Small predators are probably dealt with in the

same way, and it is likely that similar alarm signals are produced by other lycaenid larvae when threatened.

The most common form of caterpillar-ant interaction is on a 'take it or leave it' basis, with the larvae secreting nectar when asked but not being dependent on the ants. Nevertheless, because ants are so numerous in most places, the majority of the caterpillars do come into contact with them, and if in the vicinity of a nest they may be constantly attended and 'milked' on a regular basis. With the exception of the harvester ants, which are specialist seed-eaters, almost any species of ant may be involved in this relatively loose association. Nearly all the European blues, as well as many of the hairstreaks and coppers, associate with ants in this way, and the association does not necessarily stop with the larva. The pupae of many of these species also exude ant-attracting secretions and are commonly taken into care by the ants. They may be installed deep in the nest, where they are regularly licked clean. Even resting larvae, notably those of the Adonis Blue and the Chalkhill Blue, may be temporarily sheltered by their guardians and are commonly covered with soil when moulting, which is a particularly dangerous time for the larvae. Although the larvae and pupae can survive perfectly well without the ants – apart from the greater risk of attack by parasites and predators – their secretions are obviously important to the ants.

The other main form of caterpillar-ant association is an obligate one, with a much closer bond between the two insects. The caterpillars are regularly tended by the ants and are taken into the ants' nests at a certain stage of development. Although the ants do not need the larvae, the latter cannot survive without the ants. And the ants must be of a certain type; not just any old ant will do at this level of association. The best known butterfly having an obligate relationship of this kind is the Large Blue, now endangered in most parts of Europe as a result of land-use changes detrimental to the ant population (see p. 305).

A lycaenid larva showing Newcomer's Organ and the pheromone-producing tentacular organs. When not in use the latter are withdrawn into the body

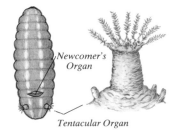

Newcomer's Organ

Tentacular Organ

THE LARGE BLUE LIFE-CYCLE

A female Large Blue lays her eggs singly in the flower heads of wild thyme

During the first three instars the larvae feed on wild thyme

The adult Large Blue is on the wing in June and July

Ants licking the 4th instar prior to picking it up. The larvae then pulls its head back into the thorax to make it easier for the ant to pick it up

After emergence from the pupa the adult, ignored by the ants, crawls out of the nest

4th instar larva is carried into the nest

In the spring the larva pupates inside the ants' nest

Mature caterpillar eating ant larvae. Workers continue to lap secretions from its body

Young larvae of the Large Blue have cannibalistic tendencies and it is as well that the eggs are laid singly – usually one per plant. After the third moult the larva loses interest in its food-plant and falls to the ground, where it waits to be picked up by an ant of the genus Myrmica. Although the caterpillar gives out little nectar while in the ants' nest, ant-attracting pheromones ensure that it is not attacked

Any species of *Myrmica* can serve as host to the Large Blue larva, but *M. sabuleti* and *M. scabrinodis* are the most suitable species and only the former is probably capable of supporting a viable population in Britain. Because the fourth-instar larva feeds entirely on the ant brood, a nest cannot support many larvae and there are rarely more than four in any nest. The majority of occupied nests actually hold only a single Large Blue larva. It is probable that about 500 ant-nests are needed to support even a small colony of the butterflies.

The Large Blue has three close relatives on the continent: the Scarce Large Blue, which prefers *M. scabrinodis* as its host; the Dusky Large Blue, which prefers *M. rubra*; and the Alcon Blue, whose larvae are found mainly in the nests of *M. rubra* and *M. ruginodis*. All are becoming rare and are threatened with extinction (see p. 304).

The first two behave very much like the Large Blue, except that the larval food plant is great burnet, but the Alcon Blue exhibits a number of interesting differences. For a start, the young larvae are not cannibalistic and although the eggs are laid singly there are often quite a number on one plant. Various gentians serve as food plants for the first three instars. The fourth-instar larva is not 'milked' before being taken to the nest, and it adopts no special 'carry-me' attitude, but the ants still know what to do with it and carry it to the nest. Whereas the other species are virtually ignored in the ant's nest, the larva of the Alcon Blue attracts a great deal of interest. Its body is covered with very small glands that continue to secrete sugary fluids, and if it is not regularly licked by the ants it becomes mouldy and dies. The ants even remove its droppings! As well as feeding on the ants' brood, the caterpillar receives some of the prey brought in by the ants and also laps up fluids regurgitated by them. A nest can thus support more caterpillars than would be possible if the guests fed entirely on the ants' brood, and as many as twenty Alcon Blue larvae have been found in a single nest.

CATERPILLARS IN WINTER

Many caterpillars can remain active through the winter as long as the weather is not too cold. This is particularly true of those soil-dwelling moth larvae known as cut-worms, which come to the surface at night and chew through an assortment of plant stems – much to the annoyance of gardeners. Relatively few butterfly larvae pass the winter in this way, with the habit being found mainly among the browns, notably the Meadow Brown and the Wall. These grass-feeding species have no problems in finding food during the winter. Activity increases and decreases with the temperature and it is interesting that, although largely nocturnal in the summer, these larvae feed mainly by day in the winter. Activity stops altogether when the temperature drops below a certain point, and the caterpillar is then said to be quiescent. But it will become active again as soon as the temperature rises above a critical point. There may be several periods of quiescence during the winter, separated by active spells of varying duration, and this kind of rest is clearly very different from the true hibernation or winter diapause shown by most over-wintering larvae. This is a state of suspended development and, as in the eggs (see p. 208), it is initiated long before the cold weather sets in. Once the wheels are set in motion, diapause cannot be prevented and it will occur in even the mildest of winters.

The Purple Emperor larva (left) passes the winter exposed, but well camouflaged, on a twig, while the White Admiral larva wraps itself in a dead leaf

Many single-brooded species have a compulsory or obligate diapause which takes place regardless of environmental conditions. Every caterpillar of these species is thus destined for a spell of suspended development. Good examples include the Silverwashed Fritillary and the Dark Green Fritillary, both of which enter diapause as soon as they leave their eggs in the summer and remain dormant until the spring. Most other hibernating larvae feed for a while and undergo at least one moult before bedding down for the winter.

Species with two or more broods in a year as a rule go into diapause only in the over-wintering generation, although some species living in drought-affected areas such as the Mediterranean region, also have a summer diapause. So what makes the over-wintering caterpillars become dormant and allows the summer generations to develop unhindered? Temperature might seem the obvious answer but, as in the eggs, an insect that waits for the actual drop in temperature before will be very unprepared to survive the inhospitable environment. Larval diapause is therefore usually triggered off by the short day-length experienced by the eggs or the young caterpillars in the autumn. But temperature can sometimes over-ride the effect of day-length. Abnormally high temperatures, for example, can prevent diapause in Small Copper larvae even when the insects are subjected to very short day-length under artificial conditions. Similarly, low temperatures may encourage diapause even when the days are long. This happens with several species living in the Alps and other mountainous regions of southern Europe. In lowland areas these species, such as the Pearl-bordered Fritillary, are double-brooded, but at altitude the cold encourages the summer larvae to go into diapause and there is thus just one brood. There is a good deal of evidence, however, that these single-brooded populations are genetically different from the double-brooded lowland populations and some of

them probably have an obligate diapause.

As we have already seen, some gregarious caterpillars build silken tents to protect themselves from the worst of the winter weather (see p. 217). Intense cold does not bother them, owing to their antifreeze, but the larvae do need protection from the drying winds and their tents certainly help them to conserve moisture. Most solitary larvae tuck themselves away amongst leaves and debris close to the ground when they hibernate. Here they have no fear of desiccation but do sometimes have to face the problem of flooding. However, most larvae can cope with short periods of inundation as the sleeping quarters, which are often in folded leaves and other small crevices, frequently trap life-saving pockets of air. The hibernating White Admiral larva prefers to stay above ground and builds itself a winter retreat or hibernaculum by fixing a honeysuckle leaf to the stem with silk and forming it into a weatherproof pouch. There are a few caterpillars that scorn any form of winter comfort. The Purple Emperor larva is a good example, spending the winter clinging motionless to a small silken pad spun in the fork of a sallow twig. Its colour matches the twig perfectly.

Prolonged exposure to cold, followed by markedly warmer conditions, is necessary to reactivate most diapausing larvae, with many species beginning the waking-up process when the temperature reaches about 8°C. A few species break their diapause spontaneously after a certain period, regardless of the temperature, but the result is always that the caterpillars wake up in the spring when fresh food-plants are available again. Some individuals may remain dormant through two or even more winters, although this is more common in species that go into winter diapause as pupae. It is a good way of ensuring that a few individuals survive if an unfavourable year comes along.

Larvae may go into diapause in any instar, but the stage is usually fixed for each species and, among butterflies, it usually happens when the caterpillars are still quite small. There are, however, a number of northern and montane species which, because of their cold environments, have a two-year life cycle and two periods of larval diapause – one in an early instar and the other usually in the final instar. Example of such biennial species include the Northern Clouded Yellow and the Pale Arctic Clouded Yellow, both from northern Scandinavia, the Arctic Fritillary and the Polar Fritillary, the Baltic Grayling, and several species of *Erebia*. The Speckled Wood is of particular interest in that it can overwinter as a caterpillar or as a pupa. Those that feed-up quickly and pupate in the autumn produce adults much earlier in the spring than those that overwinter as larvae.

THE CATERPILLAR'S ENEMIES

With an adult butterfly capable of laying several hundred eggs, it is obvious that if all the offspring survived to maturity we would suffocate in clouds of fluttering wings. The fact that we do not suffer such a fate is due to hordes of natural enemies, most of which, as far as European butterflies are concerned, attack the caterpillars. As with the eggs (p. 209), these enemies fall into two main classes – the predators that gobble up caterpillars in large numbers, and the parasites for whom just one caterpillar provides a lifetime's larder. Pathogenic fungi and bacteria also kill plenty of caterpillars, but the most important micro-organisms in this respect are the viruses. Affected caterpillars 'wilt' and often hang limply from the food-plant with fluid oozing from their bodies but, unlike caterpillars with bacterial diseases, they do not become smelly and they do not change colour until after death. Wet weather can encourage the spread of virus infections, and so can over-crowding and poor diet – as many caterpillar breeders have discovered too late.

The main vertebrate predators of caterpillars are the birds, especially

during the nesting season, while among the invertebrates there are many bugs, beetles, spiders, and harvestmen eager to reap the harvest of caterpillar meat. Wasps also collect plenty of caterpillars and take them home to feed their grubs. All these predators are polyphagous, taking a wide variety of larvae for food.

Not surprisingly, most of the quantitative work carried out on caterpillar predation has involved the cabbage whites. In field crops it has been shown that ground beetles, harvestmen, and other invertebrates remove over 50% of the first and second instar Small White larvae. At the beginning of the third instar the birds begin to take an interest and share the caterpillars more or less equally with the invertebrate predators. Thereafter the birds are the main predators. In gardens, however, birds have been shown to be the main enemies of all caterpillar stages. House sparrows

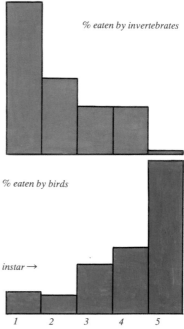

Invertebrates eat a greater proportion of the early instar caterpillars, whilst birds feed mainly on the late instars

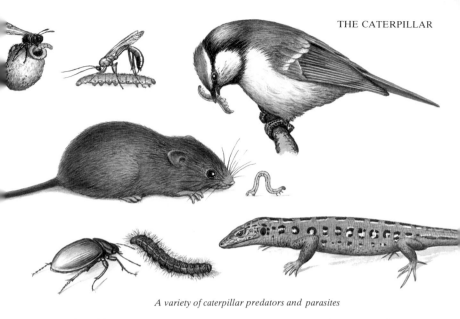

A variety of caterpillar predators and parasites

and warblers eat the youngest stages, while tits go for the older larvae and also for the pupae. The different predation patterns in field and garden crops stem mainly from the denser growth of most field crops, which can shelter far greater numbers of invertebrates. There are also fewer birds in the open fields, for many species do not like to go too far from the shelter of trees and hedgerows. Survival of the caterpillars also depends to some extent on the type of crop. When feeding on hearting cabbages, third-instar Small White larvae tend to move into the hearts where they are better protected from their enemies. Despite being more susceptible to disease germs multiplying in their accumulated droppings, about 7% of caterpillars reach full size on hearting cabbages compared with only 3% on non-hearting varieties.

Few investigations have been carried out with other species, but it seems likely that invertebrates are the main predators of early instars in the wild, with birds becoming more important as the caterpillars get bigger. Unless populations are very dense, the birds do not waste time on the small caterpillars; they wait for them to reach a size worth eating.

Ichneumons and other parasites

The best known of the parasites attacking caterpillars are the ichneumons, a very large group of rather leggy insects distantly related to the bees and wasps and placed with them in the order Hymenoptera. The larger forms, such as *Netelia* and *Ophion*, are very familiar to moth collectors, for they turn up in large numbers in moth traps. They are also attracted to lighted windows at night.

Most parasites, such as lice and tapeworms, are much smaller than their hosts and rarely cause them any serious harm. The ichneumons, however, normally kill their hosts and are commonly called parasitoids to distinguish them from the other types of parasite. Some are almost as large as their hosts.

Two families of ichneumons, the Ichneumonidae and the Braconidae, attack the caterpillars of our butterflies and moths. The braconids are, on average, somewhat smaller than the ichneumonids, but the families are best distinguished by the wing venation. Their biology is very similar, except that the braconids have a much higher proportion of gregarious species (see p. 224).

Host caterpillars are generally

A caterpillar carrying the grub of an ectoparasitic ichneumon

found by scent, and this may be helped in many instances because the adult ichneumons are often attracted to certain habitats or micro-climates to start with. They may also be attracted by the food-plant of the host caterpillar within these areas, thus narrowing down their search area even more. You can often see the ichneumons scampering over the vegetation, waving their long antennae and tapping them excitedly on the leaves as they pick up the scents of potential victims. Some species will accept a wide range of caterpillars feeding in a particular habitat or on a particular food-plant, even if they belong to widely different families, but other ichneumons are restricted to just one kind of host or to a group of closely related host species. Many species are attracted to hosts at a particular stage of development – very often just those in the first- and second-instars – but a few can utilise larvae at any stage of development and some can even use pupae as well.

Having found a suitable host, the parasite lays its egg or eggs in or on the body. Almost all the ichneumonids lay their eggs singly. When the egg is laid on the outside of the host the ichneumon is termed an ectoparasite. In this case the caterpillar is usually paralysed to some extent by an injection from the ichneumon. The host may continue to feed for a while, but it does not usually moult again and the parasite's egg or the resulting grub, feeding voraciously on the outside, need not worry about being left clinging to an empty skin. Ectoparasites generally attack moth larvae that live concealed in plant tissues. The parasites themselves are thus well protected but, to be on the safe side, they mature unusually rapidly.

Ectoparasitic ichneumonids are much less common than endoparasitic species, which incubate, hatch and grow up inside the host caterpillars. *Ophion* species are familiar endoparasites, attacking the larvae of various moths – especially the noctuids. The adult female uses her needle-like ovipositor to inject an egg into the host, and the grub, safely concealed, usually grows more slowly than those of the ectoparasitic species. By avoiding the vital organs to start with it ensures that the host larva remains alive and continues to moult, although it may become sluggish and grow rather slowly. But as the invader approaches its full size it turns to the host's vital parts and finally reduces it to a lifeless shell. This usually happens while the host is still in the larval stage, but in some instances the parasite allows it to turn into a pupa before the death sentence is carried out. The parasite itself then pupates, either in the old host skin or after making its way to the outside.

Many braconids are gregarious parasites, laying numerous eggs in a single host and thereby making efficient use of its resources. 40 or more braconid grubs may develop in one caterpillar, their total bulk being similar to that of a single ichneumonid grub and close to that of the host caterpillar itself. Solitary braconid species tend to attack smaller host species.

The best known of the braconids is undoubtedly *Apanteles glomeratus*, a tiny insect which is greatly valued for its attacks on the larvae of the Large White. It also demolishes the caterpillars of the Small White and several other whites, but the Large White is its main host. Eggs are laid in the young caterpillars and the grubs – up to 150 of them in a single caterpillar – grow plump on the host's stores of fat. They usually kill the host at about the time that it starts to look for a pupation site, and they then emerge to pupate in little yellow cocoons around the host's shrivelled skin. These cocoons are commonly seen on garden sheds and fences, especially in the autumn. Like the host, the parasite has two generations in a year.

Insects leaving their hosts in the autumn remain in their cocoons throughout the winter and emerge to attack the new generation of caterpillars in the spring – although if they have done their job well there will be relatively few Large White caterpillars for them to attack and many have to turn to other host species. In some areas there may be 100% kill of the Large White, but the butterfly is a great migrant and new individuals soon arrive to re-populate the areas. Nevertheless, *A. glomeratus* is a great ally of the farmer and the gardener. It managed to rid Australia of the Large White when introduced to combat the pest, itself introduced, in the 1930's.

Other species of *Apanteles* and closely related genera are known from almost all our butterfly larvae although skipper caterpillars seem immune from attack by these little parasites – perhaps through their habit of sheltering in leafy pouches and tubes (see p. 216). Many of these small parasites are confined to a single host species or to a few related hosts and, as with *A. glomeratus* and the Large White, they have a marked regulatory effect on the butterfly populations, often leading to appreciable fluctuations in numbers. This is especially true with host-specific parasites or with multi-host parasites in areas where only one suitable host is available. The host can be virtually wiped out over a period of years, and then the parasite dies out in the area as well. New stocks of butterflies eventually invade the area and, free from the parasites, they increase their populations dramatically for a few years – until the parasite finally finds the population.

Synchronisation with the host

It is obvious that parasites must arrange their life cycles in such a way that they are ready to lay their eggs when the host caterpillars are at the right stage, and they employ many neat strategies to ensure that this happens. We have seen that when *Apanteles glomeratus* parasitises the larvae of the Large White it is double-brooded and maintains synchronisation with its host by going into winter diapause, as a pupa, just like the host species. It seems that, even inside the host's body, the final-instar *Apanteles* grubs are affected by day-length and produce diapausing pupae when they detect the shorter days of autumn. When afflicting the single-brooded Black-veined White, however, the parasite adopts a single-brooded or univoltine life-style. Black-veined White larvae go into hibernation at an early stage (see p. 217) and the parasites pass the winter as quiescent first-instar grubs – kept quiet by the hormones circulating in the diapausing host. They cannot develop further until the host comes out of diapause, so there is no danger of the parasites' out-growing their sleeping hosts and starving to death.

Many other ichneumon grubs pass the winter at various stages of development inside diapausing host larvae. In some instances the grubs may have a true diapause, brought about by their own internal hormonal changes triggered off by changes in day-length, but in other instances, as in the Black-veined White, the grubs' winter rest is more accurately called quiescence as it is brought about by the host's hormones. But the result is the same; the parasitic grubs go to sleep with their hosts and are still in step with them when things start to move in the spring.

Some ichneumons hibernate for long periods as adults in order to keep in step with their hosts. Usually only mated females hibernate in this way, and they are ready to lay their eggs as soon as suitable host larvae are avail-

Apanteles grubs leaving a Large White caterpillar and spinning their cocoons

able in the spring. Both multi-host and single-host parasites may overwinter in this way, but those species that can use several hosts do not have to worry quite so much about synchronisation: there are usually some suitable caterpillars about. Some of these parasites regularly use different hosts for different broods.

The parasites mentioned so far all produce one brood in each generation of the host insect, but this is not always the case. It is quite possible for several broods of a parasite to develop in one batch of caterpillars if they get their skates on and mature quickly. Keith Porter has studied this development on *Apanteles bignellii*, a parasite of the Marsh Fritillary in southern Britain which produces three generations in one brood of host caterpillars.

The Marsh Fritillary lays large batches of eggs in late May and June, and the gregarious first-instar larvae are available to the egg-laying parasites by the end of July. The *Apanteles* grubs develop in the host caterpillars for about six weeks and are fully grown when the hosts are in the third instar. The parasites emerge to pupate around the shrivelled host

A basking mass of Marsh Fritillary larvae

skins in August and new adults are soon on the wing, laying eggs in fourth-instar hosts shortly before the latter bed down for the winter. The parasites remain quiescent through the winter, but are re-activated as soon as their hosts come to life in early spring. These second-generation parasites leave the late fourth-instar hosts in March and pupate in the normal way, and the resulting adults then lay their eggs in fifth- or sixth-(final) instar host caterpillars.

The parasite now brings into play its built-in delaying tactics, designed to tide it over the couple of months that the host butterfly spends as chrysalis, adult, and egg. Parasitised fifth- and sixth-instars of the host grow much more slowly than their unafflicted brethren, and by the time the parasites are ready to leave the sixth-instar larvae and pupate the unaffected hosts have streaked through their own pupal stage and many are nearly ready to emerge as adults. But the parasites still have to wait a few weeks for new host larvae to be available, and so the adult parasites go into a summer dormancy for about a month before emerging from their cocoons. These summer cocoons are much fluffier than those of earlier generations and probably protect their occupants from both desiccation and enemies.

Using caterpillars of different ages, the parasite obviously has to adjust its egg-laying behaviour in different generations, and whereas up to about 70 grubs can be found in sixth-instar host larvae, no more than five are found in third-instar hosts. But more host larvae are available in the early stages and thus a female *Apanteles* does not necessarily lay fewer eggs in total when attacking early host instars.

The Marsh Fritillary undergoes marked fluctuations in numbers as a result of parasitism. In some years there is a very high death rate, but this may be no bad thing in the long run because it prevents over-population of the restricted habitats currently occupied by this species. With the females each able to lay some 500 eggs in a small area, huge populations can build up in the absence of parasites and 'plagues' of Marsh Fritillary larvae have been recorded on numerous occasions in the past, with consequent destruction of the food-plant. The weather also has a marked effect on the populations of this butterfly as a result of differential effects on host and parasite.

In good basking weather (see p. 217) unparasitised fifth-instar larvae grow up very rapidly in the spring and may go right through the sixth-instar and into the pupal stage before the second-generation parasites emerge from their cocoons. With few larvae to parasitise, the *Apanteles* population crashes and the Marsh Fritillary population goes up. A dull spring, on the other hand, does not allow the caterpillars to raise their temperatures and speed development by basking, and there are still plenty of caterpillars available when the parasites emerge from their cocoons. Parasite numbers thus remain high and butterfly numbers stay down.

Parasitic flies
Although the ichneumons and various smaller hymenopterans are the major parasites of European butterfly and moth caterpillars, a number of flies belonging to the family Tachinidae have also got in on the act. Related to the blow-flies or bluebottles, they are generally very bristly and rather drab flies, although *Tachina fera*, a parasite of many different caterpillars, is very striking as it parades over the flowers in its orange and black livery. *Phryxe vulgaris*, another very common polyphagous species, is also conspicuous owing to its shiny black coat and rust-coloured scutellum.

All the tachinids are endoparasites and, being fairly large, they are generally solitary – although sometimes it is possible to find three or four grubs in a large caterpillar. They go for the larger host species and are well known to moth breeders. Some, as we have seen, are polyphagous, but the majority have a restricted host range and, like the ichneumons, are well synchronised with their hosts' activities. Most are single-brooded.

Tachinids have several entry routes into their hosts, but only a few species can inject their eggs directly into the caterpillars. The commonest method is for the fly to lay its eggs on the host's body and for the resulting grubs to tunnel their own way in. *Phryxe* uses this method. Another common method is for the eggs to be laid on vegetation frequented by the host species and for the grubs to seek out the hosts. This system, used by *Tachina*, does not guarantee a host and requires far more eggs to be laid, usually between 400 and 1,000, compared with under 200 eggs laid by *Phryxe*. The eggs are pre-incubated, however, and they hatch very soon after they are laid. The third method involves the laying of very tiny eggs on the host's food-plant: the eggs are swallowed by the caterpillars and they then hatch immediately, allowing the resulting grubs to tunnel into the tissues from the food canal. This method is even less reliable, for the eggs cannot seek out the host, and up to 6,000 eggs may be laid by flies using this system. Some tachinid females give birth to active grubs instead of laying eggs.

The tachinid grubs generally leave their hosts when fully grown and pupate in the soil or leaf litter, although a few species pupate inside the shrivelled skins of the host larvae. Some allow the host to pupate, and then pupate inside it themselves.

A Silver Y caterpillar carrying eggs of the parasitic fly Phryxe vulgaris *and an example of the adult parasite*

CATERPILLAR DEFENCES

A soft, squelchy, and slow-moving caterpillar might not seem to have much to offer in the way of self-defence, but a short period of watching caterpillars will reveal a surprising array of weapons and defensive tricks. There are also many hidden defences, often based on chemical warfare, that are effective against both predators and parasites.

Camouflage

The most effective defence is obviously to avoid discovery in the first place, and many of our caterpillars go in for camouflage in a big way. Green is a very common colour for caterpillars and this in itself helps to conceal them from prying eyes, but they are never plain green; natural selection over many generations has added many refinements aimed at achieving the closest possible harmony with the surroundings. Counter-shading is extremely common in green caterpillars, with the upper surface somewhat darker than the underside. The pale underside tends to cancel out the shadow, causing the caterpillar to appear less solid and to merge into the background. This phenomenon is very common throughout the animal kingdom, in creatures ranging from caterpillars to antelopes and fishes to lions. It is interesting to note in this context that caterpillars, such as that of the Eyed Hawkmoth, that habitually rest and feed in an upside-down position display reverse counter-shading, having the back lighter than the belly. Caterpillars resting on flat leaves also have to contend with the dark shadows cast on to the leaves below their bodies. The commonest way to reduce such shadows is to pull the body tightly down against the leaf. Many lycaenid larvae do this, and fringes of hairs along the lower sides of the body help many other caterpillars to hide the shadows beneath them.

Stripes, whether of various shades of green or of different colours altogether, also play a major role in concealing caterpillars by breaking up their outlines – a phenomenon known as disruptive coloration. Longitudinal stripes occur in caterpillars belonging to most families of butterflies and moths. One stripe often runs along the middle of the back and there may be several more on each side. One commonly links the spiracles low down on each side. The disruptive effect of the longitudinal stripes is especially effective in the grass-feeding satyrid caterpillars, and several pierid larvae also have prominent longitudinal stripes. The Orange-tip larva, for example, is extremely well camouflaged among the slender seed-capsules of its food-plants thanks to the broad, pale stripe that effectively splits its body in two.

Diagonal stripes are also very common, especially among moth larvae. As well as breaking up the outline, they resemble the veins of leaves and, when combined with counter-shading, they are extremely effective. The caterpillars often resemble rolled leaves and are difficult to detect even when they have eaten much of the surrounding foliage. Among butterfly larvae employing diagonal stripes to good effect are those of the Purple Emperor and the Scarce Swallowtail. Even trained entomologists sometimes fail to spot these larvae from just a few inches away. But the caterpillars have to sit properly for the deception to work, so behaviour is a vital component of camouflage.

A classic of caterpillar camouflage is provided by the larva of the Two-tailed Pasha, which feeds on the leaves of the strawberry tree in the Mediterranean region. It spends the day basking on a leaf in the full sun and, despite its bulk, manages to harmonise with its surroundings so perfectly that it is all but invisible from all angles. Pulled firmly down on to the pad of silk which it spins as a bed, the body matches the colour and texture of the leaves beautifully, and the two eye-like blotches on the back are easily mistaken for natural blemishes. The head, darker than the rest of the body, resembles a cluster of buds, while the four red spikes – so obvious when the caterpillar is seen out of its

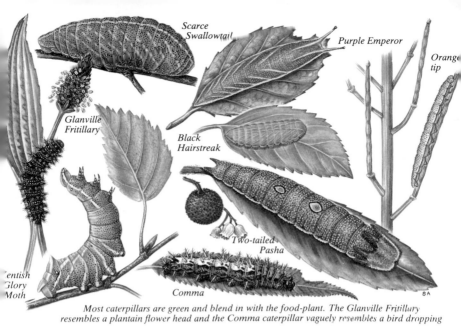

Most caterpillars are green and blend in with the food-plant. The Glanville Fritillary resembles a plantain flower head and the Comma caterpillar vaguely resembles a bird dropping

environment – look for all the world like leaf stalks when it is in its natural position, sitting on a leaf in the sunlight.

Hairs can also play a role in camouflage, especially in the early stages of a caterpillar's life. Many lycaenid larvae, for example, have relatively long hairs in their early instars and these help to conceal the larvae while feeding on hairy flower buds and young leaves. As far as most hairy caterpillars are concerned, however, the hairs act mainly as mechanical barriers (see p. 230).

Camouflage literally means deception or trickery and does not necessarily imply concealment. Many camouflaged creatures are really quite obvious, but because they bear strong resemblances to objects in their surroundings they are ignored by potential predators. This kind of camouflage is commonly called protective resemblance, to distinguish it from the simple blending in with the environment which we call crypsis, although there is no hard and fast dividing line between the two levels. The resemblance of striped caterpillars to the surrounding leaves is generally classed as crypsis, but when

they are actually seen and mistaken for rolled leaves it could equally well be termed protective resemblance. The larva of the Two-tailed Pasha actually employs both types of camouflage. Its body simply blends with the leaves, but its strange head spikes show a strong protective resemblance to leaf stalks. Such combinations are very common throughout the insect world.

Protective resemblance is exceptionally well developed in the larvae of many geometer moths, which look just like twigs and leaf stalks. Young Kentish Glory larvae cluster near the tips of birch twigs in spring and look very much like the female catkins. Among the butterflies, the larvae of the Spotted Fritillary and the Glanville Fritillary and several of their relatives bear strong resemblances to the plantain flower-spikes amongst which they feed. There are also a number of butterfly larvae that resemble birds' droppings – an excellent way of avoiding the attentions of hungry birds! These ingenious caterpillars include those of the Comma, which increase the deception by resting in a curved position as they get bigger, and the young stages of the swallowtails.

Mechanical and chemical defences

Hairy coats provide good enough protection for many caterpillars without any attempt at concealment. The spiky larvae of many fritillaries and other nymphalid butterflies are especially well protected from birds, and so are the furry caterpillars of the Vapourer and many other moths – although the cuckoo does not mind getting a mouthful of hair with each meal and will even eat moth larvae with poisonous spines. A dense coat of hair might actually protect a caterpillar from bird attack simply by making it appear larger than it really is. Dense hair can certainly give some protection against some parasites by denying them access to the body, but it does not offer complete protection; small hymenopterans might not be able to spear the caterpillar through its fur coat, but tachinid parasites which lay their eggs on the outside are not deterred and hairy larvae do tend to have a higher proportion of tachinid parasites than their non-hairy relatives. The silken tents which are spun by certain larvae also give a certain amount of mechanical protection from both predators and parasites.

The larvae of the swallowtails and their relatives in the family Papilionidae go in for chemical defence. When agitated, the caterpillar thrusts out a plump, Y-shaped orange 'sausage' from the top of its prothorax and waves it about. This action may be enough to scare small birds, but the chemical secretions from the swelling – technically known as the osmeterium – play a more important role in defence. Protrusion of the osmeterium is accompanied by the diffusion of a strong odour, which varies from species to species and probably serves mainly to deter parasites. Human observers have described the scent of the Scarce Swallowtail larva as quite pleasant – similar to lanolin is one description – while descriptions of the other species' odours range from mildly unpleasant to downright objectionable. It is unlikely that birds, with their poorly developed sense of smell, are put off

Painted Lady larva in its silken shelter

by the scent itself, but the arms of the osmeterium are often covered with a pungent fluid and this may be sprayed onto or smeared on the attacker as the osmeterium thrashes about. The fluid contains acetic acid and could well irritate the eyes of a bird or other inquisitive vertebrate. The danger past, the osmeterium is withdrawn tip first, just like the tentacles of a snail.

Warning colours

Right at the other end of the scale from the cryptic caterpillars are those that advertise their presence with bold colours or patterns. They sit brazenly on the vegetation and yet they are rarely attacked by birds or other vertebrate predators. The conspicuous colours warn the predators that the caterpillars are protected by foul tastes or other unpleasant attributes, such as irritating hairs. Good examples of such warning or aposematic colours are shown by the caterpillars of the Monarch butterfly and of the Cinnabar moth. Cinnabar larvae are black and gold and commonly increase their visual impact by clustering together on their food-plant, as do many other aposematic caterpillars. It is generally accepted that the system works because young predators try the caterpillars – often just once – and quickly learn to associate the unpleasant results with the bold colours. They avoid the caterpillars from then on. Experiments suggest that the bold coloration is more easily remembered than less conspicuous colours, but recent studies indicate that memory is not always involved. Many

Cinnabar caterpillars show classic warning coloration

young birds are inherently wary of all unfamiliar things and may instinctively shy away from warning colours at first. There may even be some kind of cultural bias away from the gaudy caterpillars if parent birds never give them to their young and if the young never see their parents attacking such larvae. Youngsters are thus likely to avoid the caterpillars for a while, but curiosity gets the better of them as they get used to seeing the insects – and then they find out why their parents left these colourful larvae alone! The punishment has to come some time to ensure that the system works and that the birds continue to take notice of the warning colours. Warnings will not work if there is nothing there to warn against. But not every bird necessarily learns the lesson the hard way: some may learn at a distance by seeing other birds' discomfort when they attack the aposematic prey.

Warning colours are useful and effective against vertebrate predators in the daytime, but they do not work against parasites or against invertebrate predators. Cinnabar moth larvae are rarely touched by birds, but during their first two instars up to 90% of the larvae are eaten by spiders and other arachnids and by beetles. These predators are obviously unaffected by the caterpillars' poisons, although not all aposematic caterpillars are taken with equal readiness. Those of the Magpie moth are

A Swallowtail caterpillar displays its osmeterium when alarmed

shunned by nearly all predators.

The poisons in the caterpillars' bodies are sometimes derived from plant toxins ingested and stored by the larvae with little or no alteration, but some are manufactured by the larvae themselves. Two main modes of action can be recognised. Phanerotoxins act immediately, often through a foul taste or burning sensation, and the prey may actually survive an attack because the predator lets go so quickly. Cryptotoxins, on the other hand, have a delayed action. The prey is usually eaten and the predator becomes sick sometime later – but it still learns to associate the unpleasant symptoms with what it ate earlier.

Because warning colours do not work until the predators have learned their lesson, a certain proportion of the prey population must be sacrificed, but this is a small price to pay for the security of the population as a whole.

Bluffing it out

Hairy coats may deter predators simply by making caterpillars appear larger than they really are. This is a kind of bluff, although the hairs are often harmful as well. Many caterpillars rely entirely on bluff to get themselves out of danger. The best examples are found amongst the moth larvae, with few putting on a better display than the caterpillar of the Elephant Hawkmoth. When disturbed, this caterpillar pulls its head and thorax back into the front of the abdomen, causing this region to swell up and display its large eye-spots. At the same time, the front end of the caterpillar lunges from side to side in a menacing fashion – quite enough to

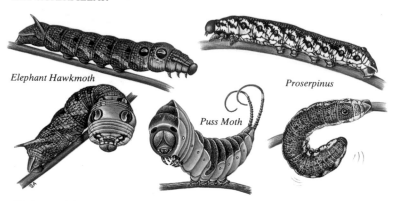

Elephant Hawkmoth

Proserpinus

Puss Moth

The larvae of the Elephant Hawkmoth and Puss Moth both pull their heads into their bodies and frighten predators with their enlarged eye-spots. Proserpinus sways in a snake-like fashion

frighten predators and many people as well, although the caterpillar is completely harmless. Less grotesque, but still alarming to predators, is the snake-like larva of the hawkmoth *Proserpinus proserpina*, which carries a large eye-spot on its rear end.

Defence against parasites

All the defences mentioned so far have been directed mainly at predators. Camouflage and warning colours are of no use whatever against the parasitic flies and ichneumons that home in on the scents of their hosts, although repellent secretions do have some protective value. The odours released by the osmeteria of swallow-tail larvae, for example, are believed to ward off some parasites seeking egg-laying sites. Violent wriggling movements, including the lashing of 'tails' by the Puss Moth larva, may also deter some parasites, and if eggs are actually laid on the outside of the body the caterpillar may be able to dislodge them by further wriggling. It may even be able to nibble the eggs, but the parasitic ichneumons commonly avoid such risks by paralysing the host when they lay their eggs.

Chemical warfare may continue after eggs have been laid in a host, with poisonous body fluids preventing the development of the parasites in some host species. Burnet moth larvae, for example, are protected by cyanide compounds and many parasites fail to survive inside them; many

may be deterred from egg-laying in the first place by the smell. But again some of the parasites are one step ahead in the never-ending battle. Several can survive successfully in the burnet larvae because they contain enzymes that are able to break down the cyanide. The tachinid *Zenillia longicauda* is a common example, attacking several burnet species. Many other successful parasites of aposematic larvae have become host-specific by becoming geared up to combat specific chemical defences.

Another form of chemical defence involves the wrapping of the parasite by special cells in the host's body cavity. This method, akin to our own bodies' attacks on invading germs, is commonly used to encapsulate and destroy eggs and young parasites by preventing them from feeding, although fast-growing or mobile grubs can fight back by breaking out of the shroud of cells as it is formed. Host-specific parasites may also have their own chemical defences that destroy the sheathing cells.

Although many parasites can develop only in certain hosts – as a result of chemical interactions – the adult females are often much less choosy. They may lay their eggs in a wide range of hosts and leave the rest to chance. What is certain, however, is that the relationships between hosts and parasites are always changing, as first one and then the other gets the upper hand in the struggle.

THE PUPA

The pupa is that stage of a butterfly's life history during which the caterpillar's body is broken down and converted into that of the adult. It is commonly referred to as a resting stage, because it does not eat or move about, but there is tremendous activity inside the pupa. The re-building job may be completed in less than a week, although the adult insect may not actually emerge from the pupa for several months or even years. The word chrysalis is now commonly used for the pupa of a butterfly or a moth, but it was originally used only for the pupa of a butterfly. It literally means 'golden coloured', and was originally coined for the metallic-looking pupae of some of the nymphalid butterflies.

When the caterpillar has completed its growth, it starts preparations for the big change from the crawling larva to the air-borne adult. It stops feeding and looks for a place in which it can pupate successfully. Many species, including lots of our butterflies, pupate on or close to their larval food-plants and therefore do not move far. Many moth larvae, on the other hand, pupate under the ground and may wander considerable distances before finding acceptable spots for burrowing. These fully-grown larvae can often be seen striding quite rapidly over the ground in a rather purposeful manner. Many of them change from green to dirty brown or purplish at this stage, thus making themselves less obvious.

Having found an acceptable site, the typical butterfly larva secures itself with silk in one of three ways. The larvae of the nymphalids and many of the satyrids hang upside down from small pads of silk spun on the food-plant. Some other larvae prefer to pupate the right way up and, after attaching the rear end to a small pad of silk, each spins a silken girdle or safety belt around itself to hold it securely against the food-plant or other vertical support. This is the

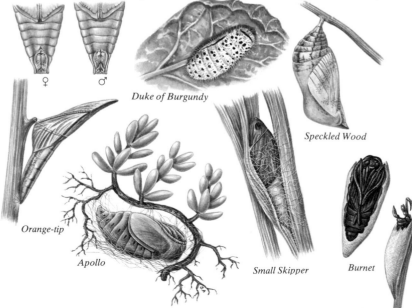

Pupae show considerable variation, including small difference between the sexes. Some, like the Burnet, have free appendages and can wriggle out of the cocoon before the adult emerges

♀　　♂

Duke of Burgundy

Speckled Wood

Orange-tip

Apollo

Small Skipper

Burnet

succinct position and it is characteristic of the pierids and swallowtails and many of the lycaenids, although some of the latter prefer to attach themselves to fallen leaves and other debris and do not necessarily pupate in a vertical position. Other larvae, including those of the skippers and some satyrids, pupate in flimsy cocoons which they spin close to the ground, in and around the grass tufts. Many skipper larvae gain extra protection by drawing grass blades around themselves as well. The Apollo larva also spins a cocoon, usually underneath its food-plant or even under a stone, but none of the butterfly cocoons could be called sturdy and the pupa is usually clearly visible through the silken web. The larvae of the Grayling and a few other satyrid butterflies actually burrow into the ground before pupating in snug little chambers, while the naked pupae of many blues are actually buried by ants after being formed on the surface.

Pupation sites sometimes vary from brood to brood. Summer generations of the cabbage whites, for example, usually pupate on the foodplants, whereas autumn larvae usually move away and commonly choose the garden fence or shed as a pupation site – almost as if they knew the cabbages would be removed during the winter, although we cannot of course credit them with such foresight. It is all down to evolution, which has favoured those insects which move away from herbaceous plants in the autumn.

Preparations complete, the larva becomes quiescent and the internal changes get under way. The period of quiescence varies a good deal, with the suspended larvae remaining still for just a day or two before wriggling out of their skins to reveal the pupae. Succinctly attached larvae remain quiescent for about three days, while those that spin cocoons may lie still for even longer – perhaps to recover from the effort of spinning! A few species, such as the Dingy Skipper, remain quiescent in the cocoon throughout the winter and do not turn into pupae until the spring.

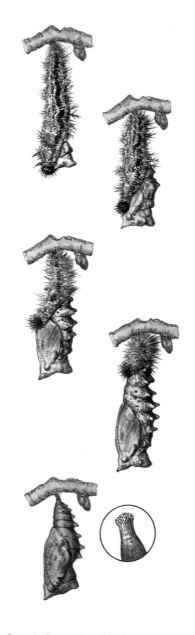

Stages in the pupation of the Large Tortoiseshell caterpillar. The inset shows the numerous small hooks making up the Large White cremaster

Before actually shedding its skin to reveal the pupa, the quiescent larva becomes shrunken and distorted and looks rather dead. The change in shape occurs because the pupa is formed inside the larval skin, and at this stage the insect is known as the prepupa. Eventually the skin splits and the pupa wriggles its way out. Here the suspended pupa has to be very careful. It does not want the old larval skin cluttering up its rear end but, with no limbs and only very limited powers of movement, how does it get rid of the skin without letting go of the support and crashing to the ground? The solution lies in instinctive reactions carried out at just the right time. The rear end of the chrysalis bears a slender projection called the cremaster and this is equipped with numerous minute hooks. The latter cling firmly to the inside of the old larval skin, which itself is firmly anchored to the silken pad by the hooks of the larval claspers. Little by little, the hooks of the pupal cremaster shuffle around the larval skin, now a crumpled heap at the tail end of the pupa, and eventually make contact with the silken pad and dig well into it to form a permanent anchorage. The old larval skin soon blows away. Perilous as the operation might seem, casualties seem very rare and the pupae are clearly very well programmed for the process. There is little problem for the succinct pupa, which is supported by its safety belt while it steps out of its larval skin, while those species that pupate in cocoons rarely bother to rid themselves of the old skins. The pupal skin is soft at first, but soon hardens.

THE PUPAL BODY

All butterfly pupae and most of those belonging to the moths are of the type known as obtect. Wings, legs, antennae, and all the other external features of the adult can be seen in outline in the pupa, although all are fused to the main body and quite immovable. Even the eyes are prominent in some pupae, although they are not functional.

The abdomen of a pupa has ten segments, although they are not all obvious, and in the obtect pupa, apart from the hooked cremaster at the hind end, it has no appendages. The cremaster itself varies a good deal. In many moth pupae it is a cluster of relatively large hooks or even a single hooked spine anchored to the cocoon or to the wall of the pupal chamber. Some of the more primitive moth pupae have no cremaster at all, while those of the burnet moths have just a cluster of blunt spines. Some of the central abdominal segments have a limited amount of movement and the living pupa will usually wag its tail end if gently squeezed – a good way of deciding whether a pupa is alive or not – although there are some butterfly pupa that cannot move at all. The spiracles remain functional throughout the pupal stage, for metamorphosis is an energy-demanding process and respiration must be maintained at all times. Small depressions mark the site of future openings of the genital apparatus, and so it is usually possible to sex the pupae without much difficulty – a useful exercise for anyone breeding insects.

The burnets and the clearwing moths have a slightly different kind of pupa, with the wings and legs partly free, although not mobile. Sometimes known as incomplete pupae, they have a number of backward-pointing spines or plates on the abdomen, which has much more mobility than is found in the abdomens of obtect pupae. Aided by the spines or plates, they can wriggle out of their cocoons before splitting open to release the adults. The black pupal skins of the

The incomplete pupa of a clearwing moth prior to the escape of the adult

burnet moths are commonly seen protruding from their papery cocoons on the grasslands in summer, and the skins of clearwing pupae can also be found sticking out from the twigs or branches in which the larvae grew up.

The most primitive moths, including the micropterigids and the eriocraniids (p. 152), have even more mobile pupae. Known as exarate or free pupae, these have the wings, legs, and other appendages hanging free from the body, just as they are in the adult, and endowed with a certain amount of movement. Jaws are present in these pupae and are used to help the pupa to escape from the cocoon.

HOW DOES IT ALL HAPPEN?

There is a world of difference between a crawling, leaf-chewing caterpillar and a flying, nectar-sipping butterfly, so how does such an amazing change take place, often within a few days, inside the chrysalis? What tells the caterpillar that the time has come for the change and that it must turn into a pupa at its next moult and not into just another larval stage? It's all done by hormones.

Just behind the caterpillar's brain there is a pair of glands known as the corpora allata, and for much of the caterpillar's life they secrete a substance known as the juvenile hormone. This ensures that the larval features are retained at each moult and that adult features do not develop. During the final larval instar, however, the brain cuts off the supply of juvenile hormone and at the final moult the epidermal cells produce a pupal skin instead of another larval skin. Development of the adult can thus proceed. Proof of the role of the juvenile hormone and the corpora allata comes from various experiments, including micro-surgery in which the glands have been removed from young caterpillars and implanted in the bodies of older larvae. Deprived of their corpora allata, and thus juvenile hormone, the young caterpillars pupated at their next moult and produced dwarf adults, while the mature cater-

pillars with the implanted glands continued to grow and delayed their change by two or three moults. Injections of juvenile hormone into mature larvae have the same effect.

Once the pupal skin has formed, the rebuilding can get under way in earnest, controlled by a complex system of hormones and enzymes. Throughout larval life, right from the earliest embryonic stages in fact, the caterpillar's body has contained small packets of tissue known as imaginal buds. Their growth has been suppressed by the juvenile hormone circulating in the caterpillar's body, but now they spring to life and their cells begin to multiply. At the same time the bulk of the larval tissues are liquefied by a process called histolysis and converted into a nutrient rich soup. Anyone who has speared a pupa while digging the garden in autumn or winter will have met this creamy fluid. The imaginal buds soon soak it up and, under hormonal control, their cells are built up into the adult organs. In fact, not all of the larval tissues are destroyed. The skin of the thoracic legs may be retained and merely re-shaped into the adult form. The tracheae are also retained for, as we have already seen, the intense biochemical activity of metamorphosis requires a lot of oxygen and respiration must continue throughout the pupal period. There is also relatively little change to the blood system.

PUPAL DIAPAUSE

The metamorphosis of a caterpillar to an adult butterfly or moth may take as little as seven days in warm weather, and a White Admiral butterfly may be on the wing only ten days after taking its last bite of honeysuckle leaf as a caterpillar. But the pupal stage often lasts a good deal longer. Many species pass the whole winter as pupae, and some moths remain in this stage for two or more years. This does not imply, however, that the conversion process takes a long time; the process comes to a complete halt at some stage and development may be suspended for several months awaiting

the return of favourable conditions.
The stage at which this diapause
occurs varies from species to species.
Many pupae remain in the 'soup'
stage throughout the winter although,
as with the Duke of Burgundy, ghost-
ly wings and partly formed legs may
be found floating in the liquid. Other
species complete their metamorphosis
soon after pupation and spend the
winter as fully-formed adults inside
their pupal cases. Strictly speaking, it
is thus the adults that survive the
winter, even if they are enclosed in
their pupal cases, but for practical
purposes it can be said that the pupa is
the over-wintering stage. A fully-
formed adult still wrapped up in its
pupal case is said to be a pharate
adult. There are also species that pass
the winter as prepupae – pupae that
have not yet shed their larval skins.

Whatever the stage at which the
pupal diapause begins, it is initiated in
the larval stage by day-length or
temperature or, more often perhaps,
by a combination of the two. It is
thought that, by absorbing some of
the light that falls on them, the
yellowish carotenoid pigments of
the caterpillars somehow register
the hours of daylight and, when this
period drops below a certain minimum, pass the information on to the
endocrine system which then prepares
the body for diapause. Genetics also
has a part to play, for not all individuals of a species are affected in the
same way. The Green-veined White,
for example, has both single and
double-brooded races in most parts of
Europe. Pupae of the single-brooded
race go into diapause in the summer,
when the days are still long, and do
not produce new adults until the
following spring, whereas the summer
pupae of the double-brooded race
develop without diapause and produce a second generation later in the
summer. In northern areas, however,
and also at high altitudes – above
about 250m in Britain – the insects
are virtually all single-brooded and it
is clear that the double-brooded strain
has been weeded out by natural selection because it cannot complete its
development before winter sets in.

Pteromalus *parasites emerging from a Small
White pupa*

As with the eggs and larvae, diapause is finally broken by the rising
temperature in spring, although other
factors, perhaps genetic in nature,
must be at work in those individuals
that pass through two or more winters
before emerging from their pupae.
The important result of the diapause,
and its subsequent breaking by the
improvement in the weather, is that
nearly all the individuals in a given
area emerge at about the same time
and thus have little trouble in meeting
and mating.

ENEMIES AND DEFENCES

Like the eggs and larvae, the pupae of
butterflies and moths have many enemies, including both predators and
parasites. Birds, lizards, and small
mammals are all fond of juicy pupae,
while other enemies include beetles,
centipedes, and some hunting spiders.
Various mites will also pierce pupae
to get at the nutritious body fluids.
The major parasites of pupae are the
ichneumons (see p. 223), including
the very common *Apechthis rufatus*
which, together with several related
species, attacks the pupae of the
Small Tortoiseshell and other nypha-
lids. The eggs are laid inside the
pupae and new adult ichneumons
emerge from jagged holes some
weeks later. But, as we shall see,
egg-laying is not always easy, even in
a relatively immobile pupa. The parasite's best chance is to find a freshly-
formed pupa whose skin is still relatively soft, and it seems to be able to
do this fairly efficiently with the aid of
its well-developed sense of smell.

The tiny chalcid *Pteromalus pupar-*

A selection of pupa predators

um is a very common parasite of the pupae of both pierid and nymphalid pupae and scores of shiny green adults can be seen emerging from a single pupa. When the time comes for these adults to lay their own eggs they must seek out soft new pupae and, with what in human terms might be called forward planning, the females can actually be seen riding on the backs of fully-grown host larvae and waiting for them to begin their transformation.

With relatively little mobility, and none at all in some species, the pupa might appear completely defenceless. It certainly cannot run away, and it cannot emit unpleasant odours or fluids to ward off attackers, but it does not lack protection entirely and the first line of defence is normally camouflage. Virtually all butterfly pupae are cryptically coloured so that they merge with their backgrounds. Even the shiny spots of many nymphalid pupae blend with the splashes of sunlight on the surrounding leaves. The caterpillars of the Large White and many other species can actually determine their pupal colours to some extent so that they blend in reasonably well with backgrounds ranging from the yellows and green of their food-plants to dark grey or even black. Experiments have shown that the pupal colour in these instances depends on the background colour

seen by the caterpillar just before pupation. Caterpillars whose eyes are covered always give rise to the normal green pupae regardless of the surrounding colour.

There are also some remarkable examples of protective resemblance among the butterfly pupae. This is a form of camouflage in which the pupa does more than simply blend in with the background; it closely resembles some natural object, such as a leaf, and thereby escapes the attentions of birds. The White Admiral pupa, for example, looks just like a rolled and shrivelled leaf (see p. 239), while that of the Black Hairstreak has an even better ploy; it looks exactly like a bird dropping stuck to a leaf or a twig (see p. 239). Numerous caterpillars and even adult moths use this same highly

Swallowtail pupae can be green or brown, depending on the background

effective ploy to fool the birds, none of which is likely to take an interest in its own excrement, but the prize for ingenuity in this sphere must go to the Poplar Admiral (see p. 80). Before pupating, the larva beds down on a pad of silk on the upper surface of a leaf and curls the edges of the leaf around itself like a cradle. The larval skin is then shed to reveal the shiny black and yellow upper surface of the pupa, which looks like it has been broken open and the yellow body fluids have oozed out from the black body. Birds, which have presumably learnt that many black and yellow creatures are distasteful, rarely bother to molest the pupa.

The various forms of visual camouflage are certainly effective against birds, but they are no defence against the parasites that seek their hosts by scent. Many pupae are completely hidden from view among debris or in the sole of the turf, while others, such as those of the Red Admiral and most of the skipper butterflies, are wrapped in leaves bound together with silk. Many moth pupae are enclosed in dense protective cocoons. All this additional wrapping provides greater concealment from predators and also makes life more difficult for any parasites trying to penetrate the enclosed pupae with their ovipositors.

The defences mentioned so far have all been passive ones, involving no action by the pupae, but detailed studies of pupae have revealed some surprising and often amusing active reactions to parasitic attack. The pupa of the Small Tortoiseshell, for example, wriggles violently when touched by an *Apechthis* parasite, although the same pupa will rarely give more than a few flicks of the abdomen if stroked with a paint brush or gently squeezed in the fingers. The contortions throw the small parasites into the air, for they find it difficult to get a foothold on the hard, shiny chrysalis at the best of times. Larger ichneumons find it easier to get a grip and plunge in their ovipositors. Several other nymphalid pupae, including those of the Painted Lady, respond in a similar way to the

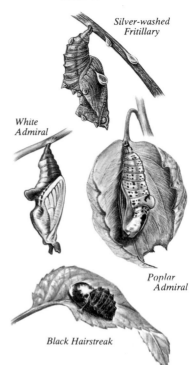

Silver-washed Fritillary

White Admiral

Poplar Admiral

Black Hairstreak

Many pupae are protected by looking like shrivelled leaves or bird droppings. The Poplar Admiral uses warning colours to deter birds

approach of *Apechthis* species, but the pupae of the Speckled Wood and other satyrid butterflies are less active and rely more on a waxy bloom on their very smooth coats to deny footholds to their *Apechthis* parasites. When experimentally wrapped in fine muslin these pupae are readily pierced by the ichneumons. The succinct pupae of the Large White and other pierids are less mobile than the suspended pupae and, although relatively thick-skinned, they are easily penetrated by the ovipositors of the larger ichneumons such as *Pimpla instigator*. Pupae in cocoons are often quite mobile and merely roll out of reach when they are touched by a probing ovipositor. They cannot go far, but they commonly 'tease' the parasite until it gives up the attack and looks for an easier victim.

Some of the smaller ichneumons are literally attacked by some pupae with particularly mobile abdomens. The margins of the abdominal plates of these pupae are sharp and often toothed, and when the abdomen is flexed these edges come together like the jaws of a gin-trap – much to the discomfort of any ichneumon probing the intersegmental membranes at the time. The trap does not remain shut for long and probably does the ichneumon no permanent harm, but it is certainly enough to send the parasite away without achieving its aim. Mites are also caught by this system, which is found mainly in the pupae of moths and beetles. Other deterrents include rustling sounds made by various pupae, either by rubbing one abdominal segment against another, as in the Hummingbird Hawkmoth, or by rubbing the abdomen against the inside of the cocoon, as in the burnet moths.

Despite their elaborate camouflage and other defences, many pupae are still destroyed by parasites and predators, and others are killed by winter floods and also by moulds. The actual numbers destroyed obviously vary from place to place and from season to season, but studies of various populations suggest that from 50 eggs – an average number from a single female butterfly – only 15 individuals are likely to reach the pupal stage, and of these only three will become adults. This represents a pupal mortality of 80%, which is much higher than the death rate observed in eggs and larvae. But as long as each batch produces one egg-laying female the population will remain more or less stable.

The pupal gin trap

ADULT EMERGENCE

As we have already seen, the butterfly or moth may remain as a pharate adult inside its pupal skin for a considerable time before it breaks out, but the time for emergence eventually arrives. The skins of many butterfly pupae become transparent at this stage, revealing the wing colours quite clearly. Most moth pupae, which are generally concealed and rather drab, simply get darker and reveal nothing of the adult coloration until the skin actually splits. The obtect pupae of the butterflies and most moths open by means of a long split running over the 'shoulders' and along the front edges of the wings. The head and thorax are then thrust through the gap and the insect gulps in air to expand its body. Gripping the pupal skin with its legs, it then drags the abdomen free. The process is easy to watch in suspended and succinct pupae, although often completed frustratingly quickly, but it cannot normally be seen in those species that pupate in cocoons or under the ground. In these instances the adults have the further problem of escaping from their silken shrouds or burial chambers. Muscle power is sufficient in many instances, but some of the tougher cocoons have to be softened by special fluids from the mouth. The structure of the cocoon may also assist escape, as in the Emperor Moth whose coarse cocoon fibres are arranged in such a way that the adult can force its way out but enemies cannot get in – a sort of lobster-pot in reverse!

The micropterigid pupae actually cut their way out of their tough cocoons with large jaws (see p. 236), although it is really the pharate adult that provides the motive power, and we have already seen on p. 235 that the burnet and clearwing pupae wriggle part way out of their cocoons or pupal chambers before rupturing to release the adults. Brute force is involved here, with the head of the clearwing pupa bearing a hard point which breaks through the cap of the pupal chamber. The legs and other appendages of these incomplete

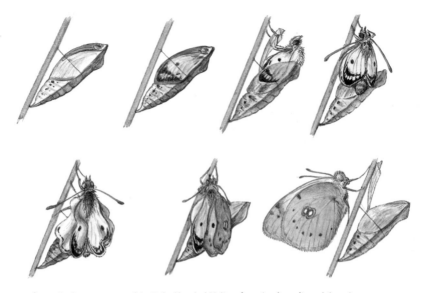

Stages in the emergence of the Pale Clouded Yellow from its chrysalis and the subsequent expansion of its wings

pupae generally become free before the skin splits to release the adult.

Although the legs are fully functional when the new adult drags itself from its pupal skin, the wings are still small and crumpled and the insect must quickly find a convenient support to which it can cling while expanding and drying its wings. Species with suspended and succinct pupae often just cling to the empty pupal skin for this final drama, but those which pupate on or under the ground may have to wander some way before finding a suitable vertical support. The imago must not begin to expand its wings until it reaches a suitable place, for the soft membranes are easily damaged and if they do not have sufficient room to expand they will end up crippled and the insect will be unable to fly.

Expansion of the wings is brought about by pumping blood into their veins. They usually reach their full size within about half an hour, although another hour or two may be needed for them to harden sufficiently for flight. During expansion and the first stages of drying the wings hang down together with only their undersides visible, and the normal resting attitude is not adopted until the wings are fairly hard. Butterflies then commonly bask for a while with their wings held very flat – an ideal time for the photographer to capture their beauty. The butterflies normally emerge from their pupae only in sunny weather, often early in the morning so that their wings are ready for flight when the air warms up in the middle of the day.

During the later stages of drying, before they take to the air, the insects release a pink, red, or yellowish fluid from the anus. Known as meconium, this contains the waste products that have built up in the food canal during metamorphosis. Where large numbers of butterflies or moths emerge at one time the vegetation and ground below may become densely spotted with this material, giving rise to tales of 'blood raining from the heavens'. Once rid of this burden, the insects are ready for the adult quest for food and a mate, although for most of them life will last no more than a few days and maybe only hours.

241

THE ADULT BUTTERFLY

HOMES AND HABITATS

Butterflies are not randomly distributed through time and space. Each species has a particular flight period and a definite range, outside of which it is unlikely to be seen. The flight period may be as little as two weeks in a year for some species with restricted distributions, but it is a good deal longer for most butterflies when the complete range is taken into account. This may be a simple result of climate, with individuals in the south of their range appearing several weeks earlier than those in the north, but the pattern is often complicated by different breeding habits in various parts of the range. Many species have two, three, or even four broods in southern and central parts of Europe, while northern populations and those high in the mountains are commonly single-brooded (see p. 237). The broods commonly overlap in the south, where butterflies such as the Small Heath may be on the wing from March until October. In northern Europe this same species has just a single brood in July. In the very harsh climates of the far north and the mountain peaks the summer might not be long enough for even one brood, and several hardy species have overcome this problem by evolving a biennial life cycle. Eggs laid in one summer do not produce adults until two years later.

Whatever the length of the flight period, individual butterflies rarely live very long before succumbing to their numerous enemies or to old age. The average life span of the adult has been calculated at only 4–5 days, although those species that hibernate as adults obviously live very much longer – usually nine or ten months. The Brimstone commonly survives for about a year, of which as much as seven months may be spent flitting about the countryside.

Apart from the highest mountain-tops, butterflies occur virtually everywhere in Europe, from the shores of the Mediterranean to those of the Arctic. Several fritillaries regularly fly over the North Cape and one of them, the Arctic Fritillary, is probably the most northerly of all butterflies. It has been seen flying in Greenland less than 1,000km from the North Pole. Seven butterfly species – the Green-veined White, the Green Hairstreak, the Small Copper, the Common Blue, the Painted Lady, the Small Tortoise-shell, and the Dark Green Fritillary – are regularly found throughout Europe, although not necessarily breeding everywhere, and a few other species are almost as widely distributed. The majority of butterfly species, however, have much smaller ranges. Some montane species, for example, occupy just a few square kilometres of mountain-top (see p. 303). Climate is the major factor con-

The flight periods of some common butterflies.

Although single brooded the

| January | February | March | | May | June |

Brimstone

Duke of Burgundy

Provence Hairstreak

Mar

trolling the ranges of the butterflies, although it may not act directly on the insects. It may be that the larval food-plant is restricted by climate, and this is just as effective in restricting the range of the butterfly. As one would expect from its warmer climate and greater variety of vegetation, southern Europe has far more butterflies than the north. France, for example, has about 235 species, while Finland has only 108. The British Isles have only 59 regular breeders, including three summer visitors, the artificially maintained Large Copper and the recently re-established Large Blue. But the Channel is more to blame than climate in denying us a greater number of butterfly species. High mountains also have fewer species than the surrounding lowlands – again the result of lower temperatures and fewer kinds of food-plants.

Most species are adapted to particular habitats, such as woodland or grassland, and therefore occur only in these specific areas within their total ranges. Many of them require extremely precise conditions for successful breeding. The Adonis Blue, for example, is confined to areas of chalk and limestone because its larvae feed only on horseshoe vetch and a few related leguminous plants which are themselves confined to calcareous soils. But the mere presence of the food-plant is not quite enough for this butterfly; it also needs sun-drenched south-facing slopes and the turf must not be more than about 3cm high for efficient egg-laying. There are thus many areas in which the food-plant grows but which do not support the Adonis Blue. The Black Hairstreak is another species limited by fussy habits. Its larvae feed on blackthorn, which is abundant everywhere, but the butterfly needs mature bushes fringing the sunny rides and glades of old woodland. This cannot be just any old woodland; in England the species is restricted to a narrow strip of the East Midlands where the traditionally long coppicing rotation has maintained plenty of mature blackthorn as well as sunny clearings.

There are, of course, a number of less fussy species. The Dark Green Fritillary, for example, is equally at home on moorlands and chalk downs, while the High Brown Fritillary is a woodland insect in Britain and Northern Europe and an inhabitant of upland heaths in the south.

OPEN AND CLOSED POPULATIONS

Even more catholic in their choice of habitat than the species just mentioned are the migrants, such as the cabbage whites and the Painted Lady. Some of these travel thousands of kilometres in a summer and these true migrants (see p. 264) are commonly joined by other travellers, including the Brimstone, the Green-veined White, the Orange-tip, and the Comma. They all sweep across the countryside, stopping here and there to feed or mate and lay eggs and then moving on to the next suitable habitat. These butterflies can thus be found more or less anywhere within their overall ranges and they are said to have open populations. Most of the

adow Brown has a long period of emergence, and therefore a long flight period

uly   August   September   October   November   December

Autumn Ringlet

Silver-spotted Skipper

Meadow Brown

butterflies that visit our gardens belong to this group. With the exception of the Brimstone, their larvae tend to feed on weeds or field crops in temporary habitats. Adults and larvae not only have different diets, but also usually feed in quite different places.

The 'stay-at-home' butterflies, which account for about 75% of all British species, form discrete colonies scattered here and there over suitable habitats. Neighbouring colonies have little or no contact with each other, even when separated by only short distances, and such populations are said to be closed.

Closed populations are typical of permanent habitats, such as woodland and grassland, where adult and larval foods are all available in one place. As long as the habitat remains suitable, the colonies can flourish for many years in the same place, although numbers obviously fluctuate from year to year. Most colonies are quite small, usually with no more than a few hundred individuals, but where there is a large and uninterrupted tract of suitable habitat the population of a single colony can be enormous. The grassy hillsides of southern Dorset, for example, support colonies of the Lulworth Skipper containing hundreds of thousands of butterflies. At the other end of the scale, there are short stretches of roadside verge supporting colonies of the Common Blue numbering no more than 20 or 30 individuals each year.

Some woodland butterflies

WOODLAND BUTTERFLIES

About one quarter of Europe's 360 butterfly species breed regularly in woodland habitats. In the British Isles 42 of the 58 breeding butterflies – 72% – are regularly found in woodland. These figures are not surprising when it is realised that most of the land was wooded up until quite recently. What is surprising, however, is the small number of butterflies whose larvae actually feed on the trees and shrubs – only 11 species in the British Isles and 33 in the whole of Europe. Even the widespread oaks support only three species of hairstreak. Birch is occasionally nibbled by Camberwell Beauty and Brown Hairstreak caterpillars, but beech and lime have no regular takers among the butterfly larvae. The conifers also have no attraction for butterfly larvae, although many adult butterflies will perch on these and other trees to sunbathe and to drink honeydew. It is a different story with the moths, however, whose larvae use all our native trees as food-plants.

Purple Emperor

Comma

Silver-washed Fritillary

White Admiral

Wood White

The majority of woodland butterflies use herbaceous plants as larval food-plants, so the butterfly fauna of a forest depends very much more on its management than on the species of trees and shrubs present.

Dense coniferous plantations with little ground flora support very few butterflies, although the Speckled Wood may stake out territories in the scattered sunny spots (see p. 284). The richest butterfly woods are those with plenty of open spaces, where sunlight can reach the ground and encourage the growth of a thick herb layer. Wide rides and grassy clearings, even in coniferous woodlands, support numerous grass-feeding species, such as the browns and skippers, as long as there are plenty of nectar sources for the adult butterflies. Mobile species like the Peacock and the Small Tortoiseshell also visit the rides and breed there if their food-plants are available. Stinging nettles are not normally found in established woodland, but crop up readily enough after disturbance of the ground.

Purple Hairstreak

Ringlet

Green-veined White

Speckled Wood

Many of the butterflies seen along the mown rides and glades are, of course, grassland species that have simply taken advantage of the shelered strips of grass. There are, however, a number of true woodland butterflies, including many of the fritillaries, that require a succession of fresh clearings in which violets and primroses can grow amongst the regenerating trees and shrubs. Traditional coppicing – the cutting of selected areas of woodland to ground level every 10–15 years – has long maintained this succession of clearings, and with it the populations of the dependent butterflies.

The decline in coppicing has led to a severe decline in the populations of several woodland butterflies in Britain, but its re-introduction as a major form of management in various woodland nature reserves is helping to reverse the trend. The Heath Fritillary, once in grave danger of extinction in England, is now surviving in good numbers thanks to the restoration of coppicing, although it is still one of our rarest butterflies and protected by the 1981 Wildlife and Countryside Act. The more extensive woodland on the continent, much of it still regularly coppiced, has allowed woodland butterflies to flourish there in greater numbers. Less intensive management of the land has also allowed the woodland butterflies to survive quite happily in the scrubby areas that have sprung up around the edges of many tracts of woodland.

GRASSLAND BUTTERFLIES

Grasslands of one kind or another dominate the landscape nearly everywhere in the British Isles and they also cover a large part of continental Europe. As well as the familiar enclosed meadows and pastures and the vast tracts of rough grazing in the uplands, they include considerable areas of roadside verges and woodland rides and clearings. More than half of the European butterflies are associated with these various grasslands, and 32 of the British species regularly breed in such areas.

Some grassland butterflies

Spotted Fritillary

Clouded Yellow

Marbled White

Common Blue

Silver-spotted Skipper

The browns, blues, and skippers are the main groups of grassland butterflies, and they are commonly joined by a number of fritillaries, especially on the continent. The browns all utilise grasses as larval food-plants, and so do most of the skippers. Many of these butterflies can be found in the dense grass of roadside verges and similar habitats, as long as there are reasonable numbers of nectar-yielding flowers. The other species grow up on the legumes and other flowering plants that grow amongst the grasses, a rich variety of plant life thus encouraging a wide range of butterflies. Many different species of burnet moths can also be found in grassland areas.

Soil, aspect, and altitude all have a role in determining the butterfly species inhabiting an area, but management is of over-riding importance. Most grasslands have been 'improved' during the last 50 years or so by adding artificial fertilisers and by re-seeding them with high-yielding grass mixtures. The wild flowers have thus been lost, and most of the butterflies have gone with them. Few of the enclosed grasslands now support more than a few browns and the occasional Clouded Yellow that survives on the cultivated clovers. To find many grassland butterflies one now has to concentrate on the wilder grasslands of the steep slopes. The chalk downs of southern England and northern France are still exciting places for the butterfly enthusiast, with thousands of blues and skippers to be seen in certain areas, but these grassland habitats are rapidly disappearing under a blanket of scrub now that sheep rarely graze on them and the rabbit population is held in check by myxomatosis.

The richest butterfly fields are undoubtedly the near-natural hay meadows of the Alps and other mountains, notably the Picos de Europa in northern Spain. Cutting and grazing are strictly controlled so that only a small part of the vegetation is removed each year, and only animal dung is used to fertilise the ground. The wild flowers and their attendant butterflies flourish, and it is easy to spot 20 or even 30 butterfly species in the space of a few minutes in early summer.

Each grassland species has its own requirements in terms of vegetation height. The Adonis Blue and the Silver-spotted Skipper, for example, require turf no more than 3 – 4cm high, with a fair amount of bare ground. Such a habitat is generally maintained by moderate rabbit grazing, and the reduction in the rabbit population since the arrival of myxomatosis has led to a severe reduction in these butterflies in southern England. The Chalkhill Blue and the Common Blue both breed happily in grass up to about 10cm tall, although they appreciate taller clumps of grass in which to roost, while the Marbled White and the Large Skipper like their grass between 10 and 20cm high. The Lulworth Skipper prefers even taller grass, often flitting around clumps exceeding 30cm in height and disappearing very quickly into them when the sun disappears.

These differing requirements mean that the richest grasslands in terms of butterfly species are those with a patchwork of different grass heights. This is exactly what is found on many hillsides. The soil is generally shallow on the steeper parts and supports relatively short vegetation, while the gentler slopes have deeper soil and taller vegetation. The pattern is often further complicated by rocks which approach or break through the surface here and there and alternate with pockets of deeper soil. Periodic mowing and grazing can create a similar patchwork if only small areas are treated at a time, as in the montane meadows. Light grazing by sheep and cattle has actually helped to increase butterfly populations on several grassland reserves, but great care is necessary to prevent over-grazing and the complete destruction of the sward.

ARCTIC BUTTERFLIES

The windswept tundra to the north of the Arctic tree line is in darkness for several weeks during the winter and the soil is frozen for about nine months of the year. Summer temperatures rarely rise above 15°C for more than a few days and there is little respite from the wind in this region of stunted shrubs, the tallest of which barely reach knee height. There is, however, continuous daylight throughout the summer months, and a carpet of brilliant flowers provides a feast of nectar for those insects that have managed to adapt themselves to the otherwise rather inhospitable climate.

Among these insects there are 37 species of butterflies – 13 of them fritillaries – resident on the tundra of northern Europe. A further 13 species regularly breed north of the Arctic Circle, although they do not normally venture beyond the tree line, which wriggles across the top of Scandinavia and in some places is as much as 160 km beyond the Arctic Circle.

Apart from the fritillaries, the main Arctic butterflies are various blues and coppers, a number of browns, and a few of the clouded yellows. Other residents include widespread species like the Green Hairstreak and the Green-veined White, together

Some Arctic butterflies

Northern Clouded Yellow

Lapland Fritillary

Arctic Grayling

Arctic Fritillary

Purple-edged Copper

with a number of moths. Most of them fly during June and July. The moths thus have to fly in daylight, although the same species may well be nocturnal further south. Species and races that inhabit the tundra often show modifications of the eyes associated with daylight activity. The resident species are often joined on the tundra by some of the wandering butterflies such as the Large White, the Small Tortoiseshell, and the Painted Lady – all of which have been found on the North Cape.

Compared with their relatives in the south, most Arctic butterflies are rather dark and some are distinctly drab; even the clouded yellows have a heavy dusting of black scales. Dark colours absorb heat more readily than light ones, and so a butterfly with dark wings has a big advantage in the cool northern climate. A good deal of heat is absorbed from rocks and from the ground by pressing the wings tightly down while sun-bathing, and a furry coating to the body of most species ensures that much of the heat is retained in the body.

Arctic butterflies also fly less than those in warmer climates, and when they do fly they usually keep close to the ground to avoid being blown away by the wind. In fact, they rarely take off if it is windy, and they never fly unless the sun is shining. Some northern moths have reduced wings and are quite unable to fly.

The short summer means that only those species with the shortest development times can complete their larval stages and pupate before the winter sets in. Many Arctic butterflies, as we have already seen, take two years to complete their growth, passing two winters in the larval stage or one as a larva and one as a pupa. Both larvae and pupae are well able to withstand the long, cold winters without harm. Some moths take as long as five years to mature, but there are also some that complete their larval growth in one summer, often aided by the fact that the female moths emerge from their pupae with their eggs fully ripe and ready for fertilisation – although this feature is in no way confined to moths in the far north. The female Emperor Moth, for example, commonly mates before her wings are dry and lays her eggs within minutes of freeing herself from the male.

Several of the tundra-living butterfly species also occur hundreds of miles to the south, around the peaks of the Alps and other mountain ranges. Such fragmented or discontinuous distributions are the result of the ice-age glaciations which pushed the tundra and its wildlife almost to the shores of the Mediterranean. When the ice finally retreated the cold-loving plants and animals went with it again. Some went all the way back to the far north, but other individuals settled happily on the cold mountain tops and have remained there ever since (see p. 303).

MOUNTAIN BUTTERFLIES

Conditions above the tree line on the mountains are similar to those on the tundra and, as we have already seen, several butterfly species are common to both habitats. There are, however, considerably more montane species than Arctic species. Numerous blues mingle with fritillaries and clouded yellows, but the dominant montane butterflies are the browns. The genus *Erebia* is represented by no less than 41 species in the mountains of Europe. Most of these are very dark (see pp. 116–133) and thus well suited to life on the rugged mountain slopes. Flying close to the ground is even more important here, for the wind is strong and a sudden gust could easily carry a butterfly far from its habitat. Many of the *Erebia* species are confined to very small areas – perhaps just one or two neighbouring peaks – and most of them have clearly evolved fairly recently from a common ancestor (see p. 303).

Although the browns are the dominant mountain butterflies in terms of numbers, the best known species are undoubtedly the apollos. These sturdy butterflies float majestically over the flower-strewn slopes on their beautifully patterned wings, stopping here and there to sip nectar or to bask on the ground or on warm rocks and then having to flap their wings rather laboriously to get their heavy bodies airborne again. Although their wings reflect much of the sun's heat, the apollos absorb a good deal directly from the ground and their furry bodies ensure that much of the heat is retained. The Apollo itself lives at fairly low levels in Scandinavia, but elsewhere it ranges between 750 and 2,000m. Although often seen on the upper slopes, its real home is in the clearings of the sub-alpine zone, just below the tree line.

The apollos are much sought after by collectors and have declined alarmingly in some places, although it is unlikely that collecting has had more than a very local effect. The main threat to the Apollo is the blanketing of the slopes with conifers, although over-grazing may also have played some part. The butterfly can withstand a fair amount of grazing in its habitat, for its larval food plants are stonecrops and houseleeks that grow among the rocks, but the over-grazing that has occurred in many parts of the

Alps has completely destroyed the flowers on which the adults depend for nectar. The apollos are now legally protected in many parts of Europe, although such legislation does not necessarily halt the decline of these fine insects.

Although many mountain butterflies, including the Apollo and most of the blues, like to drink from the edges of streams and other wet places – animal dung and urine has a great attraction for them – most species are to be found on the well-drained, sunny slopes where the bulk of the flowers grow. Some butterflies, however, spend all their lives on the poorly-drained moors and bogs. The Mountain Ringlet – the only truly upland butterfly in the British Isles – is a good example, usually found between 200 and 900m in Britain although it goes a good deal higher on the continent. Because they fly only in sunshine, British specimens spend most of their lives resting amongst the sodden grasses of the moors. The Large Heath is another species preferring wet, boggy habitats, although it is not confined to upland areas.

Some mountain butterflies and moths

Green-veined White

Mountain Ringlet

Alpine Argus

Emperor Moth

Apollo

Some Mediterranean butterflies

Mediterranean Skipper

Spanish Festoon

Two-tailed Pasha

Southern Swallowtail

Provence Hairstreak

Large Blue

Just as there are Arctic races or sub-species of many common European butterflies, so there are montane races of many lowland butterflies. These are often much darker than lowland races – the sub-species *bryoniae* of the Green-veined White is a good example – and they are often a good deal smaller, probably as a result of the shorter feeding season. Only a few of the montane browns have adopted the two-year life cycle.

Many day-flying moths mingle with the butterflies in the mountains, the most obvious being the burnets. Like the *Erebia* species, these have evolved rapidly since the retreat of the glaciers and have produced a bewildering array of species and sub-species in mountainous areas. Other common day-flying species include the Emperor Moth, which dashes madly over the heather moors and alpine pastures, the Small Dark Yellow Underwing, and the Black Mountain Moth and other *Psodos* species.

MEDITERRANEAN BUTTERFLIES

The Mediterranean lands were once clothed with evergreen oaks and other tough-leaved trees adapted to withstand the long, hot summers. But centuries of human occupation have had a profound effect on the region. Apart from patches of valuable cork oak – food-plant of the striking Oak Hawkmoth – very little of the original vegetation remains. Over-grazing, often followed by severe soil erosion, denuded vast tracts of land and many areas still consist largely of bare rock. Elsewhere, if not submerged by the rapidly-spreading bricks and mortar, the land supports dense scrub. Over the limestones, where the soil is extremely thin or even non-existent, the scrub is composed largely of such aromatic plants as thyme, rosemary, and lavender and is known as *garrigue*. Larger shrubs, including junipers and kermes oaks, grow in the deeper soils in the numerous crevices. The acidic rocks usually support thicker soils than the limestones and the scrub is usually taller, consisting mainly of heaths and cistuses with scattered strawberry trees. This is the famous *maquis*. Lots of herbaceous plants grow among the shrubs, especially on the *garrigue*, but they usually flower early in the year and then die down in the summer drought.

A number of butterflies are characteristic of these dry habitats and several of them fly early in the year to coincide with the spring flowers. None flies earlier than the Provence Hairstreak, which is on the wing from January until April. Its larvae feed on low-growing legumes in the spring and are safely tucked up as pupae before the summer drought sets in. Other early butterflies include the Moroccan Orange-tip and the Green-striped White, the latter managing to get two generations in between February and May. The Spanish Festoon is also on the wing between February and May. On the other hand there are species like the Mediterranean Skipper and the Pigmy Skipper that positively revel in the hot summer sunshine and often bask on the hottest rocks. Their nocturnal larvae manage to find enough green grass underneath the shrubs during the summer. Those species whose larvae actually feed on the shrubs have fewer problems and can produce two or more generations in a summer, as with the tiger blues. Small butterflies can usually find enough nectar in the small flowers of the heaths and other low-growing shrubs, but larger butterflies must look elsewhere for their food as large flowers are rarely seen on the *garrigue* or the *maquis* during the summer.

The most striking butterfly of the *maquis* is undoubtedly the handsome Two-tailed Pasha, whose larvae feed on the strawberry tree. Two generations of this large butterfly are produced each year and the adults sidestep the problem of nectar shortage by taking most of their food in the form of fruit juice. Peaches are favourites during the summer, while figs get a lot of attention from the autumn brood. Originating in Africa, the Two-tailed Pasha has now spread virtually all round the Mediterranean but it is rarely found more than a few kilometres from the coast.

GARDEN BUTTERFLIES

Never be surprised by the butterflies that visit a garden. Even the Silver-washed Fritillary will come to buddleias if the garden is in the middle of a wood, and gardens surrounded by fields commonly attract grassland species such as the Meadow Brown and the Common Blue. Rural gardens with plenty of hedges around them receive visits from the Ringlet and the Gatekeeper.

Town gardens obviously receive fewer butterfly visitors, but they do get some as long as there are a few nectar-yielding flowers for them to feed on. About twelve species can be regarded as typical garden butterflies in northern and central Europe, regularly visiting gardens in both town and country. A few additional species, including the Scarce Swallowtail, can be found in gardens in southern Europe. These regular garden butterflies all have open populations (see p. 243) and they merely visit our gardens in the course of their wanderings. Apart from the cabbage whites, the most numerous are generally the vanessids – the Peacock, the Small Tortoiseshell, the Comma, the Red Admiral, and the Painted Lady. On the continent they are not infrequently joined by the Camberwell Beauty. Other familiar garden butterflies include the Brimstone, especially noticeable in the spring, and the Orange-tip. The latter often breeds on railway embankments and in cemeteries very close to the centres of towns. The Wall Brown breeds in similar places, although it is a much more sedentary species and visits only those gardens that are very close to its breeding grounds. The same can be said for the Small Copper. The only blue normally seen in the garden is the Holly Blue, which is more mobile than most of its relatives and which

Some garden butterflies and moths

will actually breed in gardens with plenty of holly or ivy.

Apart from the Holly Blue, the only butterflies that breed in a typical garden are the troublesome cabbage whites and the occasional Orange-tip that finds the honesty or sweet rocket to its liking. Our cultivated plants are just not attractive to butterfly larvae in the main, although many are eaten readily enough by various moth larvae. Of course, the nettle-feeding Peacock and its relatives can be persuaded to breed in the garden if they are given a sunny patch of stinging nettles, and some of the grass-feeding browns may take up residence in long grass at the bases of walls and hedges, but the intensive management of the garden and the temporary nature of much of its vegetation makes it unsuitable for most of the sedentary butterflies.

Our garden butterflies are joined by a number of day-flying moths, the commonest of which is generally the Silver Y. This restless moth is usually seen as a greyish blur hovering in front of the flowers, but when it does settle the reason for its name becomes clear – a silvery Y-shaped mark in the centre of the forewing. Resident in southern Europe, the moth moves northwards in immense numbers each spring (see p. 266) and can usually be found in the smallest town garden. It is especially common among the flower beds of town parks, where it is often joined by the Hummingbird Hawkmoth. This is another well-known migrant and even swifter and more restless than the Silver Y. The two species are frequently confused when seen at flowers, but the Hummingbird Hawkmoth is much larger and browner than the Silver Y and it makes a distinct hum with its wings. The Currant Clearwing commonly sunbathes on the leaves of its food-plant, where it is easily mistaken for a large fly or one of the solitary wasps, and the Red-belted Clearwing is often seen basking on or flying around apple trees in the summer.

Hawthorn hedges are often patrolled by fast-flying male Vapourer moths in search of the wingless females. This species is also very common in towns and cities, where its hairy larvae feed on a variety of ornamental trees.

Butterfly pests
The only butterflies that can really be classed as garden pests are the two cabbage whites – the Large White and the Small white – whose larvae feed on a wide range of brassicas and often reduce them to skeletons of tough veins. The closely related

252

Green-veined White is often perse-
cuted along with its two destructive
cousins but, although a common garden visitor, it shows little interest in
brassicas. It prefers wild crucifers in
its larval stage, although it will sometimes breed on sweet rocket and
honesty in the garden. Even on the
continent there are very few butterflies that can be regarded as pests in
the garden, or anywhere else for that
matter. The Black-veined White is
sometimes a nuisance in orchards,
where its gregarious larvae damage
various fruit trees, especially plums
and cherries. The Scarce Swallowtail
larva also feeds on these trees, as well
as on wild blackthorn, but it is rarely
present in sufficient numbers to do
any real harm and the beauty of the
adult as it floats around the garden
more than makes up for the loss of a
few leaves.

There are, of course, far more pests
among the moths – in the fields and
forests as well as in the garden. With
the exception of the Hummingbird
Hawkmoth, all the species mentioned
above do some damage in their larval
stages. Silver Y larvae are indiscri-
minate feeders and nibble their way
through almost any herbaceous plant,
while Vapourer larvae do the same to
almost any deciduous tree. Clearwing
larvae are nearly all wood-borers and
they occasionally kill small branches
of their food-plants, but they are
rarely common enough to do any
serious damage.

Butterfly gardening
Many butterflies can be encouraged to
visit the garden by providing them
with the right kinds of nectar-yielding
flowers, and they repay the gardener's
hospitality by adding even more colour as they dance over the flower
beds. Most of the visitors will belong
to the typical garden species mentioned above, although some others
may arrive if there are suitable habitats near-by. Drawn by the colours
and scents, they stop off to feed and
they may stay around for the whole
day. Some may appear day after day,
but the garden butterflies are primarily wanderers and marking them

reveals that each day commonly
brings a completely different set of
individuals to the garden. This is
certainly true during the spring and
summer, although the Small Tortoiseshell and the other hibernators
become more sedentary during the
autumn and hang around good nectar
sources, such as ice plant or ivy
blossom, for several days while stock-
ing up in readiness for the winter
sleep.

The right plants can be of many
different species, but the insects must
be able to get at the nectar and many
of the best plants are wild ones or the
old-fashioned garden plants with
plenty of scent. Few modern horti-
cultural varieties are of interest to the
butterflies because, even if they have
any nectar, the insects commonly
cannot reach it. Bred primarily for
colour, many of today's varieties have
lost their scent and nectar altogether.
Many seedsmen now offer a range of
wild flower seeds specially selected for
attracting butterflies.

There is, of course, more to butterfly gardening than simply feeding
the adults. The ideal thing is to
provide larval food-plants – in the
right kind of setting – so that the
insects can breed and increase their
numbers. As we have already seen,
this means providing patches of stinging nettles for the common vanessids,
and few gardeners will have either the
space or the inclination to do this even
if the nettles can provide a tasty dish
for people as well as for caterpillars.
Thistles are necessary for the Painted
Lady, although its larvae will sometimes eat nettles, and docks are required by the Small Copper, but again
few gardeners are prepared to toler-
ate these weeds. The browns require
areas of rough grass of various
heights. This can be achieved by
setting aside patches of lawn or
orchard and allowing the grass to
grow up and flower, or just by being a
little less tidy – leaving long grass
around trees and hedges and along
the base of walls. Allowing
hedgerow ivy to flower will help the
Holly Blue.

BUTTERFLY SENSES

THE COMPOUND EYE

The eyes occupy a large part of the head and are known as compound eyes because each one is composed of thousands of separate light-gathering units called ommatidia. Each ommatidium is a slender cone, topped by a minute lens or facet and equipped with a light-sensitive cell, called a rhabdom, at the lower end. Nerves from the lower end of the ommatidium lead directly to the brain. The lenses form a miniature honeycomb pattern on the surface of the eye and are just about discernible with a good hand lens. Each ommatidium is surrounded by a jacket of pigment-containing cells which insulate it from its neighbours and, in most butterflies, prevent light from passing from one ommatidium to another. Each ommatidium thus sends its own individual signal to the brain when light stimulates the rhabdom at the base of the cone. Because each ommatidium sends a separate signal, the butterfly sees a mosaic image of its surroundings, made up of thousands of dots each representing a minute fraction of the field of view. Resolution is poor at a distance, but the system is very good at detecting light and shade and, because of the large number of lenses

in the butterfly's eye, it can also give a pretty good idea of the shapes of nearby objects. The system is also particularly good at picking up nearby movements, and this is of great importance to the insect. Moving objects, including predators and potential mates, stimulate a succession of ommatidia as they pass across the field of view, and the insect is immediately aware of them and can take appropriate action.

The butterflies also have extremely good colour vision and can probably detect a wider range of colours than any other group of animals – from deep in the ultra-violet at one end of the spectrum to well into red at the other. Colour clearly plays a major role in their lives and is used for finding food-plants as well as for recognising mates although, because of their sensitivity to ultra-violet, they do not see things in quite the same way as we do.

The skippers stand apart from the other butterflies in several respects and their eyes are no exception. The pigment is restricted to the outer parts of the ommatidia as in the night-flying moths, but the ommatidia are arranged in such a way that light entering a bunch of neighbouring lenses can be focused on one rhabdom to give a clear, bright image. The skippers obviously have very good sight, judging by the way in which they dart quickly and accurately from one flower to another.

A compound eye showing how the individual ommatidia fit together, and a single ommatidium to show how light passes through it

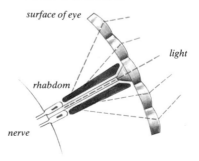

surface of eye

light

rhabdom

nerve

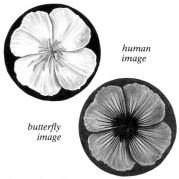

human
image

butterfly
image

An evening primrose as seen by a human and as seen by a butterfly, showing the ultraviolet reflections

THE ANTENNAE

Although the antennae are commonly called feelers, they do much more than enable the butterfly to feel its way about. They are literally covered with sensory equipment and their main role is in the detection of scent. Male moths, which find their mates largely by scent, usually have much larger antennae than the females, and in the Emperor Moth they are really enormous. The large size increases their ability to intercept scattered scent molecules carried on the wind. At the other end of the scale, female bagworm moths, which rarely leave their pupal cocoons, often have no antennae at all.

The palps also play a significant role in picking up scent and removal of the antennae does not eradicate the sense of smell, although it does reduce the butterfly's ability to pick up scents from any great distance.

Scents are detected by a variety of olfactory receptors, the commonest of which are minute hairs on the surface of the antenna and also on other parts of the body. Less commonly the hairs are sunk into little pits. Seen under an electron microscope the hairs resemble sponges, with numerous pores where the scent molecules actually lodge and stimulate the nerve endings inside. It seems likely that some hairs are able to detect only one particular odour – perhaps an important pheromone – while others can pick up several different scents, such as those of various food-plants. We do not know, however, how the various chemical stimuli are translated into nervous impulses and then sorted out by the brain.

Taste, being another chemical sense, is obviously closely related to the sense of smell. Most of the taste receptors are found on the palps and on the feet, with the antennae playing a relatively minor role. Many butterflies can be persuaded to extend the proboscis by treating one foot to a bath in dilute sugar solution. Sugars are the main feeding stimuli for adult butterflies, although many will also respond to salt solutions. But it is not just the adult food that has to be tasted. Egg-laying females have to ensure that they lay on the right food-plant, and they commonly do this by stamping their feet on the leaves to pick up the taste (see p. 201).

The sense organs involved in detecting taste are quite similar to those picking up smells. Most are thin-walled bristles, but they require much higher concentrations for stimulation than the olfactory sensors. Substances also normally have to be in solution before they can be absorbed and detected by the taste receptors.

The antennae are also involved in picking up a variety of mechanical signals such as touch and vibrations. Again, it is minute hairs, termed mechanoreceptors, that actually pick up the signals. Each hair is attached to the body by a tiny ball-and-socket joint and any deflection of the hair is transmitted to the joint and thence to a nerve fibre running to the brain. The butterfly thus knows immediately which hairs are being stimulated, but it does not necessarily have to bump into something to receive signals. Air movements are enough to disturb the delicate hairs and the insects can thus detect air currents coming towards them and passing over them. Hairs on other parts of the face are also involved with air currents and they all help the butterfly to maintain a steady flight.

Antennae generally comprise three discernible parts. The segment attached to the head is called the scape and is generally the longest. The next is the pedicel, which is generally short, and the remainder consisting of numerous very small segments, is called the flagellum. Between the pedicel and the flagellum there is a bundle of nerve endings called Johnston's organ. It is not as well developed in butterflies and moths as in many other insects, but it plays an important role in orientation during flight. The nerve endings detect stresses in the joint and thereby inform the insect of the position of its antennae with respect to gravity. The speed of air currents can also be detected by way of the push they exert on the antennae.

HEARING

It is often believed that butterflies are deaf because they have no ears. However, because sound is only very small vibrations of the air, many butterflies can detect some sounds, especially loud, low frequency ones, using highly sensitive mechanoreceptors. Most butterflies do no more than twitch when bombarded with sound and suggestions of butterflies responding to music are purely circumstantial. Many caterpillars also respond, rearing their heads and flicking their front ends from side to side when shouted at.

Many moths, mainly noctuids and geometers, possess true ears; the typanal organs, on the sides of their bodies. Their function is primarily to detect the high-pitched sounds of hunting bats and the ears thus respond to much higher frequencies than the hairs of the butterflies.

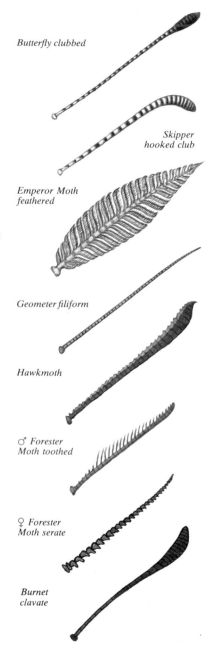

Butterfly clubbed

Skipper hooked club

Emperor Moth feathered

Geometer filiform

Hawkmoth

♂ Forester Moth toothed

♀ Forester Moth serate

Burnet clavate

A variety of butterfly and moth antennae, which are involved in a range of different sensory functions. Recent studies suggest that the complex antennae of the Emperor Moth can even pick up infra-red waves

FEEDING BEHAVIOUR

Adult butterflies and moths, with the exception of the primitive Micropterigidae (see p. 152) and the pollen-eating heliconiid butterflies of tropical America, feed solely on liquids, which they take through a hair-like tube called the proboscis. There are, however, a number of moths that do not feed in the adult state and have a much reduced proboscis or even none at all. The Emperor Moth does not even have a mouth.

The proboscis is actually in two halves which have to be zipped together to form the tube, and this is one of the first jobs that the butterfly has to do on leaving its chrysalis. Each half of the proboscis is composed of numerous horny rings separated by soft membranes, and there is an elastic strip of cuticle running the length of the upper side. Inside each half there are numerous oblique muscles, firmly attached to the walls. When not in use, the proboscis is coiled up between the palps on the underside of the head.

Butterflies and moths feed almost entirely on nectar. Almost any kind of nectar will do, although butterflies do seem more attracted to red, purple, and blue flowers than to the paler colours, but it must be remembered that the butterflies do not see colour in the same way that we do (see p. 255). Scent also plays a role in guiding the insects to the flowers as they get closer and is especially important for night-flying moths.

Scent may be enough to persuade the insect to uncoil its tongue, but some species need more stimulation than this. Taste organs on their feet or palps need to pick up traces of the sugary nectar before the proboscis will uncoil, but even then the insect will not feed unless the sense organs on the proboscis itself are sufficiently stimulated.

Uncoiling of the proboscis is brought about partly by blood pressure in the two halves of the apparatus,

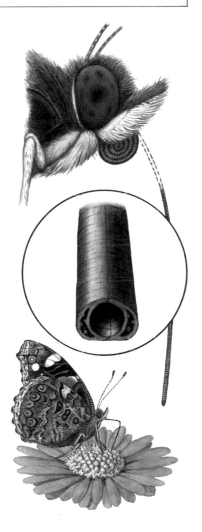

The proboscis, which at rest is coiled under the head (top), is composed of two halves fitted together to form a tube (middle). When uncoiled it is used to probe for nectar, which is made easier by the 'knee-joint' halfway along its length

but largely by the action of the oblique muscles. When coiled at rest, the upper surface of the proboscis is more or less flat, but when its muscles contract they cause the upper surface to become domed and this causes the whole proboscis to uncoil. It is then used to probe the flowers for nectar, which is pumped up by the action of muscles inside the mouth. There is usually a flexible 'knee-joint' about half way along the proboscis, enabling the butterfly to probe flowers at any angle without shifting its whole body.

Although nectar is the main food source for butterflies and moths, many species make use of other sweet and not-so-sweet substances. Honeydew, secreted by aphids and various other bugs, is an important food for the Purple Hairstreak and the Purple Emperor and several other woodland butterflies, while the moth-hunter's beer and treacle mixture attracts lots of moth species at night. Salt is also attractive to many butterflies, which often gather to suck up perspiration from human skin and from damp clothing. The blues are especially fond of such drinks. Urine is equally attractive to many blues, which sometimes gather in huge numbers on plants recently drenched by cattle. Such aggregations are seen mainly in the drier parts of southern Europe,

Black-veined Whites gather to drink from damp ground

including many mountain slopes, where the butterflies also gather to drink from muddy ground around the edges of ponds and streams and around any seepages on the slopes. The blues usually dominate these aggregations, often forming a blue haze as they flutter over the ground and jostle for position, but they are commonly joined by a number of fritillaries, skippers, and browns. The Black-veined White is also a great drinker and it is common to find hundreds of individuals fluttering around damp slopes in the mountains.

Although most obvious in dry areas, communal mud-puddling probably occurs everywhere at certain times. Green-veined Whites have

Male Common Blues acquire essential sodium from urine-drenched grass

Victorian collectors used the Purple Emperor's liking for putrid flesh to attract specimens with rotting meat

been seen milling around puddles in Britain on several occasions, and the Wood White has also been known to indulge in the habit, but in the moister climates, where water is freely available more or less everywhere, there is rarely any need for the butterflies to congregate at any one spot. Many moths also indulge in mud-puddling.

The butterflies and moths that congregate at these watering holes are nearly all males. Several suggestions have been put forward to explain this, but recent research has shown that it is the need for minerals, especially sodium, that brings the males down to the ground to drink. Sodium is required for the formation of the males' spermatophores, which are passed to the females during mating, and the males must continually top up their reserves because sodium is also essential for the proper working of the nervous system. This would certainly explain the attraction of sweat and urine for many butterflies.

Even when the ground appears quite dry the butterflies can acquire their minerals by dribbling on to the surface and sucking up the resulting solution. The organs of taste and smell tell them where to start, and it is very obvious from numerous investigations and observations that one feeding butterfly, or even a dead one placed on a suitable spot, will attract a lot more.

Dung is attractive to some butterflies, and it is well known that the Purple Emperor enjoys the putrid fluids of rotting flesh. Ripe and rotting fruit is more to the taste of some of the other nymphalids, such as the Two-tailed Pasha (see p. 251) and the Red Admiral. The latter will spend all day sitting on a soggy plum or apple and may get quite tipsy if the fruit is sufficiently well fermented. The butterflies' tongues cannot penetrate sound fruit, but some moths can with the aid of sharp spines on the proboscis and they can cause appreciable damage to fruit crops in the tropics. A few tropical moths even pierce human skin and suck blood, having probably moved on to such a diet by way of sucking fluids oozing from the eyes or from wounds.

FLIGHT AND RESTING BEHAVIOUR

The butterfly's two pairs of wings are connected to the upper edges of the thorax by ball-and-socket joints and they are moved up and down by the action of two pairs of muscles – the largest and most powerful in the body. These muscles are completely enclosed in the thorax and are known as indirect flight muscles because they are not directly attached to the wings in any way. They act by altering the shape of the thoracic walls, to which the wings are attached. One pair of these muscles runs vertically from the top to the bottom of the thorax and the other pair runs longitudinally through it. Contraction of the vertical muscles pulls down the roof of the thorax, and the pivoting system is such that the wings move upwards. Contraction of the longitudinal muscles then causes the thoracic roof to rise again and force the wings downwards.

Only a small amount of muscular contraction is needed to produce a large wing movement, and the efficiency of the system is improved even more by the elasticity of the thoracic walls. These are always ready to spring back to their original position, and thus help each set of muscles in turn.

The wings contain no muscles of their own, but several small muscles are attached to their bases and they are concerned with twisting the wings as they move up and down. High-speed photography of flying insects has shown that the wings are changing shape all the time and are never the simple flat structures that we see when the insects are at rest.

Although butterflies and moths have four wings, the front and hind wings on each side are linked together in various ways (see p. 16) and each pair thus behaves as a single wing. The veins near the leading edge of the front wing are stiffer than the rest, providing the rigidity necessary for cutting through the air.

FLIGHT PATTERNS

It is often possible to hazard a guess at the identity of a butterfly, or at least to place it in its correct family, just by watching the way it flies. Many nymphalids, for example, glide gracefully from perch to perch with just an occasional flap of the wings and none shows this better than the White Admiral and the superficially similar Hungarian Glider and Common Glider. The Scarce Swallowtail is another superb glider. The whites and yellows generally go in for more energetic flapping flight, well seen in the Large White and the Brimstone, although the Wood White cannot manage much more than a feeble flutter. The browns and blues also go in for flapping and flutttering and the smaller species, especially among the blues, are very hard to follow in flight.

The complete wing-beat ◀

During normal flapping flight, most medium-sized butterflies beat their wings 8–12 times per second, which carries them along at speeds of up to about 14km per hour, but they can fly much faster than this for short periods when disturbed. In general, the wing-beat is fastest in the smaller species and the fastest wing-beats of all butterflies are found among the skippers, whose rapid, darting flight is very different from that of the other butterflies. Burnet moths also flap their wings very rapidly, although their flight is slow and they appear to drift from flower to flower. The hawkmoths, which are among the fastest of all insects, commonly beat their wings 50–100 times per second and often produce an audible hum. Several of them, including the Hummingbird Hawkmoth and the bee hawkmoths, can hover.

RESTING POSITIONS AND TEMPERATURE CONTROL

A few butterflies, such as the Brimstone and the various clouded yellows and graylings, seem reluctant to display their upper surfaces other than during courtship and they never open their wings when perching on the ground or on the vegetation. The heaths and several of the hairstreaks also keep their wings tightly closed when perched. Most other butterflies do open their wings when they settle, but not every time; it depends very much on the temperature of the surroundings and of their own bodies and it normally occurs only when the sun is shining.

Butterflies are unable to maintain their bodies at a constant temperature but they are able to regulate their temperatures by various means and they can keep them within fairly well defined limits when the sun is shining. Their resting positions play a major role in this activity. Many species, including most of the nymphalids, sunbathe with their wings wide open and turned towards the sun so that they receive the greatest possible amount of radiant heat. Front and hind-wings may be completely separated, as commonly happens in freshly-emerged butterflies, but more often there is a fair degree of overlap. Whites and browns commonly bask with their wings slightly raised, while the golden skippers have a basking attitude all of their own, with the hind-wings more or less horizontal and the front wings inclined at a fairly steep angle.

The butterflies adopt their basking positions whenever they need to raise their body temperatures – as long as the sun is shining – but basking behaviour is especially important in the morning. It enables the insects to get their bodies up to the optimal working temperature much sooner than they would if they had to wait for the air to warm up. The flight muscles need to reach a certain temperature before the insects can fly properly and it has been demonstrated that the minimum body temperature required by several butterfly species is 25–30°C. The Swallowtail needs a body temperature of 28.7°C before it can take off, and the Silver-washed Fritillary maintains a body

Small Tortoiseshell

Large White

Comma

Large Heath

Small Skipper

Heath Fritillary

Queen of Spain Fritillary

The basking attitudes of various butterflies, from wings completely flat to completely closed. During copulation the male Queen of Spain Fritillary basks to ensure that he is warm enough to carry the female in flight

temperature of about 34°C in the sunshine even if the surrounding air temperature is only around 23°C.

Butterflies can fly at body temperatures below the optimum, but flight is then very feeble – just sufficient, perhaps, to carry the insect to a sunny spot when it wakes in the morning. Few butterflies can fly at all if the ambient temperature is below about 14°C, and in cloudy conditions the temperature must be a good deal higher than this to tempt the insects out from their resting places.

Diurnal moths raise their body temperatures to the required levels by 'shivering' and whirring their wings for a while before take-off. Nocturnal moths use the same system, but it is rarely seen in butterflies and probably plays little part in raising body temperatures.

As the basking butterfly approaches its optimum body temperature it gradually closes its wings and reduces the amount of radiation received, and once the optimum has been reached it can be maintained by opening the wings to the sun for short periods. In the middle of the day, when the ambient temperature catches up with the body temperature, the butterflies may spend much of their time feeding with wings closed, but in the cooler parts of Europe the ambient temperature rarely reaches such a level and the basking attitude is the normal one in sunny conditions throughout the day. Butterflies that never open their wings at rest control their body temperatures by altering their positions relative to the sun (see p. 275).

Flying, like any other muscular activity, produces heat and thus raises the body temperature even further. Much of the excess heat is quickly lost again to the air passing over the body, but in very hot weather some butterflies may actually have to seek shade, where they settle with wings open to dissipate the excess body heat. Even some of the hairstreaks which do not normally open their wings at all at rest have been seen with wings wide open and pressed to the ground in the shade of bushes and picnic tables in southern France.

HOW DOES IT WORK?

The precise mechanisms involved in heat regulation by butterflies are still disputed. It was once assumed that the wings absorbed heat and passed it to the blood in the veins, which then carried it to the thoracic muscles. The fact that the veins are often dark, even in pale areas of the wing, supports this theory, but more recently it has been shown that the amount of blood flowing through the wing veins is not nearly enough to account for the rapid rise in body temperature experienced by some basking butterflies. Obviously the thorax receives a certain amount of direct radiation, and it has been suggested that this is the main route through which body heat is acquired, with the wings serving merely to control the amount of sunshine reaching the body. But if the wings are not actively involved in absorbing heat it is difficult to see why many northern and montane butterflies should be darker than their lowland relatives (see p. 250).

Current theory suggests that the wings do absorb heat directly from the sun, but instead of passing it directly to the body through the blood they warm the air trapped underneath them (or between them) and the body absorbs the heat from there.

BAD WEATHER AND NIGHT

It is well known that few butterflies fly in cool, dull weather. Several species seek cover as soon as the sun goes in. Many of them simply hide under leaves and their camouflaged undersides make them very difficult to find. The browns and the blues manage to find enough shelter amongst the grasses, tucking themselves well into the tufts and holding their wings in a vertical plane so that very little rain actually falls on to them. The blues commonly roost in a head-down position, especially in grass.

The butterflies occupy similar situations at night and it is possible that falling light levels as well as falling temperatures send them in search of cover. There is also evidence that some butterflies, including some skippers and the Scarce Copper, actually select roosting sites on the eastern side of clumps of vegetation, where they will be able to bask in the early morning sun without having to move very far. With the exception of the Dingy Skipper and the closely related Inky Skipper, which wrap their wings around their bodies in a moth-like attitude, all European butterflies sleep with their wings held perpendicularly above the body in the classic butterfly position.

A typical day in the life of a male Scarce Copper. During the middle of the day, half of the time may be spent flying, but only if the air temperature exceeds 20°C

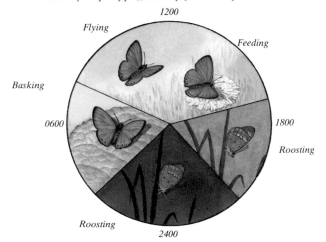

MIGRATION

It is well known that several kinds of butterflies and moths are summer visitors to the British Isles and to other parts of northern Europe. They fly up from the Mediterranean region in spring and early summer, produce one or more generations of offspring before the autumn, and then disappear. It was once thought that all of these visitors died in the autumn, but careful observations by numerous entomologists have revealed that most species show a definite, although not usually very obvious, southward movement during late summer and autumn. These southward migrations are generally more noticeable in southern Europe, where numbers are always higher, and the best places in which to see them are mountain passes; the insects tend to be funnelled into the passes and their movements are then much more conspicuous. It is also quite common to see the migrants crossing the coast at various points along the English Channel – Dungeness is a favourite spot for both birds and butterflies.

Among the European butterflies, the Red Admiral and the Painted Lady are good examples of species which display long-distance migratory behaviour. The Red Admiral is a common resident in southern and central Europe and it starts to move northwards in early spring. The first specimens are usually seen in the British Isles in March, although the main invasion occurs towards the end of May. The butterfly reaches the northernmost parts of Europe and is a fairly common visitor to Iceland, although it does not often breed there; its stinging nettle food-plant is sufficiently rare on the island for it to be grown and labelled as a specimen in the Akureyri Botanic Garden! One or two broods are produced in Britain and many other parts of Europe during the summer, and by the middle of August those in the far north are beginning to move southwards again. Increasingly colder nights probably initiate the change in direction, although studies of the Small White indicate that increasing amounts of

The routes taken by some of the common migratory butterflies

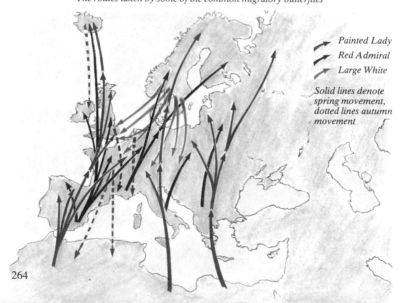

Painted Lady
Red Admiral
Large White

Solid lines denote spring movement, dotted lines autumn movement

cloud cover at dusk and dawn – which effectively prolong the length of the night – are also involved. The change-over zone gradually moves southwards, and by mid-September it reaches the south coast of Britain. To the north of this zone the Red Admiral shows a clear southward trend in its movements, although butterflies to the south of the zone may still be heading towards the north. But not all British specimens are inclined to travel. Many can be seen enjoying the autumn flowers until well into October and it is certain that most of these butterflies seek hibernation sites in this country. A few survive until the spring, and it is possibly these individuals, rather than early immigrants, that show themselves in March. However, most of the hibernators perish for one reason or another.

It is often suggested that insufficient anti-freeze in their bodies (see p. 272) is the main reason for the lack of hibernation success, and that the survivors are those that manage to find themselves some really sheltered winter quarters. This is not the whole story, however, for the Red Admiral can hibernate successfully on the continent, where winters are often much colder than in Britain. In addition, the autumn flight is more or less due south, taking the butterflies to areas with shorter winters but not necessarily milder ones. If mild winters were the main requirements, one might reasonably expect the insects to have evolved a south-westerly flight.

Although some of the butterflies leaving Britain and northern Europe fly straight down to the Mediterranean area, where they can be seen flying on sunny days throughout the winter, many stay in central Europe and hibernate successfully. The first migrants to arrive in the British Isles in the spring have probably spent the winter asleep in northern France.

The Painted Lady resembles the Red Admiral in its migratory behaviour, but it is considerably less hardy and it is unlikely that any adults can survive the winter in Britain or anywhere else north of the Alps. The insect has no resting or hibernating stage and there is little doubt that virtually all of Europe's Painted Lady population is renewed each year from North Africa, where the insects can breed throughout the year. Some come direct to Britain and northern Europe and arrive as early as March if there are favourable winds – as happened in 1985 when many migrant moths also arrived unusually early. The majority arrive in early June, and most of these have grown up in southern and central Europe – the children of the butterflies that left Africa early in the spring.

Like the Red Admiral, the Painted Lady spreads to all parts of Europe, including Iceland, during the summer and produces one or two generations in the north before the return flight begins in August. In most years the species is less common than the Red Admiral, but there are occasional years of exceptional abundance which can be linked to population explosions in North Africa, favourable winds bringing plenty of early immigrants to northern Europe, and, most important, favourable breeding conditions for the immigrants when they arrive.

Clouded Yellows occasionally reach England in large numbers. The number depends on the breeding success of the butterfly on the continent

Two well-known day-flying moths – the Silver Y and the Hummingbird Hawkmoth – are among the many moths that accompany the migrating butterflies on their spring journeys from southern Europe or beyond. The Silver Y flies throughout the year in North Africa, and for most of the year in the Mediterranean region of Europe, where its caterpillar feeds throughout the winter. Enormous numbers surge northwards in the spring, often accompanied by Painted Lady butterflies, and they reach the British Isles and northern Europe during May and June. There was a particularly large invasion of eastern England in 1936 and their myriad beating wings were said to produce a distinct hum audible from a considerable distance. A summer generation develops on a wide range of wild and cultivated plants, and then there is a fairly well marked southward flight during September and October. These autumn moths are reproductively inactive in the north, but begin mating and laying eggs when they reach the warmer climate of southern Europe. Although the species can breed almost as far north as the Arctic Circle in the summer, the larvae and pupae are killed by frost and, apart from a few adults known to have survived the winter in sheltered places, it is very unlikely that the Silver Y can survive anywhere north of the Alps.

The Hummingbird Hawkmoth resides throughout the southern half of Europe, where the adult sleeps fitfully through the winter in buildings and other sheltered spots. It wakes on sunny days and takes to the wing for a while even in the middle of the winter. Scattered individuals can be seen making their way northwards in sunny weather at any time of the year, but the major surge occurs in March and April and most immigrants arrive in the British Isles at the end of May and the beginning of June. They are especially noticeable in the sea-front gardens around the south coast, but in a warm summer the species will spread throughout the British Isles and produce a new generation in

August. The return flight begins in September and is most noticeable when the insects are funnelled into the passes of the Alps and Pyrenees. They can sometimes be seen hovering at rock faces, apparently enjoying the heat reflected from the surface.

RESIDENT MIGRANTS

Not all butterfly migration involves seasonal travel between the Mediterranean region and northern Europe or a marked expansion of the range during the summer. A number of species that are permanently resident in Britain and other parts of northern Europe exhibit distinct movements through their ranges and, although the distances may not be so great, such movements are essentially the same as those shown by the Painted Lady and its fellow travellers and thus clearly come under the heading of migration.

British residents that go in for such migrations include the Peacock, the Small Tortoiseshell, the Large White, the Small White, and, to a lesser extent, the Green-veined White. These species make similar movements on the continent and there is also a good deal of coming and going across the English Channel and the North Sea. The Large White differs from the other species in that the main immigration into the British Isles takes place in July and August instead of in the spring. The summer immigrants come mainly from southern Scandinavia and there is also a marked southward migration into Germany at this time.

Large White movements in July and August, when large numbers move south and west from Scandinavia

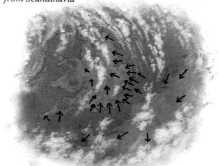

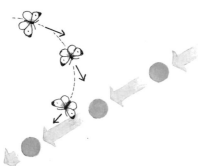

The daily movement of the Small White in autumn. By always flying towards the sun, the butterfly follows a gentle curve, but maintains an overall southward movement

The movements of the Small White have been studied in some detail by Robin Baker, who has contributed a good deal to our knowledge of migration and territoriality in many butterfly species. When not involved with feeding at flowers or breeding in the cabbage patch, the Small White flies in more or less straight lines and can reasonably expect to find another garden or similar habitat before long. After exploring this next patch for a while – perhaps for a whole day if it is a large patch and offers plenty of scope for feeding, courting, and egg-laying – the butterfly moves on again, in the same general direction that it took before. Each individual has its preferred compass direction, which it maintains by flying at a fixed angle to the sun. There is no compensation for the movement of the sun across the sky, so the butterfly actually flies in a series of gentle curves instead of in true straight lines, but this is not problem as the insect is merely searching for a new habitat and not heading for a definite locality. The important thing is that it should not double back on itself and end up in a cabbage patch that it has already explored. The length of each flight obviously varies with the distances between neighbouring habitats of the right kind, but various estimates suggest that an individual butterfly may cover about 200 km during its life.

Although individual butterflies can be seen flying in any direction, according to their personal preferences, in any given location there is a distinct bias towards one particular direction at any one time. During spring and summer, for example, the mean direction of flight in the British Isles is a bearing of roughly 159° to the sun. Nearly half of the butterflies in the region fly in this general direction, and the same is probably true in other parts of Europe as well. A major change of direction occurs later in the year and nearly half of the butterflies then start to fly directly towards the sun, which means virtually due south. This change spreads through the population in a given area within a few days and, as already mentioned, it is brought about by the lower temperatures and increasing length of the night. In northern Europe the change of direction begins in early August, with the change-over zone gradually moving southwards and lying close to the south coast of England by the end of the month. One week later the change-over zone lies half way down France. Unlike the Painted Lady, which has to get to the south as quickly as possible, the Small White flies in a leisurely fashion, just as its forbears did on the northward journey in the spring, and stops to feed and mate whenever the opportunity arises. The change of direction simply ensures that the butterflies do not lay eggs in areas where the offspring could not reach the over-wintering pupal stage before the beginning of winter.

Similar migratory patterns can be seen in many other butterflies, although the dates of the change-over at any particular latitude vary from species to species. Those that hibernate in the larval stage need not leave quite as early as those whose offspring must reach the pupal stage before winter sets in.

VISITING VAGRANTS

The British Swallowtail is a non-migratory butterfly, but the continental race is very mobile and flows to and fro across the continent in much the same way as the Small White. Occasional specimens find their way to the south coast of England, but such vagrants can immediately be distinguished from the British race by their paler colour (see p. 26). Other continental species that migrate in a similar way include the Long-tailed Blue, the Queen of Spain Fritillary, the Bath White, and the Camberwell Beauty. All extend their ranges northwards during the summer, and all turn up as vagrants in Britain, although numbers arriving here are always small and the insects hardly ever breed. Most visitors arrive in early summer, but the Camberwell Beauty almost always arrives in Britain in late summer and autumn. The species is most often found on the East Coast and the visitors are nearly all Scandinavian-bred insects which have flown too far to the west on their autumn migration. A few have been known to hibernate in Britain, and to fly again in the spring, but the species never seems to have bred in this country. As with other migrants, there are abnormally large influxes in certain years, and these usually coincide with hot summers. The highest number recorded in Britain was 436 in 1872, followed by 272 butterflies in the hot summer of 1976.

WHY MIGRATE?

One of the commonest statements put forward to explain migration is that it enables animals to escape the winter, when food is difficult or even impossible to find. Although the migrating animals certainly do avoid the worst of the weather, it is not a complete answer. Our migrant butterflies are basically southern insects and it is thus more appropriate to ask why they move northwards in the spring, when they are already surrounded by food. The conventional answer here is that migration spreads the species over a larger area and allows it to produce more offspring – the 'aim' of all plants and animals. But there would be no lasting advantage to the species if all the migrants and their offspring died in the autumn without returning something to the gene pool. Careful observations are revealing return flights in more and more migrant butterflies and moths, and so the

explanation seems a sound one.

But what actually makes the insects fly northwards in the spring? With the arrival of spring it is obvious that the area to the north of the wintering grounds becomes more suitable for the insects, and it is not really surprising that they spread into these newly available habitats and gradually move further and further north as they lay their eggs on all the available food-plants. In fact, population pressure causes the insects to explore in all directions but, as we have seen with the Small White, the majority fly to the north-west in spring and early summer. Those flying in other directions are likely to find most of the habitats already occupied. The direction of flight is clearly an innate feature for each individual and it can be inherited just like any other feature. Those butterflies and moths moving to the slightly cooler climates to the north, with their untapped food resources, tend to produce larger offspring – and therefore more eggs in the following generation (see p. 203) – than those staying in the warmer south, and as long as there is a substantial return flight in the autumn the north-flying habit will gradually spread through the population. It is unlikely, however, that whole populations would become north-flying; the dangers encountered on the long flights partly cancel out the better breeding success and ensure that other flight directions occur in the population.

So why do not all butterflies and

The Marbled White maintains a closed population, with adults and larvae thriving in the same grassy habitat.

moths migrate, if migration is so good for the species? Why do some species, such as the Marbled White and the Ringlet, stay in the same field or woodland clearing in which they were reared and rarely travel more than a few hundred metres from their birthplace? Such questions have occupied the minds of numerous entomologists, and it is now generally agreed that the most common migrants among the butterflies are those species whose adult food-plants are most often found away from the immediate vicinity of the larval food-plants and whose larval habitats are of a temporary nature. Having to fly some way to find food and new egg-laying sites, these species were pre-adapted for migration and it is easy to see how their long-distance flights have evolved from short-distance beginnings. Other notable features concerning the common migrants are the relatively high rate of formation of new larval habitats and the relatively short distance between these sites thus enabling enough butterflies to make the journey.

Migrant butterflies and moths clearly need widespread and common food-plants. The most common European butterfly travellers – the whites and the nymphalids – have larvae which feed on some of the commonest plants around. These include wild and cultivated brassicas and the ubiquitous nettles, which provide little or no nectar for the adult butterflies and which also grow in distinctly temporary communities – all criteria which

The Peacock has an open population, with adults and larvae often occupying quite different habitats

favour migration. New areas of food-plant are also created rapidly, either by natural colonisation of disturbed ground or as a result of planting by man, and the butterflies are never short of fresh egg-laying sites.

At the other end of the scale from the long-distance migrants are the closed or sedentary populations (see p. 244) of many of the browns and skippers, which spend all their lives in one small patch of grassland. The adults are happy with the flowers that grow among the grasses on which the larvae feed and, although there is no shortage of grassland sites, new sites are not formed very rapidly. Existing sites are likely to be occupied to the full, so there is no advantage for the butterflies to move away from their original homes and these species have remained sedentary. There are, admittedly, some instances of butterflies, such as the Ringlet, moving away from their homes in time of drought (see p. 308), but this is an escape-or-die reaction to abnormal conditions and there is no evidence of a return to the original habitat at a later date. Many biologists equate such movements with those of lemmings and locusts escaping from overcrowding, and describe them as emigrations rather than migrations.

The most sedentary of all our butterflies are those species whose habitats satisfy none of the criteria favouring migration. That is species whose habitats are permanent, widely separated and which form slowly, and in which both adults and larvae find their requirements in a compact area. Such butterflies include the Adonis Blue and the Chalkhill Blue, both restricted to certain areas by the specific habitat requirements of their food-plants, and the Mountain Ringlet which is restricted to certain altitudes – mainly between 500 and 800m in Britain. The British race of the Swallowtail is also extremely sedentary because its fenland habitats are few and far between, although the continental race is very mobile and far more catholic in its choice of habitat.

FINDING THE WAY

Migrating butterflies fly in very definite directions and are not passively carried by the wind, so they must have some way of knowing which way to travel. As we have already seen, many butterflies navigate by the sun, keeping it at a certain angle to their direction of flight, with or without compensation for the movement of the sun across the sky. This is clearly an innate feature, requiring no learning, but it is one which can be modified by external factors such as temperature and day-length – as shown by the sudden

Bath White

Long-tailed Blue

Pale Clouded Yellow

Queen of Spain Fritillary

Four butterflies which, depending on the weather, occasionally reach Britain and Northern Europe during their annual migration.

changes of direction of many species in late summer and autumn (see p. 267). Species that hibernate as adults also exhibit a change of direction in individual insects. Investigations with the Peacock, for example, have shown that the low temperatures and short days experienced during hibernation convert the south-flying insects of autumn into north-flying insects in the spring. The reproductive urge, which is entirely lacking in the autumn, is also switched on during hibernation and, after replenishing their batteries with the spring nectar, the butterflies soon begin courting and mating.

Navigation is also considerably modified by local topography, with many butterflies preferring to fly along hedgerows and similar linear features rather than to cross wide open spaces. Hedgerows are thus excellent places for the males to set up their territories when waiting for females (see p. 286). Wind is another major factor, involving the insects in considerable effort to maintain a correct course. In fact, several species refuse to take off if the wind speed exceeds about 12 kph. If the wind gets up while they are flying they will drop to lower levels where the wind speed is generally lower, but they will stop flying altogether if the wind gets too strong, regardless of its direction. A strong head-wind demands too much energy of the butterfly, while a strong tail-wind may carry it so fast that it cannot assess the vegetation below. The height of migratory flights is not much different from that of normal flight, with most individuals travelling within about 2m of the ground.

It has also been shown that some moths navigate by means of the earth's magnetic field, using some kind of internal compass. It is possible that some butterflies also navigate in this way, perhaps in addition to steering by the sun, but there is not as yet any clear idea as to how the internal compass might work.

HIBERNATION

Only thirteen of the European butterfly species hibernate in the adult state and six of these occur in the British Isles. All but three – the Brimstone, the Cleopatra, and the Nettle-tree Butterfly – belong to the Nymphalidae.

With the butterflies spending as much as six months asleep in one spot, good camouflage is clearly very important and the undersides of all the hibernating species display superb cryptic coloration. The Brimstone's leaf-like wings, for example, are extremely hard to spot when the butterfly is tucked up in its usual retreat amongst the leaves of holly or ivy or other broad-leaved evergreens, while the Comma and the Nettle-tree Butterfly are both very difficult to distinguish from dead leaves when sleeping in their chosen trees and bushes. Peacocks and tortoiseshells usually choose hollow trees and similar cavities in the wild, and their dark undersides render them almost invisible in such places. The Queen of Spain Fritillary usually passes the winter in the caterpillar state, but in some parts of southern Europe it hibernates as an adult. The large, mirror-like spots on its underside are surprisingly effective at camouflaging the butterfly as it sits amongst the dead grasses on stony slopes.

The hibernation of adult butterflies is rather different from that of their earlier stages and it is not generally accepted as a true diapause (see p. 208) because the insects are already fully grown and there can be no arrest in their development. There is, however, a very definite pause in the development of the reproductive organs in most hibernating species. Although the adults emerge from their pupae in the summer, they show no interest in sex at this time and their reproductive organs remain poorly developed until the spring, when mating finally occurs. The only exception to this appears to be the Cleopatra, which is said to carry mature eggs throughout its winter sleep.

Some hibernating butterflies, all well camouflaged in their natural resting places

Peacocks and Small Tortoiseshells hibernate in caves and other dark places, where their drab undersides conceal them very effectively

Beginning right at the start of adult life, or even in the pupal stage, reproductive diapause is not clearly linked to the winter sleep, although the same stimuli of rising temperatures and increasing day-length bring both to an end in the spring. Unlike truly diapausing insects, the nymphalids commonly wake on sunny days, even in the middle of winter, and fly for a few hours before going back to sleep again. This suggests that the winter sleep is more like simple dormancy or quiescence (see p. 220) brought about by harsh conditions, but the story is more complex than this because some species go into hibernation long before the cold weather arrives. The Nettle-tree Butterfly, for example, commonly disappears in August or even in July – at the height of the Mediterranean summer. The Peacock and the Camberwell Beauty also hibernate early, presumably urged to do so by the decreasing day-length as summer turns into autumn. The Small Tortoiseshell, on the other hand, stays out very late, draining the last drops of nectar from the flowers right up until the hard frosts arrive. At such times, with their sex lives in abeyance, the butterflies are remarkably sociable. Dozens of butterflies gather to stock-up with nectar for the long sleep ahead and, as long as they have enough room to spread their wings, they seem almost oblivious of their neighbours jostling for position on the flowers.

Like the earlier stages in the life history, the adult butterflies are well supplied with anti-freeze materials which enable them to survive at temperatures well below freezing point without actually freezing solid. There is clearly a pre-hibernation period during which these materials are accumulated, for an active butterfly placed in a refrigerator dies at temperatures well above those that it experiences during the winter. Apart from the storage of anti-freeze materials, there is also a change in the structure of the blood and other body fluids which makes them less susceptible to freezing.

Peacocks and tortoiseshells commonly hibernate in houses, especially in attics and other little-used rooms. When the heating is turned up in the depths of winter the butterflies often wake and fly around. They can sometimes be persuaded to drink from a small wad of tissue paper soaked in sugar solution or diluted honey, and are then best put in an unheated shed or other out-building where they can continue their sleep. They should not be put outside in the garden, unless it is a very sunny day, for they cannot fly in very cold weather (see p. 261) and would undoubtedly perish without any protection.

Warmth sometimes wakes hibernating butterflies

ENEMIES AND DEFENCE

The most important diurnal predators of adult butterflies and moths are the birds, with the lizards playing a significant supporting role in the warmer parts of Europe. Spiders, mantids, and wasps – especially the hornet – also destroy large numbers of butterflies and moths, but it is undoubtedly true that the adult insects have fewer enemies than their earlier, earthbound stages. In particular, they are not attacked by ichneumons or other parasitoids, the relatively short life enjoyed by most adults being insufficient for the development of these internal parasites.

Defences against the birds and lizards, which have good colour vision and hunt primarily by sight, centre mainly on visual features and include a wide range of visual trickery, from simple crypsis to some really elaborate hoaxes. The term camouflage, which in its widest sense simply means deception, can be used to describe all these tricks, but it is more often employed only for those instances in which an animal evades detection by blending in with its background. The butterflies and moths are experts in this field, with none being better hidden then the resting Green Hairstreak. The deep green undersides of this butterfly blend beautifully with the herbage, and concealment is improved even further because the insect keels over so that its wings lie almost parallel to the leaf on which it stands and its shadow is eliminated. The Green Hairstreak is also extremely difficult to follow in flight, alternately showing brief flashes of its brown upper surface and then melting into the background as the wings are raised to expose the green undersides.

Most butterfly undersides are actually pretty well camouflaged, with many good examples to be found among those species that hibernate. The Peacock, Small Tortoiseshell, and Camberwell Beauty all have very dark undersides that protect them in their natural hibernation sites, such as caves and hollow trees, as well as barns and attics. The Brimstone is another superb example, taking the theme of camouflage a little further. Its pale green underside bears several strong veins, and when the wings are closed the butterfly looks just like a

Despite their ability to fly, adult butterflies and moths have many enemies

273

leaf. This type of camouflage, in which an animal resembles some part of its environment, is commonly called protective resemblance (see p. 229). The leaf-like Brimstone may be quite visible, but predators ignore it because they have learned that leaves are inedible. The camouflage holds good in dull weather, when the Brimstone generally rests under a leaf, and also during the long winter sleep which is usually taken in evergreens such as holly or ivy. The Comma is an equally well protected hibernator, although here the resemblance is to a torn and shrivelled leaf and the hibernation site is a tree trunk or the dense undergrowth of a hedgerow.

False eye-spots on the wings divert a predators' attention from the body

FALSE EYES

Butterflies of the family Satyridae – the browns – nearly all possess a number of eye-spots or ocelli around the margins of their wings, with an especially large one near the tip of the forewing. Commonly occurring on both upper and lower surfaces, these eye-like markings function as decoys, drawing the attentions of birds away from the head and body and towards the less vulnerable parts of the butterfly. There is no doubt that the eye-spots – usually black with white pupils – are conspicuous to the birds, and the large number of butterflies found with clear beak marks around the eye-spots shows that birds really do peck at them. The eye-spots and chunks of the surrounding wing membranes may be torn off, but the insects can still fly and attend to the all-important business of procreation. It may be argued that a well-camouflaged butterfly needs no such decoys at all, but the easily observed Meadow Brown shows how eye-spots and crypsis can work together for even better survival.

On landing, the Meadow Brown sits with its wings together and the apical eye-spot of the forewing clearly exposed, as if inviting attack. If it is attacked it will fly away, perhaps minus a piece of wing membrane, but if it is not molested within 5–10 seconds it assumes that it is safe and

settles down to rest. The forewings are pulled down inside the hind wings and the eye-spot disappears, and the butterfly is then very hard to see. It may shuffle around to face the sun, or it may tilt its wings towards the sun, thereby reducing its shadow to a minimum and making itself even less conspicuous.

Several other satyrids behave in a similar way, but recent studies of the Grayling suggest that orientation with respect to the sun is more concerned with temperature regulation than with concealment. When the air is warm – in the middle of the day, for example – the butterfly settles with its head towards the sun or with its wings tilted over so that they are parallel to the sun's rays. Relatively few rays hit the insect in this position and it does not overheat. At the same time, its shadow is virtually eliminated and the cryptic underside makes the butterfly almost invisible in its rough, grassy habitat, but shadow reduction seems to be of minor importance when compared with temperature control. Early in the day, when the air temperature is low, the butterfly sits with its wings at right angles to the sun and throwing a deep shadow. Concealment is clearly sacrificed for a rapid rise in body temperature in the morning. It should be remembered that the Grayling is one of a number of butterflies that never bask with their wings open.

A number of butterflies have taken the false-eye idea to its logical conclusion and have evolved false heads at their rear ends, and some of these illusions are good enough to fool human observers even at close range.

The orientation of a Grayling towards the sun affects both the temperature of the insect and the size of its shadow. Early in the morning the butterfly sits side on to the sun, to warm up quickly, but casts a long shadow.

Once the butterfly has warmed up it faces the sun and casts a very slender shadow . . .

. . . or it leans towards the sun and casts virtually no shadow

The false heads are borne on the undersides of the hind wings and consist of one or more dark, eye-like patches together with filamentous outgrowths which resemble antennae – especially when the insects are at rest with their true antennae concealed between the front edges of the forewings. Prominent stripes on the undersides commonly deflect a predator's gaze away from the true head and towards the false one. Expecting the butterfly to fly away in the direction of the false head, the bird frequently aims slightly above it, and then the most it gets is a beakful of wing as the insect flies off in the opposite direction. Of course, the false antennae and perhaps the whole false head may be lost after a couple of attacks, but by this time the butterfly has probably fulfilled its reproductive function. The trickery has worked.

As with all forms of camouflage, this 'back-to-front' coloration is best developed in the tropics, where it is shown by numerous blues and hairstreaks. A few European lycaenids, notably the Long-tailed Blue and the Blue-spot Hairstreak, have embarked on this path, but they have only faint suggestions of false heads at present and their 'tails' have a long way to grow before they can be mistaken for antennae. Nevertheless, even this slight resemblance to a head can fool a few birds and be a distinct advantage. Geneticists have calculated that a feature so slight as to give protection in just one out of about 10,000 encounters will be preserved in the long run and gradually improved through natural selection (see p. 280). The blues were to some extent pre-adapted for the evolution of false heads because of their tendency to rest in a head-down position. Birds thus normally see the rear end first, and the development of the slightest resemblance to an eye or a head would have attracted them to this end even more. There would thus have been strong pressure for further refinement of the resemblance.

Scarce Swallowtail and Long-tailed Blue with false head patterns on their hind-wings

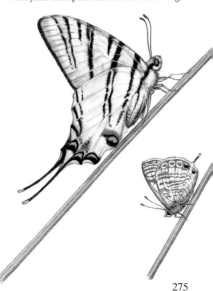

The lycaenids are not the only butterflies with false heads. The Scarce Swallowtail is perhaps the best European example. Its false head, complete with eye-spots and long 'antennae', is much more obvious than the true head as it sits with its wings closed or even half open on a flower. In common with several other 'back-to-front' butterflies, including some of the hairstreaks, it sometimes turns through 180° when it lands, reinforcing the role of the false head and confusing any following bird even more when it takes off in the opposite direction.

Eyes that scare

The eye-spots described so far are all rather small and imitate the butterflies' true eyes or heads. There are, however, many butterflies and other insects that carry much larger eye-spots on their wings. The Peacock is the most familiar European example and the function of its large 'eyes' is not to divert the predator's attack but to frighten it off altogether. When feeding, the Peacock commonly has its wings closed, showing only the sombre underside, but from time to time, and especially when approached too closely, it opens its wings and displays the eye-spots. It may also hiss quite loudly by rubbing its fore and hind wings against each other. This is too much for most small birds and they back away immediately. To them it must be like looking at the eyes of a mammal or some other vertebrate predator, but the Peacock butterfly is, of course, harmless and this kind of deception is pure bluff. Peacocks whose eye-spots have been removed by rubbing off the scales elicit little or no fear in the birds. Experimental work has shown that many small birds have an innate fear of eye-like markings – an obvious survival mechanism – and that the closer these resemble the vertebrate eye the greater the fear. Birds can become accustomed to large eye-spots, however, and the bluff works best if the display is switched on and off – especially if the eye-spots appear suddenly. This is, of course, what the Peacock does when it opens its wings. The Apollo 'blinks' the eye-spots on its hind wings by rhythmically covering and uncovering them with its forewings when a bird gets uncomfortably close. The resting Emperor Moth always has the eye-spots on its forewings exposed, but any bird or lizard daring to approach too closely gets a shock when the moth suddenly exposes the eye-spots on the hind-wings.

Observations of Small Tortoiseshell butterflies and a number of insectivorous birds suggest that some birds may actually have an innate fear of any bright colour. During such experiments the birds rarely attacked intact butterflies, but readily pecked and ate those whose wing scales had been removed to reveal the dull greyish membrane. This may well be why the Small Tortoiseshell and some other brightly coloured butterflies can bask and feed with their wings open although, as with eye-spots, the birds can become accustomed to the colours and lose their fear. The permanent display of bright colours can protect insects only when backed up by some form of 'punishment'.

When alarmed the Emperor Moth reveals a second pair of eye-spots, enough to frighten most predators

WARNING COLOURS

We have already seen how bold colours and patterns combined with an unpleasant taste can protect caterpillars from birds and some other predators (see p. 230). No deception is involved here because the insects are advertising themselves as the poisonous or unpalatable creatures that they are, but warning colours are the foundations on which mimicry is based and mimicry is definitely a form of deception (see p. 278).

Caterpillars with warning colours do not necessarily turn into butterflies and moths with warning colours, and even when they do the colours may not be the same. The black and gold Cinnabar caterpillars, for example, produce black and red moths. The orange and black Monarch butterfly also develops from a largely black and yellow larva. The same poisons or other unpalatable substances are usually present in both larvae and adults of the same species – often derived from the larval food-plant and passed on to the adults.

Relatively few European butterflies have been examined biochemically, and warning or aposematic coloration linked to poisonous or unpalatable substances in the body has been convincingly demonstrated only in the Monarch, the festoons, and some of the whites, although many other butterflies may be unpalatable because of their texture. The unpalatability of the Large White is due to mustard oils derived from the larval food plant, and is advertised by the bold black and white colouring. The Monarch relies on poisons called cardenolides for its protection and the American entomologist Lincoln Brower neatly showed that these are obtained from the larval food-plant by rearing larvae on cabbage instead of on the normal milkweeds. He found that the resulting adults had no stored poisons and were perfectly acceptable to various birds, provided that the latter had not previously had nasty encounters with butterflies reared on milkweeds. Incidentally, these results also show that not all birds are

Burnet moths exude poisonous fluids from mouths and feet when attacked

inherently afraid of bright colours.

Aposematic coloration is more widespread among the European moths and is especially well developed in the day-flying burnets. These conspicuous red and black moths, usually with a metallic green or blue sheen when freshly emerged, exude pungent fluids from glands around the mouth when they are disturbed. Few predators will press home an attack when confronted with these fluids, but those that do continue the attack get an even nastier shock; the burnet pumps cyanide-containing fluids out through joints on the thorax and legs. There is, of course, very little cyanide – to which the burnets themselves are relatively insensitive – but there is quite enough of this poison to punish all predators and ensure that they do not attack burnets again. The moths can thus sit freely exposed on the flowers without risk. Their movements are sluggish, and so 'confident' are they in their defences that they often allow themselves to be picked up.

The burnets are the most poisonous of our moths, with the Five-spot Burnet being more toxic than most of the 33 species found in Europe. Not surprisingly, the great majority of poisonous moths are day-flying, and thus able to benefit from warning coloration. Among them are several tiger moths, the Cinnabar – although this is not fully diurnal – and the syntomids.

MIMICRY

The Broad-bordered Bee Hawkmoth and the Narrow-bordered Bee Hawkmoth both display remarkable similarities to bumble bees as they feed at flowers. Their darting flight is quicker than that of bumble bees, and they also hover in front of the flowers instead of alighting on them, but their furry bodies and transparent wings – most of the scales fall-off during the first flight – are still sufficient to fool most birds and also many naturalists. This is a fine example of Batesian mimicry – named after Henry Walter Bates who first described it – which is the resemblance of a harmless and edible species, known as the mimic, to an unpalatable species, known as the model, which is protected by some degree of warning coloration. The mimic gains protection by coming to look like the model, and this form of mimicry is clearly a form of deception. Many other fascinating examples can be found in the insect world, with bees and wasps among the commonest models and hover-flies and moths among their commonest mimics. The clearwing moths, resembling several different kinds of social and solitary wasps, are perhaps even better mimics than the bee hawkmoths, for the larger species buzz like wasps as well as looking like them. There are no clear-cut examples of this kind of mimicry among the European butterflies but they abound in the rich butterfly faunas of the tropics where Bates made his original discoveries in the 1850's.

Model and mimic must inhabit the same area and fly at more or less the same time if predators are to mistake one for the other, and the model must normally be more common than the mimic. If the mimic were the commoner of the two, or if it appeared earlier than the model, young predators would meet it more often than the model and thus associate the colour pattern with good food rather than with a painful experience. But the mimic need not always be less common than the model, especially if the model appears a little earlier than the mimic. A number of experiments have shown that some birds can remember an unpleasant experience for a very long time, and so an early encounter between a bird and a distasteful model can protect the edible mimics for much of their lives. In tropical regions many butterfly mimics exist in two or more forms, each resembling a different model species. This allows the mimics to become common without risk of exceeding the population of its models – although it may well be more common than any of its individual model species.

Many biologists have included protective resemblance (see p. 229) in the definition of mimicry, arguing that there is little difference between resembling a leaf or a twig and resembling another animal. Both phenomena are certainly forms of deception, and both have come about through the agency of natural selection (see p. 280), but there is one fundamental difference between them. Animals which resemble leaves or other objects in their environment are

The Hornet Clearwing Moth gains protection from birds by resembling a Hornet

Hornet Clearwing Moth

Hornet

The burnet mimicry ring in which all the insects share a similar pattern

attempting – unwittingly, of course – to evade detection, whereas the mimics are advertising themselves; they want to be noticed and mistaken for their unpalatable models. After many years of argument and debate, filling hundreds of pages in learned journals, this distinction seems to be gaining general acceptance.

There is another form of mimicry, much more common among the butterflies and moths of Europe, in which two or more unpalatable species share a common pattern of warning coloration. There is no deception here, because all the species involved are advertising their true nature, but all are gaining a considerable advantage by mimicking each other. Birds and other predators have to learn just one colour pattern before they avoid all the species sharing that pattern, and so each species in the mimicry ring loses fewer individuals to predators than it would if they all had different patterns. It is not always possible to say which are the models and which are the mimics in these situations and all the participants are generally

known as co-mimics. This type of mimicry is called Müllerian mimicry, after the German zoologist Fritz Müller who described it in 1878.

Although theoretically quite different, in practice it is not possible to draw a clear dividing line between Batesian and Müllerian mimicry because predators have different tastes and an insect that behaves as a Batesian mimic with respect to one predator may be a good Müllerian mimic with respect to another. The Broad-bordered Bee Hawkmoth probably comes into this category, for feeding experiments with young and inexperienced birds have indicated that it is distasteful to some species.

Dozens of similarly coloured species may join a Müllerian mimicry ring. They may be closely related but they can also be drawn from totally unrelated groups. Within such a ring there is normally a wide range of palatabilities, ranging from the very toxic to the mildly distasteful. The club may also be joined by a number of true Batesian mimics. All benefit by sharing a similar colour pattern, but the similarity need not be exact. Only a very slight similarity, perhaps causing just one predator to hesitate and turn away on just one occasion, can prolong an insect's life and give it a chance to reproduce and pass its protective characters on to the next generation.

The white butterflies of the family Pieridae form an extensive mimicry ring centred on the Large White which, owing to its large-scale storage of mustard oils, is the most toxic of the group and unpalatable to most birds. The other pierids store smaller amounts of mustard oils or none at all, and some may actually be palatable to certain birds, but all are protected to a significant degree by their resemblance to the Large White. The marbled whites of the family Satyridae also belong to the club, although they normally have more black on them. They are rather distasteful – perhaps more so than some of the smaller pierids – and they clearly have a Müllerian relationship to the whites.

The cyanide-containing burnet moths form another extensive Müllerian ring, together with such diverse insects as the Cinnabar moth, beetles of the genus *Trichodes*, froghoppers of the genus *Cercopis*, and assorted heteropteran bugs such as *Graphosoma italicum*. These are all red and black and all are distasteful, some of them excessively so. It might be argued that the burnets all have the same basic coloration because they are closely related and not because they have copied each other. This is largely true, because they have not actually converged as many other mimics have (see p. 281), but the advantage of sharing a common pattern has prevented the various species from diverging too much and they are true mimics in the Müllerian mould. There is, however, one interesting example of divergence from the red and black pattern. *Zygaena ephialtes* is a common burnet exhibiting considerable variation across the continent of Europe. In central regions it sports the typical red and black coloration of its cousins, but in much of the south it occurs in a very different guise – black with white and yellow spots. This is the *coronillae* race and it occurs only in areas inhabited by the Nine-spotted Moth (*Syntomis phegea*) or other *Syntomis* species. These moths are also black with white and yellow spots and it is clear that the burnet has abandoned its normal dress to join the syntomid club. It is rather odd that this should have happened because the syntomids are only mildly toxic, although still highly unpalatable, but they are very much commoner in the south than the red burnet complex and the frequency of encounters clearly makes up for the mildness of the punishment when it comes to teaching the predators a lesson. Where *coronillae* overlaps with the red and black *peucedanoides* the two interbreed and produce the intermediate forms illustrated here.

Zygaena ephialtes *is a very variable burnet.* Z. e. coronillae *has abandoned the typical red and black colouration and is an excellent Müllerian mimic of the Nine-spotted Moth.*

NATURAL SELECTION

Camouflage in all its forms, including the most complex examples of protective resemblance and mimicry, is a product of evolution, brought about by natural selection along the precise lines suggested by Darwin in his famous phrase 'the survival of the fittest'. Predation by birds has been the main driving force as far as the butterflies and moths are concerned. Many experiments, involving the release of camouflaged and conspicuous insects in a variety of environments, have confirmed that birds really do select a far greater proportion of the uncamouflaged insects than of the cryptic ones. Survival of the fittest – those that are most suited to the environment in question – is thus a fact, and these 'fit' individuals are the

Z. e. coronillae

Nine-spotted Moth

Z. e. peucedanoides

Z. e. icterica

Z. e. ephialtes

ones that survive to breed and pass their characteristics to the following generations. With the least fit being weeded out by birds and other predators in each generation, there is naturally a gradual improvement in the fitness of the whole population, and this is what we mean by natural selection. Of course, natural selection needs something to select in the first place, but it requires no great stretch of the imagination to accept that, among all the butterfly and moth species, some quite fortuitously had slight resemblances to leaves or bark. Natural selection then had its raw materials and each species began to evolve along a certain path, resulting in the amazing examples of camouflage that exist today.

Mimicry can be explained in just the same way if we again accept that, at some time in the past, some species exhibited chance resemblances to others. Such resemblances need have been only very slender, but if one species was protected by warning colours, the other, whether palatable or distasteful, would have gained some advantage. With the best mimics having the best chance of survival in each generation, the resemblances could only improve. This increasing similarity of unrelated species is known as convergence. The clearwing moths probably embarked on their mimicry of wasps when, very early in their history, a chance variation gave them virtually transparent wings. After that the various species diverged, evolving colour patterns and behavioural quirks to match the various kinds of wasps. The Hornet Clearwing has even evolved a buzzing flight tone similar to that of its unpalatable model. Behaviour is clearly very important in mimicry. Little would be gained by a mimic if it evolved the colours of its model but behaved in a totally different way, and the same thing holds true for protective resemblance. A caterpillar, for example, can match a twig in every facet of colour and texture, but if it does not hold itself at the right angle it will always be detected for what it is.

Normal and melanic Peppered Moths

Evolution is not just something that happened long ago. It is happening today and the insects' defences are still being perfected. But they will never be 100% effective; the birds have to eat and so there is always pressure on them to evolve sharper eyesight to keep pace with the insects' camouflage. Environments change too, and camouflage which works at one stage might not be so useful at a later stage or in another area, so evolution may change direction. This has been well illustrated by the evolution of melanic (black) forms of the Peppered Moth and some other species during the last hundred years or so as a result of smoke pollution in industrial areas.

INVERTEBRATE ENEMIES

Camouflage and warning coloration are of little use against spiders, which generally lie in wait, with or without a web, for their prey to arrive. Vibrations rather than visual signals tell the waiting spiders when a meal appears. Most of the spiders seem unaffected by the toxins of the distasteful butterflies and moths and some species will even eat burnet moths that blunder into their webs. There are some moths, including the Magpie, that are immediately rejected and hastily cut from the webs, but it is their taste and not their warning coloration that saves them, for the spiders will always try a bite first.

Crab spiders commonly lurk in flowers and grab butterflies coming to drink the nectar. There is some experimental evidence that butterflies – and bees and hover-flies – avoid certain flowers carrying artificial dark marks in the centre. This reaction could possibly keep them away from lurking crab spiders, but many of the latter are already one step ahead and they match their chosen flowers extremely well. Although such camouflage is more often regarded as a protection against birds, it clearly gives the spiders an advantage in terms of catching prey as well. Some of the crab spiders, notably *Misumena vatia* which is sometimes called the White Death, can change their colours, albeit rather slowly, to match a range of yellow and white flowers. Butterflies and other insects landing on occupied flowers are very quickly grabbed just behind the head – the most efficient spot for quick paralysis – and drained of their body contents. The spiders are in no way intimidated by large prey and a spider a mere 10mm long has no hesitation in attacking, and over-powering, a Swallowtail many times its own size. Unlike most other spiders, the crab spiders do not crush the bodies of their prey and it is not uncommon to find drained corpses of otherwise perfect butterflies clinging to the flowers where they died.

Mantids catch large numbers of butterflies and moths in southern Europe and, although relying on sight, they seem totally unperturbed by any warning colours or foul tastes.

A well camouflaged crab spider feeding on a Glanville Fritillary

Holding the victim firmly in its spiky front legs, the mantis usually eats everything, including the wings. Dragonflies and robber-flies catch some of the smaller butterflies in the air and take them to perches for consumption. Dragonflies eat most parts of the body, although they often drop bits of the wings, but robber-flies are purely liquid-feeders and make do with the body fluids. Hornets commonly bite the wings off before attempting to carry their victims to the nest.

Mites and midges

Small red mites are commonly found attached to the bodies of butterflies and moths, especially to members of the family Satyridae. The Marbled White and the Meadow Brown seem especially prone to attack and often carry a dozen or more mites. The latter are actually the young stages of several species of the families Trombidiidae and Erythraeidae. They gorge themselves with the butterflies' body fluids by plugging their mouth-parts in to the soft inter-segmental membranes, often at the base of the wings. They fall off when replete and do not seem to do the butterflies any real harm. The adult mites are free-living predators of other mites and small insects, usually hiding themselves in grass and other dense vegetation – hence the frequency with which the grassland satyrid butterflies are infested. But not all the mites found on butterflies are necessarily parasitic; some are simply hitch-hikers, clinging to the butterflies for a while without feeding and then dropping off to explore new habitats.

Magpie Moths are even poisonous to spiders

FINDING A MATE

Meeting the opposite sex and ensuring the continuation of the species is the prime function of every adult butterfly, and a large proportion of its daily activity is devoted to this end. Observations of individual insects suggest that during the breeding season – which is virtually the entire adult life for most species – far more time is spent in sexual pursuits than in feeding. Among some of the day-flying moths, including the Emperor and the Vapourer, feeding has been abandoned altogether in the adult state.

Most butterflies use a mixture of visual and olfactory signals to bring the sexes together, while most moths, both nocturnal and day-flying, rely purely on scent. It is usually only the female moth who has the alluring scent or pheromone (see p. 289) and she can attract males over surprisingly long distances. Investigations with Emperor Moths and their relatives show that the males, equipped with large feathery antennae, can detect and locate calling females several kilometres away. The pheromone is produced by the virgin female and released when she extrudes her scent organ from the tip of her abdomen. Wafted on the breeze, the scent particles are intercepted by the male antennae, which are clothed with thousands of sensory cells (see p. 255), and they stimulate the male to fly upwind. Such a response automatically carries him towards the female, but he commonly loses the scent on the way and then resumes his typically fast and erratic flight. This is likely to bring him into contact with any female scent drifting about and to set him back on course. Eventually, he will arrive at the calling female, but he is unlikely to be alone; males will have been attracted from a wide area and it is usually a matter of first come, first served. The female stops calling after accepting a mate but the scent lingers for a time and the disappointed suitors continue to circle around her and may even try to push the triumphant male aside. Entomologists commonly use this assembling behaviour of the Emperor and other moths to obtain specimens, and such is the pulling power of the female pheromone that marked males have been known to cover 1km in less than 10 minutes on their way to rendezvous with a captive female. Even a container in which a calling virgin female has been confined for a while will attract quite a number of males.

COURTSHIP TERRITORIES

Among the butterflies it is almost always the male who initiates courtship behaviour, employing one of two main strategies for making contact with the female. The majority of species adopt some kind of territory and, from a convenient perch, they defend it against other males of the same species while waiting for females to arrive. This is commonly known as the sit-and-wait strategy. Other species, including the Silver-washed Fritillary and many of the blues, have a patrolling strategy and fly incessantly through their habitats in search of females. But there is no rigid dividing line between the perchers and the patrollers. Quite a number of territory holders leave their perches periodically and fly around their territories to check for strangers, and in so doing are behaving just like patrolling species. The true patrolling species often stick to one small patch or beat within the habitat, but they do not defend any particular area and cannot be said to have a true territory; they merely defend the air space around them, wherever they happen to be at the time, and this serves to space out the males quite effectively. The Speckled Wood actually swaps from sit-and-wait to patrolling behaviour and vice-versa according to local conditions.

The resident male Speckled Wood, basking in his sunspot, flies up to investigate any intruder

The resident usually wins

The territorial behaviour of the Speckled Wood butterfly has been studied in detail by several entomologists and it is well known that in most parts of Europe the males adopt and defend patches of sunlight on the woodland floor or on low-growing vegetation, rather than defending particular areas of the woodland. The sunny spots are attractive to females, especially in the afternoons, and are thus good places for acquiring mates. But the male does not have to be territory holder in order to get a mate; at any given time there are plenty of males patrolling in the canopy and observations indicate that these butterflies do not go short of partners. The relative proportions of perching and patrolling males depend on the habitat and the weather. In cloudy conditions, when there are no sunny spots, all the males take to patrolling the canopy in search of females. Patrolling also becomes the dominant strategy in warm weather and in open rides where large areas are bathed in sunshine. Perching behaviour is more important at lower temperatures, as long as there is some sun, and in dense woodland where sunny spots are relatively scarce.

Perching males commonly take up position on sunny leaves or twigs about a metre above the ground, and in a large sunny spot an individual may remain on its chosen perch for a considerable time. In smaller sunny spots, however, the insects must continually move perches in order to remain in the sunshine. Anything flying in the vicinity of the territory causes the resident male to fly out to investigate, and if the intruder is another male of the same species there is commonly a spiral flight in which the two butterflies rise into the air and bump into each other several times. The 'fight' is quickly over, however, for serious damage to either butterfly would not be in the interests of the species as a whole, and the intruder almost always flies away into the trees. The resident then drops back to his perch. The whole interaction takes place in the shaft of sunlight above the territory. In places where there is severe competition for relatively few sunny spots the spiral flights may last somewhat longer than they do elsewhere, but still the resident almost always wins. Just how the resident male transmits its 'I was here first' message is not known, but perhaps the simple act of flying up to meet the intruder is sufficient to establish the status. Experience and age may also be involved, making some individuals better territory holders than others, and in such instances the resident male may not be the winner. Contests sometimes take the form of horizontal chases, especially

A male intruder is engaged in a spiral battle, which almost always ends with the intruder leaving the area and the resident returning to his sunspot

in woodland rides and other large areas of sunshine, but the result is usually the same, with the resident butterfly returning to his perch.

The approach of a female Speckled Wood naturally provokes a totally different reaction in the territory-holding male. He breaks into a dance routine similar to that of the Grayling butterfly (see p. 291) and the female settles on the ground to watch. If she is sufficiently impressed by the male's performance and his scent is sufficiently alluring, the couple eventually fly up into the trees and mate.

The size of the Speckled Wood's territory is clearly related to the butterfly's ability to spot intruders. Sunny patches up to about 14 sq. metres rarely contain more than one perching male, but larger patches of sunshine often contain two or more males, spaced out so that they do not really notice each other. Because more females are attracted to large sunny spots than to small ones, the males are all likely to be satisfied.

It was commonly thought that, once a male had adopted a sunny spot in the morning, it stayed with the spot and moved around with it, often for much of the day, until the sun disappeared from the area. Some males certainly stay for an hour or two, but they get restless after that and usually fly up into the trees, perhaps to try a bit of patrolling or else to feed on honeydew on the leaves, for the butterflies never seem to feed in their sunny spots. Some males stay in a particular sunny spot for only a few minutes, but within minutes of their leaving their places are taken by other males descending from the patrolling population in the canopy. New spots forming when the sun first reaches a clearing are also quickly occupied by males coming down from the trees. A newcomer immediately takes control of the sunny territory and has no trouble at all in seeing off an intruder within seconds of taking up occupation. This suggests that scent-marking plays no part in defending a territory and that it is the act of flying up from the perch that gives the resident the edge in the battle. On rare occasions when two butterflies arrive simultaneously – usually at a fairly large sun spot – both fly up to do battle when they see each other and then, both believing themselves to be the rightful owners, they engage in a rather more prolonged battle than usual. Such arguments are eventually settled, possibly because one of the combatants is a better territory holder than the other. Because sunny spots come and go quite rapidly, and because the butterflies move in and out quite quickly, it is likely that all males become territory holders at some time in their lives, but they might not all acquire mates in their territories.

With territorial behaviour developing only in certain habitats and under certain weather conditions, it is even likely that more mating takes place among the patrolling than among the perching population.

In southern Europe, where sunshine is never in short supply during the summer, the Speckled Wood shows an interesting reversal of its territorial habits. Instead of seeking sunny spots, the butterflies – represented here by the orange-spotted ssp. *aegeria* – make for the shade. Males and females meet and mate here in the normal way, but such a shift is clearly advantageous when the female comes to egg-laying, for only in the shadier spots can she find the green grasses that the larvae will need; elsewhere the grasses are brown and shrivelled.

The Swallowtail and the Scarce Swallowtail are both strongly territorial but, unlike the Speckled Wood, they make regular rounds of their territories to see off any intruding males. Their perches are commonly thistles or other prominent flowers, from which they get a good view of the surrounding area. Their territories may cover as much as 5,000 m². The Two-tailed Pasha is another extremely territorial butterfly, perching in sunny spots and making regular sorties over its domain. Every intruder is investigated; small birds are regularly chased away, and more than one inquisitive entomologist has had his face slapped by these powerful butterflies. Although most butterfly territories seem to be concerned exclusively with courtship and mating, the Two-tailed Pasha also seems to have an eye for food when selecting its patch for the day.

The Peacock has an open population (see p. 243) and covers a remarkably large area during its long life, but the male's territorial defence is not unlike that of the Speckled Wood. Territories of about 50 m² are established in the middle of the day in spring and early summer, after a morning of basking, feeding and searching for a suitable patch. Sunny hedgerows and the borders of woods are commonly selected as territories, for the females, in common with those of many other species, tend to fly along such linear features and interception is more likely here than in open fields. Territorial males fly up to investigate intruders, and the mere appearance of the resident may be sufficient to persuade another male to carry on flying. At other times, however, the two butterflies will engage in a bit of aerial skirmishing, chasing each other in a series of spiral

The territorial combat of two Peacock butterflies, as described by Robin Baker

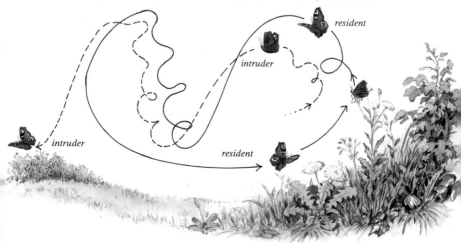

resident

intruder

intruder

resident

ascents and plummetting dives for perhaps 10 or 15 seconds before the resident male disengages and streaks back to his territory, leaving the intruder to continue on his way. Such encounters may carry the butterflies as much as 200m from the disputed territory.

As with the Speckled Wood, an intruder may slip in unseen if the resident male is already occupied with an earlier intruder, and then the returning resident may have to work a little harder to retain his territory. A single skirmish like that already described may be sufficient to drive the invader away, but a second round is often necessary and the intruder may even come back for a third. When this happens the argument is finally settled in the air; the butterflies spiral upwards and each strives for the uppermost position, and the ultimate winner is usually the one managing to hold this position in two consecutive spirals. Here it is obviously fitness rather than residential qualification that determines the outcome and decides which male returns to rule the territory.

When a female arrives in the territory the resident male investigates her in the normal way and, if he gets the 'come-on' signal, he abandons his territory and follows her across country until she goes to roost in the evening. Mating takes place, after the formalities of courtship, in the female's chosen bedroom. The next morning sees the male searching for a new territory, often several kilometres from that which he defended during the previous afternoon.

The male Red Admiral adopts territories similar to those of the Peacock, but studies in North America suggest that it does not occupy them until late in the afternoon. A male may then remain on station for about 2½ hours, although he gives up earlier in cool and cloudy weather. Like the swallowtails, he makes regular inspections of his territory – with about 30 flights an hour recorded in the American studies – and spends the rest of the time on a favourite

perch. Intruding males are engaged in spiral flights, but these do not normally carry the insects far from the territory and the resident quickly drops back to his perch.

The male Small Tortoiseshell usually adopts a territory in or close to a patch of stinging nettles – the larval food-plant – and, like the Peacock, generally takes up residence in the middle of the day. He defends his patch against rival males in much the same way as the male Peacock, but if no females approach during the first hour or two he moves on to find another territory. Many males thus occupy two distinct territories during an afternoon. Towards the end of the afternoon the males become less aggressive towards each other and three or four individuals may end up in a nettle bed that supported only one butterfly earlier in the day.

When a female does arrive in a territory and makes herself known to the resident male, he persuades her to land and then drops down just behind her and guards her jealously, periodically stroking or tapping her with his antennae. If a rival male arrives the resident flies up and leads the newcomer a merry dance for 100m or more before zooming back to his female and clouting her with his antennae to usher her into a more concealed spot. The invading male may return and further chases may take place if he discovers the pair again, but the resident male usually wins all such skirmishes. Towards evening the female drops down into the nettle patch and the male quickly follows her to mate in secrecy.

COMMUNAL COURTING GROUNDS

Not all male butterflies are quite as hostile to their brothers as the territorial species described above and a number of species actually make use of communal courting grounds. Many select hilltops and other prominent landmarks for their assemblies, but a careful look will reveal that the congregating butterflies are nearly all males. The females make only brief visits to the hilltops and leave as soon as they have acquired mates. The Bath White and several of its relatives are well-known 'hilltoppers', with the Moroccan Orange-tip sometimes producing dazzling 'displays' on the hilltops of Provence and on some of the cliffs in the Rhône Valley. It might be thought that the males' bright colours serve to entice the females to the courting grounds, but there is no real evidence to support this idea (see below). Other familiar 'hilltoppers' include several fritillaries, the Wall Brown, and the Holly Blue. Males of the latter species have been known to form a blue haze around the top of a small hill, while the females flew up to visit them from the ivy-clad thicket below.

Although these hilltop courting grounds are often densely populated, the males still try to avoid each other and each adopts a small individual territory within the habitat. Exactly the same thing happens with the Purple Emperor, whose males flock to a 'master tree' – usually a tall oak – and adopt small branches as their individual territories. They battle with each other in much the same way as the Speckled Wood males as they wait for females to arrive at the tree.

Several northern butterflies go in for communal courting grounds and this is clearly a good system in areas where the weather frequently discourages prolonged flying. The Pale Arctic Clouded Yellow is a good example, with all newly-emerged adults congregating at selected flowery patches on the tundra to choose their mates. There are some similarities here with the leks of the black grouse and some other birds, although there is no obvious display by either sex to bring the butterflies together. A true lek is purely a display ground, whereas these butterflies are gathering at important food sources. A closer approximation to lekking behaviour is shown by the Rock Grayling which, in both upland and northern regions, gathers on sunny rocks in the middle of the day. The males perform a dazzling aerial ballet, causing a mating frenzy amongst the females!

A similar performance is enacted by the males of some of the day-flying long-horn moths, such as *Adela reaumurella* and *Nemophora degeerella*. These insects float around the trees with a lazy-looking rising and falling motion and their long white or white-tipped antennae apparently signal to the females. The latter gather on the foliage to watch the dance and are gradually carried off by the males. The Green Hairstreak also congregates around certain trees and bushes, commonly selecting small hawthorns. Both sexes are involved in these aggregations and it seems likely that a good deal of scent is released. If the emission of scent is regarded as a display – and it can be just as important as visual signals – it seems reasonable to regard the Green Hairstreak as a lekking butterfly.

COURTSHIP

As stated earlier, the male almost always makes the first move in butterfly courtship. This is true whether he is a percher waiting for a female to fly into his territory or a patroller actively searching for females. Only extremely frustrated females are likely to fly towards males. Darwin thought that the females were attracted by the bright colours of the males and that they picked out the brightest ones as mates, but extensive research has failed to produce any clear evidence that this is so. In many species, notably among the browns and some of the hairstreaks, the male is actually less colourful than the female, although some might well be decorated with ultra-violet reflections which are invisible to the human eye. All the evidence points to male scent being the major factor in sexually exciting the female. Male colours are primarily for recognition by other males. Some males are actually repelled when they see each other's colours and this helps to space the insects evenly throughout the habitat, especially in some of the patrolling species. Ultra-violet reflections may also be important in this respect.

Anything of approximately the right size and colour and showing the right kind of movement is likely to attract a male in the first instance, although movement is probably less important in the patrolling species, which often find females resting on the vegetation. The detailed wing pattern probably plays little part in the initial attraction in most species, although experiments with models of female White Admirals suggest that any alteration to the width and spacing of the white bands makes the models less attractive to the males. The spot pattern of the female Silver-washed Fritillary is the main stimulus for the patrolling male, but it has to be moving in the right way as well. Males are not attracted to stationary females but when, as in the experiments of Dietrich Magnus, female wings are rotated on a cylinder so that the black spots move at the correct speed the males immediately become interested. The Idas Blue is another patrolling species which has been studied in some detail. In this species the females rest with their wings closed and observations suggest that the males actively search for them. It seems likely that the males home in on the characteristic pattern of the female underside, and the same is probably true of the closely related Brown Argus. It is quite possible that strong ultra-violet reflections help the males to locate the females.

After the initial meeting, which commonly occurs in the air, the all-important pheromones take over and the eager male soon discovers whether the object of his attentions is worth pursuing; it may be another male or a recently mated and unreceptive female more interested in laying eggs, or it may even belong to a different species. Unwilling females generally immediately reject the male. Such rejection behaviour may involve both visual and chemical signals. The unreceptive Grayling female, for example, sits and flutters her wings, and several skippers behave in a similar fashion. Many female pierids, including the Brimstone and the cabbage whites, make their feelings known by flying straight up into the air until the male gets the message and gives up the chase; a behaviour that is very easy to observe above the garden cabbage patch. The butterflies may also land on the vegetation and hold the abdomen vertically in the air. This is the typical pierid rejection posture, and it is also used when the female is accosted while at rest. It may appear to be an invitation, but it is virtually impossible for the male to get at the tip of the raised abdomen. It also seems likely that mated pierids release a repellent pheromone from the exposed tip of the abdomen. But not all unreceptive females show obvious rejection behaviour. Some just fly away, while

Unreceptive females indicate their unwillingness to mate in a variety of different ways. The Grayling flutters her wings, the Brimstone flies into the air and the Large White holds her abdomen vertically

Grayling

Large White

Brimstone

the female White Admiral simply closes her wings and denies the male the visual stimulus he seems to need to continue his courtship. Scent alone is probably enough to stop many courting males. As soon as a male Silver-washed Fritillary touches a mated female with his antennae he is turned off by an anti-male pheromone – possibly deposited by an earlier, successful suitor (see p. 295).

If the male gets all the 'come-on' signals from the female the two butterflies alight and the real courtship begins. It may be a very simple affair, as in the Monarch, or a prolonged and complex ritual involving visual, chemical and tactile signals. 'Courtship' in the Monarch has actually been described as little short of rape, with the male almost battering the female to the ground and then copulating with her immediately, although he does not press home his attack if she gives a rejection signal. During more typical butterfly courtship pheromones are produced by both sexes and, acting only over short distances, they stimulate the insects to begin the final stages of the performance. Several pheromones may be involved, together with various movements or other visual signals, and only when stimulated by the right signals from its partner can the insect move on to the next stage. In at least some species the male pheromones appear to inhibit flight in the female and to keep her in one place. Many females certainly alight very rapidly after the initial flirtation with a courting male.

The butterflies' courtship pheromones themselves are very volatile materials belonging to several chemical groups, including fatty acids, alcohols, terpenes, and ketones. Some are detectable by the human nose. The male pheromone is commonly just a single substance, but female pheromones are more often mixtures of two or more compounds. They are all secreted in minute amounts, and at just the right time in the courtship routine to trigger off the next stage. Each species has its own very specific pheromones which are meaningful only to other butterflies of the same species, and the pheromones clearly play a major role in keeping the species separate. It is commonly stated that reproductive isolation is maintained by differences in the genitalia (see p. 293), but the pheromones may be even more important, for they come into play at a much earlier stage in courtship and normally prevent any attempt at cross-mating.

Most male butterflies produce their courtship pheromones on their wings and distribute them through specialised scent scales or androconia (see p. 20). These scales may be scattered all over the wing surface or aggregated into well-marked patches called sex brands. Some species emit their pheromones through tufts of slender hairs called hair-pencils, although these organs are much more common among moths than butterflies. They may be found on the wings, the legs, or the abdomen. Most female pheromones emanate from glands in the abdomen.

Hair pencils, used to release pheromones, are found on various parts of the lepidopteran body

Angle Shades

Plain Tiger

Many male butterflies flutter their wings during courtship and this might appear to be a visual display, but it is usually a way of wafting the male pheromones from his wings to the receptive organs on the female antennae. In some species the female must actually touch the male's androconia with her antennae in order to pick up sufficient aphrodisiac (see p. 292), and among the skippers the female antennae actually pick up a coating of 'love-dust' – fragments of the hairlike androconia – from the males' wings. The female may show rejection behaviour at any time during courtship, and this may be a sign that the male's pheromones are not sufficiently stimulating – perhaps due to age or general lack of vigour. She may break away from the liaison and wait for a more vigorous suitor, for she must not waste time with a male who might not in the end be able to fertilise many of her eggs. The female can thus 'choose' a mate on the basis of his performance, although she does not seem to be able to distinguish visually between an old and ragged male and a fresh specimen.

The whole sequence of courtship and mating has been studied in a number of butterfly species, with some of the most detailed being Niko Tinbergen's work on the Grayling. This is a perching species and the male will fly up to investigate anything of approximately the right size that flies into view. Using models, Tinbergen and his colleagues showed that shape is not particularly important, but that the model must 'fly' with the right kind of skipping or bouncing motion; models towed smoothly through the air were not particularly attractive to the males. Even colour seems to be of minor importance, for males seem more interested in black and red models than in the natural browns and greys displayed by this species.

A receptive female Grayling that is chased by a male soon drops to the ground. The male lands next to her and, guided by the sight of her antennae, he shuffles around for a face-to-face confrontation. With his wings

Stages in the courtship of the Grayling, beginning with the chasing flight (top), followed by the antennal stimulation and side-stepping dance which leads to copulation

291

vibrating rapidly, he begins to rotate his antennae, but the female remains motionless and apparently unimpressed. The male's fanning movements increase and then, with his antennae firmly planted on the ground, he tilts his body and wings forward to enclose the female's antennae. Continued movement of his wings ensures that the female's antennae collect plenty of the exciting pheromone from the extensive patches of androconia on his forewings, and that she is ready for the next stage. A side-stepping 'dance' brings the male just to the side and rear of the female and, if the pheromones have done their job, a slight nudge from the male will cause the female to raise her wings slightly and expose her abdomen – all the invitation that the male needs to curve his abdomen round to make contact with her genitalia.

The female may reject the male's advances at any time during the courtship by simply fluttering her wings. This may indicate that she is not warm enough, or it may be that the male just does not have enough to offer in the way of excitatory pheromones (see p. 291). Males that have been experimentally denuded of their androconia go courting eagerly enough, but are always rejected before reaching the final stages.

Several other browns, including the Great Banded Grayling and the Wall Brown, go in for similar displays, although they do not all rub their wings over the female antennae when bowing to her. Most of these butterflies prefer to go courting in the sunshine, but the Ringlet is an exception. It lives in shady places, often in very damp woodlands, and can be seen courting in very overcast conditions, even sitting and displaying on foliage that is dripping with water after rain. The damp atmosphere is ideal for carrying the courtship scents and there is no need for close contact between the male wings and the female antennae. The Ringlet thus has no need of concentrated sex brands and the androconia are scattered all over the wing surface. Ringlet populations tend to rise after a wet season, and there was a dramatic fall in the British population after the two drought years of 1975 and 1976. But it is not clear whether such fluctuations reflect mating success or the amount of food available for the larvae. There is also evidence that many of the butterflies left their normal haunts during the droughts and moved across country in search of more congenial conditions.

The Wood White is a patrolling species whose courtship has been studied in Sweden by O. Wiklund. The male approaches anything white and of vaguely the right shape, and if it turns out to be a female the two butterflies flutter weakly through the air together. If the right signals are exchanged the female lands on the vegetation and the male alights in front of her. He never seems to land beside any other white butterfly, so the female pheromones clearly play

Attracted by the female's pattern, the male Silver-washed Fritillary flies underneath her repeatedly, until she settles on a leaf. Settling in front of her he rubs his wings against her

COPULATION

Having got the female into the right mood with his pheromones, the male is ready for the final act. He commonly takes up a position to one side and slightly astern of the female, but still facing in the same direction, and then curves his body round to probe her with the tip of his abdomen. This caressing is the final trigger needed to bring the genitalia into action and the 'excitement' of the two butterflies is visible as the genitalia meet and copulation begins. At this point the male usually turns to face in the opposite direction.

The male genitalia are centred on a chitinous ring just inside the end of the abdomen and the most prominent parts are two valves or claspers which are usually hinged on the rear edge of the ring. They can usually be seen fairly easily right at the tip of the abdomen, although they are clothed with hair, and they gape open if the abdomen is gently squeezed near the tip. The valves bear numerous bristles and other outgrowths and their function is to grasp the tip of the female's abdomen during mating. They are usually aided in this by a hook, known as the uncus, which projects from the rear of the chitinous ring. In most members of the Lycaenidae, however, the uncus is replaced by a pair of lobes. There are commonly other backward-pointing hooks around the uncus and all help to grip the female's abdomen and line it up ready to receive the penis or adeagus.

The male Wood White (right) excites the female by twirling his antennae around her head

an early role in the proceedings. He puts his tongue out at her, although it is not known what pleasure he gives or receives from this behaviour, and points his antennae at her head. He then sways in such a way that his antennae describe circles around the female's head. The white undersides of the antennal clubs are prominent and undoubtedly play a part in exciting the female. A willing female then bends her abdomen towards the male, probably releasing an excitatory pheromone at the same time, and copulation takes place almost immediately. A mated female, if she even allows herself to get to this stage, bends her own antennae out of the way and never bends her abdomen towards the male. The male will not attempt copulation unless it is initiated by female.

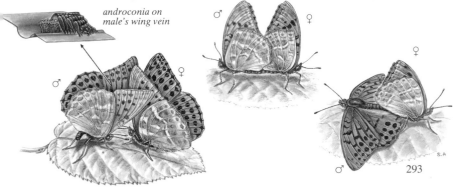

antennae to transfer excitatory pheromones from his androconia. She then allows him to mate with her. During mating the male often basks with his wings open (After Magnus).

androconia on male's wing vein

293

The latter is a horny tube which is thrust out between the valves when the two insects are properly coupled and which transmits the spermatophore to the female. Valves, uncus, and adeagus all vary in shape from species to species and are often of great help in separating closely related species.

The differences in genitalia help to ensure that different species cannot mate successfully, although some closely related species can pair up if their equipment is not too dissimilar.

The female genitalia are almost entirely concealed within the abdomen and the most important part as far as identification is concerned is the bursa copulatrix. This is a rather thin-walled sac which receives the male's adeagus and spermatophore during copulation. Its surface bears a number of chitinous and often spiny patches and the shape and arrangement of these, as well as the overall shape of the sac, are important in identification of the species, although the differences between female genitalia are often less than those between the male structures. The bursa copulatrix opens on the underside of the eighth abdominal segment by way of a duct of variable length.

When everything is lined up, the male's penis or aedeagus is thrust into the opening of the female's bursa copulatrix ready to pump in the sperm. The latter is accompanied by various other protein-rich secretions which harden around it and form a capsule known as the spermatophore. Because it is fluid when pumped into the female, it takes on the shape of her bursa copulatrix. It is thought that the females of some species use the proteins of the spermatophore for nourishment and possibly even to increase their egg-production. If a female has already mated the new male may have to dislodge the remains of the old spermatophore with his genitalia. Although he usually does not get rid of them completely, eggs are always fertilised by the last spermatophore received by the female.

Sperm transference may take place as soon as the butterflies have linked up, but the insects remain *in copula* for anything from a few minutes to several hours. Copulation is particularly drawn out in *Parnassius* species, in which the male also has to fit his mate with a 'chastity belt' (see p. 295). Observations also suggest that for a given species copulation takes longer at lower temperatures, although females commonly refuse to accept courtship if the temperature is not above a certain level. Older males also seem to spend longer copulating than younger ones. A male that has mated before produces smaller spermatophores than a virgin male and the older male is clearly less suitable as a father – but the female will not know this unless the male also has a reduced pheromone output, in which case she might well reject him during the initial courtship, before he gets anywhere near copulation.

It is normal for the Monarch and its relatives to fly *in copula*, but the majority of butterflies prefer to copulate on the ground and they take to the air only when disturbed. Because the insects are linked tail-to-tail, one individual clearly has to take the lead and carry the other, and in most cases the sex of the carrier is species specific. Among the blues and the whites it is usually the male that does the carrying, although the Black-veined White is a notable exception. The female does the work in most skippers and browns and many fritillaries, although the male does the carrying in some of the fritillaries and while copulating he often basks to ensure that he is warm enough for take-off should it be necessary (see p. 262).

The female normally terminates copulation – possibly informed by the pressure of the spermatophore that she has acquired – and struggles free. The two insects rarely have any further contact, although the males of a few tropical species are believed to hang around and chase off rivals while the females lay their eggs – eggs which have, of course, been fertilised by the defending males.

A mated female Small Apollo with the sphragis in position

THE AGE OF CONSENT

Male butterflies can sometimes mate on their first day, but most have to wait for their pheromone stocks to build up. They usually emerge a few days before the females and spend the time spreading themselves around the habitat. One big advantage of this is that they are likely to move some way from their sisters and thus reduce the likelihood of inbreeding. Females can mate on the day of emergence for, with an average life of only 4–5 days ahead of them, there is no point in procrastinating; they must get on with the business of mating and egg-laying as soon as possible. Some species, including the Small Apollo, regularly mate before their wings are fully expanded. With the female virtually helpless, there is little or no courtship in such instances. Females of some of the tropical birdwing butterflies get their mates even earlier; the female pupae give off pheromones that attract males in the way that the Emperor Moth does, and the males then wait for the adults to emerge from their pupae.

HOW MANY MATES?

Male butterflies are nearly always ready to mate and it is quite common for individuals to have four or five liaisons during their brief lives. Some non-European butterflies have been seen to mate more than a dozen times. Some individuals even manage two matings in one day, although observations on a number of species suggest that mating on alternate days is the norm. More matings normally lead to more offspring and so, other things being equal, natural selection favours those strains whose males manage the most matings. But this is not so for the female. Her best strategy is to mate once and then spend the rest of her life laying eggs, although there is evidence to suggest that multiple matings may increase the fecundity of some species. Some female butterflies, notably those of the genus *Danaus*, can mate ten times or more – as shown by the number of spermatophores retrieved from their bodies – but 1–3 matings is more normal and studies of various species reveal a distinct trend towards female monogamy.

Some females simply become unreceptive to the males' advances after copulation and show various forms of rejection behaviour, although they may accept another male if they live long enough. In many species, however, there are definite mechanisms designed to prevent a second mating. The best known and most efficient of these is the sphragis or 'chastity belt' fitted to the *Parnassius* female during her one and only mating. Produced by the male, it is a horny structure which plugs the female's genital opening and also forms a rather prominent pouch under her abdomen – perhaps making her unattractive to other males right from the start. Male *Parnassius* butterflies probably mate less frequently than other butterflies as well, for the production of the sphragis must be a considerable drain on their resources. Females of some species release anti-male pheromones when they have mated, and in some tropical species it has been shown that these scents are deposited in the female's abdomen by her first and probably only mate. It is quite possible that such anti-sex pheromones may be present in many butterfly species. Another very simple, but effective method of reducing the number of female matings is for the mated females to move to slightly different habitats from those frequented by the males and virgin females. This happens in many hill-topping species (see p. 288), and in some regions the Orange-tip has also been shown to switch habitats after mating.

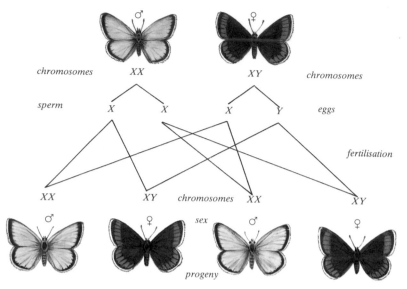

Inheritance of the sexual characteristics in the Atlas Blue butterfly

THE GENETICS OF SEX

The sex of butterflies and moths, like most other features of an animal, is genetically controlled and is determined at the moment of fertilisation. Among the butterflies and moths the male body cells each contain two sex-determining chromosomes, conventionally known as X-chromosomes, while female body cells contain just one X-chromosome and a much smaller Y-chromosome. The latter carries very few genes and plays no active part in determining the sex of the individual, although it is still known as a sex chromosome. This situation is completely the reverse of that found in mammals, where the female carries two X-chromosomes and the male has one X and one Y.

When eggs and sperm are formed the chromosome pairs split up and one of each pair goes to each sex cell. Each sperm thus contains an X-chromosome, while half the eggs contain X-chromosomes and the other half contain Y-chromosomes. At fertilisation the X-bearing sperms join with X-bearing eggs to produce males and with Y-bearing eggs to produce females, the two sexes being produced in more or less equal numbers.

As well as differing in their primary sex organs, male and female butterflies and moths often have different colours and patterns and may be of different sizes, all of this being determined by the number of X-chromosomes in the cells. A single X-chromosome in a cell causes it to develop female characteristics, while two X-chromosomes lead to the development of male features appropriate to the cell's position in the body. Among the vanessids, such as the Red Admiral and the tortoiseshells, the two sexes are almost identical as far as their external features are concerned, but at the other end of the scale there are butterflies in which the two sexes are so different that they are commonly taken for different species. Examples include the Orange-tip, the Brimstone, and most of the blues. Species in which the two sexes are visibly different are said to show sexual dimorphism.

Gynandromorphs

The fertilised egg is converted into an embryo by way of numerous cell divisions, with each new cell developing features appropriate to its position in the body. Thousands more cell divisions take place as the insect grows up and it is quite common for 'mistakes' to occur during these divisions, leading to a range of abnormalities in the body. Most of these abnormalities are lethal and the affected insects usually die at an early stage, but mistakes involving the sex chromosomes do not necessarily interfere with the normal working of the body and the insects often grow up with nothing worse than an abnormal sexuality.

The best known of such abnormal butterflies are the bilateral gynandromorphs, in which half of the insect is male and half is female. The dividing line is right down the middle and the situation results from a mistake in the first division of the fertilised egg. This division produces two cells, one of which gives rise to the left-hand side of the body while the other produces the right-hand side. If one of the two X-chromosomes is lost from a cell during this first division, that cell and all those on the side derived from it will have only one X-chromosome

Genetic mistakes during development can give rise to full blown bilateral gyandromorphs, or to small patches of the opposite sex's coloration as in the Brimstone

and thus produce female characteristics, while the other side retains its male features. Clearly, such bilateral gynandromorphs can develop only from eggs originally destined to be males, for only these have two X-chromosomes to start with. The loss of a Y-chromosome from a female cell has no effect on its sex, and loss of its one X-chromosome leads to death.

Bilateral gynandromorphs have been discovered in nearly all species of butterflies, although some species seem more prone to this abnormality than others. Certain populations also seem to be affected more than others. The Irish race of the Common Blue, for example, produces a greater proportion of gynandromorphs than the British race. The phenomenon is, of course, most obvious in the blues and other species with marked sexual dimorphism. As well as differing in colour, the two sides may differ in the size of their wings and legs. The genitalia, of course, are part male and part female and the insects cannot mate. It is doubtful if they even try courtship, for one half would presumably try to behave as a male and the other half as a female.

Mistakes occurring later during the insect's development lead to smaller areas' being affected – just those parts derived from the cells involved in the mistakes. Small patches of female coloration may occur on an otherwise male wing, and with mistakes occurring at a very late stage it is possible to get patches of male colour on an otherwise female wing. This happens when a female cell divides and sends two X-chromosomes to one of the new cells instead of sending one X and one Y. The other new cell would receive no X-chromosomes, but at this late stage it does not matter that the cell dies.

VARIETIES AND SUB-SPECIES

As we have seen on p. 25, butterflies and moths are subject to considerable variation even within a species. Any individual deviating from the normal pattern of its species is called a variety, but this term has no specific scientific value and is used indiscriminately to cover several different kinds of variation.

An aberration is a variation that appears irregularly or randomly in a population as a result of some genetic or environmental disturbance. Good examples include the melanic varieties of the White Admiral – ab. *obliterata* and ab. *nigrina* – in which the white patches are obliterated to varying degrees, and also the various heavily-marked varieties of the Silver-washed Fritillary. Collectors have always been keen to acquire aberrations, and many have resorted to treatment of the pupa with high or low temperatures (see p. 299) or to prolonged in-breeding to obtain abnormal specimens. Genetically produced aberrations can be passed on to succeeding generations but, because abnormal individuals usually have less chance of acquiring mates in the wild, the aberrations are rarely passed on in practice. They crop up again only when the particular genetic mistake recurs.

Forms are varieties which occur on a regular basis and make up a fairly constant or significant proportion of the population. An aberration can, of course, evolve into a form if it confers some advantage on the individuals and is able to spread through the population. This happened with the Peppered Moth, whose melanic form is now common in many parts of Europe although regarded as a rare aberration 150 years ago. Insects with two or more forms are said to be polymorphic.

The Silver-washed Fritillary normally has a bright orange ground colour, but in certain areas, notably England's New Forest and some of the larger forests of the Alps, 10 to 15% of the females have an olive-green ground colour and are known as form *valezina*. They maintain themselves at a more or less constant fraction of the population via a mixture of genetic and environmental factors. The *valezina* coloration is produced by the presence of a single gene which is dominant to that producing the normal form, and any female possessing this gene will take on the *valezina* form even when the normal gene is present. It is believed that the greenish *valezina* is less vulnerable to predation in the denser woodlands, and thus has an advantage over the normal form. One would therefore expect it to increase dramatically, as did the melanic form of the peppered moth, but this clearly is not happening and the reason seems to be a genetic one. The 'pure' or homozygous *valezina* form, possessing two *valezina* genes, is apparently unable to survive and there is thus a considerable loss of this gene in each generation. This loss just balances the advantage conferred by the greenish coloration and maintains the *valezina* population at 10–15% of the total Silver-washed Fritillary population in the area. Such a situation is known as balanced polymorphism.

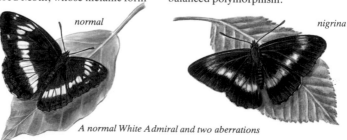

normal

nigrina

A normal White Admiral and two aberrations

A typical Small Tortoiseshell (top) with aberrations produced by rearing at high (left) and low (right) temperatures

It has also been suggested that *valezina* females are less successful than the normal forms in attracting mates, and that this might actually balance out the advantage of camouflage. This seems an unlikely explanation, however, because most *valezina* females captured in the wild have actually mated!

The *valezina* gene is carried by 10–15% of the male butterflies as well, and is passed on to some of their offspring. A normal female can thus produce *valezina* offspring if she mates with a male carrying the gene. But for some reason the gene cannot assert itself in the male body and the males always exhibit the normal coloration.

The Clouded Yellow exhibits a very similar example of balanced polymorphism among the females. Most of these share the deep yellow colour of the males, but about 10% of the females are dirty white and are known as form *helice*. They are often confused with the Pale Clouded Yellow, although the latter has much narrower black borders to its wings. Like the

obliterata

valezina form of the Silver-washed Fritillary, *helice* is produced by a single dominant gene, but we do not yet know what genetic or environmental factors combine to maintain the polymorphism.

Polymorphism, with two or more forms existing side by side in the same population, is found in many other butterflies, especially in the tropics, and is also very common among the burnet moths. The Six-spot Burnet, for example, has a well known form – f. *flava* – in which the red coloration is replaced by yellow. The frequency of these forms may be less than 1%, but they are nevertheless maintained by heredity rather than by repeated mutations or 'mistakes'. Such mutations occur at a very much lower rate. Whereas *helice* and *valezina* are produced by dominant genes, the rarer forms are due to recessive genes which do not dominate the normal ones. The character manifests itself only in those individuals carrying two of the recessive genes – one from each parent – and these homozygous individuals are much less common than the heterozygotes which carry normal genes as well. The heterozygote obviously has some advantage over the other forms, otherwise the recessive gene would disappear altogether. Equally clearly, there must be some serious drawback to the recessive form which prevents it from becoming more common.

SEASONAL VARIATION

Several double-brooded species exhibit marked differences between the two broods and, although not flying together, they are clearly parts of the same population and thus legitimately known as forms – although there is not necessarily any genetic basis for the distinction and the phenomenon is more often called seasonal polyphenism than seasonal polymorphism.

The best example is certainly that of the Map Butterfly from Central Europe. Butterflies of the spring generation (f. *levana*) resemble fritillaries, whereas the summer form (f. *prorsa*) could be mistaken for a small White Admiral. The two forms were once thought to be different species, but the differences are brought about purely by environmental factors. Although once thought to be controlled by temperature, the variation has now been shown to be due to the varying day-lengths experienced by the larvae. Autumn larvae experience short days, leading to a long pupal diapause which, in turn, leads to the fritillary-like spring brood, whereas the long days of summer produce non-diapause pupae and the darker coloration of the summer brood. By exposing autumn larvae to artificially long days they can be made to produce f. *prorsa*, and summer larvae subjected to short days will produce f. *levana*. Temperature can also have some effect; by cooling summer larvae or pupae and prolonging their development it is possible to produce intermediates between the two adult forms and also some *levana* adults. But it is not possible to produce *prorsa* adults by warming up autumn larvae or pupae, for day-length has already programmed them for a lengthy development into f. *levana*.

The Comma exhibits a more complex polyphenism, involving the normal rich chestnut form and the paler f. *hutchinsoni*, which also has a rather less ragged appearance. The species hibernates in the adult state and all the hibernators are of the normal form. They mate in the spring, but the resulting larvae then follow one of two courses. One group matures rapidly, producing f. *hutchinsoni* in July or even earlier, while the second group develops slowly and does not mature until August as a rule. These slow developers all produce normal adults which go into hibernation soon after emergence. Meanwhile, the *hutchinsoni* adults have mated and produced a second generation of larvae. These produce 2nd-generation adults in September and all are of the normal form. They hibernate and in the spring they mate freely amongst themselves and also with the slow developers of the previous year. It is not known what causes the spring larvae to segregate into two groups – the fast-breeding, double-brooded population and the slower, single-brooded one.

The life-cycle of the Map Butterfly

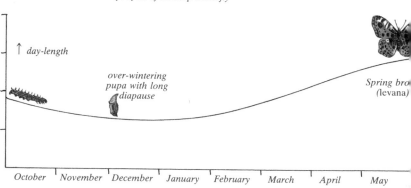

↑ *day-length*

over-wintering pupa with long diapause

Spring bro(od) (levana)

October | November | December | January | February | March | April | May

SUB-SPECIES

When a widely distributed species is broken up into isolated populations by natural barriers such as mountain ranges and seas the separated populations commonly evolve along slightly different pathways. Guided by the local climate and other factors, they gradually evolve a number of small, but nevertheless distinctive features. When the differences between two of these separated populations are such that, although they are still able to interbreed, they can be distinguished simply by looking at them, they are called sub-species (see p. 25). The English Swallowtail population, for example, differs from the continental ones in several details (see p. 26) and belongs to the sub species *brittanicus*. Continental populations, which are double-brooded in most places, belong to the sub-species *bigeneratus*.

It is, understandably, quite common for islands to have their own sub-species, and the Small Tortoiseshell provides a very good example with its ssp. *ichnusa* confined to the islands of Corsica, Sardinia, and Elba. Mountains also tend to have their own sub-species and no butterfly shows this better than the Apollo, which has more than a dozen sub-species scattered over Europe and many more elsewhere. Over 160 sub-species have actually been listed, although this is taking 'splitting' to the extreme and it is unlikely that there is anything like this number of truly recognisable sub-species. A species

with more than two distinct sub-species is said to be polytypic.

Sub-species are also commonly known as races, although some entomologists reserve this term for variations which are not quite so clearly distinguished from the original populations.

Isolation is not always necessary for the development of sub-species. An insect with an extensive distribution may experience totally different conditions at opposite ends of its range and thus develop some very different features. This can lead to the formation of true sub-species, although in this instance they may be connected by intermediates right across the range. Such a series of gradual changes is called a cline. Genes are exchanged between neighbouring parts of the range, but sheer distance prevents any real mingling of the genes from the two extremes and thus maintains the identity of the two sub-species.

There are several examples of clines among the European butterflies, the best documented being that of the Speckled Wood. This butterfly has two very distinct sub-species – *aegeria* with cream-coloured spots and *tircis* with orange spots – but there is a continuous variation across the range and it is not possible to say exactly where one sub-species takes over from the other. The very variable Spotted Fritillary is also a clinal species and it exhibits at least three clines; from the lowlands of Central Europe into the mountains, from the mountains to the low-lying Mediterranean areas, and through lowland France to link the northern and Mediterranean populations. The intermediates between these clines are often very difficult to identify.

Clines and sub-species can develop only in the more sedentary butterflies, where there is only limited movement between neighbouring colonies and thus a very restricted gene flow. It is very obvious that the strongly migratory species, such as the Peacock and the Red Admiral, show virtually no geographical variation. The mobility of these species ensures that no

summer brood
(*prorsa*)

non-diapausing
pupa, produced
by long summer
days

ne   July   August   September   October

The Speckled Wood cline, showing how the insect changes gradually from northern Europe to the Mediterranean

population is isolated from another for very long.

If two sub-species remain isolated, with no gene-flow between them, they may eventually diverge so much that they become completely separate species. Even if they meet later they cannot breed with each other because they are no longer compatible. Behaviour and genitalia may have changed so much that mating is impossible, and even if mating can occur the differences in genetic make-up will normally prevent the production of viable offspring. But sub-species do not inevitably progress to full species; only if sufficient mutations occur and if the local conditions are sufficiently

different to favour extensive changes can the process reach this conclusion. Even sub-species cannot develop without the occurrence of mutations affecting the appearance of the insects. Quite a number of sedentary species show little or no variation throughout Europe, although some of their populations might be quite isolated. The Common Blue and the Gatekeeper are good examples, but lack of variation in their appearance does not mean that they are not adapted to various climates. Behavioural and physiological adaptations are usually more important in this respect than mere changes of colour and pattern.

Because the climate and even the face of the earth are always changing, albeit very slowly, barriers that once isolated populations and led to the evolution of new species can be swept away. The new species are then able to mingle, and as long as they all have different requirements they can live side by side without competition.

SPECIATION IN THE ALPS

The Pleistocene glaciations had a marked effect on the landscape of Europe and also on its flora and fauna. The present-day distribution of many butterflies can be attributed directly to the effects of the ice-sheets and a good number of species owe their very existence to the ice ages. This is best illustrated by the numerous species of *Erebia* living in the Alps. At the height of the glaciation much of Central Europe resembled

today's northern tundra and undoubtedly carried a similar assortment of grass-feeding *Erebia* species. Most of these would have been pushed down from the north as the climate deteriorated, and when the ice started to retreat these cold-loving butterflies began to go with it. Some went right back to the north, but many followed the ice up the mountains and became isolated there, cut off from other members of their species by the 'inhospitable' lowlands. This happened three or four times during the Pleistocene and led to the numerous local species that we know today, some of them confined to just a few neighbouring peaks. Several different species may occur on one mountain, but they usually avoid competition with each other by occupying slightly different altitudes (see below).

At the height of a glaciation a given butterfly species may have been widely distributed on the tundra

As the ice retreated the butterflies moved up the mountains and each population evolved in a slightly different way

When the ice returned the insects were forced down again and they spread over the tundra

When the ice retreated again the insects again climbed the mountains, with each species occupying a particular level. Further divergence occurred, and in theory one original tundra species could have produced nine new species

BUTTERFLY POPULATIONS

EXTINCT AND VANISHING SPECIES

Eight butterfly species have disappeared from the Netherlands since the end of the Second World War. The Purple-edged Copper became extinct there in 1946 and was followed during the next 26 years by the Large Blue, Dusky Large Blue, Scarce Large Blue, Pearl-bordered Fritillary, Spotted Fritillary, Lesser Marbled Fritillary, and Scarce Heath. Luxembourg, Belgium, and Denmark have all lost species in recent decades, and 1979 saw the disappearance of the Large Blue from Great Britain. The publicity surrounding this last extinction undoubtedly had a beneficial effect in creating a general awareness of butterflies and the need for their conservation, and the Large Blue has now been re-introduced into some carefully managed habitats (see p. 312). Several other rare species have been saved from extinction, at least temporarily, by proper management of their habitats, but it seems that the Large Tortoiseshell has now been lost as a breeding species in Great Britain.

The only other butterfly species to become extinct in Britain in the twentieth century was the Black-veined White, which died out in the 1920s, but its loss was not altogether unwelcome because it was something of a pest in the orchards of southern England. It remains common enough on the continent. The English Large Copper (*Lycaena dispar dispar*), however, which formerly occupied the Fen country has now gone for ever, exterminated by a variety of causes in the middle of the nineteenth century. The Large Copper living, somewhat precariously, in England today (see p. 312) is the Dutch subspecies *L.d. batavus* and differs in a number of respects from the original natives. Many other local races or sub-species have undoubtedly disappeared over the years. The New

The Mazarine Blue, which mysteriously disappeared from Britain in the 1800s

Forest Burnet (*Zygaena viciae ytenensis*) has not flown in England's New Forest since the 1920s, although another sub-species, *Z.v. argyllensis*, maintains a shaky existence at a single site in Scotland.

The species mentioned so far have not become extinct in Europe as a whole, but several species are in real danger of disappearing in the near future. They are the Corsican Swallowtail, Cranberry Fritillary, Bog Fritillary, Scarce Fritillary, Large Blue, Scarce Large Blue, Dusky Large Blue, Alcon Blue, Large Copper, Dalmatian Ringlet, and False Ringlet. In addition, the False Comma and the Bavius Blue are regarded as endangered, although these butterflies are rather special cases because both are on the extreme edge of their range in Europe. Most of these endangered species exist in Asia, although their status there is generally unknown, but the Corsican Swallowtail flies only in Corsica and Sardinia and extinction there would be the end of the species.

In addition to the thirteen endangered species listed above, which account for about 3.5% of Europe's butterflies, a further fifty species are classed as vulnerable (see endpaper). Many of these are considered to be endangered in certain countries. Most European species have actually declined in numbers in the last few decades.

Why do butterflies become extinct?
Several factors have been implicated in the decline and extinction of our

304

butterflies, but the prime factor has always been the alteration or complete destruction of the habitat. All over Europe woods have gone under the plough, and meadows that supported clouds of butterflies have either been covered with bricks and mortar or 'improved' so that they are no longer of interest to many butterflies (see p. 246). The extinction of the English Large Copper was clearly initiated by a major change in the habitat – the drainage of the fens during the eighteenth and nineteenth centuries. The butterfly quickly became restricted to quite small areas and populations continued to fall because reed-cutting and peat-digging were abandoned in most of the remaining fens and the butterfly's food-plant, the great water dock, was crowded out. Butterfly collectors probably dealt the final blow by homing in on the small populations in the few remaining localities. The last butterfly was recorded in 1851.

Marked declines in woodland fritillaries followed the abandonment of coppicing and other changes in woodland management (see p. 245) which resulted in the loss of the clearings needed by the butterflies and their food-plants. The Heath Fritillary suffered more than most butterflies in Britain and very nearly disappeared, but careful management of its remaining localities has enabled it to build up its numbers again and it has been successfully re-introduced into some of its old haunts where coppicing has been resumed. The loss of the Chequered Skipper from the English Midlands during the 1970s was also due to changing woodland management.

The extinction of the Large Blue in Great Britain was due to the loss of rabbits and the reduction of sheep grazing, which made the pastures less suitable for the single ant species which is essential for the survival of the butterfly (see p. 220). The Large Blue and its relatives are also under threat on the continent, but now that the host ants' requirements are known it should be possible to maintain the surviving populations by regular graz-

Scarce Large Blue

Cranberry Fritillary

False Ringlet

Violet Copper

Drainage of wetlands has threatened many butterfly species throughout Europe

Dusky Large Blue

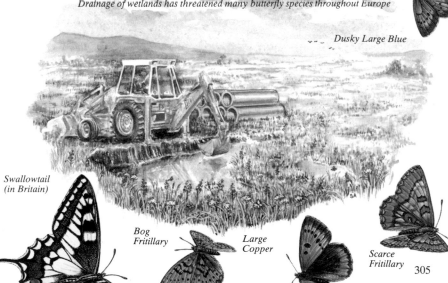

Swallowtail (in Britain)

Bog Fritillary

Large Copper

Scarce Fritillary

305

ing of the habitats to keep down the coarse grasses.

Long-term climatic changes, as opposed to annual fluctuations in the weather (see p. 308), may also be involved in the decline of certain butterflies, although populations have not been studied for long enough for definite links to be established. It is possible that the Black-veined White's extinction in Britain was due to some subtle change in the climate. Always on the edge of its range here, the butterfly spent its last few years confined to a small part of Kent, and it has been suggested that spraying of the orchards may have been the final straw. Another theory is that a slight increase in rainfall during the early years of this century allowed pathogenic fungi to increase and wipe out the butterfly. Mystery also surrounds the extinction of the Mazarine Blue in Britain. Always local, but not uncommon in some areas in the first half of the nineteenth century, it disappeared in 1877 and, apart from scattered specimens presumed to have been released by collectors, it has not been seen since. Like the Black-veined White, the butterfly remains common over much of the continent. The reasons for the decline of these two species are likely to remain a mystery, although it is well known that species on the edge of their range are susceptible to small climatic changes unless they are really well established. Small populations are particularly vulnerable in such situations.

Pesticides are commonly blamed for the decline in butterfly populations but, although the widespread use of pesticides began at about the time the insects started their post-war decline, it is very unlikely that they had any major effect. Insecticides are usually confined to agricultural or forest crops, which support very little butterfly life in any case. Drift can cause problems, of course, especially when spraying from the air, but its effects are usually very localised and the doses are very small. Herbicides have perhaps caused more trouble, for they are commonly used to keep

down the vegetation on roadsides and have undoubtedly killed off some of the grassland and hedgerow butterflies, but again the effects have been very local. Cars and lorries speeding along the roads may well kill more butterflies than the occasional dose of pesticide.

Butterfly collecting, popular for over 200 years, has also been blamed for the loss of butterflies and, as we have seen, probably did play a part in the disappearance of the English Large Copper. But it is unlikely that any extinctions have been caused entirely by collecting. Normal collecting is unlikely to harm healthy populations, but it is a potential threat to species whose populations have been reduced for other reasons. Closed populations of low-flying and easily caught butterflies, such as the Heath Fritillary, are particularly at risk, but only when the adult population falls below about 250 insects. High-fliers, such as the Purple Emperor, have nothing to fear from collectors because it is impossible to capture more than a very small number of them.

BUTTERFLIES ON THE INCREASE

Although there has been a general decline in butterfly numbers in Europe, the signs are not all bad and many species are holding up well in the less populated areas. In Finland, for example, a survey of about 50 species has shown no real change during the last 25 years. Even in Great Britain the populations of many species are maintaining their levels in areas where the habitat remains suitable – on nature reserves, for example – and it is still possible to see clouds of blues on some grassy hillsides. A few species have even been increasing their ranges.

The White Admiral was very rare in Britain in the early part of the twentieth century and was confined to the New Forest and a few neighbouring woods, but it underwent a remarkable expansion in the 1930's and by the early 1940's it was found over much of

England south of a line from the Severn to the Humber. A succession of warm summers was primarily responsible for the build-up, for it has now been shown that high temperatures, especially in June, speed-up the development of the larvae and pupae and thereby reduce the time available for predators to find them. Changes in habitat, notably the abandonment of coppicing, also contributed to the spread of the White Admiral, for the butterfly likes partial shade and prefers to lay its eggs on the rather spindly growths of honeysuckle that are found in more mature woodlands. The species is also found in the rides of many coniferous plantations. There have been some losses since the peak populations of the 1940's, due mainly to the destruction of a number of woodlands, but the butterfly seems to be maintaining itself well in most of the newly colonised areas despite somewhat cooler summers. In fact, it has colonised several new sites in recent years. Numbers shot-up in the very hot summer of 1976 when a high proportion of larvae, already numerous following the good summer of 1975, produced adults, but the increase was not maintained because the drought caused the deaths of many of the young larvae during the autumn and the 1977 population was actually quite low.

The Comma has had a rather similar history in Great Britain. It was widely distributed, although not necessarily common, during the eighteenth and nineteenth centuries, but then the population crashed and the butterfly withdrew to a small area around the River Severn. It remained relatively common there in the early part of the twentieth century and began to spread again in the 1930s. And it is still spreading. Attempts have been made to link the decline of the Comma with the decline in hop-growing, for hops were certainly a major food-plant during the nineteenth century, but the butterfly disappeared from many areas where hops continued to be grown and it seems more likely that a climatic factor was at work. Cold, wet winters

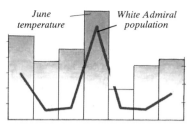

June temperature — *White Admiral population*

The White Admiral population closely follows the average June temperature

may have been responsible for the decline, for the butterfly certainly shrank back to an area with a combination of both mild and dry winters. When it began to spread again its main food-plants were stinging nettle and elm, but both are quite closely related to the hop and it is not surprising that the caterpillars were able to utilise them when hops were no longer common.

The fact that both the Comma and the White Admiral have suffered severe population crashes and then recovered much of their former ranges within a few decades suggests that these fluctuations might be part of a long-term cycle. If so, it is possible that some of our other declining butterflies will pick themselves up in the future, when the right climatic conditions come round again – but only if we maintain their habitats in a suitable condition.

The Speckled Wood and the Wood White have also increased their numbers in Britain in recent years. The Speckled Wood is a shade-loving butterfly and man's neglect of woodland has certainly aided its increase. It also thrives in the rides of many coniferous plantations as long as there is sufficient grass for its caterpillars and as long as it can find a few sunny patches to mate in (see p. 284). This species pays little attention to flowers and feeds mainly on honeydew. The Wood White has also colonised many young coniferous plantations, but surveys in established woodlands show that it is likely to die out again as soon as the rides become too shady. Wide rides, perhaps up to 20m across, would help this attractive and delicate little butterfly to continue to increase.

SHORT-TERM FLUCTUATIONS

Superimposed on any long-term population trends there are many annual or seasonal fluctuations – the entomologist's good and bad years. The weather is clearly a major factor here, acting either directly on the insects or indirectly through their food-plants and natural enemies. Most butterfly species increase their numbers during good summers and decline in years with low temperatures or high rainfall.

We have already seen how the White Admiral responds to high temperatures by speeding up its development and thus running less risk of being eaten. Conversely, its numbers can fall, as they did in Britain in 1980 and 1981, when summer temperatures, particularly those in June, are on the low side. Small Copper populations crashed alarmingly in some areas in the 1960's, when a succession of damp, cloudy summers prevented the females from laying more than a small proportion of their eggs, but numbers quickly rose again when good summers returned. There was a further crash after the 1976 drought, however, because the larvae starved on the shrivelled food-plants. This summer was actually too hot for many butterflies and reduced populations were reported for numerous species throughout north-west Europe in the following year. The Ringlet fared particularly badly in Britain because both adults and larvae require a lush grassy habitat, but numbers recovered well in most places, and by 1980 – the damp year which saw a fall in White Admiral populations – the Ringlet was considerably more abundant than in the pre-drought years.

But not all butterflies were adversely affected by the drought. The ubiquitous Meadow Brown, with its tolerance of a wide range of environmental conditions, carried on as if nothing had happened, and the Small Skipper actually increased its numbers in 1977, aided by the fact that the larvae hibernate without feeding and were thus unaffected by the drought.

It is unlikely that bad weather, as opposed to long-term deterioration of the climate, would ever cause widespread extinction of butterflies because weather usually has only local effects. Abnormal weather conditions have been known to wipe out local populations, however, and several small colonies of the Adonis Blue were destroyed by the 1976 drought. This is a very sedentary species and was unable to re-colonise these sites from neighbouring areas where the species had survived the drought. Prolonged and severe flooding destroyed the introduced colony of the Large Copper in England in 1968, although a reserve stock escaped and was available for re-stocking the fenland habitat in the following year.

Migrant species, such as the Painted Lady and the Clouded Yellow, show very large fluctuations from year to year in Britain and other parts of northern Europe. Thousands arrive in some years, while hardly any are seen in other years. Such fluctuations are undoubtedly traceable to weather conditions in the Mediterranean area

The Ringlet population crashed after the 1976 drought, but gradually rose again during the wetter years that followed

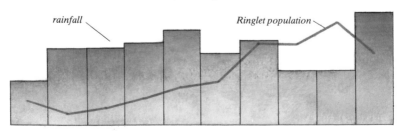

which somehow affect the numbers of insects setting out on the northward journey. Wind is an important factor, for strong or prolonged winds from the south always bring reports of unusual numbers of migrants. They breed in Britain and in the north, as long as local conditions are suitable, and late summer populations may then be extremely high.

Biennial species in the north and in mountain regions may be common in one year and rare in the next, simply because the two populations are not equal in size (see p. 23). In parts of Norway the Polar Fritillary appears only in alternate years. In theory it would be very easy for a biennial species with two separate populations to evolve into two separate species, but in practice there is usually sufficient intermingling of the populations to keep the gene pool more or less uniform. Individual butterflies may swap groups by maturing in one year or by taking three years to mature instead of the normal two years.

Predators and other natural enemies also commonly cause seasonal fluctuations, although these are usually short-lived and very local in their effect. Wasps, for example, have been known to remove whole broods of Peacock caterpillars from the nettles around their nests, thus reducing the local population for a time – although with a mobile species like the Peacock the effect is not readily noticed in the adult stage.

The effect of both predators and parasites can be modified by the weather. Large numbers of insectivorous birds die in severe winters and the consequent reduction in predation may lead to an upsurge in butterfly populations in the following summer. A wet season at any time of year can have a detrimental effect by encouraging the growth of parasitic fungi which attack larvae and pupae. Parasites of all kinds also tend to increase in numbers following an increase in their hosts, so here we have an automatic mechanism for regulating populations and cutting numbers back to normal proportions (see p. 225).

BUTTERFLY MONITORING

Much of the data given in this section on butterfly populations has been obtained from the Butterfly Monitoring Scheme, which the Institute of Terrestrial Ecology has been running in Britain since 1976. The scheme is designed to show up changes in butterfly numbers in selected areas all over the country. Participants in the scheme walk along a fixed route or transect at least once a week and count the numbers of each species seen within fixed limits – between the edges of the path or track, for example, or perhaps within 5 metres of the observer. With less than 60 resident species, and considerably fewer in any given habitat, it is not too difficult to identify most of the British butterflies in flight. The transects pass through as many different habitats as possible in each area, thus maximising the number of butterfly species likely to be seen.

The figures obtained are used to calculate a weekly index of abundance for each species, the index being the average number of each species of butterfly seen on each transect. This method does not give any estimate of the total population, but there is a good correlation between the index of abundance and actual population estimates obtained by other means. The scheme is thus a reliable way of recording fluctuations from year to year and, most important, gives an early warning of declines, allowing conservation measures to be taken in good time. Many local recording schemes, often carried out on a county basis, also help in detecting population changes.

Few population studies have been carried out on the continent so far, but it is hoped that monitoring schemes will be started in the near future. Monitoring by transect will, of course, be slower than it is in Britain because of the greater number of species involved and the need to capture at least some of them for accurate identification, but it will provide much valuable data on which effective conservation measures can be based.

BUTTERFLY CONSERVATION

With so many species declining throughout Europe, a great deal of effort is now being devoted to the conservation of the species and populations that remain. Both official and voluntary bodies are involved in this work, although few of these organisations are concerned purely with butterflies or even with insects. The United Kingdom has always led the field, but with the encouragement of the International Union for Conservation of Nature and Natural Resources and the Societas Europaea Lepidopterologica most other European countries are now assessing their butterfly populations and taking steps to ensure their survival.

LEGISLATION

Many countries prohibit the collection of certain butterflies. Luxembourg and East Germany have imposed total bans on collecting anything other than the cabbage whites, and a similar ban applies in most parts of Austria. West Germany prohibits the collection of most butterfly species at any stage of their lives and there are heavy fines for breaking this law. Most large moths, including the hawkmoths, are also protected in these countries as are most day-flying moths.

There are also collecting bans in certain areas of other countries. The French Department Alpes de Haute Provence, a favourite collecting ground for many years, now bans all collecting of butterflies and moths except by children under twelve years old using nets no more than 20cm in diameter. It is even illegal to carry a butterfly net in the Laggintal area of Switzerland, this legislation being designed to protect the very rare Rätzer's Ringlet which is confined to this area and flies in just a few scattered localities. Collecting is, banned in all European national parks and reserves, although permits can be obtained for scientific purposes.

NATURE RESERVES

Protection of the habitat must always be the aim of butterfly conservation, for loss of habitat is the major threat to butterflies everywhere and even a minor alteration can have a serious effect on the survival of a species. In the face of all the demands on the countryside, nature reserves are playing an increasingly important role in the conservation of butterflies and other forms of wildlife. It has recently been estimated that one fifth of the British butterfly species will be largely or entirely confined to reserves of various kinds in the near future. The picture is similar in several other parts of Europe.

If we are not to lose some of our threatened species altogether, steps must be taken to safeguard adequate areas of habitat for each species and, bearing in mind the existence of many sub-species, these protected areas should be set up in as many regions as possible. Wetlands are especially important conservation sites, for land-drainage has already reduced them to very small proportions and eight of the currently endangered European butterflies (see p. 304) are wetland species.

Many species with closed populations can maintain thriving communities in areas of less than 5 hectares, and some manage on less than one hectare. Butterfly reserves thus do not need to be extensive, but they do

The very rare Rätzers Ringlet

Moderate grazing is essential for the welfare of many grassland butterflies. Several species actually declined when reserves were fenced against rabbits

need to be able to support a minimum of about 250 adults if they are to survive the natural fluctuations brought about by unfavourable weather. Most existing reserves are much larger than the minimum required and, if properly managed, should have no difficulty in holding on to their butterfly populations.

It may be thought that acquiring and fencing a piece of land is all there is to setting up a nature reserve, and that once this is done the wildlife will flourish unaided. Unfortunately, nature does not work like this; vegetation does not stand still, and in most parts of Europe neglected land quite quickly returns to woodland. Few European butterflies live in mature woodland, and so a good deal of work is necessary to maintain their required habitats. But before this can be done, detailed research is needed to find out precisely what conditions are required by each species at each stage of its life cycle. Several kinds of butterflies, including the Heath Fritillary, have actually been lost from nature reserves because their requirements were not fully understood.

Although the Heath Fritillary flourishes in grassland in southern Europe, most of its more northerly populations (ssp. *athalia*) require open woodland of the type that was continually being created by coppicing in earlier times. As coppicing declined, so did the butterfly and it has become one of Britain's rarest species with only 31 known colonies in 1980. It is one of four butterflies

protected under the 1981 Wildlife and Countryside Act. In an early attempt to conserve the species, two woods with healthy populations were acquired as reserves, but the butterfly quickly died out in both woods because its dependence on the earliest stages of woodland succession was not appreciated in time. Research by Dr M. S. Warren has now shown exactly what the butterfly and its larvae require and the appropriate management of its remaining British localities has led to a marked increase in numbers in the last few years. Butterflies have even been re-introduced to some of their old haunts. The future of this species in Britain now seems secure but it is unlikely that it will survive outside the specially managed reserves.

Grazing by sheep and rabbits once kept the grasslands open and suitable for many butterflies. The reduction in grazing over the years, especially since myxomatosis decimated the rabbit population during the 1950's, has been a prime cause of the decline of various grassland blues and skippers. These butterflies continued to dwindle on reserves until the importance of turf height was realised, and the Large Blue actually became extinct on one reserve after it was fenced-off to keep out collectors, as the fence also kept out the vital grazers. Carefully managed grazing of reserves, aimed at maintaining a variety of turf heights (see p. 246), is now making the future much brighter for several other grassland butterflies.

RE-INTRODUCTIONS

The idea of re-introducing butterflies to areas in which they have become extinct is not new and many attempts have been made over the last few decades, with varying degrees of success. Some naturalists disapprove of 'interfering' in this way, but where the original extinction was simply through loss of habitat it seems perfectly good conservation to attempt a re-introduction – as long as suitable habitat can be re-created and maintained.

The Large Copper was re-introduced to the English fenland in 1927, although this was the Dutch race (*Lycaena dispar batavus*) and not the original English race (*L. d. dispar*). The latter became completely extinct in the nineteenth century. The scheme has not been entirely successful and the population has had to be reinforced regularly from captive stock, but work is now in progress to discover precisely what conditions are best for the butterfly in the hope that it will be able to hold its own unaided in the future.

More recently, the Large Blue has been re-introduced to Britain and, although the work is at any early stage, the results are encouraging and it is hoped that the butterfly will again be a permanent member of the British fauna. As already mentioned similar success is being achieved with the Heath Fritillary. The Black Hairstreak has also been successfully re-introduced into some of its earlier haunts, but attempts to re-establish the Swallowtail in England's Wicken Fen have met with failure because the necessary wet habitat could not be maintained.

Reintroduction should only be attempted with professional guidance, for it is important to select the best stock and to ensure that it is of the correct race. Normally, it should be taken from the nearest available locality. Mated females are generally chosen for release, as they do not carry ichneumons or other internal parasites that might affect the next generation. Even a few such females can provide a good nucleus of eggs.

The Adonis Blue population of one reserve climbed to about 4,500 just two years after 65 adults were re-introduced to the area. Britain's largest Black Hairstreak colony is believed to be the result of releasing about twelve adults more than 30 years ago.

CONSERVATION IN THE GARDEN

Gardens are important refuges for many forms of wildlife, and the thousands of hectares clothed with nectar-filled flowers are valuable feeding grounds for adult butterflies. Apart from the cabbage whites, however, very few butterflies actually breed in gardens – because our cultivated plants are rarely suitable for the caterpillars.

A certain amount of untidiness on the part of the gardener may encourage a few more species to lay their eggs. The Holly Blue, for example, may breed if ivy is allowed to flower in the hedge or on the garden wall. Some butterfly enthusiasts allow nettles to spring up to encourage the Peacock and other vanessids, and as long as the nettles are in the sun for at least a part of the day the butterflies will often oblige with some eggs. But these butterflies are all mobile species with open or wide-ranging populations and are unlikely to remain to adorn the garden. Garden breeding can augment the total population if carried out over a wide area but at present it is doubtful if enough gardeners encourage suitable plants for them to make any significant contribution to the wild butterfly populations.

Even if it is not possible to provide food and shelter for caterpillars in the garden, there is still much to be gained from attracting the adults with flowers. The gardener gets the pleasure of watching the butterflies as they pollinate the flowers, and the garden itself acts as an important re-fuelling station for the insects, providing them with the energy necessary for the next stage of their journey to the breeding habitats. Moths, bees, and several other insects should also visit the flowers, adding further interest to the garden.

WHY CONSERVE?

There are several practical and aesthetic reasons for looking after our butterfly populations. They are extremely useful as pollinators of both wild and cultivated flowers and they are also useful indicators of a healthy environment. Butterflies are among the first animals to disappear when the habitat deteriorates, and if we take steps to maintain them we are likely to keep the whole environment in reasonable shape. Slightly less important, although more easily understood by most people, is the immense pleasure that butterflies can give us as they fly around us. It would be a sad reflection on today's society if our descendants had to grow up without these delightful insects to brighten the countryside.

Gardens can be made attractive to butterflies by growing the right kinds of nectar rich flowers

John Wilkinson

GLOSSARY

Aberration A variation from the normal pattern of a species, of rare and irregular occurrence and brought about by genetic or environmental factors (p. 298).

Aedeagus The male's penis.

Aestivation Dormancy during very hot or dry summer weather.

Allopatric Occupying distinct geographical areas with no mutual contact: applied to two or more species or sub-species.

Anal angle The inner angle of the hind wing.

Anal veins The hindmost veins of the hind wing, basically three in number although one or more may be missing (p. 17).

Androconia The scent-releasing scales of male butterflies and moths.

Annulate Composed of ring-like sections.

Apterous Wingless.

Brachypterous With wings noticeably shorter than the normal for a species or group.

Cell Any one of the spaces between the veins of a wing. Cells which are completely enclosed by veins are closed cells, while those that reach the wing margin are open cells. *The* cell is the large cell occupying much of the basal half of the wing, although this is also called the discal or discoidal cell (p. 17).

Chitin The tough, horny material that makes up the bulk of the insect's outer covering.

Chrysalis The third of the four life stages of a butterfly or a moth. Also known as the pupa, it is the stage during which the larval body is re-built to form that of the adult.

Claspers a) The hindmost pair of legs of a caterpillar. b) Those parts of the male genitalia, also known as valves, which grip the end of the female abdomen during copulation (p. 293).

Cline A population or series of neighbouring populations occupying a large area and displaying continuous and gradual variation from one end of the range to the other (p. 301).

Cocoon A protective silken case, sometimes incorporating hairs and other materials, made by many fully grown moth caterpillars prior to pupation. Butterfly caterpillars rarely construct cocoons.

Compound Eye An eye made up of several or many separate units called ommatidia. Each ommatidium has its own hexagonal lens or facet, giving the surface of the eye a honeycomb appearance when seen under a lens (p. 254).

Costa The front vein of the wing, usually very close to the front margin and sometimes actually forming the costal vein. Also known as the costal vein.

Costal fold A narrow groove, near the front edge of the forewing in certain skipper butterflies, which encloses the androconia.

Costal margin The front edge of the wing: sometimes abbreviated to costa, but this term really refers to the associated vein.

Cremaster The hook or hooks at the tail end of a chrysalis or pupa, commonly attaching it to its support.

Cubitus The major vein in the rear half of the wing, forming the lower margin of the cell. In dealing with Lepidoptera, but not other insects, it is also known as the median. It generally has two branches – veins 2 and 3 of the butterfly wing (p. 17).

Diapause A state of suspended development occurring at some stage in the life history of most insects living in cold and temperate regions – generally during the winter.

Dimorphism The occurrence of two distinct forms in a population. Those species in which the sexes are markedly different, as in many of the blues, are said to show sexual dimorphism. Species in which spring and summer generations differ are said to show seasonal dimorphism, although this phenomenon is more accurately called seasonal polyphenism (p. 300).

Discal area The central area of the wing, including the outer part of the discal cell (p. 17).

Discal cell The large cell in the basal half of the wing: usually referred to simply as *the* cell.

Dorsum The rear margin of the front wing, especially in moths – in many of which this margin is the uppermost when the insects are at rest.

Ecdysis The moulting process, during which caterpillars shed their outer skins (p. 214).

Eruciform Caterpillar-shaped, with a more or less cylindrical body and with both thoracic legs and abdominal prolegs.

Exarate pupa A pupa in which the appendages are all free from the body. Among the Lepidoptera, such pupae occur only in a few of the more primitive moth families (p. 236).

Exuvia The cast-off outer skin of a caterpillar or other insect: generally used in the plural – exuviae.

Femur The third segment of an insect leg and usually the largest, although not necessarily the longest.

Form A regularly occurring variety making up a fairly constant proportion of a population (p. 298)

Frenulum A device for coupling the front and hind wings in many moths (p. 11).

Gynandromorph An insect which, as a result of a genetic mix-up during development, is part male and part female – often half and half and then known as a bilateral gynandromorph (p. 297).

Hibernation Winter sleep or dormancy, usually but not always involving diapause (q.v.).

Humeral vein   A small branch from the base of the subcosta in the hind wing of some butterflies and moths. It runs forward and supports the enlarged front part of the wing.

Imago   The adult insect.

Instar   The stage in an insect's life between any two moults, except that the first instar is the stage between hatching and the first moult and the final instar is the adult insect, after its final moult.

Integument   The outer covering of the insect body.

Jugum   A small lobe projecting from the rear of the front wing in certain moths and resting on the hind wing to couple the two in flight.

Larva   The name given to caterpillars and other young insects that bear no resemblance to the adults and pass through a pupal stage before becoming adult (see Metamorphosis).

Media   The longitudinal vein in the centre of the wing of most insects. Its basal region is absent in most butterflies and moths, or is fused with the cubitus (q.v.), but its outer part is represented by veins 4, 5, and 6 in the front wing. In butterflies the cubitus is often called the median vein.

Metamorphosis   The change of form that occurs as an insect grows up. It may be complete, as in butterflies and moths and other insects that pass through larval and pupal stages, or incomplete as in grasshoppers and dragonflies which have no pupal stage and which change gradually into the adult form.

Micropterous   Having extremely short wings.

Micropyle   The minute pore through which sperm enters an insect egg for fertilisation.

Obtect Pupa   A pupa in which all the appendages adhere firmly to the body, as in most butterfly and moth pupae (p. 235).

Ocellus   A simple eye, capable of little more than differentiating between light and dark. Most butterflies and moths have two ocelli, one behind each compound eye, although they are usually concealed by the scales. Caterpillars also have ocelli low down on their heads, but these are more strictly called stemmata.

Ovipositor   The egg-laying apparatus of the female, best developed in crickets and other insects that lay their eggs in crevices or inside plant tissues. Some moths have a small, retractile ovipositor, but most lepidopterans have none at all and merely pump their eggs out on to the surface of the food-plant.

Palp   A sensory appendage springing from either the labium or the maxilla (or both) and generally concerned with smell or taste.

Polymorphism   The regular occurrence of two or more distinct forms in a given population (p. 298).

Polyphenism   The occurrence of two or more distinct *seasonal* forms in a species or population (p. 300).

Post-discal Area   An area of the wing just beyond the central discal area (p. 17).

Prepupa   The quiescent, fully grown larva before it moults into the pupal stage. Compared with the active larva it often appears rather small and shrivelled (p. 235).

Proboscis   The tongue of butterflies and moths.

Proleg   One of the fleshy legs on the rear half of a caterpillar, equipped with minute hooks which maintain a firm hold on the food-plant (p. 211).

Pupa   See Chrysalis.

Pupation   The act of turning into a pupa or chrysalis.

Race   A sub-species characteristic of a particular region or habitat.

Radial sector   The vein forming much of the anterior border of the cell and then branching to form veins 7, 8, and 9 of the front wing.

Radius   The main longitudinal vein in the front part of the wing, forming the basal part of the anterior margin of the cell and then giving rise to the radial sector.

Retinaculum   The hook holding the frenulum (q.v.) in place under the front wing (p. 11).

Seta   A bristle.

Sex brand   A patch of specialised scales, including the scent-releasing androconia, found on the wings of some male butterflies.

Space   The area of wing membrane between any two neighbouring veins (p. 17).

Species   The basic unit of classification – the individual kind or type of organism.

Spiracle   A breathing pore, by which the internal breathing tubes (tracheae) open to the outside world: best seen in caterpillars (p. 214).

Sub-costal vein   A small vein running very close to the front margin of the wing and forming vein 12 of the front wing, although often indistinct. It is commonly fused with the radius in the hind wing to form vein 8

Succinct pupa   A pupa attached to its support, usually in an upright position, by a silken tail-pad and a silken girdle around its middle.

Suspended pupa   A pupa hanging upside down from a single point of attachment (p. 234).

Sympatric   Occupying the same area: applied to two or more species.

Tarsus   The foot of an insect, consisting of from one to five segments – usually five in the Lepidoptera.

Tegulae   The pair of lobes or scales overlying the bases of the front wings like 'shoulder pads': usually densely covered with scales.

Termen   The outer margin of the wing.

Tibia   That part of the leg between the femur and the tarsus.

Tornus   The angle at the rear of the front wing: also called the anal angle, although this is more commonly restricted to the hind wing (p. 17).

Trachea   One of the fine air-carrying tubes that permeate the insect body and open at the spiracles. The finest branches are known as tracheoles.

Venation   The arrangement of veins in the wing.

INDEX

Figures in **bold** type refer to entries in the field guide section; those in *italics* refer to illustrations elsewhere (often with mention in the text on the same page).

INDEX

similar species, but they are not full descriptions and should always be read in conjunction with the illustrations. Where two or more sub-species exist, these diagnostic features refer to the nominate sub-species (see p. 301), as long as this occurs in Europe. Both sexes (♂ = male: ♀ = female) are described where they are significantly different. The following abbreviations are used in the descriptions:

ups	upperside
uns	underside
upf	upperside of forewing
uph	upperside of hind wing
unf	underside of forewing
unh	underside of hind wing
fw	forewing
hw	hind wing
pd	post-discal (p. 17)

HAB describes the type(s) of surroundings in which the species is most likely to be found.

ALT gives the altitudinal range (in metres) within which the species is normally found. sl = sea level. Lower limits are unknown for quite a number of upland species, especially in central Europe, and only a maximum altitude may be given:
<1500   up to 1500 metres.
Minimum altitudes are given for some montane species:
>1500   above 1500 metres.

FLIGHT indicates the months during which the adults are on the wing somewhere in Europe. 5–8 means that a species can be found from May until August, although it is not necessarily on the wing for the whole of this period in any one place. In general, a species flies earlier in the southern parts of its range than in the northern parts. But many species are double-brooded in the south and single-brooded in the north, flying in spring and late summer in the south but only in mid-summer in the north. Unless otherwise stated, there is only one brood.

FP gives the food-plants of the larvae where known, although they are still unknown for quite a number of species.

EGG gives the months during which the eggs may be found although, as explained under flight, they will not necessarily be found throughout this period at any one place. The colour is given where it may help with identification, together with the position on the food-plant and an indication of whether the eggs are solitary or in batches. The eggs of some species are unknown.

LARVA indicates the months during which the larvae may be found, although not necessarily in an active state. Many double-brooded species can be found in the larval state throughout the year in some part of Europe or other. The larvae of some species are unknown.

PUPA again indicates the months during which pupae may be found, followed by information on the location of the pupa where this is known. Suspended pupae are those hanging from their hind ends, while succinct pupae are held in an upright position by a silken girdle binding them to the food-plant or other support. The pupae of some species are unknown.

WINTER gives the over-wintering stage. Over-wintering larvae are generally hibernating but some, particularly in the milder regions, remain active and feed sporadically through the winter.

VAR gives the important variations which are briefly described and distinguished from the nominate sub-species (see above). Geographical races or sub-species are indicated by the abbreviated scientific name followed by a third name in italics: e.g.
A.u. ichnusa – the sub-species *ichnusa* of the Small Tortoiseshell *Aglais urticae*.

Many non-geographical variations are known as forms and are indicated by f. followed by a name in italics: e.g. *Colias croceus* f. *helice* – the pale form of the Clouded Yellow *Colias croceus*.

NOTES add anything of interest concerning the recognition of a species, its distribution, or its habits.

STATUS indicates whether or not a species is threatened in any way – usually by human activity. The three categories used here are those used by the International Union for Conservation of Nature, and it must be remembered that these categories are based on the degree of threat and not on the degree of rarity. A species can be quite numerous in a given habitat, but if that habitat is threatened with destruction the insects living there will obviously be under threat.

Endangered (E) means that a species is in danger of extinction and that it is likely to disappear in the near future if the causal factors continue to operate – the causal factors generally being habitat destruction in one form or another. Most endangered species are already confined to just a few small areas, although these may be widely scattered.

Vulnerable (V) means that a species is likely to move into the endangered category in the near future if the causal factors continue to operate. These species are generally declining throughout their ranges, as a result of changing land use, and many of them occupy vulnerable habitats.

Rare (R) means that, although not in any immediate danger, a species is at risk. Such species are usually very local or thinly scattered over wider areas – but not necessarily rare in terms of numbers at present.

A species may be threatened throughout its European range or just in the countries listed, the decision as to whether it is threatened or not being based on the observations and opinions of numerous entomologists in various countries. A species which is threatened throughout its European range is indicated by the appropriate letter without any countries following.

? following status indicates that not enough information is known to make a true assessment but it is likely that the insect is at risk to some extent.

Species that are stated to be **Legally Protected (LP)** in various countries enjoy some form of legal protection – usually a ban on collecting and trading. All butterflies apart from the cabbage-feeding whites are so protected in East Germany and Luxembourg and also in most parts of Austria, and to save space in the species accounts these countries are not mentioned in the butterfly section.

SEE ALSO At the end of each species account there may be a number of page references directing the reader to further information on the biology of the species concerned.

MAPS give the normal range of each species, including areas covered by regular annual migrations. Sporadic occurrences by vagrants have not been mapped.

General Abbreviations Throughout the species accounts B stands for British Isles: N stands for northern Europe, C for central Europe, S for southern Europe, SW for south-western Europe, and SE for south-eastern Europe. For the purposes of this book, northern Europe is all that part of continental Europe north of 55°N: central Europe lies between 45° and 55°N, but also includes the whole of the British Isles: southern Europe lies south of 45°N. South-western Europe is taken to cover areas west of Nice, and south-eastern Europe lies to the east of Nice.